BERTRAND RUSSELL
and the Pacifists
in the First World War

BERTRAND RUSSELL

and the Pacifists
in the First World War

JO VELLACOTT
Assistant Professor of History, Acadia University

ST MARTIN'S PRESS
NEW YORK

For information write:
St. Martin's Press, Inc.,
175 Fifth Avenue, New York, N.Y. 10010

Printed in Great Britain
First published in the United States of America in 1981

Library of Congress Catalog Card Number: 80–53409

ISBN 0–312–07705–X

CONTENTS

PREFACE

When I first became interested in Bertrand Russell's activities during the First World War, there was little in print to flesh out his own short dry comments in the *Autobiography*. He had opposed the war, supported the Union of Democratic Control, worked with the No-Conscription Fellowship, been tried twice and jailed once for offences against the Defence of the Realm Act. His published writings from the period testified to his absorption with the social and political bases of peace and war, to the near exclusion, till 1918, of his philosophical interests.

None of this was sufficient to tell me what Bertrand Russell really did during the war, who were his companions, what were his day-to-day activities. In spite of Russell's later fame or notoriety for his willingness to lay himself on the line in anti-nuclear demonstrations, the presumption among scholars tended to be that, because Russell was noted for qualities of mind, his involvement in pacifism during the First World War must have been of a predominantly cerebral nature.

Over a long period of time I found and read many letters, minutes of meetings, informal reports, short articles, rough notes on activities of the No-Conscription Fellowship and ephemera of many kinds written by Russell and by others among his friends and enemies. I came on new information on opposition to the First World War, on the problems and issues, and on the people who were swimming against the tide. I found that the man who had written later of his intense solitude and sense of isolation from his fellows had written at the time: 'I can't describe. . . how happy I am having these men to work with and for—it is *real* happiness all day long.' Transitory, perhaps, but he meant it, and it affected him.

I came too to see how personal was the background to Russell's writings of the period. I now read this passage from *Principles of Social Reconstruction* as movingly autobiographical and am happy to take it as the theme of my book:

Instinct, mind, and spirit are all essential to a full life; each has its own excellence and its own corruption. Each can attain a spurious excellence at the expense of the others; each has a tendency to encroach upon the others; but in the life which is to be sought all three will be developed in co-ordination, and intimately blended in a single harmonious whole.

Writing the book has been exciting. I write, I hope, as a scholar; austere standards of research and the use of evidence are important to me. I have not attempted to hide my sympathy with my subject; at the same time I have imposed little of my own interpretation on the material—I believe it interprets itself. I hope it informs about the complex development of a flawed but great human being; if it raises some questions about history and human nature at large I shall be more than satisfied.

I dedicate the book with love and respect to two people who began it all: Bertha Cruze, who taught me to love books; and Jean W. Rowntree, who taught me the excitement of history; and both of whom taught me so many other things as well.

Jo Vellacott
Ban Righ Foundation
32 Queen's Crescent
Queen's University, Kingston, Ontario
December 1979

ACKNOWLEDGEMENTS

Kenneth Blackwell, the Bertrand Russell archivist at McMaster University, deserves more of my gratitude than I can express for his inspiration and unwavering encouragement through many vicissitudes, no less than for his skilled and painstaking assistance at every stage of the writing of this book. Warm thanks go to his wife, Kadriin Timusk, for her help on many occasions and in many ways.

In the history department at McMaster University, my appreciation goes to the late H. W. McCready, from whom I received every help and encouragement until a few months before his death. Richard Rempel, his successor, has also been most supportive.

From beginning to end, Thomas Kennedy of the University of Arkansas has shown generosity and a willingness to share scholastic resources and insights far beyond what I had any right to expect. Conrad Russell, John Slater, Peter Brock, John Rae and Louis Greenspan read the manuscript at an early stage and gave generously of their time in making valuable suggestions and comments. Comments from the late Lady Russell, Jay Winter, Alan Cassells, Charles Beer and the late Lady Constance Malleson have also been helpful. The responsibility for errors of fact or interpretation of course remains mine.

Those who have helped my research in many different ways are too numerous to mention and some names must inevitably be omitted. I would especially like to mention Arthur Marwick, who encouraged me at an early stage, the late George Gascoigne, who showed me his bleak little watercolours done with smuggled materials in prison, Lady Helen Pease, the late Fred Haslam and Lord Brockway. The encouragement of my colleagues in the Conference on Peace Research in History has also been helpful. Darlene Booth and Diane Kerss at the Bertrand Russell Archives gave untiring assistance. Soo Newberry and John Isaac were invaluable research assistants; Mary Newberry gave informal help at an earlier stage. For the last stages in preparation of the manuscript and for the index I am warmly grateful to Pat Stephenson for her meticulous assistance and her wise comments.

My acknowledgements to the following archival collections and libraries and to the archivists are in most cases no mere formality; I have greatly appreciated the interest which has encouraged the work. My indebtedness to the Bertrand Russell Archives, McMaster University, Hamilton, Ontario, will be obvious and can hardly be overstated. Previously unpublished writings in McMaster's copyright are © Res-Lib, 1980. Acknowledgements are also due to Bruce Jones and the staff of the Cumbria Record Office, Carlisle, for the use of the Catherine E. Marshall papers; to the Rare Book Staff of the Thomas Cooper Library, the University of South Carolina, Columbia, S.C., for the use of the Lord Allen of Hurtwood papers; to Bernice Nichols and the staff of the Swarthmore College Peace Collection, Swarthmore, Pennsylvania, for the use of the British peace collections; to June Moll and the staff of the Humanities Research Center, the University of Texas at Austin, for the use of the Ottoline Morrell, D. H. Lawrence and Siegfried Sassoon papers; to the British Library of Political and Economic Science, London, for the use of the E. D. Morel papers; to Jack Brennan and the staff of the Western Collections of the University of Colorado at Boulder for the use of the archives of the Women's International League of Peace and Freedom; to Edward Milligan and the staff of Friends' House Library, Euston Road, London; to Grace Pincoe of Friends' House Library, Toronto, Ontario; to Richard Storey of the Historical Manuscripts Commission; to the Clerk of Plymouth Monthly Meeting of the Society of Friends; to the staff of the Public Record Office, London, for assistance and for quotations from documents covered by Crown copyright; to the Imperial War Museum for use of the Anti-War Movement (1914–1918) collection.

I am grateful for the financial assistance provided by the Canada Council, the Province of Ontario, McMaster University, and the Hamilton University Women's Club (via the Jean Gall Memorial Scholarship). I have also been supported by a Fellowship at the Institute for Advanced Studies in the Humanities at the University of Edinburgh, by a Calouste Gulbenkian Fellowship at Lucy Cavendish College, Cambridge, and by a period as Scholar-in-Residence at Queen's University, Kingston, Ontario.

I am grateful to the following for permission to use copyright material: George Allen and Unwin for Russell's *Autobiography, Practice and Theory of Bolshevism, Principles of Social Reconstruction, Roads to Freedom, Mortals and Others,* Alan Wood: *Bertrand Russell: The Passionate Sceptic;* Oliver Lodge for letter dated April 1, 1916 from Sir Oliver Lodge to Bertrand Russell; Professor C. F. Cornford and Dr. Hugh Cornford for unpublished correspondence of F. M. Cornford; Miss Joan Allen for writings of Lord Allen of Hurtwood; Mrs. T. North Whitehead for letter dated April 16, 1916 from A. N. Whitehead to Bertrand Russell; Professor James A. Leith for a quotation from *Modern Revolutions;* the Bodleian Library and Alexander Murray for correspondence of Gilbert Murray; the London School of Economics and Political Science for quotations from Beatrice Webb, *Our Partnership.*

CHAPTER 1
RUSSELL IN 1914

To those whose interest in Bertrand Russell is limited to the study of his philosophical thought, the First World War may seem an unfortunate interruption. Although he had not confined himself exclusively to the academic life, he was known in 1914 above all as a distinguished philosopher and mathematician, a Fellow of the Royal Society since 1908, co-author with A. N. Whitehead of *Principia Mathematica*, president of the Aristotelian Society in 1911 and 1912, the holder of a lectureship at Trinity College, Cambridge. His work on the interrelation of philosophy, mathematics and logic had gained him a world-wide reputation, particularly in the United States, where he spent the spring of 1914 as a visiting lecturer at Harvard. It is true that since 1913 he had believed his philosophical progress halted because of what seemed to him unanswerable criticism from his most brilliant pupil, Ludwig Wittgenstein, which had thrown him into deep and long-lasting despair about his work.[1] But few would have doubted that he was settled in an academic career in which he would advance steadily to even more impressive heights.

Russell's social contacts were wider than those of many academics. He had friends among his colleagues, but many of his close acquaintances had not chosen to follow an academic life. He had been one of a circle of quite exceptional men during his student days at Cambridge, and some of these were to become part of the intellectual and artistic social constellation known as the Bloomsbury group. He remained on the fringe, but his intimacy with Lady Ottoline Morrell from 1911 on threw him more frequently among them, and he was a familiar figure in the circle. More austere and disciplined than many of them, more dedicated academically than most, and probably more hardworking than any, he was nevertheless accepted. His presence was welcomed, yet even in a group which affected to regard wit more highly than compassion, his caustic tongue and demolishing logic were feared. Ideas and aesthetics were the stuff of life to the Bloomsbury group, and they lived for the most part in a world where it seemed inconceivable that civilised man would again take arms against civilised man. A number were to be pacifists when the war came, if only from a fastidious distaste for the gross reality, an inability to accept the obscenity of war.

In his personal life, Russell had known happiness and bitter unhappiness. His marriage to Alys Pearsall Smith had broken down, ending with a long period during which they lived together in a mutually destructive relationship. No worse indictment of Russell's part in the failure could possibly be found than his own self-justifying journal,[2] kept only for a few years at this time, in which he shows himself self-righteously seeking narrow intellectual solutions for problems that were transparently rooted in the emotions, and assuming for his own protection a controlling remoteness and superiority that left his wife always in the wrong, and were as unlovely as the jealous control she apparently tried to exert over him. Russell thought his own responses dictated entirely by reason, and assumed that it was a fault to allow emotion an influence: but he suffered. Beatrice Webb wrote a remarkable description of what she saw in him:

Bertrand Russell's nature is pathetic in its subtle absoluteness: faith in absolute logic, absolute ethic, absolute beauty, and all of the most refined and rarified type—his abstract and revolutionary methods of thought and the uncompromising way in which he applies these frightens me for his future, and the future of those who love him or whom he loves. Compromise, mitigation, mixed motive, phases of health of body and mind, qualified statements, uncertain feelings, all seem unknown to him. A proposition must be true or false; a character good or bad; a person loving or unloving, truth-speaking or lying.[3]

The last three years before the war found Russell once more taking the risk of entering into a close relationship, and with it beginning a period of personal expansion which was to take him at least a few steps from the man of Webb's description. The intimacy with Lady Ottoline Morrell which began during this period was of the utmost importance in his development, perhaps, in all-around significance, second only to the effect of the war years. Lady Ottoline provided Russell not only with a measure of sexual liberation, but at the same time with a substitute for the mother he did not remember, and a therapeutic relationship akin to that of prolonged individual psycho-therapy. A friendship on which so many incompatible demands were made could never be wholly fulfilling, but Russell's gains were marked.[4]

With Lady Ottoline, Russell explored fresh areas of interest. He re-examined his spiritual beliefs, discovering in himself a capacity for mystical experience which was not new—he dates his well-known 'conversion' episode as early as 1901,[5] and one of his best-known writings on religion was written in 1903[6]—but which he had not previously examined closely with another person. Lady Ottoline held herself to be intensely religious, and when her influence on Russell was at its height he went farther to meet her than he later believed justified. But the position he ultimately adopted was not greatly different from that expressed in 'A Free Man's Worship', where he declared himself unable to find any evidence of God, but stressed the need of man to reach out to man in common humanity, transcended by a creative idealism. Only by this profound paradox of religious man in a godless world was he able to satisfy his mysticism without offending his scientific intelligence. The war gave the vision a new and agonising reality.

Another area which Lady Ottoline helped Russell to face was the function of passion. Russell, like many people, had learnt to deny expression to intense feelings: he feared even the acknowledgement of violent and destructive impulses. To Lady Ottoline he admitted that he believed himself a man of violent nature—at the age of sixteen he thought he had come near to strangling a friend after an argument—and he was scarcely able to find any way of meeting this violence within except by the sternest repression, rigid self-control and recourse to rationalisation. In this too the war was to force a self-confrontation.

Lady Ottoline and his academic career had taken up most of Russell's time in the three years just before the war, leaving him little time for politics, but although he had earlier resisted family pressure to follow in the footsteps of his grandfather, Lord John Russell, by making a career as a politician, he had always followed political events with keen interest and ever since his graduation there had been a tension between the demands of politics and the claims of the scholarly life. He had entered the arena when he thought principle was at stake, selecting his causes not as an ambitious young politician might have, but purely for the importance—as it seemed to him—of the issues. He wrote and spoke in favour of free trade,[7] he stood for Parliament as a women's suffrage candidate,[8] he threw himself into the election campaigns of 1910 in support of curbing the power of the House of Lords. He gained some political experience, but although the going was rough at times—the women's suffrage cause in particular laid him open to some near-violent heckling—he was not forced at any time before the war to step out of his inherited role as a member of the ruling class (indeed as an aristocrat) with all the assurance of ultimate security and deference which this gave, and with the almost unbridgeable gulf which it fixed between him and the English common people.

After each of his forays into the political field Russell retreated, apparently with relief, into the life of scholarship, and by 1914, in spite of Lady Ottoline's complaints that he was too much of a don and a prig, Cambridge seemed to have triumphed over Westminster. Although he was disillusioned by the failure of the Liberal government to deliver all the expected reforms when the incubus of the Lords' veto was removed,[9] and although the handling of the miners' strike in 1912 moved him to indignation, he rested content with his Cambridge lectureship from 1910 until the outbreak of the war. On the whole, he could be comfortable under a Liberal government—nothing, it seemed, was likely to go too far wrong.

Russell's political thought emerged slowly in the absence of crisis. The causes he espoused show him to have been in practice on the left wing of the Liberal Party, an occasional reference suggests sympathy (stopping short of action) with those who advocated revolutionary social change,[10] he was well-informed on Fabian socialist thought but rejected the emphasis on the centralised state.[11] But there is nothing approaching an integrated political philosophy, although his attitudes were seldom inconsistent with the liberal idealism in which he had been brought up.

Russell had never defined liberalism or what the Liberal Party meant to him and it may be presumptuous to attempt it on his behalf. Liberal values were part of his way of life, as he believed them to be part of the ethic of his country. At a personal level they included fair dealing, toleration, a belief in progress, a disbelief in original sin, something near to worship of civilisation (which meant to him the freeing of the mind to reach new heights), and a reliance on reason and on its power to convince. For the nation and between nations, assumed common goals were maximum liberty for the individual, opportunity for personal fulfilment for as many people as possible, reliance on negotiation rather than force, a fair distribution of economic and political powers and the usual concomitants of justice, such as freedom from harassment and from arrest without warrant. For all these to flourish, peace was a precondition, as well as a good in itself. The whole tone of the thinking is rational and attractive—reminiscent, indeed, of Enlightenment thought—and it makes as little allowance for the vagaries of the impulses of humankind at large as Russell had made for the emotions of his wife and himself in his assessment of the predicament into which they had fallen.

To do Russell justice, he had begun to recognise by 1914 that some of these principles would be more realistically regarded as desiderata than taken for granted as common too all reasonable men. Belief in the liberal principle of the rule of law was already tempered by a suspicion that bad laws could sometimes be changed only by breaking them. He had a respect for democracy but less for its political machinery, which he found imperfect, out of date, biased and tending to concentrate power far too much. As for the Liberal Party, he expected it to act as the custodian of the values he held dear. He was already quite cynical about politicians, believing them self-seeking and untrustworthy, but he supposed that the body of Liberal supporters held the same values as he did, and he was confident that the number and vigilance of the Liberal voters were sufficient to prevent the politicians from throwing overboard the liberal ethic in any important respect. The State and the Liberal Party were not entities of importance—they were no bigger than the sum of their parts—and as long as right-minded people predominated, there was little to fear. The people he knew best were all Liberals, and he believed they could be trusted to reject any gross irrationality. War was so irrational as to be literally unthinkable.

These very deeply-held assumptions (based, paradoxically, surely more on emotion than on reason) made it seem unnecessary for Russell to formulate his ideas clearly on just those matters which were suddenly to jump into prominence in August 1914. On the conduct of foreign policy he had little to say and took no action. What he did say bears out somewhat tenuously his claim to be a pacifist, if this term be taken in the loose connotation of the time, more nearly equivalent to the term 'internationalist'. With the pacifists or 'peace men' he deplored the arms race, supported international arbitration, took exception to the build-up of hostility to Germany, and occasionally criticised the methods, means and objectives of foreign policy as conducted by Sir Edward Grey. But on most of these points Russell wrote very little even in his private correspondence, and no issue among them stirred him to public action or published writing. He later claimed to have been one of the earliest critics of the policy of the Entente, resigning from the Coefficients dining club on the issue, before Grey took office; but he certainly did not make it the subject of continuing study.[12] In all, there is little to except him from the perceptive indictment of Irene Cooper Willis, who accused 'the average Liberal . . . in the pre-war period' of displaying

a semi-indifference to foreign policy . . . which was to a great extent temperamental. . . . The conception of conflict between nations, on which foreign policy was based, was distasteful to him; he had no wish to acknowledge it. He was internationally minded; he believed in concord between nations, and so ardently that he did not question overmuch whether concord between nations actually existed.[13]

As for evidence of a positively pacifist outlook, Russell does not appear to have spent any significant amount of time or thought on the principles or practice of pacifism between his alleged conversion of 1901 and the outbreak of war in 1914. He discussed Tolstoy's views with George Trevelyan in a brief correspondence in 1904, but showed reservations about the admiration shown by Trevelyan at that time for the extreme of Christian anarchist pacifism.[14] Interesting, too, is the attention he gave to an essay in which William James propounded the view that people in fact want war, for itself and as a mystic rite. Russell was later to claim that this thought had come to him, with horror, for the first time in August 1914, but his review of James's *Memories and Studies* in 1911 shows that intellectually the concept was familiar and convincing to him well before the war. James's paper (first given as a speech to a group of pacifists) obviously struck a responsive chord in Russell. He went on to praise the companion essay in which James suggested peaceful alternatives, and summed up the two papers: 'Men's energies need an enemy to fight, but all progress demands that the enemy should not be human.'[15] Russell's ability to agree so strongly with James's terrifying premise and yet to bury it so comfortably in Liberal optimism is revealing.

Russell in 1914 was on the whole well content with his environment. He saw the social and political systems of his day as imperfect but likely in time to be modified rationally. Meanwhile, he and others like him had facilities for advancing the achievement of creative intelligence, which was the meaning of civilisation. But in some more personal areas he was less content and much less certain. Underlying his classical liberal optimism was a deep-rooted emotional pessimism, and he was subject to moods of despair. He was extraordinarily vulnerable to criticism, and inclined in his turn to make harsh judgements. Just before the war, too, the intellectual defences against emotional exposure that he had earlier built were crumbling, and he was developing a new awareness and painfully seeking a new balance between the forces within himself of reason, impulse and spirit.

The war was to turn upside down this picture of a man secure in his environment but personally uncertain.

CHAPTER 2
STRANGE DEATH

'The war and risk of war is quite awful—I try not to realise it—the horror of it is too great.' So wrote Russell to Lady Ottoline on 29 July 1914, just six days before Britain declared war on Germany—and it is his first clear reference to the possibility of British involvement. Like most Britishers who professed any interest in public affairs, his whole concern the previous week had been with the crisis in Ireland, with the international tension as no more than a background threat.[16]

When Russell suddenly realised not only the certainty of a European war, but the probability that Britain would take part, the first days of August turned into a nightmare for him, and he flung himself desperately into the last-minute campaign for British neutrality. There were in fact many people who shared his horror at the prospect of war and his conviction that Britain should stay out of it, and the campaign commanded far more widespread support than is generally remembered. But effective opposition was debilitated by two factors: the speed of events, and simple disbelief compounded by the fact that the Liberal Government in power was thought to be committed to internationalism and peace.[17]

When at last—following the German declaration of war on Russia—thinking people began to recognise that the drift toward war had been replaced by a forced march, demonstrations and meetings were held everywhere, petitions, letters and manifestos were composed. But just as the protest began to gather momentum, the British Government declared war.

Russell's opposition was total, and a matter of simple conviction. Later he gradually defined and limited his pacifism, but in early August 1914 he knew only that the war was a great evil which he must oppose. His reputation as a thinker inclines one to search for intellectual grounds for his attitude, but he himself later ascribed it to the mystical experience of 1901, and his description of that five-minute episode[18] may also be read as an epitome of his whole development during the first years of the twentieth century. Whatever the process by which he had come to stand where he did, he had not expected to be isolated, and his revolt against

British intervention was matched by a sense of betrayal when almost the whole nation seemed to support the action.

At his beloved Cambridge, the young men who should have been the inheritors of reason were going off to kill and be killed, in the name of the civilisation of which the war made a mockery, and their elders, senior academicians, the supposed repositories of wisdom and objectivity, appeared to Russell to have turned into a rabble of warmongers. Liberal values were going down like ninepins: suddenly no one cared for freedom of speech, truth, the recognition of a common humanity, or even academic integrity. In all this welter of unreason, he might have been able to take some comfort had he found himself standing as a rock of reason, but he did not have this solace. He was engulfed by a rage and violence against the warmakers that came near to matching the fear and hatred against the enemy which he saw on every side and recognised as part of the climate of war. At times he was overcome by the feeling that all thought and reason had been 'swept away in a red blast of hate'.[19] He bitterly condemned the Liberal Government for the pre-war diplomacy which, he believed, had directly led Britain into the war, and he was appalled at the suspension of rational judgement by his academic colleagues and his Liberal friends. It was his fellow-Liberals by whom Russell felt let down in 1914, and his reaction against the betrayal was personal, extreme, and near violent. His sense of loss can be understood, but the intensity of the experience was extraordinarily acute. Giving up Liberalism was like giving up the food on which he had been reared. He wrote to a friend: 'You were right about the Liberals. I have done with them. I had never believed anything so frightful could happen—I felt as if it meant an end of all happiness for the rest of our lives—but perhaps we shall emerge into a saner world'.[20]

His thoughts turned in the first hours of the war to the formation of a new political party made up of a combination of Radicals and Labour, and he drafted a long letter to the *Nation*.[21] He claimed 'that no man whose liberalism is genuine can hereafter support the members of the present Cabinet',[22] and he thought the new party must dedicate itself to ensuring effective democracy in every branch of government, including foreign policy; the forces for peace were great and must see to it that in future they exercised control. The letter was not published and was probably never sent. Possibly it is even unfinished: Russell may have lost faith in his proposals even as he wrote them down, or lost it in Massingham, the editor of the *Nation*, upon whose change of heart between 4 and 5 August he was later to comment.[23] In any event, unless the letter had been followed by a sufficient public response to inject courage into the potential political leadership and to enlist the support of at least one major Liberal organ, there could have been no hope of success.

While it was easy to condemn pre-war diplomacy, the question of Britain's involvement, given that she found herself in the position resulting from that diplomacy, was less straightforward, and in spite of his later scathing condemnation of those who turned from neutralists on 4 August to supporters of the war on 5 August, Russell was not quite so dogmatic or so settled in his views at the time. On 5 August, he wrote that he felt terribly alone, partly as a result of a letter from Evelyn Whitehead in support of the war, and a conversation with J. A. Hobson, who had campaigned for neutrality but had now gone over completely because of Belgium. He went on: 'One can only suffer and wait. But I do see the point of those who believe in the war, and it is a comfort, because it makes it easy not to hate them. And I think at the very last it could not be helped; but until the very last it could have been.'[24]

This small degree of sympathy with the Government position evaporated when it was revealed during the following week that the German ambassador had, on 1 August, asked Grey to state the terms on which Britain would remain neutral, and that Grey had refused to do so. The Government White Paper[25] in which this was stated gave a detailed history of the diplomatic steps which had preceded Britain's declaration of war—an interesting example of a document that could be entirely coloured by the glasses of the reader. Put out by the Government to justify British intervention, it did just that for all who read it in the hope that it would do so; and for others, who could not believe such a catastrophe was necessary, it proved a mine of evidence that entry into the war had been neither justified nor inevitable.[26] Russell's views on war guilt were confirmed by reading it, and it provoked his first public wartime statement. He wrote again to the *Nation*, and although Massingham was now supporting the war, he gave space in the issue of 15 August to a long letter. Russell first described the immediate effect of the war. He saw the whole fabric of society torn down and civilised values reversed, so that killing became a virtue instead of a crime, and he went on to indict the diplomats and statesmen: 'a set of official gentlemen, living luxurious lives, mostly stupid, and all without imagination or heart'. As for the White Paper:

No literary tragedy can approach the futile horror of the White Paper. The diplomatists, seeing from the first the inevitable end, mostly wishing to avoid it, yet drifted from hour to hour of the swift crisis, restrained by punctilio from making or accepting the small concessions that might have saved the world, hurried on at last by blind fear to loose the armies for the work of mutual butchery.

Behind the diplomats, Russell continued, lay the forces of national greed and national hatred, concentrated and utilised by the Government, the press, the upper class and the makers of armaments, and encouraged by 'a whole foul literature of "glory" and by every text-book of history with which the minds of children are polluted'.[27]

Yet Russell found he had to stop short of willing German victory, although he was unable to see that any good could result from British success as an ally of Russia. 'And if we succeed,' he wrote, 'the only Power that will ultimately profit is Russia—the land of the knout.'[28] With less overt bitterness, he wrote in a letter of 21 October that 'as far as one can see', British victory would be much better for the world than the victory of Germany would be.[29] He strove for a more positive anti-war position, but was unable to find an attitude at this time that differed in its central emphasis from that adopted by radical Liberal papers, now turned Liberal Government apologists and committed to the comforting view that 'Being in . . . we must win'.[30]

All, of course, believed that the conflict would soon be over, but short war or no short war, Russell at least was not prepared to subscribe to the moratorium, tacitly being observed by press and politicians, on criticism of diplomatic methods and constitutional deficiencies which had contributed to bringing Britain into the war, though he made a distinction for public purposes between this and the personal attack he longed to make on Grey's part in it. In a long letter to Lady Ottoline he urged that Philip Morrell should go on pressing in Parliament for reform and standing out for 'some real participation of the democracy in foreign affairs'. The letter ends with a piece of insight, added almost as an after-thought. Thinking in terms of the statement Philip was to make he wrote: 'The two things to say are (1) that war is an infamy (2) that even without us France and Russia were quite strong enough to hold their own and that no *decisive* victory of one side is in the interests either of England or of Europe.'[31]

Russell could well have pressed their final point, which contains the germ of the demand for a negotiated peace and provides the way out of the dilemma of who would best handle victory. He had all along spoken of the need for avoiding a harsh and humiliating peace, but it is possible that his disillusionment with governments was at this period so complete that he saw no hope in any agreement which might be reached by existing rulers, and believed that famine would have to bring revolution before solutions would be possible. Liberal internationalist opinion per-haps lost an opportunity when it failed immediately to follow up its unsuccessful campaign for neutrality with constructive and continuing pressure on the Liberal Government to declare the terms on which peace negotiations could be opened, to seek mediation from the neutral nations, and to welcome any signs of German readiness to negotiate.[32] These demands were to be urged by Russell in his writings for American journals in 1915, and with even more vigour in his Welsh campaign of 1916, but their advocacy was left too late, and since it came only from women, pacifists and socialists it gained little respectability.

Meanwhile Russell longed for a sense of personal involvement on the side of peace. He felt it imperative to let his friends and the public know where he stood, but he found his welcome in the press sharply curtailed. Massingham had given him his one chance, but now that the Liberal journals had all settled back into uncritical support of the Government—together with denigration of the enemy, for a Liberal war must be a holy war—they were not anxious to entertain the views of the unregenerate. Russell turned to the *Labour Leader*, which published five articles (and a short Christmas message) by him before the end of 1914, and others as occasion arose. The first article was provoked by H. G. Wells's contention (in the *Nation*, 15 August) that this war was a war to end war—the catch phrase that later turned so sour. Russell countered that war would be abandoned only when people were so convinced of its enormity that they would refuse to fight even in a just cause.[33]

Russell was intensely interested in what he saw as the psychological factors—the fear and hatred between peoples which were a root cause of war, and which he held were fostered and exploited by unscrupulous statesmen. At the same time, he set himself to learn more about the process of exploitation, and to explore the practical problems of maintaining peace. What was new to him, and of great importance, was the weight he now gave to the concept that no explanation would suffice and no system could hope to succeed that did not take into account the impulses by which people were driven as well as those aspects of behaviour which appeared to be motivated by reason. He set to work to do what seemed to him at first the only thing possible while the war lasted, which was to think out 'how wars come and how they might be avoided, and then, after the peace, do all one can to bring other people round'.[34] Tentatively as Russell worded this project, it was quite a sweeping one: what he saw the need for amounts to the formulation of a complete political philosophy, and we can recognise the seed which was to come to fruition a year later in *Principles of Social Reconstruction*.

At first Russell saw the problem primarily as one related to foreign policy, and he found himself more ignorant than he liked to be of the process and history of recent developments on the international scene. Although he never comfortably admitted this deficiency, he read extensively to make up for it. He admitted to being 'amazed' by E. D. Morel's *Morocco in Diplomacy*,[35] and carefully explained to Ottoline Morrell the preoccupations which had resulted in his knowing less about the Moroccan crisis of 1912 'than about most political things'. He was excited by the report of the Carnegie Commission on the Balkan Wars, which he described as 'written as history ought to be written', adding that 'if the young were taught by such books, there would be no wars between civilised countries'.[36] He wrote a short magazine article on the report as early as October 1914, but it was rejected by the *New Statesman* (which was, so Russell said, 'shocked by it') and did not appear until 11 March 1915, when it was published in the *Labour Leader*.[37] What Russell praised was the emphasis laid in the report on the sufferings of the common people, and the clarity with which it emerged that these were the product of war and ought to be of more consequence than any diplomatic gains. Everything he read reinforced his view of the culpability of statesmen and diplomats, and by December 1914 he was planning a book which would expose the methods of foreign policy.[38]

Working out his views was important, but insufficient. Russell tried to assuage his restlessness by helping Ottoline Morrell in the work of visiting and supplying relief to the so-called enemy aliens, many of whom were suffering serious deprivation.[39] He toyed with the idea of a personal peace mission to Germany.[40] More realistically, he planned a trip to America, where he knew he had a considerable reputation, might hope to exert an influence, and might even be able to meet with President Wilson.[41] People in England, he thought, were not yet ready to discuss post-war internationalism, but in the United States the seed might fall on fertile ground. Russell planned to advocate a league of neutrals while the war should last, followed by a post-war scheme of arbitration treaties between all the major powers, to be enforced by mutual guarantees. 'I am more and more convinced', he wrote, 'that stable peace requires all disinterested nations to form a police force in any quarrel. Mere humanity is not strong enough.'[42] But plans for the trip fell through, partly because Russell felt he neither had nor was prepared to beg for any approval from the British Government.

The Union of Democratic Control provided something of an outlet. Russell gave a good deal of time and attention to it from its embryonic stage in the very first days of the war, and was more closely connected with it in the early weeks than has previously been recognised, although he appears as a learner and a critic rather than as a leader. His activity in the neutrality campaign led to his inclusion in the informal meetings, held after the war broke out, among the small group who still admitted to holding that British intervention had been a mistake: included were such men as E. D. Morel (the UDC secretary from its inception), J. R. MacDonald, Norman Angell, Charles Trevelyan, Arthur Ponsonby and Philip Morrell. They had little to say on how to end the war, but planned to begin their active work as soon as peace came. To Russell they all seemed painfully right-minded, but totally lacking in the necessary strength and political courage. In some of his private comments Russell's pre-war friends would have recognised his acerbic intolerance of fools—as when he referred to the group's talk of starting a new party as 'eight fleas talking of building a pyramid'.[43] But their objectives were acceptable: the establishment of Parliamentary control over foreign policy, and (when peace returned) the opening of direct negotiations with democratic parties and influences on the Continent 'so as to form an international understanding depending on popular parties rather than on governments'. The third aim was to obtain peace terms that would not lead to future trouble by humiliation of the enemy or by artificial frontier changes.[44] Initially, all this was to be kept under wraps until some future date when the country should be secure from danger, but of course there was a leak, and the *Morning Post* (10 September 1914) announced the discovery of a sinister pro-German conspiracy.[45] The ensuing decision to come into the open led to the loss of much moderate and influential Liberal support—or, as the UDC's recent historian has it, to the rejection by the Liberal left of its last chance to become politically effective within the context of the party.[46] But Russell, as might be expected, was delighted that members of the Union now had to stand up and be counted, and he was happy to see the base broadened by the formation of branches and the affiliation of like-minded groups throughout the country.[47] Indeed, the Union could not go fast or far enough for him. Although his UDC pamphlet, *War: the Offspring of Fear*,[48] with its suggestion that there might be other perspectives than the British, was sufficient to provoke Christabel Pankhurst into calling on Russell and the Union to go to Germany where they would find themselves among their friends, the right-wing press attacks did not gather momentum until the Union began to hold public meetings in the spring of 1915, and for almost six months it was relatively undisturbed.[49] To Russell, with his longing for dramatic action to end the war, the UDC fell far short of the apocalyptic force he would have liked to see, but he would work with it as long as there was no better alternative.

His obsessive inability to adjust to the fact of the war had made it impossible for Russell to settle back into a semblance of his usual life and wait for it to end. His personal and professional life were both affected. On the personal side, an early casualty had been his relationship with Helen Dudley, a young American to whom he had made a thoughtless commitment during his spring visit to the USA, and who had arrived in England during the first week of the war. Probably the affair had little future in it in any event, but as it was, when she arrived Russell 'could think of nothing but the war' and treated her very shabbily.[50] For Russell, possibly, the episode presaged a readiness for independence from Ottoline Morrell, but although Lady Ottoline had been on the point of ending their intimacy, she put up an immediate and well-rationalised resistance to his suggestion of another attachment; and at the same time all Russell's dependence on her returned under the stress of war.

Russell found that his interest in things academic were gone. The publication of an important book of his Lowell lectures in Boston (*Our Knowledge of the External World*)[51] moved him little, and though he gave the Herbert Spencer lecture at Oxford on 18 November, he complained while he was writing it that 'it is terribly hard to think about philosophy'.[52] To make matters worse, his teaching load had almost disappeared—one of his courses was attended only by 'two Americans, an Italian, a Jap, and a woman—not a single male Englishman'; while one of this rare breed still attended the other.[53]

When the end of 1914 came, no dramatic—or even satisfying—means of voicing a protest had come to hand, and yet in a sense Russell had already set foot on a path that was not to be trodden by any other distinguished academic in Britain. The apostasy or indifference (as he saw it) of his friends was incomprehensible to him. While they justified intervention (in the case of Gilbert Murray), took government service (in the case of J. M. Keynes), withdrew fastidiously (as Lytton Strachey), or concentrated on schemes for a better post-war world (as Lowes Dickinson or Leonard Woolf), Russell strove to become involved in action, and worked not with academics but with politicians and journalists of the dissident Liberal wing, the Independent Labour Party and the UDC.

CHAPTER 3

SEEKING SALVATION

By the end of 1914, most of Britain had settled into a wartime routine—but not Bertrand Russell. His restlessness increased, and he longed to leave Cambridge and work full time for peace— perhaps writing, travelling and speaking abroad. He thought he might work 'through the Labour people and foreign socialists':

> ... it is clear the Socialists are the hope of the world; they have gained in importance during the war. I would swallow socialism for the sake of peace, What I can do further in philosophy does not interest me, and seems trivial compared to what might be done elsewhere. . . . I can't bear the sheltered calm of university life—I want battle and stress, and the feeling of doing something.[54]

But the opportunity to do something dramatic was a long time in coming, and meanwhile, with growing desperation and occasional bursts of hope, he did whatever came to hand to further the cause of peace. He embarked on more substantial pieces of writing, turning his attention first to foreign policy, and planning a book that should be 'a merciless savage attack on the whole tradition of diplomacy in all countries',[55] and might even turn into a post-war 'bible of democracy in foreign affairs'.[56] Irene Cooper Willis, who was studying Spinoza with him, worked as his research assistant, gathering material from the newspaper files of the British Museum. Russell became excited about the enterprise, which he saw as leading towards two books, one a small volume dealing with British foreign policy since 1906 and the other an ambitious work covering Europe from 1870 and suggesting international reforms. For the time being, he put the larger work aside, while the other began to take shape as 'Principles and Practice in Foreign Policy', a frankly propagandist work, setting out to show how sharply practice departed from declared principles. The historical illustrations he had in mind were bitterly negative: for example, under the heading 'Treachery of the Government', he listed: '(1) "Respect for Treaties—Morocco"; (2) "Defence of Democracy—Russia in 1906"; (3) "Protection of Small Nations—Persia"; (4) "Prevention of War—Entente, and Naval Scare of 1909".'[57]

Long before the book was complete, Gilbert Murray's defence of British policy (*The Foreign Policy of Sir Edward Grey, 1906–15*)[58] goaded Russell into using the work he had done for a reply, which was published as *The Policy of the Entente: A Reply to Professor Gilbert Murray*. [59] The dispute was conducted with venom, Murray referring to Russell (and others) as 'pro-Germans', Russell declaring that Murray wrote 'under the tutelage of the Foreign Office'. With obvious justice, each accused the other of bias. Russell was even more bitter than he allowed Murray to see; Gilbert and Mary Murray were old friends of his and this exacerbated the contempt he felt for Murray's orthodox Liberal Party stand on the war. [60] In letters to Lady Ottoline, Russell made savage personal comments on his former friend whenever he mentioned him, [61] using phrases that it is to be hoped returned as coals of fire when Murray generously and effectively set himself to help him obtain first-division treatment after his conviction in 1918. [62] Much later, Russell admitted that 'Gilbert's kindly feelings were less liable to lapse into savagery'. [63].

After the publication of his reply to Murray, Russell lost interest in continuing the major work on foreign policy and went on to other things, particularly pursuing the idea of influencing public opinion in America, which he saw as the one great power which genuinely loved peace. He believed the States could be of crucial importance in bringing an early end to the war and in moulding the post-war world, and he was sure his reputation there would ensure him an audience. When his plan to visit the States had fallen through in November, he had accepted an opportunity instead to write a number of articles for the *Atlantic Monthly*. In the first of these, 'Is a Permanent Peace Possible?', [64] he pulled together many of his thoughts on the causes of war, from underlying instinctual patterns to the shortcomings of human institutions. He declared that pre-war diplomacy had taken no account of the interests of the peoples, which rested on international economic co-operation, not on national prestige or territorial acquisition. The existence of instinctive fear and aggression, carried over from a much more primitive period, enabled unscrupulous leaders to manipulate whole populations into ferocious war against their fellows, with whom they had no real cause of quarrel. After emphasising that the end of the war must be accompanied by neither great gains nor humiliating losses for either side, he went on to advocate radical changes to ensure more stable international relations. He stressed the role he hoped would be played by America, both at the Peace Congress—to be held in Washington with Woodrow Wilson presiding—and afterwards. His thought about the means of preserving peace had developed beyond the series of arbitration treaties he had earlier projected; he now suggested a continuing international council, which, though only roughly sketched, foreshadowed in broad outline the League of Nations.

The other articles published in the *Atlantic Monthly* in 1915 were 'The Future of Anglo-German Rivalry' (July), and 'War and Non-Resistance' (August), a controversial piece[65] in which Russell envisaged how it might be if Germany invaded England and was met by total passive resistance (the term 'non-resistance' is misleading) rather than by armies and guns. A fourth article, 'How America Can Help to Bring Peace', was withdrawn at the last moment at Russell's request, after the sinking of the *Lusitania*.[66]

In February 1915, Harvard cabled to invite Russell to lecture there in the fall, but he turned down the offer with little hesitation, mainly because he believed he had nothing new to say in philosophy, and did not want to think about it just then.[67] He thought his *Atlantic* articles gave him the chance to communicate things of more vital importance, and would go himself for nothing less than a specific peace mission. When the possibility of this again came up in May, his interest revived. Following the International Women's Peace Conference at The Hague in April, a group of delegates had made a tour of the belligerent and the neutral countries of Europe, and had talked with major statesmen in most of them.[68] One of the most impressive and influential of the women was Jane Addams, well known in the States for her social work and as a spokeswoman for peace. Shortly before returning to America she urged Russell to go with her, in the hope of influencing President Wilson and the public toward the strengthening of American neutrality, and if possible toward the initiation of a combined and continuous mediation, seen as an instrument for clarifying war aims, facilitating bargaining, and gradually leading up to the opening of peace negotiations. Russell took up the idea with enthusiasm, and was at one point ready to sail within a week. He attempted to see Grey or Asquith before leaving, but was unsuccessful. At the last moment, he changed his mind and decided it would be unwise to go. Hope for the success of the mission had diminished when Addams approached the British Ministers about it and found their attitude discouraging. Russell began to have doubts about her, especially after meeting an American who told him mendaciously that she was viewed in Washington much as the Pankhursts had been in Downing Street, and was 'about as welcome there as the black plague'.[69] How much credit Russell gave to this grossly exaggerated view is not clear, since in the same letter he said his support might prove damning to her. Certainly he knew himself out of favour, and his revulsion against the Government had not perceptibly diminished with the progress of the war; he wrote to Ottoline Morrell that he could not bring himself to beg their goodwill, adding 'If I could, I would have them all guillotined. Something very deep in me rebels against asking favours of them; I feel as if I should lose my integrity, because some hypocrisy would be necessary.'[70] So, for the time being, the plan was set aside.[71]

The Union of Democratic Control continued to provide Russell with another outlet for his drive to further the causes of peace. He gave an extraordinary amount of time to it during 1915, though the tasks he undertook were relatively humble, and he made little attempt to influence policy; he attended conferences and council meetings, he lectured frequently, and he helped to found a branch at Cambridge.

Although large public meetings were avoided by the UDC until March 1915, there were many small bodies considering affiliation, already affiliated, or just interested, who were anxious to have a speaker from the Union, and from December 1914 on Russell was kept busy, mostly in London and Cambridge, but at times as far afield as Manchester and Glasgow. He addressed well over thirty meetings in 1915 on subjects such as 'The terms of the peace settlement', 'War and human nature', 'Nationality', 'The principles of peace', and 'The causes of the war'; he found most of his audiences receptive, and he gained confidence as a speaker.[72]

The first public meeting held by the UDC was in Cambridge and owed much to Russell. After the first enthusiasm for the war had worn off and the first wave of eager undergraduate volunteers had enlisted and departed, Russell found that among those who remained there was much sober thinking. Even some who believed they must fight saw the war as having been unnecessary and sought means of preventing future conflicts. By the end of November 1914 Russell thought hopefully that peace feeling in Cambridge was growing, and he planned to organise it as soon as the Christmas vacation was over, working with G. H. Hardy, a Fellow of Trinity and the holder of a lectureship in mathematics.[73] Now that some of his old friendships had become sources of little but pain because of his unorthodox views, Russell spent quite a bit of time with such men as Hardy and F. W. Simpson, a Trinity College chaplain whom Russell found 'a great solace—he is so full of pity for all',[74] a remark it is hard to imagine coming from the pre-war Russell.

Response to the new Cambridge branch of the UDC, formed in mid-January, was good; a month later there were about 150

members, and Russell decided to ask E. D. Morel to come and
address a large public meeting, which he hoped would attract
many outside the membership. He did not expect any disturbance;
indeed at this time, to his surprise, the new branch had met with
little hostility. In a letter to Ottoline Morrell he said. 'At first the
bloodthirsty old men tried to thunder against us, but no one paid
any attention. It is an odd sensation to have summoned up all
one's courage and then find it wasn't needed.'[75] Morel consented,
probably seeing Cambridge as a fairly safe milieu for a first
experiment in large open meetings, and the gathering took place
on 4 March. The attendance was not quite as good as Russell
could have wished, but it went off without a hitch; Russell
reported that Morel had spoken well and that the audience had
been enthusiastic.[76]

The UDC officials were pleased with the way the meeting
went, and followed it with others in major provincial centres. But
Russell had underestimated the persistence of opposition in Cambridge. Already his article 'Can England and Germany be Reconciled after the War?', which appeared in the *Cambridge Review* on
10 February, had provoked criticism, published in the next issue.
Russell accepted the opportunity to answer it the following week,
but does not seem to have taken it too seriously, feeling that the
'old fogies' who attacked him were easy to answer.[77]

By the middle of May the hopeful mood had left him. The
growing horrors had turned a few against war, but had caused
others to harden their attitudes. W. E. Armstrong, a pupil of
Russell's who had enlisted early in the war, had been changed by
what he had seen and suffered; as soon as he had sufficiently
recovered from the loss of a leg, he became a UDC supporter.[78]
But for a while Russell was sure all he had done to spread reason
among the young had been undone—especially by the use of gas,
the effects of which were described by their friends in the
trenches.[79] The undergraduate secretary of the Cambridge branch
of the UDC, an enthusiastic supporter since December 1914,
resigned in May 1915 in disgust at German excesses, and adopted
an ultra-patriotic stance.[80]

Russell began to find his position at Cambridge intolerable. Out
of sympathy with the objectives of the war, he had from the
outset been extremely sensitive to a feeling of alienation from
young men who were leaving to go and fight—at first so eagerly,
later with more reluctance but with the same sense of duty. He
thought them brave but misguided, and he came to feel as
estranged from England as from the individual young men. To
make matters worse, he was giving no courses by this time, and

had no regular commitments except for informal gatherings on Thursday evenings, when he invited students to his rooms for open discussion.[81] The university that had been for him the growing edge of civilisation, and the seed-bed of his own ideas, had suddenly ceased to have meaning.

Months before, Russell had made up his mind to ask for time off, to begin at the start of the long summer vacation, intending to use the time for some kind of peace work.[82] His attempt to free himself temporarily from his lectureship was soon complicated by news that the Trinity College Council was planning to offer him a research fellowship, an appointment which would give him tenure, better pay, and a voice in the College government.[83] At first he was given informally to understand that acceptance would not interfere with his desired leave, but by the time he made formal application in May for permission to be absent for the Michaelmas and Lent terms, the position had changed. Leave was not at first refused outright, but he was told that as a research fellow he would be expected to devote the time of absence to the systematic study of philosophy and mathematics, which he at once replied that he did not plan to do, adding: 'I have always found that my philosophical work is improved by occasional excursions into other fields, from which one returns with renewed freshness of outlook. I am quite sure that the *uninterrupted* pursuit of philosophy would be injurious to my work in that subject.'[84] But feeling against the UDC ran high in Trinity College Council by this time, and its members could not stomach the idea of releasing one of their number to make an excursion into pacifist work. His request for leave was finally refused. According to his information, only the two members of the Council who belonged to the UDC voted for him—the division 'was on strict party lines'. Although it had been Ellis McTaggart, Russell's former mentor, who had mentioned to Russell in February that he might expect to be offered a research fellowship and that it would not interfere with his plans to take leave, he was now the prime mover against Russell. Russell contemplated resigning from Trinity, but instead wrote to propose a compromise solution, suggesting that he might forego the research fellowship but continue as lecturer, taking two terms off. His resignation would have been an embarrassment to them, but Russell was probably right when he said they would be relieved by his rejection of the senior appointment, especially as it carried a vote in the College government, 'which', Russell commented bitterly, 'it is feared I might use to further the advancement of learning'.[85] It was the Council's acceptance of his proposal which opened the way for his dismissal in 1916.

The incident brought home to Russell the isolation of his position, and he could hardly wait for the term to end, so that he could leave the community from which he now felt so estranged. He wrote to Lady Ottoline: 'I find it unspeakably painful being thought a traitor. Every casual meeting in the Court makes me quiver with sensitive apprehension. One ought to be more hardened.'[86] In his reaction to charges of lack of patriotism, Russell was experiencing a feeling common among war resisters. Later, when he worked closely with the young men who were refusing to be conscripted, he found it extraordinarily painful to refuse what seemed to almost everyone else to be the highest service to that country. But in 1915, he was particularly vulnerable because he believed himself almost alone.

Russell had many reasons to be depressed in the early summer of 1915. His personal difficulties included an inability to adjust to Ottoline Morrell's move to Garsington and distress at the wasteful death of the young Cambridge poet, Rupert Brooke.[87] Optimism about an early end to the war was no longer possible: it was becoming clear that advances on the western front, if they came at all, would be costly and slow, and hopes of a successful second front were diminished by the expensive ill-fortune (or mishandling) of the Dardanelles expedition. Germany's use of gas had been horrible to Russell: for Britain to use it was far worse and filled him with shame.[88] The bombing of London and the sinking of the *Lusitania* thickened the atmosphere of hatred.

The formation of the Coalition Government on 20 May 1915, was part of the process of settling into a long war. Russell had at the time little faith indeed in any government and the change did not greatly surprise or alarm him. Some of his predictions for the new regime were gloomy—for instance, he recognised that it brought conscription closer[89]—but he hoped its follies would speed its downfall, and he looked forward to this with impious relish. He wrote:

The Cabinet amuses me. By way of increasing its warlike efficiency, they take in Balfour and Lansdowne because of the energy and foresight with which they conducted the Boer War, Carson and Bonar Law because they have bought and sold (respectively) guns from and to the Kaiser for use against us. It suggests Gilbert and Sullivan. I rejoice in Winston's discomfiture, I am glad Fisher is gone, and I think Ll. George will do well. But in the main they are a hopeless jumble, and I expect they will make a much worse mess of things than the late Cabinet. But they will last until Larking gets up a rebellion and cuts their heads off. May we live to see that day.[90]

He was also cynically amused by the fall from favour of Kitchener, whom he saw as 'a savage ruffian, without humanity or mercy'.[91] At about the same time, the newly-published report of the Bryce

Committee on German atrocities in Belgium confirmed his view of the moral destruction wrought by war. The use of atrocity-mongering to stir up hatred had bothered him from the beginning of the war, and he found the Bryce report far from impartial or careful as to evidence but believed enough emerged to make it incontestable that horrors had been committed. He doubted if these were all on one side, and was sure they would increase as militaristic attitudes became more firmly entrenched on the Allied as on the German side.[92]

Russell left Cambridge in June with a feeling of relief, and a determination to find a means of spreading his opinions as widely as possible. The Union of Democratic Control still provided his chief forum, but at the same time set some limits to what he was free to say. He was in full agreement with all four points of the Union's programme, which had now crystallised as democratisation of foreign policy, no transfer of territory without the consent of the population, abandonment of the balance of power concept in favour of an international council, and reduction of armaments.[93] But he was increasingly ill-at-ease with a campaign that could be effective only after the war came to an end, which no longer seemed likely to be soon. This was the crux: a policy predicated on a short war was not relevant if the war was to go on for several years. After the formation of the May coalition the UDC executive moved towards more active pressure for a negotiated peace, but they did not incorporate it in their platform until the end of 1915.[94] The organisation was not moving fast enough for Russell. In addition, the decision of the UDC not to take a stand against conscription alienated him and gave point to his feeling that it had nothing to say in the present. More and more he found that loyalty to the UDC line prevented him from speaking out, and made him 'stiff and constrained'.[95]

In spite of his longing for understanding from those who were important to him, Russell did not sympathise with the UDC's over-sensitivity to mud-slinging, and the anxiety of its executive to avoid any hint of subversiveness.[96] Private criticism wounded him—he felt it deeply when his aunt, Agatha Russell, reflecting the press view, accused him of lack of patriotism[97]—but public opprobrium troubled him little. The UDC, despite its efforts, became the target for virulent attacks from the right-wing press, being made a symbol for all that was sinister and pro-German, and represented as a spy-infested, traitorous organisation, secretly financed from enemy sources (the last accusation probably being fed by the proneness of Quakers to the giving of anonymous contributions). By advertising the time and place of meetings, the

Daily Express did its best to make the attacks physical as well as verbal, with some limited success.[98]

Russell's opposition to the war was of course widely known by mid-1915, and led to his being included on a number of occasions when those of like concerns met together, but in the main he found meetings of pacifists futile. Of a Representative Peace Conference sponsored by the Society of Friends in June 1915, he wrote to Ottoline Morrell: 'One might as well send a Quaker deputation to Etna to ask it not to erupt. Peace now means defeat for England and the nation is a long way from willingness to accept defeat.'[99] He was even more appalled by a prestigious public meeting on the 'Pacifist Philosophy of Life' held on 8 and 9 July, at which the speakers included, in addition to Russell himself, Goldsworthy Lowes Dickinson, J. A. Hobson, Carl Heath and Vernon Lee. Russell commented: 'They were an awful crew. Pacifists are really no good. What is wrong with mere opposition to war is that it is negative. One must find other outlets for people's wildness, and not try to produce people who have no wildness.'[100] This is an interesting echo from his pre-war comments on William James.

Meetings of this kind at least served the purpose of enabling the opponents of the war to get to know each other. Gradually Russell began to except two groups from his general condemnation. He was favourably impressed by the women of the newly-formed International Committee of Women for Permanent Peace (shortly to become the Women's International League) whose concern for suffering humans appealed to him more than the idealistic theorising with which even the UDC was often content.[101] And he began to see the same immediacy and relevance in the No-Conscription Fellowship, an association of young men pledged to resist compulsory military service. He wrote to Lady Ottoline:

Irene [Cooper Willis] said she went to a meeting of the No-Conscription Fellowship, and found it far more inspiring and better than the U.D.C. . . . I feel moved to speak for them. . . . I grow less and less interested in the politics of the war, and more and more to feel the important thing is to denounce all war. If one could have made any defence of Germany, I daresay I should not have felt as I do. But Germany seems to me very nearly as bad as the most rabid people say, and yet I feel it is wrong to fight Germany.[102]

But Russell did not make a serious commitment to the Fellowship until the Military Service Bill became law in early 1916. Instead, he continued to lecture for the UDC, dividing his time between this and a new possibility which fortunately opened to him just as he left Cambridge on his leave of absence.

The direction in which he channelled his energies in the summer of 1915 owed much to a friendship with D. H. Lawrence, which was of short duration but important in the development of Russell's thought. They became acquainted early in the year, and within a few weeks an intense exchange began. Lawrence visited Russell in Cambridge for a weekend early in March, and left him 'gasping in admiration' at his intuitive perceptiveness. Lawrence came prepared to attack, and found Cambridge contemptible. Far from standing up for his once-beloved university, Russell put up no defence, receiving Lawrence's criticisms of his friends and acquaintances as if they stemmed from a source of truth not revealed to himself.[103] After he had gone, Russell (who seldom wrote nonsense) said of Lawrence, in a letter to Ottoline Morrell; 'The mainspring of his life is love—the universal mystical love—which inspires even his most vehement and passionate hate.'[104]

Once they were apart, Russell's critical faculties recovered somewhat and he began to foresee disagreements between them; but when he visited the Lawrences for a weekend in June, he was once more captivated, Lawrence's enthusiasm helped him in a difficult time, and, in practical terms, one plan had an important outcome. They decided to prepare and deliver jointly a series of lectures. Ideas came thick and fast, and even at the earliest stage the skeleton is recognisable of what was to be fleshed out as Russell's seminal work, *Principles of Social Reconstruction*.[105] He wrote in some excitement to Ottoline Morrell that he and Lawrence had talked of lecturing during the coming autumn,

on his religion, politics in the light of religion, and so on. I believe something could be made of it. I could make a splendid course on political ideas: morality, the State, property, marriage, war, taking them to their roots in human nature, and showing how each is a prison for the infinite in us. And leading on to the hope of a happier world.[106]

He was not only excited by the subject matter of the proposed lecture series, but saw them as a possible start to a new career: 'Won't it be delightful,' he wrote, 'if I can establish myself in London as an independent teacher like Abelard? I should so love the freedom of it.'[107]

Russell began work immediately, and by the end of June he sent an outline to Lawrence. The gulf between them at once became clear, at least in so far as it affected their views of the State. Russell was seeking a viable alternative to the form of central government with which he had become so disillusioned, and was influenced at this time by his reading about French syndicalism.[108] He saw the decentralisation of the State as a means towards making popular control more effective, and more of an integrated part of man's function as a social animal. Although Lawrence spoke of the need for a socialist revolution, there was no place for democracy in his political philosophy, which, as Russell later recognised, tended more to a proto-Fascist system, in so far as it was at all systematised in Lawrence's mind. The views which Russell wished to express were emerging with enough authenticity for him to feel confidence in them, but not necessarily in his own power to stand by them.[109] He was particularly disturbed by Lawrence's accusation that he was disguising his own basic lustfulness and cruelty under a mask of insincere peace propaganda.[110] His secret fears of the violence within him made this indictment most threatening; he still feared a loss of control, and Lawrence's savage words made him question his own motivation. Lawrence showed insight in recognising and making use of Russell's sensitivity on this score, but his attack —which is one with which pacifists are familiar—lacks rational argument. Recognition of the violent nature of humanity, including one's self, may sensibly be advanced as a reason for adopting a pacifist position, rather than being a bar to such a position. The pacifism that is not based on such self-knowledge is open to serious question,[111] as Russell was beginning to recognise.

The partnership broke up, and with a struggle Russell was able to dismiss Lawrence's criticism and carry on with the writing of his lectures. His extraordinary vulnerability to criticism from those close to him was demonstrated again when Ottoline Morrell added her complaints—mainly on the ground that he was giving too much attention to the work—and he was momentarily ready to give up the whole project.[112] But the subject had become important to him, and he had to go on.

The encounter between Russell and Lawrence may be explained dialectically, with Russell's initial views representing the thesis of intellect, Lawrence's reaction the antithesis of emotion, and the lectures emerging as the synthesis. The purpose Lawrence had served for Russell was to offer him the extreme: after striving and failing to accept it uncritically, he was able to move to a balanced position in which credit could be given to instinct and emotion without discounting intellect or doing violence to his 'scientific temper and . . . respect for fact'.[113]

By October, Russell was working well on the lectures, although the delays of the summer caused him some anxiety about his ability to complete them in time.[114] He later said they 'came out in a spontaneous manner',[115] but in fact when they were nearly finished he was complaining that they had practically driven him into insanity.[116] Perhaps the explanation is that in spite of the difficulties surrounding their writing, the form and subject matter emerged from a deep level of his subconscious, so that he did not feel he directed the process.

The lectures were delivered at Caxton Hall, London, on Tuesday evenings from 18 January to 7 March, 1916, and published in November. The central theme is that it is not reason that causes or prevents wars. Most human actions, Russell claimed, stemmed from 'impulse'. Men's impulses were essentially non-rational and unconsidered. They were neither good nor bad in themselves and the direction of their force could be toward life or it could be toward death. But Russell did not believe the direction was random—whether impulses would be creative or destructive was largely determined by social institutions. In successive lectures he examined some of the most important human institutions—the State, war, property, education, marriage, religion and the churches. While each had come into being to serve one or other purpose of some validity at the time, each had come to exist for its own sake and was now inappropriate, restrictive of liberty and productive of only harmful impulses. Without liberty, people were not free to reach their creative potential, but were filled instead with fears and hatreds of each other which could lead only to destruction. The changes Russell proposed were all in the direction of freeing people from compulsion, of giving them a greater control over their own destinies, of replacing meaningless conformity based on fear with active intelligent participation. The results he envisaged went far beyond the mere removal of cause for war, and had a positive creative aspect, evolutionary rather than utopian. Improved institutions were not to preserve man in a safe and static system, but to free him for development of instinctual, intellectual and spiritual excellence.

The important position given in these lectures to the function of impulse was new in Russell's writing, and it owed something to Lawrence's influence. But it is wrong to regard Russell as having taken over any concept ready-made from Lawrence. All the evidence indicates that in so far as Russell's political philosophy derived anything from the encounter, it was not from listening to Lawrence's ideas. Russell's progression had been from the rigidly controlled and arid intellectuality of his early years, through a fearful attempt, facilitated by Ottoline Morrell, to come to terms with the passions, and through the terrifying unleashing of anger in himself and others when war broke out, towards an integration of the different sides of personality. Lawrence (propelled, significantly, by Lady Ottoline) came into Russell's life just at the time when he had to resolve the apparent contradictions and face the implications of the integration in his own life and as it bore on the lives of mankind at large. The ideas which Lawrence laid before him struck Russell as nonsense, although his initial attraction to him and his wish to please Ottoline Morrell made him try hard to appreciate them.[117] It was not what Lawrence said about emotion as much as the way in which he seemed in himself to epitomise the life of feeling that struck Russell with such force, and caused him to open himself uncritically for a brief while to the impact of the other's personality, as he had done with few people before. The experience was traumatic, but the self-examination which followed contributed significantly to the clarification of his thought on the relation between instinct, reason and spirit.

Besides being a vitally important formulation of Russell's political philosophy, the lectures were abstractly autobiographical. Russell spoke from his own experience when he said:

Instinct, mind, and spirit are all essential to a full life; each has its own excellence and its own corruption. Each can attain a spurious excellence at the expense of the others; each has a tendency to encroach upon the others; but in the life which is to be sought all three will be developed in co-ordination, and intimately blended in a single harmonious whole.[118]

Russell had of course great hopes that his lectures would prove a positive force for good. As they proceeded he saw them as a 'rallying-ground for the intellectuals',[119] whom he hoped to spur on to personal and political action. In fact, response both in spoken and in written form was good, and he had cause to be well satisfied with the reception of the series.[120] But he began to see that what came from the depths of his own conviction could yet be accepted by his audiences merely as a delightful intellectual exercise, words with which their minds could agree without that moving of their instincts and spirits that would result in action. By the time the lectures were delivered, he had given up the idea of following them with other series for London audiences. For him, if not for most of his hearers, the coming of conscription at last brought an opportunity for the kind of radical action he was advocating.

CHAPTER 4
RUSSELL FINDS WORK TO DO

Russell saw the introduction of conscription in early 1916 as another step in the laying-waste of civilisation and the rape of liberal values which were the inexorable consequences of the continuing war. But almost simultaneously he came to believe that what looked like the ultimate triumph of militarism might instead be the means to its defeat. He hoped resistance to compulsory service would be widespread, and he thought the example might make articulate the latent popular opposition to the war he still believed existed. The theoretical basis of opposition to conscription dove-tailed nicely with his political philosophy as he had expressed it in *Principles of Social Reconstruction*: it was a direct rejection of war, it was an individual's refusal to have his conscience overborne, and it was a challenge to the too-powerful central state. Far more than all this, Russell was excited at the opportunity at last to translate theoretical and verbal disapproval of the war into action. He wished he was of military age, so that his defiance could be direct, but he soon found there was plenty of work for supporters who were not themselves liable for service. He was tired of writing and speaking words which did not seem to affect people's behaviour or the course of events—what was the good of giving lectures if they just made people feel comfortable and broadminded without any practical outcome?[121]

To be part of the resistance of the conscientious objectors seemed enormously important—a chance to tilt at the whole system by which wars came about and possibly even to overthrow it. In his lectures Russell had spoken of the 'supreme fire of thought and spirit'[122] which alone could save future generations, and he came to see this as incarnate in the young men of the No-Conscription Fellowship. Certainly for some of those who had chafed at the lack of a channel for effective dissent the enactment of compulsion brought almost a sense of relief: there was a world of difference between refraining from volunteering and refusing to be conscripted.

The No-Conscription Fellowship had been formed as early as November 1914, when Fenner Brockway, the young socialist editor of the *Labour Leader*, had called together a group of men of military age who would not be prepared to take the part of combatants if conscription should come.[123] From the outset the leadership had been shared by socialists and Christian pacifists, a dichotomy (though not a clearcut division) which was to be a source both of strain and of strength throughout the life of the Fellowship.[124] Russell was soon to be very closely involved in the dynamics of interaction between the individuals and at times the factions which made up the NCF National Committee. His later description of himself as having differed from both socialists and Quakers and as having felt throughout 'the pain of solitude',[125] does not do justice to the closeness he felt at the time to the ardent young men of both persuasions, although he did maintain a certain philosophical objectivity of approach which was sometimes useful in the divisive problems confronting the leaders.

By the time Russell gave himself to the work of the No-Conscription Fellowship important decisions had already been made, in which a large part was played by Clifford Allen, the dynamic socialist who was chairman of the Fellowship throughout its existence. Full membership was limited to men of military age, but provision had been made in May 1915 for the inclusion of 'associates', persons not liable for conscription because of age or sex.[126] An ideological basis of membership had been decided upon, by a process that was in itself unusual. Having attracted the interest of a large number of men, Brockway, Allen and their small planning committee set out to find the common factors in the beliefs on which these men based their inability to accept compulsory service. There were diverse views, but by the first convention of the Fellowship, held in London on 27 November 1915, Allen was able to report that underlying all other reasons, 'there was one objection to conscription which we shared with intense fervour, and that was a belief in the sanctity of human life'.[127] This was adopted as the ground on which the NCF would base its objection to conscription, and on this basis socialist agnostics, Christian pacifists, and ethical humanists worked together.

So simplified a formula could mean different things to different people. What really drew Russell to the young men of the Fellowship was that he shared their view that a stand against conscription was the first step to a better world: this practical consideration weighed more with him than the theoretical basis and indeed, once adopted, the phrase 'the sanctity of life' had been little discussed. For many it meant that the taking of life was never justified, but Russell would certainly have been more in sympathy with the gloss put on it by Allen at the time (and spelled out more explicitly in retrospect) which was that human life was so important that control over life and death must be set apart from other categories of men's actions. The decision to give his own life or take that of another could not be taken out of the hands of the individual, resistance to compulsion in this matter, rather than the ethics of killing, thus becoming the crux.[128]

The new element introduced when the young leaders of the Friends' Service Committee came in during the summer of 1915 was to be of such great importance during Russell's association with the NCF that a brief outline of what they brought with them is essential. The Society of Friends had not easily met the challenge of war. Contrary to popular belief, Quakers are not bound to any pacifist creed, but must continually seek the light corporately and individually. All shades of opinion on the rights and wrongs of the war and on the obligations of Friends were found among members in the early months. Only gradually did the Society move toward a meaningful corporate reaffirmation of the historic peace testimony, with conscription acting as a catalyst. When a special adjourned session of London Yearly Meeting[129] was held in January 1915 following the introduction of the conscription bill, a clear consensus was reached, in a crowded Meeting, uncompromisingly reaffirming opposition to all war and even taking a stand against the principle of alternative service. This was not a unanimous decision even of those present, nor did it attempt to bind the conscience of any Friend, but it enabled the men of the Friends' Service Committee, into whose hands leadership in matters concerning military service had largely passed, to feel behind them the support of their Society. If the Quakers could be said to have an official voice on conscription, it was from this time on that of the FSC. It was the strength of their conviction that led the Society to agree not to seek any special status or exemption for Quakers as such, and to their close involvement with the No-Conscription Fellowship. Alfred Barratt Brown and John P. Fletcher, moving spirits in the FSC, joined the National Committee a few weeks later, as did Edward Grubb, the elderly Quaker (a radical of an earlier generation) who served the Fellowship as treasurer for the rest of its existence, and who formed a relationship of much warmth and mutual respect with the younger men, Quakers and non-Quakers alike. But the FSC men had still a good deal to contend with in their own Society, many of whose members continued to differ from them over such matters as alternative service, and this was to contribute at times to their assumption of an intransigent and apparently intolerant stance (deplored by Russell) towards those members of the NCF who differed from them.

Another decision of far-reaching consequence had been made when the NCF gave approval in principle to the rejection of compulsory alternatives to military service, although the option was to be left 'open to the individual judgement of each member'.[130] When this resolution was passed at the Convention of November 1915, the time of trying to guess what the Military Service Bill might contain was nearly over. The Government's cautious steps towards compulsion finally culminated in the introduction of a bill on 5 January 1916, making military service obligatory for single men between the ages of eighteen and forty.[131]

To Russell, compulsory military service was the epitome of illiberalism, although he had long realised that a Liberal Government which had swallowed intervention in the war would not be likely to strain at conscription. Opposition in the country, in Parliament and in the Cabinet was rapidly whittled away or disarmed. Labour—whose united resistance had been feared by the Government and hoped for by the anti-conscriptionist—was bought off ('bamboozled', as Russell put it[132]) by the promise that there would be no industrial conscription, the Irish Members by a clause excepting Ireland from the operation of the Act, and possible Liberal opponents (especially in the Cabinet) by the inclusion of the conscience clause. Both the NCF and FSC refrained from publicly advocating any exemption clause, though the NCF may have privately laid before potentially sympathetic parliamentary groups a proposal for a statutory declaration of conscientious objection, to be made before a justice of the peace.

Whatever the Cabinet's motivation (and it was certainly more to placate queasy Liberal consciences than to meet the needs of the known objectors), there is no doubt that to make any provision for conscientious objection was an exceptional and enlightened step at that time.[133] But the changes were made at a late stage in the drafting, and much of the benefit of the clause and perhaps even more of the respect which might have accrued to the framers of the bill were lost as a result of two factors: gross ambiguity in the wording, and the placing of the onus for its interpretation on unsuitable tribunals inherited from the Derby scheme, which had been a last-ditch attempt (in late 1915) to raise men voluntarily. Tribunal members, originally selected as patriotic recruiters, did not easily understand that they were now to be impartial dispensers of judicial decisions.

When it was decided to add a conscience clause, the alterations made in the bill were minimal. To the list of grounds[134] on which exemption could be claimed were added the words, 'on the

ground of a conscientious objection to bearing arms'. The clause
dealing with certificates of exemption was amended to read: 'Any
certificate of exemption may be absolute, conditional, or temporary, as the Military Service Tribunal think best suited to the case,
and in the case of an application on conscientious grounds may
take the form of an exemption from combatant duties only.' A
further amendment tagged on the following words: 'or may be
conditional on the applicant being engaged in some work which in
the opinion of the Tribunal dealing with the case is of national
importance'.[135] The proposers of this were two Quakers, Arnold
Rowntree, of whom Russell did not have a high opinion, and
T. E. Harvey, with whom Russell was to tangle later on the very
issue of alternative service.

Asquith, perhaps thinking of his Garsington friends,[136] must be
given the credit for having the clause framed in such a way that the
right to claim conscientious objection was not limited to those
who could give evidence of religious grounds, a point on which
he was insistent despite representations from the War Office,[137]
and the dubious political value of his stand. Such a concession was
particularly pertinent to the NCF, yet Asquith's speech on introduction of the bill disgusted Russell and destroyed any illusion
that the Prime Minister understood the position of the radical
objector. In it Asquith painted a picture of the typical conscientious objector as refusing only to bear arms, but ready and eager
to perform any military duties that did not involve him directly in
the taking of life: such a man would be content to claim
exemption only from combatant service. Russell thought this
interpretation rendered the conscience clause almost worthless.[138]

The Military Service Act passed the third reading, with only
thirty-eight votes against it, on 24 January 1916. Russell had
joined as fully as the pressure of his lectures would permit in the
effort of the NCF and the newly-formed National Council
Against Conscription to prevent its passage. The latter organisation had been brought into being at the eleventh hour in an
attempt to rally a wider spectrum of opponents of conscription,
and it attracted many small and large Labour groups as affiliates.
Besides many well-known Labour people, the executive included
women activists, Christian and socialist pacifists, radical Liberals
and a number of unattached intellectuals and Bloomsburyites.[139]
Russell rejoiced in the sight of Lytton Strachey and Robert
Smillie, the president of the Miners' Federation, working together. He himself went to a few meetings of the National Council
Against Conscription[140] but was increasingly drawn to the No-
Conscription Fellowship because of the deeper personal commit-

ment that was forced on the men liable for service who were its members.

As the potential role of the objectors became clearer and conscription no longer seemed just another hopeless defeat, Russell offered his services to the Fellowship. He recognised the quality of Clifford Allen (whom he had probably met on such occasions as the Representative Peace Conference), although at first he did not find him attractive, saying of him, 'Allen is just like a dissenting parson, but he is vigorous and able and has a really great gift of leadership'.[141]

At this time Russell did not really expect the tribunals to deal harshly with the objectors, and when the first reports of seemingly harsh decisions began to appear he was appalled: but the emotions he experienced were much more complex than simple aversion. His letter to Lady Ottoline revealed more of his great need for personal commitment than he would have been likely to allow to show elsewhere. 'The tribunals are monstrous,' he wrote, '—the law is bad enough, but they disregard it and are much worse. It is simply a madness of persecution. . . . I felt horror of the men on the tribunals, for their persecuting spirit, but I rather envy the men they persecute. It is maddening not to be liable.' In the same letter he wrote that the spirit among the resisters was a real ferment, 'like the beginning of a new religion', and he wrote too of the new vigour and life that were filling him.[142]

The ambivalence expressed here by Russell was common and perhaps inevitable among those who had pledged themselves to resist compulsory military service, and particularly among the militant leaders of the NCF.[143] Although they could not but approve the inclusion in the Act of a conscience clause, such provision for exemption was not a primary objective. Their stand was anti-war and anti-conscription: they were prepared for resistance rather than for appeal. They soon made the decision to work within the frame-work set up by the Act as far as it met their needs, but saw it as a vehicle for opposition to militarism and to the continuation of the war rather than as a means to exemption, a hard attitude for their friends and sympathisers to understand, and one which at times carried some of them to extremes and divided them from their fellows. Yet it was a logical development of the type of thinking Russell had been doing, and which he had put into *Principles of Social Reconstruction*. The conscience clause might make those who still supported the Liberal party feel that something of liberalism had been saved, but for those who wanted to throw their weight against what they saw as the whole military system, conscription provided a *casus belli* and the conscience clause merely gave them an arena.

In spite of the prospect of new and exciting work to be done Russell found himself temporarily drained of energy and purpose after the last of his lectures was given on 7 March 1916. The mood did not last long: characteristically he dispelled it by taking a two-week walking holiday with friends.[144] Two important, and very different, channels were opening to him. Besides his hope of being of service to the NCF, there was now at last a firm commitment to go to the United States. A renewed invitation had come from Harvard in January to lecture there early in 1917.

Russell still believed American attitudes to be of great importance and thought a term spent at Harvard would enable him to exert some influence without interference from the Foreign Office, which he was sure would not let him go to America except to teach. There were other arguments to be taken into account (for example, it would be helpful financially), but one of the most attractive features of the proposal, and one in which it differed from the 1915 invitation, was that in addition to a course in logic he was to give one on ethics 'with reference to the social and international applications', which he considered would be more difficult but more worthwhile. He realised the trip would interrupt the peace work he hoped to be able to do in England, and he was reluctant to take on such a heavy load of preparation just as the lecture series he had found so taxing came to an end, but on balance he decided the opportunity should not be missed, and he sent off his acceptance.[145]

Russell's leave of absence from Cambridge was drawing to an end, and he would have to go back for the months of May and June. But his duties there were very light and the long summer vacation would follow, so he could expect to have time free for peace work and the preparation of the Harvard lectures. Meanwhile, there were a few weeks before he had to return to Cambridge. His interest in the No-Conscription Fellowship was still very much alive, and now the eagerness was not all on his side. Catherine Marshall was determined to involve him fully.

Marshall, one of the most important figures among the anti-conscriptionists of the First World War, has been curiously neglected by history. She had played an extremely significant role in the development of political strategy by the National Union of Women's Suffrage Societies (the non-militant wing of the women's suffrage movement), for which she worked almost full-time from 1908 to 1914. During late 1914 she had worked in various ways, in accordance with the policy of the National

Union, to protect the interests of women in the dislocation caused by the war, and at the same time she had spoken out for the urgent need to re-think the structure of international relations in order to prepare for a new attitude when peace came. The issue of education for peace, and specifically of support for the International Women's Conference at The Hague in April 1915, had split the executive of the National Union, and in the face of the intransigence of its president, Millicent Fawcett, all the officers, including Marshall, and over half the executive had resigned, many of them—again including Marshall—going on to form the British section of the Women's International League for Peace and Freedom which emerged from the conference. During 1915 Marshall devoted much of her time to the new organisation, and met with the NCF leaders and Bertrand Russell at several pacifist gatherings. When the Military Service Act was imminent, she worked for the National Council Against Conscription, but by March 1916 she was devoting most of her time and political know-how to rallying support for the No-Conscription Fellowship.[146] While Russell was on holiday she began to write to him almost daily, 'beseeching help' on behalf of the Fellowship, and as his lethargy dissipated he responded with a return of enthusiasm. He returned to London on 1 April, and promised all his free time from then until 25 April to the service of the conscientious objectors.[147]

Marshall had not exaggerated the need. Events were moving rapidly and the pressure on the resources of the NCF was intense. The 1916 Military Service Act differed radically from more recent conscription laws. Coming as it did when other means of producing men had been milked dry, it was designed to enlist men for immediate use rather than to keep up and regulate a steady flow. In effect, it conscripted a 'class' of men—the single men between the ages of eighteen and forty who had not enlisted voluntarily. This would be sufficient only for the needs of the next few months, and the first Act was indeed succeeded in May by a second, enlisting the married men. Meanwhile there was no attempt to divide those liable under the Act into groups to be taken in order. All those covered by its provisions were deemed to have enlisted and all were immediately liable for service. All, therefore, who wanted to apply for exemption must do so at once.

The NCF, undaunted by its failure to prevent the passage of the Act, set to work at once in the new context. Nation-wide, the members now needed not only encouragement from the leaders to maintain their stand but also information and advice on innumerable points of law and procedure,[148] on how to fill in their appeals,

on how to conduct themselves in front of the tribunals, on what
they might expect to happen to them and when. On some of these
points policy had to be hammered out by the National Committee
behind closed doors, before there could be agreement on what
advice to give. Meetings were held everywhere, material was sent
out to branches and to individual members, advice centres were
set up, the maintenance department (charged with support of
COs' families) prepared itself in earnest, funds were raised (privately), leaflets were planned, supporters were organised to watch
and report on tribunals, speakers were sent to branches and to
sympathetic groups such as Independent Labour Party gatherings.[149]

Russell came into the Fellowship not as a member but as one of
the so-called associates, people excluded from full membership
because either age or sex placed them outside the scope of the Act.
The main focus for his work was initially the Associates' Political
Committee. When this group first met formally, in mid-March,
there were four members, Russell, Brailsford, Marshall and J. S.
Middleton, the Labour Party's assistant secretary. With this
combination of political, journalistic and literary talent, the direction of its work is not surprising—the members took on the task
of working toward repeal of the Military Service Act by propaganda and political pressure, tackling it on a scale out of all
proportion to the Committee's size. The second main function of
the group was to stand by to take the place of National Committee members liable to arrest if the organisation should be declared
illegal, and this was why there was no hurry to make them full
members. 'The question of carrying all our eggs in contraband
baskets is a serious one, but . . . the National Associates' Committee appears the only way out', wrote an NCF official to
Herbert Peet of the Friends' Service Committee.

Meeting on 17 March 'to consider methods of agitation', the
Committee wasted no time.[150] Russell was still on holiday, and
did not go to the first two meetings, but he must have been in
close touch because his name came up a number of times and tasks
were confidently assigned to him. By the time of the NCF's
second National Convention on 8 and 9 April 1916, the group had
laid the groundwork for much of its future work, making use in
particular of the wide political skill and knowledge gained by
Marshall   in   her   work   with   the   non-militant   suffrage
movement.[151] The information and propaganda network set up
kept the cause of the conscientious objectors in the public eye
throughout the war. There was nothing but applause and appreciation from within the Fellowship at this time for the efforts of

the political Committee, although later some forms of political action were to be called in question.

In spite of his late start, Russell's contribution to the work was substantial. By the meeting of 4 April he had set to work on several areas. Another member of the Committee was compiling 'a list of prominent people willing to write or sign letters and a list of London and Provincial papers willing to publish such letters', and Russell was writing 'a series of letters to be used in this way, designed to meet every sort and kind of misunderstanding'.[152] Unfortunately, there is no evidence as to whether such letters were ever in fact published over other people's signatures. In April the *Labour Leader* asked to be supplied with a weekly page of information and news about the conscientious objectors, and Russell may for a time have written this in rotation with others.[153] He had also promised to write a leaflet or leaflets, and to help look after general literature.

Russell took an active part in the liaison with Parliament. He offered to undertake 'a certain amount of lobbying',[154] and on at least one occasion he was responsible for getting in touch with lukewarm supporters in the House of Commons about a proposed deputation. More satisfying must have been his connection with Philip Snowden, the one MP who needed no urging to challenge the administration of the Military Service Act whenever occasion offered, and who spoke against it in the debates on the Consolidated Fund Bill on 22 March, and on the adjournment on 6 April. Even on the first occasion, so soon after the Political Committee first met, they were ready to provide material for Snowden or any other critic of the Government who might take part in the debate. Snowden made the principal speech on the conscription issue, but it is not certain how much he was assisted by the NCF group on that date. A deputation from the Fellowship met with him on 25 March, and when the 6 April debate came along Russell undertook to prepare the case for him.[155] As a known opponent of the Military Service Act, Snowden had other sources of information besides the NCF—for example, numerous individuals with grievances wrote to him—and he did not speak for the NCF, but there can be little doubt that he accepted Russell's priming (on behalf of the Committee) as to what were some of the most important points to be stressed. On 22 March, he had attacked on a wide front, citing examples in respect to every kind of conscript or applicant for exemption, although giving particular attention to the problems faced by conscientious objectors.[156] On 6 April his whole attention was given to the latter. He spoke of the inequality of treatment meted out by different tribunals, and criticised the military representatives. He asked what would happen to applicants whose exemption was refused, or who had been given non-combatant service which they could not accept: in particular he repeated a concern which he had voiced on 22 March that they would be taken to France where they might be shot. At best, as he pointed out, those who did not obtain the exemption they sought, and who then refused army orders, were in the unenviable position of being subject to punishment by the same military authority against which they were protesting, a situation which he described as 'indefensible'. In conclusion, Snowden asked for 'the cessation of all these prosecutions, and the release of all these men, pending some impartial inquiry into the administration of the Act and the devising of some new machinery for dealing with this difficult class of objectors', and for a statement that would allay the anxiety which was felt. Snowden's two speeches were printed in pamphlet form by the Independent Labour Party, and were widely distributed by the NCF.[157]

Snowden's speech well reflects the temper of the early weeks. The operation of the MSA was still only in its first phase and there was a great deal of uncertainty as to what the future would bring. The tribunals were in full swing, and there were enough inequalities and injustices in some of the decisions they handed down to provide grist for the NCF's propaganda mill. But actual hardship had scarcely begun: most of the members who had failed to get exemption had gone home quietly to await the arrests which began in the first week of April, even as Russell and Snowden prepared the speech.

Russell had also offered to prepare sympathisers in the House of Lords for a possible debate there, but sympathisers among the Lords were even harder to find. Allen met with Lord Courtney[158] who, in spite of advanced age and near blindness, remained one of the most consistent and courageous supporters whom the conscientious objectors had in the Lords until his death, at the age of eighty-six, in 1918. Lord Parmoor was supportive,[159] and Russell's brother, the Earl Russell, was prepared to take up the cause at times: Russell had taken some pains to influence him before the Act was even passed. Frank Russell is not always given all the credit he deserves for the support he offered to his maverick brother during the war, providing him with accommodation when he needed it, championing him within the family when his anti-war attitude caused embarrassment,[160] and later visiting him in prison. He was also responsible for one unusual triumph for the conscientious objectors when, by means of skilful wording, he forced the House of Lords to allow a motion to be carried which by implication was critical of army treatment of the objectors.[161]

Russell was active on behalf of the Political Committee in another important way. The Committee took seriously the 'conversion' of influential individuals. They thought it worth going to a lot of trouble to get the right people to see them, or write to them, or answer their letters in the press.[162] Russell devoted considerable effort to this (in addition to influencing his brother informally). The Bishop of Oxford became a special project of his. Much could be hoped for from episcopal support—a bishop might be a spokesman in the House of Lords, could provide a weighty signature on a memorial or an impressive voice in a deputation, and might have a strong influence on sections of the public. Charles Gore, Bishop of Oxford, was known to be a man of liberal and humane views, and had raised the interest of the Fellowship by a letter to *The Times* on 14 March in which he protested against the attitude being shown by some of the tribunals in their dealings with the conscientious objectors.[163] Russell undertook to request his signature to a planned memorial to the Government, influenced perhaps by the fact that Lady Ottoline Morrell was acquainted with the Bishop. Russell kept in close touch with him, pressuring him to sign the memorial—which the Bishop refused to do—and later to serve on a deputation—which he agreed to.[164] In these early days Russell, in common with others among the NCF leaders, had trouble recognising that the logic of the conscientious objector's position, and particularly of their refusal of alternative service, was not as apparent to all as it was to him. Later, as the evangelical optimism of the leaders diminished, they became better able to respect the boundaries of the sympathy to be expected from people such as the Bishop of Oxford, who could be counted on for courageous support whenever there were cases of apparent injustice or brutality, but who were not to be converted to complete agreement with the stand of the objectors.

Russell's attempts to make converts were not limited to working on those who were showing some (but not enough) sympathy. He was described as being 'on tap . . . for answering letters from important people who need persuading or convincing',[165] and some letters have recently been found which he drafted in answer to individuals who refused when approached with a request to sign the memorial to the Prime Minister. Frank Marshall, Catherine Marshall's father, of Hawse End, Keswick, had, it seems, sent the document out with a covering letter from himself, perhaps to local people of distinction or to those known to him personally. Unfavourable or critical replies which he received were sent on to his daughter in London, and she passed them to Russell.[166] The exchange is worth quoting at some length, since it illustrates facets of the opposition to the NCF, and shows in Russell's words the direction in which the leaders wished to influence the thinking public. It is also of interest that the letters were written for use over someone else's signature—perhaps the first, but certainly not the last time, Russell worked as a ghost-writer on behalf of the COs.

Sir Oliver Lodge, physicist, first principal of Birmingham University, and president (1913) of the British Association, explained his inability to sign the memorial in terms which must have become all too familiar to officials of the NCF:

I am not able to sign the document you enclose; for, while sympathising of course with the intentions of those who have drafted it, I feel that the Tribunals have an extremely difficult task. And I learn of artificial consciences being fostered by agitators, and of rehearsals being gone through, and texts learnt up, for the purpose of evading responsibilities.

Conscientious Objection of a real kind can hardly be widespread, and even in that case people of wrong-headed views must be content to suffer from them to some extent.

Russell's draft reply (undated) is in his own handwriting with the exception of the first sentence, added by Catherine Marshall, which reads: 'My father has sent on to me your reply to his letter'. Russell's draft reads, in full:

I am sorry that you are not able to sign the memorial to the P.M. No doubt it is true that the Tribunals have had a very difficult task: to judge of the genuineness of a conscience which leads to conclusions that seem strange is always difficult. But I am afraid no one who has followed the proceedings of the Tribunals closely can deny that, in many cases, the strength of their prejudice against conscientious objectors has prevented them from performing their difficult duty in a judicial spirit. The stories of "artificial consciences fostered by agitators" have no foundation in fact. Spontaneously, the small minority who find themselves opposed to all war have been drawn together by the need of sympathy; their combination is no more "artificial" than the British Association.

After all, conscientious objection to war, though it cannot but seem strange to those who feel the importance of victory for the cause of the Allies, is no new thing. It has been for 250 years a fundamental principle of the Society of Friends; it was a tenet of the Christian Church until the time of Constantine, and was one of the chief reasons for the early persecutions.

You say that "conscientious objections of a real kind can hardly be widespread." But I can assure you from personal knowledge that many among the conscientious objectors have that kind of dogged unyielding courage which makes them perfectly willing, if necessary, to incur any penalty, even death, rather than take part in what they believe to be wrong. I think it will be found that the number of these among men liable to the Act is at least 10,000. To treat these men as "shirkers" shows a complete misunderstanding of their character.

You say: "People with wrong-headed views must be content to suffer for them to some extent." They *are* content to suffer, not only to some extent, but to any extent. But ought we to be willing to make them suffer? The principle you set forth is the very principle by which religious persecution is always justified.

The views for which Galileo suffered were even less widespread in his day than conscientious objection to war is now; the harm which was feared from their prevalence was greater than any which we fear from the Germans, since it was thought they must lead to eternal damnation. Yet we have decided that it was a mistake to persecute them, and we do not persecute those who believe that the world is flat. If the views of the conscientious objectors are equally foolish and equally rare, can they not be allowed to die out through their own absurdity? And if by any chance they contain some germ of wisdom, shall we not risk being associated by future ages with Nero and the Inquisition and the fires of Smithfield?

Another critical letter forwarded by Frank Marshall came from Sir Michael Sadler, the vice-chancellor of the University of Leeds. His main ground for refusing to sign the memorial was that he thought the Leeds tribunals had 'shown great consideration for the conscientious objectors and have treated the cases which have come before them with patience and insight'. He would not, therefore, wish to do anything which might imply dissatisfaction with these tribunals. Further, he favoured compulsory alternative service, and hoped new proposals would 'remove all reasonable grounds for objection to the enforcement of the obligation upon all'. Russell's draft reply (which, like the letter to Sir Oliver Lodge, had a first sentence written in by Marshall) suggested that Sadler might record his satisfaction with the fairness of the Leeds tribunal while pointing out that other tribunals had been less fair, and often treated any conscientious objector who did not happen to be a Quaker as if he were a criminal and a shirker, an utterly untrue implication:

There are among their number men of great intellectual eminence, Fellows of Colleges, who have done original work of high value. There are many men who believe (as the early Christians did) that the teaching of Christ forbids war. There are many others—and these have almost invariably failed to receive the slightest consideration from the Tribunals—who, while not being members of any definite religious organisation, have a profound belief in the brotherhood of man, and a belief (perhaps fanatical, but shared by many of the greatest religious teachers, and finding intellectual expression in the philosophy of Spinoza) that hatred can only be conquered by love, that the reign of force cannot be destroyed by force, and that only spiritual weapons can destroy militarism.

Russell went on to restate the case against persecution, in what seem rather high-flown terms:

For this faith and belief they are willing to suffer any persecution, even death. For their sakes I can scarcely wish that they should be spared, since their suffering must enoble [*sic*] their cause to many thousands who now despise them and see nothing but selfishness in their abstention. But for the sake of the nation, I hope that the crime (as I cannot but think it) of punishing a profound and sincere spiritual belief will not be committed, and that a way will be found by which their fervour and zeal may be of profit to the community.

Sadler's hopes regarding alternative service were answered concisely:

> I am afraid most of them would not feel that their case would be met by non-combatant service, or by any change of occupation with a view to organizing the nation's resources for war. They would feel that, if they undertook such service, they were setting free others to fight, and were participating indirectly in the guilt (as they believe it to be) of warfare. I think if you place yourself, in imagination, at the point of view of those who believe that all war is wicked, you will see that no other course of action is open to them.

The draft replies quoted above are of some interest as examples of epistolary skill as well as for their subject matter. In his replies, Russell did three things: he wrote precisely in answer to points raised by the correspondent; he drew upon his knowledge of the other's interests and background (Lodge championed an unpopular cause, the investigation of psychic phenomena); and he conveyed the values of most importance to the NCF at the time. At least once, he seems to have yielded momentarily to the temptation to use his wit toward defeating his opponent rather than toward conversion—one wonders whether Lodge really relished the comparison between the British Association and the NCF. But Russell and the Fellowship were in earnest in the hope and belief that they could convert people to support of the cause of the objectors. Something central to Russell's pre-war philosophy was involved here; his faith died hard that intelligent people, exposed to reason, must see its force.

The achievements of the Political Committee in the first few weeks of Russell's association, which also marked the beginning of its existence, were remarkable, but on the debit side, there was a certain unconscious arrogance in the Committee's style, a difficulty in seeing the point of view of their opponents, an almost chiliastic tendency to divide the world into the converted and the unconverted.[167] In this, Russell was a prime offender, especially in the early days, although the characteristic was widespread among the NCF leaders.

Until his return to Cambridge at the end of April, Russell worked cheerfully under the direction of Marshall and Allen, more as a literary hack, brainstormer and runner of errands than as an executive, and during this time he wrote that he was busy, loving the people he worked with, and 'as happy as a king'. His euphoria had two main and complementary elements in it. First there was his relief at being thoroughly occupied in work which he considered worthwhile, with people to whom he felt increasingly drawn. He found the young men of the Fellowship delightful, full of fun and ability, and his respect for Allen was slowly turning to affection.[168] Secondly, and probably at this time of even greater importance, there was the belief that the conscientious objectors could win their struggle. On 2 April he wrote to Lady Ottoline that there was '*real* hope of mitigating the lot of conscientious objectors', and a week later (after the Convention) he went much farther, writing, 'I really believe they will defeat the Government and wreck Conscription, when it is found they won't yield'.[169] He doubtless believed, as he told Lodge, that there were 10,000 men who would stand firm. The care he took with his draft replies showed his faith that people like Lodge and Sadler could be convinced, by the power of words and the example of these men, that what they were supporting was inconsistent with their own liberal ideals. More important, he thought that recognition of this betrayal would lead them to join in the opposition to what he saw as persecution.

This optimism informed and justified the whole plan of the Political Committee during March and into April 1916. Although Marshall headed her scheme 'Agitation on behalf of Prisoners', it was to be more than a mere campaign for averting hardship and injustice: it was conceived as the means by which public and Parliamentary opinion would gradually but inevitably be brought in behind the conscientious objectors, who were not passive sufferers as much as the vanguard of the attack on militarism.

It was a great relief to be with young men who were willing to die rather than to fight, and Russell was encouraged to find that some at least of the early supporters of the war were expressing changed opinions.[170] At this time he said little about the deeper aspects of pacifism, but he took comfort from the strength of conviction of the people with whom he was now beginning to work. His feeling of alienation from England, his need to find an acceptable way to serve the country for which so many were unacceptably giving their lives, made him particularly receptive to Allen's strong and well-developed faith that the objectors would, in the long run, be helping to bring about the needed changes in the nation, and were immediately and directly helping to prevent the establishment of a principle that was the negation of what England was supposed to be fighting for. Russell would have echoed Allen's view that 'Here, at last, was an immense opportunity for work of national importance'.[171] This, too, was to be the spirit of the Convention held in April 1916.

CHAPTER 5

CONSCRIPTION: A FOCUS FOR OPPOSITION

Russell's devotion to the No-Conscription Fellowship was sealed by his attendance at the emergency National Convention held at Devonshire House in London on 8 and 9 April, 1916, when he had been working full time for the Fellowship for just over a week. The eager and in some cases fearful young men who attended were well aware that it was a crucial time for them, and for Russell it was an exceptional opportunity to gain an understanding both of the most important personality in the Fellowship and of the most vital issue with which the organisation would have to deal. Clifford Allen, the chairman, dominated the gathering, and the question of alternative service permeated the discussions. Few of those present were ever to forget the occasion.

The timing of the gathering was exactly right. The passage of the Military Service Act had brought to an end the long period of uncertainty, and the few weeks since the measure had been in force had shown that many men would not be satisfied by the decisions of the tribunals. Arrests were just beginning.[172] The time of preparation was over and the test lay immediately ahead. The branches were functioning effectively and were extremely active—as is evidenced by the number of resolutions forwarded in time for publication with the agenda of the Convention—and the central organisation was busy and growing, but the need was felt for a common reaffirmation of purpose and unity, and for an exchange of information and views: there were also essential policy decisions to be made. No individual could predict exactly what form his ordeal might take, which made greater the need for confidence in the leaders and a feeling of solidarity and mutual support among the members.

One problem in particular was causing concern to the leaders and had to be brought to the members at the Convention. To those who, like Russell, saw resistance to conscription as an attack on the whole militarist system, it was clear that schemes of alternative service would be a threat to its success. The confusing terminology of the 'conscience clause' of the Military Service Act was a problem to the administration as much as to the objector. The difficulty of defining and identifying the conscientious objector was to result in the Army finding itself with men who were not conscientious objectors according to their tribunals, but who maintained that they were. In addition, the Act set up three categories of exemption: absolute exemption; exemption from combatant service only; and exemption on condition of taking work of national importance.[173] Absolute exemption was claimed by most members of the No-Conscription Fellowship, but was granted to very few, even after the second Military Service Act in May 1916 removed the ambiguity and made it clear that this form of exemption could legally be granted to claimants on conscientious grounds.

The existence of the other two categories, exemption from combatant service and exemption on condition of performing work of national importance, made it necessary to provide or to define types of work which would meet these criteria. In early March the Non-Combatant Corps was created, and to this were sent all men granted certificates of exemption from combatant service only. The response of the NCF leaders was immediate and united, and seems fairly to have represented the views of the members. A firm letter was sent to the Prime Minister on 14 March, in conjunction with the Friends' Service Committee, stating that the Corps in no way met their objections, and that they could take no part in such a unit. The letter declared that no form of military service would be acceptable, and for all but a few, no civil alternative if it in any way contributed to the prosecution of the war. Many objectors, the authors claimed, would not change their occupations except to work more directly for peace.[174]

As far as the rejection of non-combatant military service went, this statement did no more than express the decision of the convention in November 1915, at which the members had resolved to refuse any alternatives which involved taking the military oath.[175] No such clear position had been arrived at concerning civilian alternative service, and the part of the statement relating to this seems to reflect the direction in which the leaders were moving rather than any knowledge of what might be expected from the members. Among the leaders, the Quakers had been the first to adopt an uncompromising stand against alternative service, but long before the April Convention, almost the whole of the National Committee was firmly committed to this view.[176]

Initially, the provision for exemption on condition of being engaged in work of national importance had been left in the hands of the tribunals, who had the right to judge each case on its merits, but had no responsibility for helping applicants to find work which would be acceptable. The tribunals had made some use of it in cases of hardship, and appropriate use in cases where men genuinely could not be spared, together with more questionable use at times, as when all the servants of the local hunt were granted exemption by the Market Drayton tribunal.[177] As it applied to conscientious objectors, it was harder to clarify and harder to implement.

Trying to meet the need, the Government took its second step into the field of alternative service by setting up the Pelham Committee in April 1916. This body was officially appointed by the Board of Trade, of which its chairman was an assistant secretary, but although it had a wide potential influence it had virtually no power, and was in any event far too late in getting into operation to be of any service to the first wave of men to appear before the tribunals.[178]

By the time the NCF Convention assembled, Russell knew, as most of the members must have done, where their chairman stood on this crucial question: Allen had made it clear he strongly favoured the rejection of all forms of alternative service. He, on his part, had seen resolutions submitted by some of the branches which expressed a hope that some form of true national service would be made available, although there were more suggesting support for his uncompromising position. When it came to his expectations of the members, Allen's state of mind seems to have been ambivalent: at times he simply asssumed the Convention would endorse his view; at other times he made a real attempt to make room for other opinions.[179]

Preparations for the Convention were thorough, although hurried. According to Russell, 'great and successful efforts' had been made to prevent the *Daily Express* and the Anti-German Union from finding out where it was to be held.[180] The *Express* had in fact advertised the meeting widely and with ill-will. Perhaps fortunately, it had overreached itself with its claim that because the newspaper had published the place of meeting the 'Hole-and-Corner Peace Cranks' had changed the location from Devonshire House to the Brotherhood Church.[181] On 6 April, the chairman had written to the commissioner of police to warn him that an attack on the gathering was feared.[182] In spite of Russell's cheerful view and the confusion of the *Daily Express*, an angry crowd did gather outside Friends' House, Devonshire Place, where the Saturday sessions were held, a circumstance which greatly heightened the dramatic tension without causing serious incident. A few of the demonstrators climbed in, but left shortly, apparently disarmed by kindness.[183]

The Fellowship managed to throw most of its enemies off the track without bewildering its friends, and although one planned speaker was unable to get in, most managed well, and platform and hall were both filled. The excitement was palpable, but controlled. In a letter to Lady Ottoline, Russell gave his impressions:

The spirit of the young men was magnificent. They would not listen to even the faintest hint of compromise. They were keen, intelligent, eloquent, full of life—vigorous courageous men, full of real religion, not hysterical at all—not *seeking* martyrdom, but accepting it with great willingness—I am convinced that at least half will not budge an inch for any power on earth. The whole assembly was full of fun, and never missed a chance of laughter.

It was the very last moment. Most of them will be arrested within the next few days, and taken to camp. What will happen there, no one knows. I don't think they will be shot, tho' they certainly can be, at any rate if they are taken to France.

Russell was greatly impressed by the extraordinary quality of Clifford Allen's leadership, to which the atmosphere gave full scope. He commented on the speed with which the Convention dealt with 'immense masses of business':

One saw how business was done in the French Revolution. Allen wields the sort of power over them that leaders had then. He is a man of genius—not at all simple, with a curious combination of gifts. At the opening of the Conference, when he first rose, they wanted to cheer him till they were hoarse, but he rang his bell and held out his hand for quiet: they stopped at once, and he began 'Will you turn to p. 1 of the Agenda'—it is like the way Parnell treated the Irish Members. I have never seen any one comparable to him as a Chairman.[184]

The agenda listed more business for this first session than even such a chairman could hope to cover. The sixty-three resolutions forwarded by the branches took up eight pages of the printed agenda, and represented the views of over forty branches, a remarkable achievement since not more than about three weeks' notice of the meaning had been given. Many of the proposals were subsumed under one or other of the major issues which the National Committee planned to raise.[185] The subject matter and tone of the other resolutions were wide-ranging, and reflected the heterogeneity of the organisation Allen was trying to weld into unity. The largest number naturally concerned the response to the Military Service Act, and the functions of the Fellowship. But Russell must have been glad to note that six branches called for support of the campaign for peace by negotiation, an issue he was anxious to see pressed, and one which had important bearings on the relation of resistance to conscription to the whole opposition to the war. A strong resolution was passed urging 'the Government to end the war by immediate peace negotiations', and pledging the Fellowship's assistance to the campaign,[186] an emphasis which gave scope to Russell to follow one of his particular concerns within the framework of the NCF.

Two major groups of resolutions concerned 'Agitation on behalf of Prisoners' and 'Alternative Service'. Because the subjects were of such importance, the specific resolutions were set aside so that the topics could each be considered as a whole. It was the first session of the Convention, devoted to the question of alternative service, that so fired Russell's imagination and impressed him with the force of Allen's leadership. The rejection of the Non-Combatant Corps was confirmed unanimously, but consideration of the Committee's recommendation that civilian service be refused took longer. The resolution passed was not one of those prepared beforehand, and possibly its form and certainly its almost unanimous adoption were not easily reached, although Russell believed at the time that it reflected the convictions of those present. Unfortunately there is no detailed record of the discussion, but clearly some members did not want to adopt in advance a totally negative attitude to whatever proposals the Government might be going to make. The resolution, which was finally passed with two dissentients, supported the National Committee's position but stopped short of closing the doors of the NCF to all whose consciences allowed them to accept some form of alternative service:

This Convention re-affirms its deeply-held belief in the sanctity of human life, and declares its loyalty to the principles of peace and human fellowship. It therefore refuses to take part in war, and further declares that it cannot accept any form of alternative service, the result of which would be the more efficient organising of the country for war, or the advancing of militarism as exemplified in the M.S.A.

Similarly, whilst leaving the decision open to the conscientious judgment of each member, the Convention endorses the recommendation of the National Committee that all final certificates other than absolute exemption be returned.[187]

There is some awkwardness in the wording of the resolution, which reads as if it had been phrased and re-phrased during a long struggle, but the final ambiguity of the first paragraph may have been no mistake, and indeed shows skill in providing a formula acceptable to both absolutists and alternativists.[188] Yet even here, the strength of the moral pressure towards complete rejection of alternative service is apparent, and the proviso for individual conscience as the final arbiter, though present, is the weakest part. A public display of division was averted: and the corollary of this, of course, was that the vote did not give a clue as to the numbers, even of those present, who could personally accept compulsory civilian service. None of the leaders seems to have remarked this, and Russell for one came away believing that alternative service had been categorically rejected. Later, he was to be brought up sharply against the potential conflict between the claims of the individual conscience and the needs of the Fellowship for a united and uncompromising stand, and was to decide for the right of the individual to differ, but at the Convention he was swept along by Allen's rhetoric. Essentially he agreed and was to continue to agree with Allen that rejection of alternative service was the better and more logical position, but what was really at stake was whether the NCF should allow only one way to its members.

How much the decision was the product of the charisma of Clifford Allen is hard to assess. We have seen how deeply Russell was impressed by Allen's power on this occasion, and a number of those present recorded similar observations. One of the most striking descriptions was written years later (probably by R. C. Trevelyan):

I had met Maynard Keynes on his way to the Treasury, and we went in together, and watched the proceedings for an hour or so from the gallery. What most impressed both of us was the masterly skill with which Allen controlled and as it were conducted the debate, in which it seemed that half the audience at once were impatiently claiming the right to have their say. He stood there, calm and alert, by word, glance, or gesture of the hand now calling on one speaker, now checking and for the moment silencing another, imperturbably and good-humouredly dominating the stormy assembly of young men, many of them with passionately conflicting points of view.[189]

The decision of the National Convention regarding alternative service was unquestionably arrived at by democratic process, but it provides an interesting example of the effect which a powerful and attractive personality can have on that process. Was Allen aware of his own power? It is hard to believe that he can have been completely ingenuous. Fortunately his belief in the right of the individual conscience was never completely submerged, though it occasionally had a hard time of it. One senses that he would have been very glad if he could have persuaded the Convention into such unanimity that provision would scarcely have had to be made for those who would take a different stand, but he did in fact remain loyal to the idea that in the final analysis a man had the right to decide for himself on the basis of conscience. In the excitement of the occasion few seemed to have guessed at the difficulties into which Allen and the Fellowship would be led by the ambivalence of establishing one position as the official policy of the organisation and permitting another to individual members.

During the afternoon session Russell left the hall for a while: he and Dr Salter, the Quaker physician from Bermondsey, went to bail out a young CO and bring him back to the meeting 'where he received a great ovation', and announced that he was reading one of Russell's pamphlets when he was arrested. Russell was not a scheduled speaker, but at some point he had an opportunity to say a few words, and he also received 'a great cheer'.[190] Russell missed most of the supporting speakers, who were widely representative, giving point to the function of conscription in focussing pacifist sentiment. They were Philip Snowden, Sir John Barlow (an older Quaker and clerk of London Yearly Meeting at the time), Robert O. Mennell (of the Friends' Service Committee), Dr John Clifford (a leading Baptist who supported the war but expressed opposition to conscription),[191] Helena Swanwick (of the Women's International League) and George Lansbury (the well-known Christian Labour pacifist, and a member of the Fellowship of Reconciliation) who spoke in place of Robert Smillie, the president of the Miners' Federation of Great Britain, who had been unable to get in.

Allen's main address, given in the same Saturday afternoon session, was the dramatic highlight of the conference. Allen did not at first revert to the alternative service question which had been so crucial in the morning meeting, and which was a great moment to him. Indeed, he emphasised that a prior question was that the administration of the Military Service Act had, in his view, broken down. He laid even greater stress on what were to him the fundamental issues, the struggle for liberty and the firm moral basis for anti-militarism. But his few comments on alternative service were reserved for the end of his speech, where they must have been most telling. The crescendo reached by the hostile crowd outside coincided with the climax; it says something for his spellbinding that the disturbance enhanced rather than detracted from his effect. So menacing was the sound from outside that in order to avoid provocation a silent form of applause was adopted: instead of clapping, the audience signified approval by the waving of white handkerchiefs. In this atmosphere, Allen again voiced his suspicion of all kinds of service acceptable to the Government. Finally he moved the general resolution or pledge, which was accepted unanimously. In it those present declared their solidarity and that of those they represented with the men already arrested, acknowledged the spirit of sacrifice of the fighting soldier, renewed their determination, whatever the penalties awaiting them, 'to undertake no service which for us is wrong', and expressed confidence that in this way they were advancing the cause of peace.[192] Russell was as deeply moved as the most impressionable man present.

After this, the rest of the Convention's business might have been expected to be anti-climactic, but Russell's mood of exaltation (shared by almost all of those present) lasted throughout the Sunday sessions, held at a hall in north London. While the tone of Saturday's meetings had been inspirational, Sunday's were concerned more with implementation. The morning session was of great interest to Russell, as it was here that Catherine Marshall presented the plan of campaign developed by the Associates' Political Committee, and exhorted the branches to make use of every possible opportunity to influence public opinion and apply political pressure. The account in the *Labour Leader* was brief but adulatory:

The whole of Sunday morning's session . . . was devoted to a consideration of the details of an unrelenting agitation on behalf of arrested members. The agitation is being organised by a committee of prominent people, and as the proposals were outlined by Miss Catherine Marshall, probably the ablest woman organiser in the land; it became clear that the Government will have to face a formidable campaign if it does not immediately meet the situation.[193]

Marshall's proposals were detailed and specific: what she was effectively doing was taking the branches into partnership in the planned campaign. In her peroration she spoke of the need for prompt action whenever occasion arose, stressed the importance of careful records, and in particular urged local workers to keep headquarters fully supplied with information, promising in return that the head office would try to keep the members up to date with all developments.[194] She stressed the importance of keeping the cause always in the public eye, and Russell was in full agreement, believing as he did that it was through widely-publicised protest that the COs' cause would take effect.

Later on Sunday, C. H. Norman spoke on the legal rights of the conscript (rights he himself was to exploit to the full) and J. P. Fletcher on what men could expect to happen to them after arrest. More resolutions were discussed, and between sessions committee meetings were fitted in.[195] After these 'two delirious days and nights of conference' Russell went home and wrote to Lady Ottoline:

It has been a wonderful 2 days—the most inspiring and happy thing that I have known since the war began—it gives one hope and faith again. . . . I can't describe to you how happy I am having these men to work with and for—it is real happiness all day long—and I feel they can't be defeated, whatever may be done to them.[196]

There was a great deal of work to be done following the Convention, and the NCF leaders set about it refreshed. Russell and Marshall were now working closely with the National Committee and seem to have been party to all their discussions, although the fact that technically they attended only by invitation was shortly to prove its usefulness.

In the days immediately following Allen's triumph at the Convention, it seemed to Russell, as to the other leaders, that the logic of the absolutist position would prevail, and that out of the confusion of varied opinion on alternative service the Chairman had induced order and unity. The National Committee set to work to give publicity to the mood and decisions of the Convention, issuing an open letter to the Prime Minister, arranging a deputation to Parliamentary sympathisers, and making use of press contacts. The strategy of the time was to urge a complete review of the administration of the Military Service Act, but the leaders made full use of the mandate they felt they had received to make this demand from an absolutist position, suggesting that no form of alternative service would help alleviate the situation.

For at least a week Russell continued in the state of euphoria which the Convention had induced in most of the participants. In this mood he took part in the publicity campaign, writing a letter to the *Nation*, which appeared on 15 April under the heading 'A Clash of Consciences'. He described the Convention in glowing terms, speaking of the men who were present as 'filled with a profound faith, and with a readiness for sacrifice at least as great as that of the soldier who dies for his country'. His theme was the need for understanding between the majority, who felt it their duty to sacrifice everything for victory, and the minority who felt it their duty to sacrifice everything for peace and brotherhood. He explained the attitude to alternative service simply and without qualification:

Many schemes of 'alternate service' have been proposed as a possible means of compromise. But compromise is difficult for these men; if they are asked to change their occupation, they feel it is in order to facilitate the prosecution of the war. They have a far stronger desire than most men to be of service to the community; but it is their belief that a stand for peace is the greatest service they can render to the community. For this reason every hint of compromise was rejected by the Convention with the utmost determination. Their belief may be wrong, or it may be right; but no one who has seen them can doubt that it is sincere and unshakeable.

Unfortunately Russell erred in describing the decision of the Convention as having been without hint of compromise. The meaning of the resolution turned out to be extremely difficult to interpret to outsiders, empowering the National Committee as it did to present the absolutist position to the Government in the name of the whole Fellowship and yet at the same time obliging the Committee to recognise the right of individual members to take alternative service. There is a logic here—only so could the organisation remain true to its witness against militarism and at the same time to its stand for freedom of conscience. But the argument was too subtle to make good publicity. The outcome was to exacerbate the threat implicit in any offer of civilian service: it might divide the membership; its rejection might alienate public opinion; it might provide the Government with an excuse to treat even more harshly those who refused it. In one thing Russell was right: there was indeed a considerable body of men (and it included most of those whom he had come to know and love on the National Committee) who would remain absolutists to the end. But there were many who would not choose this route, and in the end the number of absolutists fell far short of Russell's predicted 10,000.

Russell soon found that the creation of the Pelham Committee (although its effect was at first slight), and the reaction of the NCF against it, had had an adverse effect on public opinion and his liberal friends; those who wished the conscientious objectors well were the most confused by their stand. The improvement of the provision for work of national importance had owed much to certain of these well-wishers, and was felt by many to offer a solution which should be acceptable to all reasonable men. Russell felt bitterly that some so-called friends showed little understanding of the CO's position and were conspiring to weaken it.

An influential man among those who wanted to put an end to persecution was Gilbert Murray, whose friendship with Russell had already been tarnished by disagreement over Britain's entry into the war. On 15 April, Murray, obviously believing that on this issue Russell would see him as on the side of the angels, wrote from Oxford about certain individual conscientious objectors he was trying to help. At the same time he was working toward a more general remedy, which he saw in terms of alternative service. He wrote:

You are no doubt in touch with Harvey; there is a small group of us here, mostly Friends, who are trying to do what we can for the Objectors. I feel clear that the right thing is to put them under some Civil Power and not the Military, and let them have the advantage of this new Board of Trade Committee on alternative service.

Immediately after writing this letter and before Russell had time to reply, Murray heard about the Convention and wrote again. The news of the resolution had taken him by surprise:

I find in pleading for the C.O.s that the pitch is terribly queered by the resolution of your N.C.F. Convention rejecting any form of alternative service. I did not know about this, but it cuts away the ground from my proposal to put the C.O.s under civil authority instead of military.

Have you any positive proposal to make by which the act could be administered or modified? Or are you out merely to break it by agitation? If (1) can you suggest any method by which a conscientious objector to military service can (a) Prove that his objection is a matter of conscience, and (b) Show that he is ready to make some sacrifice approximately comparable to that which his fellows are making. If you have any such plans let me know quickly. If (2) you are out merely to break the act by agitation, I see nothing for it but the C.O.s to endure imprisonment and, if necessary, death. It seems that Lincoln had conscientious objectors shot. But even in America it did not seriously affect public opinion. Worse luck![197]

Russell replied at once (17 April) and at great length. He denied that there was anything surprising about the decision of the Convention, which, he said, 'expressed what has been throughout the attitude of about three quarters of the Conscientious Objectors, and indeed to my mind the unavoidable attitude for those among them who are capable of logical thought'. He went on to attack Murray's associates, revealing considerable bitterness:

Harvey and a few other elderly Quakers, against the corporate opinion of the Friends, particularly of the Young Friends (who are the ones directly concerned), have arrogated to themselves the right to say what conscientious objectors ought to do, and have concealed from the authorities the fact that they disagreed from those for whom they professed to speak. The result has been the production of schemes which never could have been accepted, and which no one in touch with C.O.s would have ever regarded as affording a possible solution of the problem.

Russell's main point was valid and important. The young Quakers whom he knew—Barratt Brown and Fletcher—were the most uncompromising opponents of alternative service in the Fellowship, and they spoke for the Friends' Service Committee. Harvey must have been aware of this strong body of absolutist opinion among the Young Friends, and he knew that the Adjourned Yearly Meeting of January 1916 had by consensus expressed firm support for them and for an unconditional opposition to militarism. It was probably an injustice to impute conscious misrepresentation to Harvey, as it is likely that he did not see himself or expect others to see him as putting forward any offical point of view, and Friends were not bound to follow the line approved by Yearly Meeting. But it was inevitable that the willingness of individual Friends to support and take part in schemes of alternative service should be felt to undercut the stand of the Friends' Service Committee and of the NCF. The Friends' Ambulance Unit indeed became a source of embarrassment and annoyance to the absolutist Quakers, particularly as there was a well-founded rumour that its expansion to provide alternative service for many more objectors was being considered. The story of the relation between London Yearly Meeting, the Friends' Service Committee and the Friends' Ambulance Unit contributes to an understanding of the extremely uncompromising attitude of the young Service Committee leaders, which was an element in the dynamic of NCF leadership throughout the war. The Unit had been formed early in the war, but had never received official sanction from Yearly Meeting, although it had not been rejected outright and was still asked to report to that Meeting. While the original grounds for refusing to sponsor the Unit were the assistance it gave to the Army and its own quasi-military organisation, its position was still more seriously called in question when the Military Service Act was passed. The Unit's organising committee obtained a certificate of exemption for its members, and the tribunals sometimes made service in the Unit a condition of exemption. Some men found the work no longer acceptable when it became a form of compulsory alternative service, and surrendered their certificates, returning to England to await arrest with the other absolutists. The fact that General Childs (Director of Personal Service at the War Office and directly responsible for conscientious objectors) later referred to the Friends' Ambulance Unit as having been of 'great assistance' to the War Office shows that there was justification for the reservations of the Society of Friends over recognising it.[198] Nevertheless, its defenders quite understandably held that it offered an alternative fully and properly acceptable to the consciences of many men, and could not see why the absolutists should rule out this option.

This was the background of Russell's response to Murray. He went on to explain the situation further as he saw it. He stressed that the basis of conscientious objection for most of the men was the belief that it was always wrong to take human life. He himself thought that there were (rare) exceptions to this, but he affirmed the general principle as it applied to war between civilised states. He then pointed out that not all COs held the same view of alternative service, and with a return of acerbity he claimed that the NCF,

unlike you and the Tribunals, makes no attempt to judge the individual conscience, and has never made any recommendation to its members as to what they should do in this matter. The vote at the Convention was a vote as to what the Fellowship collectively could accept; but the vote was not intended to bind the separate members in any way, though undoubtedly it expressed what most of them felt to be the right course for themselves as individuals, as well as for the Fellowship.

There was some justice and some lack of consistency in what

Russell wrote. In admitting that some COs did not object to alternative service so long as it was not directly connected with the war, he surely deprived himself of the right to object to the setting up of a scheme by which suitable employment might be offered to such men before they entered the Army. And the NCF leaders had, of course, made a recommendation regarding alternative service: it would have been more exact to say that they had not attempted to dictate to the members. But what Russell was reacting to was Murray's evident expectation that such a scheme would be acceptable to all objectors. Russell may well have been right in holding that such ignorance and lack of understanding of the absolutist position was neither necessary nor justifiable in one who claimed to be a friend of the COs. The position had been stated often and clearly.

Russell dealt with Murray's request for a plan to improve the Act or its administration by disclaiming the ability to speak for the NCF on this, but the proposals he outlined were those being put forward by the leaders and by their close sympathisers whenever opportunity served.[199] In brief, what was suggested was an immediate inquiry into the action of the tribunals, and the suspension meanwhile of all proceedings against conscientious objectors, with those who had already been arrested being released from prison or military custody.

As to Murray's concern about equality of sacrifice, Russell expressed astonishment at the question:

The sacrifice of the C.O.s is immensely greater than that of the men at the front. So far as I can see, the risk they run of being shot by the military authorities in France is as great as the ordinary soldier runs of being shot by the Germans. . . . Like ordinary deserters, they would merely appear in the casualty lists; the public would not know the manner of their death, and you would not believe it. Those who escape this fate will have long terms of hard labour or solitary confinement in military prisons. And every imaginative person knows that obloquy and the active contempt of those among whom one is compelled to live is far harder to bear than the prospect of death.

Russell made use of arguments here which the NCF was careful to keep out of its public propaganda, and he exaggerated; he was angry, and yet he was (correctly) assuming that Murray shared many of the same basic values. In concluding, Russell denied that the primary objective of the Fellowship was the defeat of the Act by agitation. Although they would be glad to bring others to their view, the COs would have to act as they were doing even if they knew they 'should all be shot and public opinion would be unaffected'.

Murray does not seem to have been convinced by Russell's

arguments, but he was not driven away by Russell's hostility. He continued to work for what he thought would be improvements in the administration of the Act. At the end of April, Philip Morrell wrote to Russell about a memorandum which was to be presented to the Prime Minister, describing it as 'the Gilbert Murray scheme': Ottoline Morrell rather unexpectedly was described as 'a kind of godmother to this G.M. scheme'.[200] No details of what Murray was planning are known, but he evidently went on believing that the Government and the conscientious objector could be induced to work together in good faith for a solution to the problem, pinning his hopes on alternative service as a large part of that solution.

Some of the bitterness in Russell's letter to Murray may be explained by his continuing pain at his estrangement from his old associates. His efforts to explain his new friends to his old friends were part of his service to the NCF, but they also reflected his own need to be understood. The cause he was now pursuing seemed to him so overwhelmingly just that he could scarcely believe others could not see it. He was often disappointed. He reopened the subject with the Whiteheads in a letter (not now extant). On 16 April, Whitehead wrote an uncompromising reply. He had hoped, he said, to avoid discussion: 'Where feeling is acute, and divergence deep, discussion among intimates is often a mistake.' His view was that exemption should be limited to those who had already evidenced 'adherence to some code of thought which involves burdens as well as exemptions. . . . I would not exempt men who produce their objections ad hoc'. Like Murray, he could see no equality of sacrifice on the part of the COs. He pointed out that in ordinary religious persecution, 'the orthodox remain in comfort', while in the present situation it was those who obeyed the state who 'go through horrors . . . compared to which the punishment of prison—with a good conscience—is exceedingly trivial. . . . Frankly, the outcry is contemptible'.[201]

There was no hope of a meeting between this point of view and Russell's. Yet it was such people as the Whiteheads, above all, that Russell longed passionately to be understood by. It was just because of the needless waste (as he saw it) of such young men as their sons, to whom he was very close, that Russell opposed the war, and yet their parents saw him as trying to belittle the cause for which the young men were fighting. The Whiteheads' war-time letters to Russell leave one with the impression that the two men would have allowed the differences to drive them apart on intellectual grounds, concealing the emotional content and the hurt. But Evelyn Whitehead repeatedly wrote at a level of deep feeling, and it seems to have been this which kept the lines of communication open as they passed through all the things that affected each so deeply and so differently, from Russell's deviant views to the death in action of one of the Whiteheads' sons, Eric, at about the same time as Russell went to prison in 1918.

In the *Labour Leader* of 20 April, 1916, there was a letter signed 'F.R.S.', which it has been suggested[202] was written by Russell. Both the pseudonym and the style make this plausible. If Russell did write it, he put into it all the wormwood of his feelings at the time. It was a savage satirical proposal, in mathematical style, that some more direct, economical and humane means than war should be found for killing half of Europe's young men, maiming one quarter, and driving the other quarter insane. It is tempting even to surmise that it may have been a response to Whitehead's letter, and that the signature was a deliberately thin disguise.[203]

Russell remained convinced of the rightness of the absolutists' case, but the intractability of his former friends began to undermine his belief in the power of reason to convince. At the same time, persecution, politically so desirable and emotionally so glamorous in anticipation, was proving less welcome in reality. Russell found himself deeply sensitive not only to the sufferings but to the weaknesses of the conscientious objectors.

CHAPTER 6

REALITIES OF RESISTANCE: LEADERS AND MEMBERS

While Russell and the National Committee worried about the effects of possible schemes of alternative service, the majority of the conscientious objectors were taken into the army with little choice. Russell was soon in the thick of the hard facts of conscription. The routine procedure was that men who had not been granted an acceptable exemption were arrested by the civil police, convicted of desertion, fined a small sum and handed over to the military authorities. If they had been refused exemption altogether they were taken to an ordinary army unit, if they had been exempted from combatant service they went to the Non-Combatant Corps. In either case, members of the NCF were committed to refusing to obey military orders.

Russell quickly became aware—more so than some of the other leaders—of a difference in make-up and motivation between those who headed the organisation and some of the members: the unity expressed at the Convention did not go as deep as he had thought at the time. Russell shared Allen's vision of the refusal to fight as part of a larger movement which would overthrow the militarist system and end the war, but it did not follow that every man could identify with the wider cause. Many doubted their own heroism, especially when they were away from the spellbinding Allen. They were determined not to kill and not to be willing soldiers, and some knew that this personal objective might take all their courage and strength of purpose. They had no wish to take on the whole military machine and would welcome alternatives that mitigated the severity of the test.

The day after the National Convention Allen himself had to appear before the London Appeal Tribunal. For many NCF members, each of the formal steps which led to prison was painful and its outcome a foregone conclusion, but Allen's nature and his political and legal sophistication turned his progress into an extended adventure. The story, from his application to the Battersea local tribunal, which was heard on 14 March 1916, to his court-martial in late August, is too lengthy to be told here. Allen never missed an opportunity for application, for argument, for appeal. The Fellowship extracted all the publicity possible from every stage of his case, in which a curious duality was displayed. On the one hand, he based his claim to exemption on the purest principle, and his written statements were lucid, sincere and moving expositions of socialist internationalist pacifism: on the other hand, his successful attempts to tie his court-room opponents in legal knots were entertaining, but were thought by some of his friends[204] (as well as all his victims) to be inappropriate. Russell was not among his critics, enjoying fully Allen's brilliance and appreciating his underlying sincerity. In his eyes Allen was the champion of the very ideals so important to Russell himself, standing 'for the brotherhood of man, for belief in the international ideal, for the conviction that hatred between nations is unnecessary and war a futile crime.'[205] Whether the chairman's manoeuvres were good for the Fellowship cannot be judged. But the seriousness of his purpose was never in question, and Russell knew he had no hope or wish to stall indefinitely but would inevitably go to prison in the end, and knew also, with dread, that Allen's health was so poor that the risk he faced was greater than for the average conscientious objector. Meanwhile, the running of an efficient organisation was made more difficult by the arrest or anticipated arrest of one after another of its officers and workers.

The fate of some of the members less well able to defend themselves troubled Russell. Two in particular caught his attention. On 10 April, Ernest F. Everett, a member of the Liverpool branch of the NCF, was courtmartialled at Kinmel Park, Abergele, and sentenced to two years' imprisonment with hard labour—the first to draw the maximum sentence at hard labour.[206] Russell had already agreed to write leaflets describing particularly harsh treatment, and on 15 April he wrote an account of the Everett case in the leaflet *Two Years' Hard Labour for Not Disobeying the Dictates of Conscience*. It was this which led to his first trial under the Defence of the Realm Act.[207]

At the same time, Russell learnt of persecution of another type. On April 11, a young objector called Eric Chappelow was arrested and taken to Kingston barracks. When he refused to put on uniform he was subjected to considerable public humiliation and on 14 April a full-length photograph of him dressed in a blanket appeared on the front page of the *Daily Sketch*, with a mocking description of the treatment he was receiving and the salutary effects it was said to be having. This type of thing was anathema to Russell,[208] and no doubt Chappelow's sufferings were severe. A poet, and known to a number of well-known literary people, he was a sensitive, rather naive young man who barely had the courage of his convictions. On 13 April he wrote an agonised description to C. P. Sanger of the treatment he was experiencing. His sense of isolation and his fear of being unable to withstand the pressure came through clearly. The case could not be handled and used for propaganda in the same way as the Everett one. Copies were made of Chappelow's letter, for private distribution, and Russell wrote to several influential people in the hope of instigating intervention. Among those who replied, Gilbert Murray promised to do what he could, and Bernard Shaw suggested basing a question in the House on the fact that Chappelow had a useful job with the London County Council and had been recognised as genuine and granted exemption, which had been rescinded by the Appeal Tribunal on the representations of the Military Representative. Philip Morrell, with support from Harvey, did ask a question on 18 April, amid much contemptuous barracking by one of the 'honourable and gallant' gentlemen in the House.[209] No attempt to temper the wind for Chappelow was successful. Two weeks later he was court-martialled—still in his blanket—and sentenced to six months' imprisonment. Just before this ordeal he wrote a further letter to Sanger, showing a mounting terror of insanity or death, and asking desperately whether the NCF was agitating for the objectors and specifically whether Russell had been able to do any more for him.[210] Russell, to whom the destruction of integrity was the deepest evil, must have suffered at his own impotence. Chappelow was sent to serve his sentence in Wandsworth, at that time the most notorious of the military detention barracks, and when Marshall wrote to him on 30 April, her letter was returned as unsuitable, and she was not allowed to visit him. Chappelow survived his troubles and does not seem to have given in, although Sylvia Pankhurst later claimed he regretted the stand he had taken.[211] At least such cases lent support to the NCF's claim that conscientious objectors should be transferred to the civil authority, one of the cardinal points for which they were pressing at the time.

These realities gave Russell a more sober view of the task of the No-Conscription Fellowship. He could not welcome martyrdom if he was not to be among the martyrs and when some of those who were were so sickeningly vulnerable. Allen's challenge to the authorities was one thing, the victimisation of men like Chappelow quite another. Russell wrote to Ottoline Morrell in gloomy tones of the nature and fate of the conscientious objectors: 'No doubt a good many are cowards; people are unspeakably cruel about cowardice—some have gone mad, some have committed suicide, and people merely shrug their shoulders and remark that they had no pluck. Nine-tenths of the human race are incredibly hateful.'[212]

Russell's view of the limitations of some of the men had an important bearing on his thoughts about alternative service, and he was much less certain than he had been about the outcome of the Convention vote. Two weeks after the Convention he wrote to Marshall:

As regards the general situation; It is clear to me (a) a scheme of "national importance" could be got now, if the N.C.F. would take it (b) total exemption cannot be got till a good many have suffered severely (c) probably a large number of the N.C.F. will, individually, become willing to accept work of national importance after a period of solitary confinement on bread and water (d) that such success as we can hope for depends wholly upon ascertaining and making widely known all cases of persecution (e) that a good many men will be morally broken, and for ever degraded in their own eyes, and that the general level of moral self-respect will probably be lowered for centuries. If I thought most would hold to what they have voted in the Convention, I would think the vote right; but I dread their yielding.[213]

Russell's predictions were to prove extraordinarily accurate, but more important was his realisation of the human factors involved and his attainment of a compassion that comes hardly to idealists. His theoretical agreement with Allen remained total: logically, he thought, the absolutist position was the only consistent one, given pacifist principles to start with. Both he and Allen were personally opposed to the acceptance of alternative service, both believed the final decision had to be left to the individual. But to Allen this latter concession was a matter of intellectually-held principle rather than of deeply-felt conviction, and he could seldom resist putting moral pressure on men's consciences to bring them into line with what he saw so clearly to be right. Russell took perhaps a lower but certainly a more realistic view of human nature than was implied when Allen urged all to choose the more difficult path. Russell's approach was genuinely humanitarian, stemming from a recognition without condemnation or contempt that some men were less strong than others, and a horror of anything that would destroy people morally by forcing them into a situation beyond their capacity for endurance. The argument was completely tangential to the whole question of whether acceptance of alternative service was morally right, and it raised without answering a profound question of the relation between courage and conviction; it was based not on logic but on great concern for the self-respect of the individual. Russell was surely growing away from the need to see everything in black and white.

What Russell was saying was important and greatly needed to

be said, but there was little more that could be done at this time than to offer the compassionate view as a leaven among the leaders, who were not yet ready to hear of any compromise. The National Committee had adopted as a point of policy the practice of backing decisions unanimously outside the committee room, once they were made. Necessary as the show of unanimity may have been felt to be, it led those of the members at large whose view was that of the defeated minority at the Convention to believe at times that they were totally without sympathisers among the leadership. The alternativists had some justification for feeling like this in the weeks following the Convention, especially as they were indeed under-represented on the National Committee. As Russell clearly feared, the man who could accept alternative service appeared in all official NCF writing of the period as something of a weak brother, although only by implication. During April, May and June of 1916 the Fellowship presented in its public propaganda a consistent opposition to all forms of alternative service.[214] In writing for the members, the chairman was no less uncompromising in his support of the absolutist position, but he usually devoted a sentence or two to reassuring the alternativist, and one of his *Tribunal* editorials is given over mainly to this. In it, Allen urged men to follow their own consciences and declared quite specifically that he would consider it a privilege and a duty to assist those who could take alternative service as well as those who must refuse it. He urged members not to let the issue divide the Fellowship.[215] From about the beginning of May, too, the NCF officially, if reluctantly, offered advice on how to apply to the Pelham Committee.[216]

This was toleration for alternativism. Perhaps no more had been promised, possibly no more could be offered at this time, and it had value. But equality it certainly was not. Allen's promised assistance was practical, but it did not extend to allowing alternativists to justify their stand, and from April to June no breath of alternativist heresy found its way into the columns of *The Tribunal*. The man who wanted to justify his ability to take work of national im-portance had to turn to the columns of the *Friend*, the *Labour Leader*, or such other journals as would print his letters.[217] The NCF continued to present a superficial unity regarding alternative service until the introduction of the Home Office Scheme in July 1916 forced the issue into the open, and greatly increased the number of men to whom a choice was available. The resentment felt by some of the alternativists against the National Committee continued to smoulder and was to be one of the most serious problems facing Russell during his chairmanship in 1917.

While most of Russell's attention was being given to the

immediate concerns of the NCF and to helping objectors as best
he could, his association with the leaders of the Fellowship, and a
closer contact with the Independent Labour Party incident upon
his NCF work, helped him define the change that had been taking
place in his political attitudes. He had considered socialism
seriously as the most viable option ever since the war began: now
he discovered he stood indeed within the ILP camp, but already to
the left of centre within that organization. On 22 April he went to
Newcastle where the National Committee was meeting to enable
members to attend the ILP conference held there over the Easter
weekend. The presence of the strong NCF section at the gathering
was significant in confirming the anti-war and anti-conscriptionist
stand of the ILP, and it brought home to Russell how far he had
moved politically since the beginning of the war.

The NCF has been described by Colin Cross as 'in practice a
satellite or ally of the ILP'.[218] Russell would certainly have
disagreed with this description, and in fact neither organisation
can fairly be described as subservient to the other. The NCF
members within the ILP were a 'ginger group', trying to pressure
the party into a more radical position. Although it is true that the
ILP represented the NCF interests in Parliament, this owed less to
positive party policy than to the conviction of Snowden and the
importunity to the NCF. Russell had often expressed dissatisfaction with the stance of the ILP leaders, his views being those of the
radical NCF wing of the party. His description of the Newcastle
conference showed his new position:

Like the nation, the I.L.P. has a Govt. which is trying to thwart and deceive the
rank and file – trying to be friends with the powers that be, not to come out
strongly about the war, and so on – Anderson is the brains of the Govt.,
Snowden was not on the platform, and led the attack on the Govt. – with the
support of a great majority of those present. Snowden was really fine. Most of
the N.C.F. young men were delegates, and several of them spoke. There was a
certain jealousy of their vigour and success on the part of the others – I find I
now regard the I.L.P. as they regard official Liberals – as lukewarm mugwumps,
using the phrases of democracy to cover inaction – so one travels! But Snowden
is really admirable.[219]

Russell had to leave before the conference was over, but after he
left Dr Salter moved a resolution that the socialists should refuse
support to all wars, which was passed almost unanimously. The
Parliamentary ILP indeed seems to have been forced or shamed
into supporting the NCF rather than the other way around.

As he had foreseen within a few weeks of the beginning of the
war, Russell had 'swallowed socialism for the sake of peace'. In
Principles of Social Reconstruction he had worked out his own

political philosophy, and it had turned out to be akin to decentralised socialism of a very idealistic kind. Many of the young men whose socialism prevented them from serving in the army were equally idealistic, and none saw any reason why their ideals should not translate into practical politics.

For Russell, his anti-war stand, his support for the conscientious objectors and his political position were all part of the same thing. The war was a bitter evil, kept going by abuse and imbalance of political power, and at present the only hope of leadership to end it lay in the refusal of the conscientious objectors to compromise with militarism. Their stand was working directly to confuse and weaken the Government, and still more exciting was the hope that the example of their resistance might mobilise and make articulate the desire for peace which Russell was convinced was latent in the common people. Not only was socialism the one political force with any declared opposition to this particular war, but also, Russell believed, some form of socialism provided the only hope that the peace which followed the war could be on a new basis. He saw the ignorance of the masses, their fears and discontents, and their gullibility as all part of the root cause of war, and believed that for peace to last, power must rest in an informed, satisfied and participating public. In 1916 there seemed little hope that the refusal of the people to go on fighting would be sudden and dramatic, but Russell believed the stand of the conscientious objectors might begin the process.

Russell's discouragement with Parliamentary politicians was confirmed again the day after he got back from Newcastle, when he spent two and a half hours at the House of Commons trying to get in touch with the so-called anti-conscriptionist group to arrange for a deputation from the NCF and the Friends' Service Committee to meet with them to explain the Convention's decision on alternative service.[220] He did not serve on this deputation, but he was included on a more unusual political occasion, when Lloyd George invited Allen, Marshall and Russell to lunch with him at Walton Heath. The purpose was clearly to enable the Minister to sound them out on the attitude of the Fellowship toward alternative service, and to see whether they were as intransigent as the tenor of their public pronouncements indicated. Russell described the visit in a letter to Lady Ottoline Morrell:

I had a queer adventure today. Lloyd George was led to think he might as well find out at first hand about the conscientious objectors, so he had Clifford Allen and Miss Marshall and me to lunch at his place near Reigate, fetching us and sending us back in his own motor. He was very unsatisfactory, and I think only wanted to exercise his skill in trying to start a process of bargaining. Still, it was worth something that he should see Allen and know the actual man. It will make him more reluctant to have him shot.

I feel convinced the men will have to suffer a good deal before public opinion and Government will cease to wish to persecute them. I got the impression that Ll. George expects the war to go on for a long time yet; also that he thinks the whole situation very black. He seemed quite heartless.[221]

To Marshall he admitted being depressed by the interview, and added 'I think all depends on the men holding firm and their punishments being given wide publicity'.[222]

On 24 April, Russell wrote that 'mercifully' the rush would end when he returned to Cambridge on the coming Saturday.[223] He did go back to Trinity College, although not until late on the Sunday (when he left a National Committee meeting to do so), but although he 'kept' the spring term which ran from April until June, there was no break in his NCF involvement. All term he never spent a weekend in Cambridge. He attended National Committee meetings almost every Saturday and sometimes on Sunday as well, and there were few weeks when Fellowship business did not bring him to London at least once during the week as well. While he was in Cambridge he was sometimes engaged in matters concerning the conscientious ojectors there, and the Cambridge tribunal irritated him so much that he attacked it in an article entitled 'Folly, Doctor-like, Controlling Skill',[224] which for some reason remained unpublished. But he confessed, 'The C.O.s here are not the sort I like best—they are conceited and superior, with no love'. Possibly the view was reciprocated: Lady Helen Pease (Helen Bowen Wedgwood), who worked with the Cambridge branch of the NCF, remembers Russell as being of little use to them, and clearly believes he sought notoriety by tangling with the authorities.[225] He may have spent some time beginning to prepare his lectures for Harvard, but he had no heart for the writing of philosophy, and found it a great trial to fulfil a long-standing engagement with the Aristotelian Society. Still, he managed to address the Society on a peace-related topic, 'The Nature of the State in View of Its External Relations'. Of Cambridge, he wrote that it had a military air: 'I hate being here—one lives to the sound of the word of command—they drill in the cloisters all morning'.[226]

Excitements related to the No-Conscription Fellowship pursued him; at the end of April he told Lady Ottoline that the police had been making enquiries, and it looked as if they might be preparing to prosecute the National Committee for conspiracy; he and Marshall would not be affected, as they only attended by invitation.[227] When action was taken against the Committee it was on grounds of its having published the leaflet *Repeal the Act*, said to be in contravention of the Defence of the Realm Act. Summonses were issued on 10 May to all the National Committee whose signatures appeared on the leaflet—all, that is, except the chairman, who was presumably left off the list because his case under the Military Service Act was expected to come up again shortly. Morgan Jones, who was in prison by the time the trial came to court, was brought from his cell and sat between two policemen. C. H. Norman's sufferings in Wandsworth military prison, which were to be very severe, were already beginning, and he was not brought to court.

Russell came up to London to attend the trial on 11 May. On the face of it, the case against the Committee was not strong. On 21 March, the Home Secretary, Herbert Samuel, had declared in the House of Commons that agitation for the repeal of the Act could not be considered illegal;[228] and it was only by a very wide interpretation that the leaflet could be considered 'prejudicial to the recruitment and discipline of His Majesty's Forces'. Nevertheless, the Committee anticipated conviction and were concerned only with making the most of the publicity value of the case. In this they had the unconscious and unwilling co-operation of their opponents. The public prosecutor, A. H. Bodkin, lacked both lucidity and a sense of humour, and in the course of a long speech came out with a statement that was a delight to the anti-conscriptionists. 'War,' he said, 'will become impossible, if all men were to have the view that war is wrong. There will be no soldiers to carry it to its logical conclusion.' The NCF later made a poster of this dictum, which resulted in the prosecution of the printer, with Bodkin briefed for the prosecution.[229]

Russell found the occasion impressive and encouraging. In a letter written on the day after the trial, he described the witness of the defendants:

Mr. Grubb was very good – usually he seems a rather mild bespectacled old Quaker, but yesterday he showed a stubborn immovability which was very impressive – he was not at all nervous, but showed that it would be utterly useless to try to bully him. They asked him if he would think it right to resist the State in the matter of Military service and he said "Yes, as my ancestors did in the 17th century." My brother, who was sitting next to Mathews the director of public prosecutions, thought fit to chaff him at this point, and whispered "Really, Mathews, the role of Torquemada doesn't suit you." Mathews became white with passion, and almost shouted "Don't *speak* to me, your opinions are quite unpopular enough already." My brother got the impression that they are quite likely to prosecute me. Then Fenner Brockway went into the box – a pink-cheeked boy, *very* handsome, with a gay smile – even the prosecution

couldn't *help* loving him. His opinions were as firm as his appearance was
charming; the contrast was curious. They could hardly believe that he had
already been 5 years editor of the Labour Leader. Barrett [*sic*] Brown was another
Quaker, and Leyton Richards a Congregational Minister – I thought they would
have to put them in prison, but I suppose they didn't dare. Ld. Derby looked an
awfully stupid man – almost wanting. . . the Trial was extraordinarily dramatic – seeing the two points of view contrasted one got a sense of the helplessness
of the forces of the State in face of resolute men – it was clear that the State could
only defeat itself by severity.[230]

Characteristically, the NCF did not measure its success in court
by the outcome of the case. The members of the National
Committee were all convicted and fines to a total of £800 were
imposed. After hesitancy on the part of some members, they
decided to appeal, but the appeal was dismissed. Russell's first
response had been that it would be unwise for the members to
refuse to pay their fines and accept a prison term instead, both
because the Fellowship needed them and because he thought the
effect on public opinion would be better in the long run if they
paid up. He thought it likely the Government would proceed to
more extreme measures shortly, such as a prosecution directed at
The Tribunal. But the Committee soon decided not to pay the
fines, except for the older members, Grubb and Leyton Richards.
W. J. Chamberlain, Walter Ayles, Barratt Brown and Fletcher
served sentences of two months' imprisonment. Brockway was
with them when they went into prison on 17 July, but he only
served part of the sentence: by previous arrangement with him,
the National Committe paid his fine and had him released in early
August to take the place of Allen, when the latter was finally
arrested under the Military Service Act.[231] In spite of Russell's
wish to keep the the National Committee out of prison, at least
for the present, he did not think he himself would be free for long.
He lunched with his brother on the day of the trial, and Frank
Russell tried to persuade him to avoid imprisonment. Russell
apparently countered every argument except his brother's final
one, which was that imprisonment might make Russell religious,
which the latter admitted certainly '*was* a consideration'.[232]

Russell had regarded the public humiliation of Chappelow as
'the limit of brutality',[233] but these words were unfortunately not
prophetic and cases of physical abuse began to occur. The
question of the ill-treatment of conscientious objectors was a
complex one, although to Russell it simply seemed that things
were happening which he could not have believed possible in
England or any country with pretensions to being civilised. The
Army as well as the objectors was faced with a situation which
was new and for which it was ill-prepared. The opponents of

conscription rightly claimed too much had been laid on the shoulders of the tribunals, by forcing them to pin a label on every claimant to conscientious objection. He was either a genuine objector to all forms of service and therefore qualified for absolute exemption, or he was an objector to military service and merited conditional exemption, or he was recognised as an objector to combatant service, or he was – despite his claim – not a geniune objector at all. Where the label was appropriate or was accepted by the claimant no problem arose. Those few who obtained absolute exemption were of course content; many of those who obtained conditional exemption accepted this willingly; more than half of those placed in the Non-Combatant Corps were men whose scruples did not bar this service; and among those who were refused all exemption there must have been some who were uncertain or insincere and who now accepted their fate and made the best of military life.

With all these the Army had little trouble.[234] But the Act had made no provision for men who continued to call themselves conscientious objectors when the tribunals had declared they were not, or for men offered an unacceptable type of exemption. The Adjutant-General summed up the position as he saw it:

It cannot be too clearly understood that once a man is handed over by decision of a tribunal to the military authorities, it is not for the military authorities to consider the reasons such a man may have for refusing to do his work. It is the clear duty of every Commanding Officer to do his best with the legitimate means at his disposal to make every man who is handed over to him into an efficient soldier.[235]

From the Army's standpoint the logic of this was indisputable, and for the first few weeks unit commanders struggled to deal with the conscientious objector on the basis of his insubordination, not of his convictions. Some of the NCF leaders appeared almost to welcome the severities and inconsistencies to which the objectors were subjected in this difficult situation, and one cannot deny their propaganda value to the cause, but Russell's repugnance at what seemed to him the denial of humanity and justice grew steadily.

Three of the earliest cases illustrated three different methods which were used. Everett was treated courteously—indeed his officers and non-commissioned officers laboured long to persuade him by words of the unwisdom of his course. When he proved intractable, he was courtmartialled and given a very heavy sentence, but one, it should be noted, which carried with it an automatic transfer to a civil prison. (Hard labour could be served only in a civil person, while detention implied confinement in a military prison.) Chappelow, as we have seen, was dealt with informally in a way which his officers presumably believed, as did the *Daily Sketch*, would soon bring him to his senses. When it did not, he was courtmartialled and sentenced to detention. In the third case, that of a man called Sara, his refusal to obey the order to put on his uniform was met with physical force. Although he was quite roughly treated initially, his officers did not persist, and he too was soon court-martialled and sentenced to detention.[236] Some were not so lucky and underwent prolonged attempts to force them into obedience.

Lieutenant Colonel Brooke, the commandant of Wandsworth Detention Barracks (already mentioned in relation to Chappelow's case), achieved notoriety for his attempts to break conscientious objectors, but had the misfortune to engage in a battle of wills with C. H. Norman, perhaps the most aggressive of all the NCF leaders, and the first to be arrested. Like Allen, Norman was not a helpless victim, but he differed from Allen in having an abrasive personality that provoked abuse. On first meeting him Russell had recognised the courage he was soon to demonstrate so materially, but had confessed that he had not particularly liked him, 'except on public grounds',[237] and later Russell himself was to find out just how awkward Norman could be. Norman took his 'red bible'—the *Manual of Military Law*—with him when he was handed over to the Army, but this did not prevent him from being sentenced to two years' imprisonment and sent to Wandsworth to serve the sentence. Here, over a period of three weeks, he suffered long stretches of confinement in a strait-jacket that was too small for him and caused him to faint, was force-fed even after he decided to give up his hunger-strike, and was verbally abused by Brooke. He was still intransigent and very probably provocative, although he denied this. Brooke would not allow Norman's father to see him even when a visit was due, and was in such a state of rage that he declared injudiciously that he was going to report Norman to a higher authority 'in order to get permission to inflict still severer penalties on him'. But the victim had already managed to smuggle out an account of his experiences, and the NCF obtained corroborative evidence. In an emergency, Marshall used her most influential contacts. Within hours the Prime Minister heard of Norman's plight from at least three sources, within days Brooke was removed from his command, and within weeks Norman was again court-martialled and sent this time to serve at hard labour in a civil prison.[238] Russell must have taken some consolation from the effectiveness of the NCF's intervention, but he believed Norman had suffered lasting moral damage.

Cases like this were extreme, and even the NCF would later have admitted that they were exceptional, and that Brigadier General Childs, director of personal service at the War Office, dealt with them promptly when they were exposed. But the fact remained that the ordinary harsh discipline of an Army detention barracks took on the colour of brutality when it was applied to a man whose conscience would not let him stop committing the crime for which he was being punished. General Childs had to establish a new department to deal with the complaints which poured in. Initially, and understandably, he could see no reason for any special treatment. He believed the Army could deal with the conscientious objector as well as it could with any other insubordinate soldier, and he was concerned only about the effect of their example on other soldiers, and the harm that might be done by publicity. He blamed the NCF, 'a pernicious organization whose propaganda is that of conversion of the community at large to anti-war principles'.[239]

Gradually the picture changed, and it became clear that the solution proposed by the friends of the conscientious objectors, and stressed, for example, in the speech which Russell had helped Snowden to draft, was also the best for the Army. If sentences were to be served in civil, not military, custody, a continuing threat to discipline would be removed, as well as the occasion of constant outside criticism. A way of doing this was found in Army Order X, promulgated at the end of May, which gave directions that if a man charged with insubordination claimed his disobedience was the outcome of conscientious objection, he was to be sentenced at court martial to a term at hard labour, which could only be served in a civil prison.[240] The main inadequacies of this solution were that it did little to help the many men already sentenced, and that there were always a few officers who would evade it or delay the court martial. It also meant that the objectors automatically received the harshest form of civil imprisonment: the conditions of hard labour were punitive in the extreme.

The No-Conscription Fellowship regarded such concessions as useful, though limited, and took some credit that the determined refusal of the objectors to obey orders had forced the Army to acknowledge the existence of conscientious objectors among the men who were sent to them as soldiers. But what faint hope there had been—and it surely had had little reality outside the hearts of the NCF—of obtaining the suspension and complete review of the Military Service Act as it related to conscientious objectors had gone. For Russell, the indifference of his former friends, the hardness of the politicians, and the realisation that not all con-

scientious objectors were willing heroes had combined to destroy
the inflated optimism induced by the National Convention of
early April. Indeed, by the end of the month a second Military
Service Bill was introduced,[241] extending conscription to married
men while making only a few minor concessions to improved
administration. But the new Act remained innocent of anything
that would help in the definition of conscientious objection—if
indeed such definition were possible. Although Asquith had
refused to let application on grounds of conscience be limited to
religious objectors, no guidelines had been spelled out in either
Act. Army Order X, curiously, came closest to providing a way
of identifying the conscientious objector which (given a broader
application) might have satisfied the men themselves, since it
rested a man's right to be given special treatment entirely on his
own word that his refusal to obey was the result of conscientious
objection. But even while boasting of the benefits of the new
order, senior War Office men, and most notably Earl Kitchener,
the Secretary of State for War, were hoping to restrict its
advantages to the 'conscientious objector with religious views'.
As long as they arrogated to themselves the right to say who was a
conscientious objector, there was no security in any provision
designed to protect the objectors.[242]

In the early summer Russell became even more acutely aware of
what could result from confusion in the administration of the Act,
ambiguities in wording, a political climate leading to hostility and
mistrust between the Army and the Government, and military
fears of the spread of conscientious objection. All were part of the
background to one of the gravest ordeals faced by the conscientious objectors, when thirty-four men were sent to France and
condemned to death. The man who resisted had always known
that his resistance carried the possibility of being shot. Russell was
in no more doubt than General Childs as to the legal right of the
Army to carry out this extreme penalty, and claimed to believe
Lloyd George quite capable of choosing to crush the movement
even if it meant shooting 5000 people.[243] On 6 May, the *Herald*
published a letter from Russell under the heading 'Will They Be
Shot?' in which he pointed out that the law offered no protection
for objectors who had not obtained an exemption they could
accept, who could legally be taken to France and shot. He
emphasised that those objectors who had not been recognised by
the tribunals were deemed by the military authorities to be
ordinary soldiers, and he urged that the first step to a solution was
to place all those who claimed conscientious objection in civil
custody instead of subjecting them to the army discipline against

which they must rebel. He believed that most officers would be glad to have the objectors removed to civil custody.

The very day after this letter was published, the first resisting conscientious objectors were being brought together for shipment to France. Russell believed that if men were to be condemned to death they would first be sent overseas and this was the view acted on by the Army as well as by the NCF, although strictly speaking it does not seem to have been legally impossible to shoot a man for continued disobedience even within England. Spokesmen for the Government were conspicuously less well-informed about the legal possibilities, or more wilfully blind. The Military Service Act provided that a conscientious objector should not be shot as a deserter, but the wording suggested that this only applied to the initial failure to report. Anxiety among the friends of the objectors increased when units of the Non-Combatant Corps began service overseas in France, and meanwhile it was almost commonplace for officers and non-commissioned officers to hold over the resisters the threat of being sent to France and shot. Snowden repeatedly pressed for reassurances that COs would not be sentenced to death, and the Government easily gave them, and was still giving them when the men were condemned.

A good deal of mystery and some controversy surround the story of the thirty-four sent to France and of their rescue. Russell was active at certain crucial moments, and his anxious interest throughout is borne out by the amount of material bearing on the case which was retained in his files on the NCF.

When the first seventeen men, known resisters, were transported to France in early May with a contingent of the Non-Combatant Corps, the NCF and the Friends' Service Committee heard of the departure even while it was taking place. The leaders at once made contact with their most influential supporters. Allen drew up a comprehensive plan to be put into effect if it should be needed, making provision for every member of the Cabinet to be telephoned (each by a different person), for action by the Society of Friends, for 'Mothers' Deputations', for an approach to be made to Northcliffe, for someone to go to France, for 1000 telegrams to be canvassed.[244] Most of this proved unnecessary, but on 9 May, before hard information was available, questions were asked in the House centring on one of the Quakers about whom a query had been raised a week before. Asquith replied in vague phrases, but expressed confidence that the death penalty would not be inflicted.[245]

At this juncture Russell was able to play a part. The NCF was keeping a very close watch on developments, and happened to be in a favourable position to reach the ear of the Prime Minister just as the crisis unfolded. A deputation of Associates and sympathisers had made arrangements to meet with Asquith on 11 May to discuss with him alternative service and the new Military Service Bill. The members of the deputation were Philip Morrell, Snowden, Marshall, Russell and the Bishop of Oxford. Because of a delay caused by the debate on the Irish crisis, the Bishop had to leave without seeing Asquith, but he left his views in a letter.[246]

This may have been Russell's first face-to-face meeting with Asquith since Britain's intervention in the war had sparked in him intense feelings of hostility towards the Prime Minister. He was pleasantly surprised and greatly encouraged by the meeting. He wrote, 'The old man knew so much about the question that one could not doubt the genuineness of his interest. He was very sympathetic and talked almost as if he were one of us—how weak he is to yield on every occasion. . . . I rather like him'.[247] Asquith assured the members of the deputation that the Government did not intend the COs to become liable to the death penalty. From this time on, the Associates kept in close touch with Asquith. Previous accounts have stressed the importance of Gilbert Murray's intervention, but new evidence shows that the NCF Associates, after their fortuitous initial meeting with the Prime Minister, were responsible for keeping him supplied with information—at his request—throughout the duration of the crisis, and in their turn were taken quite fully into his confidence. The Commander-in-Chief, Sir Douglas Haig, was directed that no conscientious objector in France was to be shot for refusal to obey orders, and although the order was not made public, notice of it was at once given to Marshall.[248]

The matter did not end there. Although the Prime Minister was now alerted and concerned, conscientious objectors continued to be sent to France, and the promulgation of Army Order X at the end of May did not prevent the passing of the death sentence on some of them. In spite of the constant pressure from the objectors' organisations, and in spite of the apparent intention of the Government to prevent any more from being sent, twenty-four more were in France by 1 June, and in the middle of June four men, and then thirty more, were sentenced to death. In every case the sentence was read out, and—after a pause—commuted to ten years' penal servitude.[249]

Russell and the other friends of conscientious objectors had throughout been extremely critical of the actions and attitude of the Under-Secretary of State for War, H. J. Tennant. Tennant had acted too late to prevent the removal of the second batch of men to

France; had been party to an attempt to confuse the public as to the distinction between men serving willingly as non-combatants and the resisters;[250] and had pleaded powerlessness when asked to bring the men back.[251] But his biggest public blunder occurred when news reached the House of Commons on 22 June 1916, of the sentencing of the first four men to death. Tennant's reply to the question relating to the report of the incident was extraordinarily incautious. He dismissed it as just another false rumour, saying there was no question of the conscientious objectors in France being sentenced to death, and he indicated that such a sentence could be passed only for desertion in the face of the enemy. By the following Monday, he had to retract both his denial of the news and his view of the state of the law.[252]

Russell raged at such incompetence or malevolence, describing Tennant in a letter to Lady Ottolines not only 'ignorant' but a 'lying, dishonourable fool'.[253] Tennant cannot be exonerated from charges of inexcusable and frightening ignorance and a measure of ill-will towards the conscientious objectors. Undoubtedly they had caused him a great deal of trouble, but the trouble was not made less by his attitude. Russell wrote a scathing indictment:

Mr. Tennant's speech in the House of Commons on June 20, as well as his replies to questions on the subject of C.O.s, show that his multifarious duties have prevented him from acquainting himself with the facts of the persecution for which he is responsible to the House of Commons.

He admits that C.O.s "may be, and possibly are, in some instances, in danger of being treated with injustice and in some cases with brutality." Who could have guessed the truth from this bland official language? "*May* be"? "*Possibly* are"! Day by day and week by week the facts have been brought to Mr. Tennant's notice in the form of questions; invariably he has been compelled to give the same answer, "I have no information." It is clear that if the facts brought to his notice by the questioners had been in any degree inaccurate, he would have had no lack of information.

He professed not to be able to understand why hon. Members were anxious that he should redeem his promise that C.O.s should not be sent to France. He said that as regards men in combatant corps there is not much distinction between their treatment in France and in England. And he could see no reason why C.O.s in the N.C.C. should not be sent to France. But in France a C.O. who obeys his conscience necessarily renders himself legally liable to the death penalty. Mr. Tennant does not know the law in this matter.

Russell went on to describe Tennant's blunders when the question of the original four sentenced to death was raised, adding 'of this, as of everything relating to C.O.s, Mr. Tennant was wholly ignorant'.[254]

Not long after, the men who had been sentenced to death were returned to England to serve their sentences in civil person, and to be offered the Home Office scheme when it came into operation. Other resisting conscientious objectors were sent to France later, but none was again condemned to death.[255] Whether they had been sent to France as the result of a deliberate plot among high-ranking Army and War Office officials remains an open question;[256] the evidence suggests their danger might have been considerable if their plight had not been revealed. Russell had found Asquith undeniably anxious about them, and if the Prime Minister feared for their lives, their friends surely had cause for concern. Asquith's mistrust of the Government's own servants in the War Office and his reliance on the NCF are clearly shown in the arrangements he made for an exchange of information. The conclusion is inescapable that the credit for making it impossible to shoot resisting conscientious objectors must go to the No-Conscription Fellowship. Other persons played a part—news from the men sent to France leaked back by a number of routes and (for instance) seems to have reached Murray as soon as it did the Fellowship. But no one else was in a position to do everything the NCF did, receiving swift and accurate information at every stage, confidently able to promise to keep the Prime Minister informed, knowledgeable of every detail of the law, and backing its persuasiveness with enough public and Parliamentary exposure of the facts to rouse opinion and create pressure on the Government. They were aided by the fact that there was something in the notion of shooting resisting conscientious objectors that Liberal opinion, jaded though it was by two years of war, could not stomach.

It may have been a very fortunate coincidence that Russell and Philip Morrell served on the deputation of 11 May. However hostile Asquith knew them to be to his policies, they were of the class he aspired to and among his acquaintance. It is possibly not irrelevant that he had loved the same woman they both loved. He was comfortable with them and he did not doubt their word, and seems to have been relieved to have a reliable source of information which he did not trust his military advisers to supply.

The episode illustrates a likeable quality in both Russell and Marshall. However important was absolute resistance, however desirable martyrdom might be for propaganda purposes, no man was allowed to suffer severely or to be exposed to risk of death if it could be prevented without compromise of principles. Whenever such a case came up, it took precedence over all else, and Russell and Marshall did what they could to rescue the victims, though even within the Fellowship they were sometimes subject to criticism. In this instance, they made commitments to confidentiality which limited the use which could be made of the incident for propaganda purposes, and they brought all the private influence they could to bear on the seat of power rather than employing only the slow process of educating the public.

Russell derived one small portion of balm from the incident. When Evelyn Whitehead read of the men sentenced to death, she wrote in great agitation begging his pardon for having dismissed the dangers and for having thought that he had believed an exaggerated statement. Although she still considered conscription probably necessary to crush German militarism, she wrote that she was entirely with him in his efforts to avert 'such a calamity'.[257]

CHAPTER 7
PERSONAL PEACE CAMPAIGN

On 12 May 1916, Russell wrote to Lady Ottoline. 'I long to stomp the country on a stop-the-war campaign. The time has come. By June 10 I shall be free; I don't think then there will be anything to do for the COs'.[258] He looked forward keenly to the end of the Cambridge term, expecting to be clear by mid-June not only from his academic obligations but—erroneously as it turned out—from the kind of crisis which had marked the first two months of conscription. Propaganda for immediate peace negotiations appealed to him as the kind of contribution most important and most suited to him; the challenge and probable danger made it the more welcome. The No-Conscription Fellowship was glad to have Russell working on the peace campaign, to which support had been promised at the National Convention,[259] and plans were made to sponsor a tour in South Wales.

But before the Cambridge term ended the Government provided Russell with a chance to take a public stance of a kind very much to his taste. The first leaflet he had written for the NCF—the one describing the fate of Everett—was being distributed by the beginning of May, and reports soon began to come in from scattered areas that the leaflets were being seized and the men and women distributing them arrested by the police, acting under the orders of the Military Authority. The Everett leaflet was not the only offending document, and was often both handed out and confiscated together with one entitled *Maximillian*, describing the sufferings of a conscientious objector in Roman times. Other items of interest to the authorities at this time were Clifford Allen's speech to the April Convention, the pamphlet *British Prussianism*, and current issues of *The Tribunal*. But the unsigned Everett leaflet attracted most attention.[260] On 17 May *The Times* published a letter from Russell under the heading '*Adsum Qui Feci*', in which he admitted authorship and challenged the authorities to prosecute him as 'the person primarily responsible'.[261]

Two weeks passed before Russell was summonsed. The responsibility for prosecuting him lay with the Home Office, and the reason for the delay is uncertain (many of the files have been destroyed

78

But if the Home Office seemed indifferent, the Foreign Office certainly was not. Relations with the United States were delicate, and pressure from her government towards an early peace particularly to be feared; the possible effect of Russell's writings on an influential sector of American opinion was already a cause for disquiet,[262] and now, just at that time, Harvard was applying to the British Ambassador in Washington for permission for Russell to take up his appointment there in January 1917.[263] Russell, who was chronically doubtful about the effectiveness of his pacifist activities, would have been flattered at the degree of influence attributed to him by Foreign Office officials whose opinions were canvassed in the last few days of May. One wrote: 'I think his effect would be disastrous in the US just now with so much peace talk about.' Another, in a minute dated 29 May, made the first practical suggestion, proposing the Home Office be asked if it was planning steps against Russell; if they were it would 'pave the way for refusing to issue a passport—which is the only real means I know of by which we can stop him from leaving the country'. Although several officials commented that no reason need be given for refusing a passport, it was understood that a conviction against Russell would strengthen the hand of the Foreign Office. A minute of 31 May, signed 'N' (Lord Newton), was particularly outspoken:

This is one of the most mischievous cranks in the country and I submit that it would be folly to let him go to America. He has invited prosecution, and I cannot think why the Public Prosecutor leaves him alone, more especially since he has prosecuted the people who distributed the seditious literature in question.[264]

The timing of the summons might suggest that the Home Office acted without waiting for Foreign Office prodding. Two detectives came looking for Russell at his London flat on 29 May, and found he had just left for Cambridge, where they caught up with him the next morning.[265] Newton's official letter from the Foreign Office to the Home Office asking about the leaflet and the anticipated prosecution is dated 1 June. But it is more than possible that a little unofficial encouragement—by telephone or personal encounter—had been given to the Home Office to do its duty. There is, of course, no reason to suspect the Home Office of wishing to be lenient, but they did want some assurance that the prosecution would not enlist too much sympathy on Russell's side. To this end, both ministries even considered taking the discreditable step of circulating deliberately defamatory articles about Russell, and may indeed have done so, though the articles have not been identified in any publication.[266]

Russell was delighted to receive the summons. Conflict with the authorities seemed to him at this time a positive contribution to the cause of peace, because of the attendant publicity, so hard to get by legitimate means. He felt he had an impeccable moral case and a good legal one, although he was sure that a conviction must result because of the cases involving those who had distributed the leaflet, some of whom had now received sentences of as much as one month at hard labour. He was stimulated by the reaction of his colleagues in the NCF:

I saw Miss Marshall and Allen and a number of the others—they were all delighted and hoping I should get a savage sentence. It is all great fun, as well as a magnificent opportunity—the sort of opportunity I have longed for—and I have come by its legitimately, without going out of my way.[267]

The long-suffering lawyer who handled the Fellowship's legal affairs was less enthusastic: Russell commented, 'I think his professional instinct is worried by these cases in which people don't wish to get off'. The lawyer was employed in an advisory capacity, and Russell decided to conduct his own case. He felt it to be so great an opportunity that he got a severe case of stage fright and slept badly for several nights, but never lost his enjoyment of the challenge.[268] He prepared his speech carefully and had it typed out in advance, although he did not plan to read it.

In accordance with the usual practice the Fellowship made the coming trial widely known. Sympathisers were privately informed, and a mimeographed letter was sent out to branch secretaries, expressing the hope that there would be a large attendance at the Mansion House for the trial.[269] Ottoline Morrell's presence was important to Russell, and his brother was also there, as were Lytton Strachey, Crompton Llewelyn Davies, T. J. Cobden-Sanderson and Evelyn Whitehead. Although A. N. Whitehead did not come, he wrote sympathetically, and Russell must have appreciated the warmth of support from this quarter.[270] Russell's NCF colleagues were also out in strength. He spoke for almost an hour (smiling all the time, according to Cobden-Sanderson) he used his prepared material but evidently felt he had improved considerably on it in the recitation, and was greatly upset to discover that by an oversight no shorthand writer had been present on the NCF's behalf.[271] The principal way in which Russell had gone beyond his written speech was in the refutation of arguments used by the prosecutor. Several attempts were afterwards made to reconstruct the text of the speech, and what was presumably believed to be the best version was finally published as a pamphlet, *Rex* v. *Bertrand Russell*, only to be promptly seized by the authorities because it quoted from the Everett leaflet.[272]

Although Lytton Strachey described the defence as 'simply a propaganda speech',[273] Russell in fact devoted considerable attention to the legal aspect. He drew attention to the Home Secretary's statement, in Parliament on 1 June, that it was not illegal to advocate repeal of the Military Service Act though it was to urge resistance to its provisions. The law recognised the existence of the conscientious objectors, Russell declared, so that it could not be assumed that every man would be able to accept the tribunal's decision; it could therefore hardly be illegal to state that some would be certain to resist. Moving on to the leaflet itself, Russell acknowledged that it was written by him, with the exception of the last paragraph, which read: 'Forty other men are suffering persecution for conscience sake in the same way as Mr. Everett. Can you remain silent whilst this goes on?'[274]

Russell went on to say he believed the prosecution resulted from fear of the effect of the leaflet on the Army. As far as recruitment was concerned, when the leaflet was issued single men were subject to conscription, and no evidence had been produced that even one married man who had intended to enlist had been turned aside from doing so by reading the leaflet. As for discipline within the Army, he could not see that learning of the heavy sentence passed on Everett could be any encouragement to others to declare themselves conscientious objectors. Russell made it clear he had not meant the Army when he used the term 'the persecutors' in the leaflet. On the contrary, he roundly declared, the persecutors were the Government and its supporters, the tribunals, the newspapers and the blind public, a definition which while legally less culpable was probably no more welcome to the official part of his audience. The true ground on which the leaflet was feared, said Russell, was the sympathy it might enlist among the general public when the true facts of the persecution were known; and he cited other instances of official attempts to prevent the circulation of such information. The leaflet, he admitted, also criticised the sentence passed on Everett, but he pointed out that this could hardly be made illegal, and used the opportunity to put in a word on the situation of the COs in France; if they were to be shot there would surely be a wide public outcry and he could not believe all those joining in this would be prosecuted under the Defence of the Realm Act. Indeed, by commuting Everett's sentence to 112 days' detention, the military authorities had acknowledged the excessive harshness of the original sentence.

In the second half of his speech Russell moved somewhat farther from the strictly legal issue to discuss wider aspects of conscience and liberty. The NCF, he asserted, had no intention of making objectors of those who had no principle against fighting, but for the nation's sake it was essential to respect genuine objectors. The purpose of the clause put into the Act to safeguard liberty had been defeated by the tribunals and by the creation of the Non-Combatant Corps. Parliament had not intended COs to be persecuted, and no remedy for the situation was possible unless the facts were known. It was not the pacifits who objected to the persecution—indeed, they were grateful for the opportunity to show they were not cowards—it was for the sake of the nation that the disgrace must not be allowed to continue. In this vein Russell launched into his peroration:

I would say, my Lord, that whether I personally am acquitted or condemned is a matter of no great importance, but it is not only I that am in the dock; it is the whole tradition of British liberty which our forefathers built up with great trouble and with great sacrifice. Other nations may excel us in some respects, but the tradition of liberty has been the supreme good that we in this country have cultivated. We have preserved, more than any other Power, respect for the individual conscience. It is for that that I stand. I think that under the stress of fear the authorities have somewhat forgotten that ancient tradition, and I think the fear is unworthy, and the tyranny which is resulting will be disastrous if it is not resisted. I would say to them 'You cannot defeat such men—'.

But the Lord Mayor (Sir Charles Wakefield) had had enough. He interposed and said, 'I have allowed you a good deal of latitude because you are not an expert. Really now you are making a political speech'.[275] Russell had nearly finished. The short passage he had been prevented from speaking was later printed in *The Tribunal*. In part it read:

Men inspired by faith and freed from the dominion of fear are unconquerable. The noblest thing in a man is the spiritual force which enables him to stand firm against the whole world in obedience to his sense of right; and I will never acquiesce in silence while men in whom spiritual force is strong are treated as a danger to the community rather than as its most precious heritage. I would say to the persecutors: You cannot defeat such men; you cannot make their testimony of no avail. For every one whom you silence by force a hundred will be moved to carry on his work, until at last you yourselves will be won over, and will recognise with a sense of liberation from bondage, that all the material force the world contains is powerless against the spirit of indomitable love.[276]

The Lord Mayor was right that Russell was now making a speech, not conducting a defence, but the content was more spiritual than political. Russell was testifying to his deepest beliefs. Evelyn Whitehead thought he had 'won over the old Mayor', but no one was surprised when the Mayor declared he had not been convinced and pronounced sentence of a fine of £100 and £10 costs or sixty-one days imprisonment. The general opinion, however, was that the Lord Mayor had acted without rancour, although

Lytton Strachey thought he 'looked like a stuck pig'. The sourest note was struck by the counsel for the prosecution, the unfortunate Archibald Bodkin, who suggested there was food for thought in that it was not until six men had been proceeded against that Russell had accepted responsibility for authorship of the leaflet.[277]

Russell's friends thought the affair had gone off very well. Marshall wrote warmly, 'you were fine today—even better than we all expected'.[278] In spite of some fear of the activities of the Press Bureau—the editor of the *Cambridge Magazine* told Russell he dare not print anything except what had been in 'the patriotic papers'[279]—the news had circulated widely. The many letters of congratulation on his stand which Russell received from friends, NCF supporters and strangers proved it had indeed been an effective means of propaganda.[280]

Russell appealed his conviction, this time using the services of a lawyer, but on 28 June the conviction and sentence were upheld. He refused to pay the fine, but there was no suggestion that the jail sentence would be enforced. Instead some of his property (including his library) at Cambridge was distrained, but his friends bought it back for him, a gesture which he appreciated but was not altogether comfortable about.[281]

The Cambridge term ended within a week of Russell's trial and after going down to Cardiff for a National Committee meeting at the weekend, Russell spent two days in London and then took ten days' holiday. He was away from 14 to 24 June and so was not in London when the NCF got the news about the COs who were sentenced to be shot, although as we have seen he was back in time to protest Tennant's ineptness.

28 June saw the dismissal of Russell's appeal, but it did not see an end to the consequences of Russell's brush with the law. While the NCF was making the most of the publicity attending the trial, those who feared Russell's influence were also getting the most possible mileage out of the situation. The Foreign Office had not waited for the result of the appeal. On 7 June a cable was sent to the British Ambassador in Washington: 'Mr. Russell has been convicted under the Defence of the Realm Act for writing an undesirable pamphlet, and no passport will be issued to him to proceed to the United States. Please inform the President of Harvard.'[282] The news did not reach Russell until 7 July, just after the start of his Welsh tour. His feelings were very mixed. He had earlier confessed to Marshall that he was wondering whether he ought to try to get out of going to America, so in some ways he was relieved, although the loss of the income was worrying, and he had already put in some time on planning his lectures.[283] Other

aspects annoyed him more: 'I loathed the thought of the exile. But you cannot imagine how it infuriates me as a piece of tyranny. I want a fuss made about it. I want it pointed out that I was going to teach logic and that the government thinks logic would put America against us.'[284]

Russell wrote equally angrily to Professor Woods at Harvard, commenting on his own trial, and on the imprisonment of working men 'for the same offence', and adding bitterly, 'This is a war for liberty'. He predicted, 'This letter will no doubt never reach you; but it may be found interesting by the Censor', a forecast which came true. No charges were laid in connection with it, but it seemed foolish to the Home Office to allow Russell to say in writing what the refusal of a passport had been designed to prevent him from saying in person: so it remains to this day in the files.[285]

Neatly conceived as was Russell's argument that the Government's position was as vulnerable to logic as it was to peace propaganda, he did, of course, intend his academic lectures at Harvard on 'ethical and social topics' to be part of his campaign for peace, and he also planned to speak elsewhere in the States on peace-related topics. And when we find Allen, Marshall and Norman Angell agreeing that Russell's American visit was so important that the use of the incident for propaganda purposes should be held back until every effort to have the passport refusal rescinded had failed, it is evident the Government was not alone in believing Russell planned to work for peace while he was there.[286] But some of Russell's supporters continued to claim that his lectures at Harvard were to have had 'nothing whatever to do with politics or the war'.[287]

Trinity College Council was hardly in less of a hurry than the Foreign Office to take advantage of Russell's conviction, although they did wait until his appeal was dismissed. On 6 July, 1916 the secretary of the Council, H. McLeod Innes, wrote to let him know that the question of his conviction and the dismissal of his appeal 'as affecting your position in relation to the College' would be considered by the Council on Tuesday, 11 July. Russell wrote to Lady Ottoline. 'Trinity is going to consider on Tuesday whether to dismiss me. I think they only *can* dismiss me for 'grave moral obloquy'— but no doubt I have incurred that.'[228] Eleven members of the Council duly met on 11 July and unanimously passed a resolution that Russell be removed from his lectureship in the College. There was some discussion of striking his name off the College books, but when it was apparent unanimity would not be possible, the idea was dropped. McLeod Innes wrote to let

Russell know of the formal decision. Russell said very little directly about his feelings on receipt of this letter. He wrote to Lady Ottoline on 15 July: 'You will have seen that Trinity have got rid of me . . . probably for *me* it is a good thing, though it is sad that Trinity should do it.'[289] Although he had already felt alienated from Trinity, the College had been of enormous importance in Russell's life and the hurt went deep. If he could not express his own feelings, he was at least able to derive some vicarious satisfaction from the reactions of others. When he went to London he saw Alfred and Evelyn Whitehead:

She is furious with Trinity; he began by being but went down and talked the matter over and came to the conclusion that the Council were not to blame. Then I saw Hardy, who is incoherent and obscene with rage and tells me Littlewood is in the same mood. Hardy will do anything that can be done. Then Miss Marshall had a dinner party—just the N.C.F. com[ee] and Norman Angell. Angell thinks it is good material for propaganda, and wants to make a good deal of it. I am of course anxious that any possible use should be made of it. I shall never go back to Trinity, so it doesn't matter offending them past forgiveness.[290]

Trinity's action profoundly disturbed many intellectuals. Twenty-two Fellows signed a memorial to the Council expressing their dissatisfaction with the action taken. In spite of Russell's belief that Whitehead was half-hearted, the latter wrote a pamphlet about Russell and circulated it privately among the Fellows of Trinity during July. Whitehead was one of the signatories of the memorial but made an unexplained reservation, 'unless the Council proposed to offer Mr. Russell a suitable academic post'.[291] James Ward, another of the signatories, came up from Cambridge especially to discuss the matter with Russell and then wrote to Marshall on 11 August, saying he was thinking of preparing a brief matter-of-fact statement covering the case of the conscientious objectors and the part Russell had played in it. He planned to send it confidentially to the Fellows of Trinity College, inviting them to join in the protest against the cancellation of the lectureship. Ward expressed particular interest in the action taken with regard to the objectors who had been sent to France, and asked for information which would enable him to decide how far he would be justified in crediting the intervention of the NCF with saving the resisters' lives.[292]

In private, individual members of Trinity reacted with shame and embarrassment. Simpson wrote to Russell:

I knew things were pretty bad; but had not imagined them quite as bad as this . . . for me it means that a thing I was proud of being I now merely continue to be: partly from a selfish attachment to my job, but partly in a hope I will not quite surrender of doing what I can when I can to make it more like the place I thought it was.[293]

Another described Trinity's action as 'both intolerant and impertinent', and F. M. Cornford wrote, 'as for the College . . . the older Dons, last time I saw them, seemed to me to be in various stages of insanity . . . I feel very bitterly that the Council has disgraced us'.[294] Nor were public protests lacking. In a leader,[295] the *Manchester Guardian* discussed Russell's conviction and Trinity's action. The writer thought the prosecution had occurred almost accidentally, the result of an initial error of judgment in charging those who distributed the anonymous leaflets. The implication that the Government had got itself into an embarrassing situation unintentionally was more convenient than accurate. The *Nation* pointed out that indignation at Russell's dismissal was not limited to those who shared his views on the war.[296] Russell had reason at least to be well satisfied with the amount of attention his case had drawn, and with the extent to which comment had been sympathetic. The attack on civil liberties was what roused liberal indignation, rather than any enthusiasm for the cause of peace. But to Russell the two were so closely allied that the distinction scarcely mattered: an awareness of the concomitants of militarism was surely one of the ingredients in a desire for peace; and he had at least been granted evidence that liberal opinion was only dormant, not completely dead.

By the time the news from Trinity College and the Foreign Office reached him, Russell was busy with his Welsh tour. The trial had caused some delay, but by 1 July he was ready to set out. The tour, which occupied a strenuous three weeks, took place under the auspices of the National Council Against Conscription as well as the NCF, with local arrangements normally being handled by branches of the NCF or the Independent Labour Party. Wales had presumably been chosen for what was planned as the beginning of a wide campaign[297] because of the strength there of the ILP, and the thought that there might be untapped wells of anti-war feeling among the Welsh working people. Strong expressions in favour of British neutrality had come from the South Wales coalfields at the beginning of the war,[298] and some of the Welsh NCF members were among those urging the Fellowship to support the campaign for the opening of peace negotiations.[299] And the extent to which South Wales industry was essential to the war effort placed, at the very least, a potential weapon in the hands of the miners. On the other hand, there had been marked public support for the war in Wales and some angry demonstrations against pacifists, so Russell can hardly have known what he would meet with on his tour.

Three types of meetings were held: private meetings of members of the sponsoring organisations; public indoor meetings; and outdoor meetings, frequently held on village commons. Russell was at once struck by the peculiarities of wartime Wales. His first meeting, at Briton Ferry on 2 July, was private, and attended by about 100 members of the NCF, whom he described as 'very good people—full of spirit—not subject to much persecution because they are all in starred industries. The streets here are as full of young men as in normal times—it is very refreshing'.[300] But it was not only in small private meetings that Russell found support. Frequently the large halls were full, sometimes with as many as 2000 people, and almost always the response was enthusiastic. Most astounding were the open-air meetings, where the audience was unselected. Russell described his experience at Port Talbot:

The state of feeling here is quite astonishing. This town subsists on one enormous steelworks, the largest in S. Wales; the men are starred, and earning very good wages; they are not suffering from the war in any way. But they seem all to be against it. On Sunday afternoon I had an open-air meeting on a green: there were two Chapels on the green, and their congregations came out just before I began. They stayed to listen. A crowd of about 400 came,—not like open-air meetings in the South when people stay a few minutes out of curiosity, and then go away—they all stayed the whole time, listened with the closest attention, and seemed unanimously sympathetic.[301]

Two weeks later, on a common outside Swansea, Russell had an even more exciting experience. As he spoke 'an immense crowd gradually assembled', and he had to shout so loudly that he became hoarse. Although, as he claimed, he did not 'mince matters', and although it was 'an entirely accidental crowd', his message met with complete agreement.[302] He also described a typical large indoor meeting:

Sunday evening I spoke at Briton Ferry—a really wonderful meeting—the hall was packed, they were all in the highest point of enthusiasm—they inspired me, and I spoke as I have never spoken before. We put a resolution in favour of immediate peace negotiations, which was carried unanimously. (I did not notice any absentions, tho' presumably the two plain-clothes men who had come to take notes must have abstained.) Those who had not already signed the peace petition signed it in large numbers. One needs no prudent reticences—no humbug of any sort—one can just speak out one's whole mind. I thought the great offensive would have excited them, but it hasn't.

So favourable was the response that Russell began to think he should have gone into some more hostile area and that at this rate he would have been better employed in town; it was a relief to address an occasional smaller meeting where a good many people appeared undecided in their minds. 'That sort of meeting', commented Russell after one of these rare occasions, 'is really more useful than an enthusiastic one. The audience were almost all miners. They seemed intelligent and thoughtful.'[303] At most of his South Wales meetings Russell found no opposition at all, although he said that he was always aware of the presence of a police shorthand writer, charged, so Russell thought, with reporting to the London police.[304] There was also at least one meeting which had to be held outdoors because the booking of a room in a convenient school in the town was cancelled at short notice by the Merthyr director of education on the grounds that it was not available for political purposes.[305]

The meeting held in Cardiff Friends' House on 7 July is important because of later repercussions. Here Russell did run into some opposition, but it seemed to him minor and indeed he clearly relished the exchange. 'I had a capital meeting yesterday,' he wrote, 'a few opponents including some soldiers but they did not interrupt. A blood-thirsty middle-aged man, who mendaciously said he was a soldier, denounced us all afterwards, but he spoiled his case by violence.' Later Russell claimed that he had 'converted' the 'men in khaki', and commented again on his pleasure at having the opportunity on that one occasion to 'reach . . . not only those who are already convinced'. At the same time he was aware of the risk he ran, and wrote:

The Police took down every word I said and I have no doubt whatever that they will get me on what I am saying. I shall be in till the end of the war. I'm wondering whether I shall come out with my mind undamaged. I should be sorry if it were injured—it is at its very best right now and there are so many things I want to do with it.[306]

But the police were in no hurry to press charges. The shorthand writer identified by Russell at the meeting was not a policeman but was E. Ellis Hughes, the chief reporter from the *Western Mail*, although the head constable of Cardiff later claimed that Hughes was there at his suggestion, and there were no less than three policemen present.[307] Lloyd George, at a later date, indignantly denied that the Government had employed spies to get an account of the speech, and said that the transcript had come voluntarily from 'a reputable journalist', an account of the incident which was substantially accurate, except that it omitted mention of the part played by the police.[308] At the time, the shorthand notes were not even transcribed; all that the *Western Mail* published the following day was an account of the question period, during which Captain Atherley Jones (Russell had been wrong in thinking him not a soldier) and Mr Lovat Fraser (a barrister) had denounced the gathering as 'a lot of miserable, pro-German, sentimental traitors'.

If the editor of the *Western Mail* and the Cardiff police were too discreet to favour publication of the speech, Captain Jones was not. The public prosecutor, Sir Charles Mathews, later wrote that the Cardiff meeting would have attracted no attention but for Jones, 'who, having nothing in the shape of argument to put forward, lapsed into such gross and virulent personal abuse of Bertrand Russell as perhaps to create some little sympathy for him',[309] a judgment surprisingly like the one made by Russell himself at the time. But the Captain who had stumbled on this nest of traitors evidently waited for three weeks for retribution to overtake Russell and then, unable to contain himself any longer, wrote to the editor of the *Daily Express*, giving a short report of the speech, and mentioning his own part in the event—he and Lovat Fraser had, he claimed, asked questions and when 'as usual' Russell 'declined to give straight answers . . . I denounced him as a traitor'.[310] This forced the hand of the Home Office; Herbert Samuel wrote to the head constable of Cardiff to ask him whether a report on Russell's speech was available,[331] so the shorthand notes were at last transcribed and the speech dispatched to London, where it caused considerable heart-searching, but eventually was to prove useful to the government.

In the House of Commons Samuel later described the Cardiff speech as 'vehemently anti-British',[312] but at the time his department was unsure whether they had an adequate case or whether it would be judicious to pursue the matter. Edward Troup, at the Home Office, brought it to the attention of the Public Prosecutor, commenting that it could not be dismissed as insignificant; Russell, he said rather condescendingly, 'writes and speaks with a good deal of misguided cleverness . . . still it is a difficult question whether we should do more harm than good by prosecuting—he would make a clever defence, and would publish it as a pamphlet'.[313] Certainly the speech, still preserved in Home Office files at the Public Record Office, was provocative. Troup was particularly concerned with Russell's statement that Russia's desire to possess Constantinople was the main cause of the continuation of the war. The authorities must also have disliked Russell's accusation, directed at all the Allied governments, that they were taking steps which would make a lasting peace impossible even when the war ended. Commenting on plans being made to follow the shooting war with 'a war of commerce', he said 'you cannot hope that the Germans are going to love their neighbours when their neighbours are engaged in starving them', a sadly prophetic remark. All the same, Mathews cautiously pointed out in a letter to Sir Ernley Blackwell (also at the Home Office) that it was not illegal to discuss terms of peace and government policy, that it would strain even the Defence of the Realm regulations 'to bring any but an infinitesimal part of the speech within them', and that prosecution would lead to publicity. But while rejecting a straightforward prosecution, Mathews made interesting proposals, suggesting that the Official Press Bureau should be instructed 'that under no circumstances is any meeting attended by B.R. ever to be mentioned in the press', nor should correspondence relating to it be published, and whatever Russell might print should be instantly seized by the police. (Evidently government officials conceded that the victory in the public trials of the National Committee and of Bertrand Russell during the early summer had gone to the NCF.) In his reply. Blackwell agreed that prosecution was unwise, and he also doubted the practicality of a blanket prohibition of reporting;[314] but within a few days of this exchange a different approach to silencing Russell was to be tried, and the speech provided a useful peg. Russell himself never saw the transcript, but he saw a few passages later which were sent by the Home Secretary to Charles Trevelyan, and told the latter that they did not express what he said at all accurately.[315]

None of this, of course, was known at the time to Russell, who was perhaps as surprised as, if less disappointed than, Atherley Jones at the failure of the government to prosecute him at once. The theme of the Cardiff speech was that of his whole tour; that the continuation of the war was unnecessary and the product of self-serving on the part of the powerful. The people, Russell implied, should demand that the Government open the way for peace negotiations to begin.

The tour continued. A large indoor meeting at Merthyr Tydfil on 9 July was one of a series organised by the Merthyr and District Peace Council. Earlier speakers in the series had included Ponsonby and Trevelyan. Although it was a fine Sunday afternoon, the attendance was good and the audience responsive. It is not difficult to see why the Government would be made uneasy by Russell's declaration on behalf of himself and an approving audience (reported this time in the Merthyr *Pioneer*) that the real division was not between the Germans and the Allies, and that they stood nearer to the German friends of peace than to the English friends of war.[316] In spite of some disappointment at finding himself talking to the converted, Russell found the tour to be a great personal release. He wrote: 'It is glorious to be speaking out at last, saying what one thinks, facing what may come of it. It is such a liberation of pent-up passion.'[317]

Russell was profoundly moved by the enthusiasm with which

he saw his advocacy of an immediate peace by negotiation received. In addition to the joy of speaking openly, the tour gave him a deeper knowledge of how people lived and a renewed faith in the judgment of the common people.[318] The response to the campaign is also of interest as providing a rare insight into the state of feeling among a section of the inarticulate public. There are obvious limits to the value of such evidence—it has no statistical exactness, it deals only with a small section of the population, it is reported by a sympathetic source—but as far as it goes it may be at least as reliable as the massive and successful wishful thinking of the Northcliffe press.

Even while his tour was still in progress, Russell's changed circumstances obliged him to take stock of his personal situation. Refused a passport to take up his appointment at Harvard, and deprived of his lectureship at Trinity, he found himself suddenly without a regular job or income. Socialistic as the NCF might be in its sympathies, it was out of the question for the leaders to accept payment for their organisational services;[319] the gentlemanly tradition of voluntary service had to be preserved. Professional services, however, were fortunately different in this respect from services rendered directly to the Fellowship, and a plan was soon proposed to enable Russell to carry on his personal peace campaign much in the way he had originally hoped, but for pay. On 15 July, in a letter to Ottoline Morrell, he wrote:

Allen has a scheme for me to give a course of lectures in the autumn like the one I gave at Caxton Hall in the spring but more popular—to be given in large towns simultaneously, free, but at the expense of local Quakers—each tour to pay me £100! I like the plan from every point of view and I expect it will come off.

Later in the same letter, when discussing his dismissal by Trinity, Russell elaborated on the proposal, turning it—as he so often did with a new project—into something of a pipe dream:

I will make myself a teacher of all the working-men who are hungry for intellectual food—there are many throughout the country—I am always coming across them. I am amazed at the number of them at my meetings who have read my 'Problems of Philosophy'. I foresee a great and splendid life in that sort of thing—dealing with political ideas, but keeping out of actual politics. And I want to enlist all the teachers and men of education who have been turned out for being C.O.'s. There are numbers of them. Think of building up a new free education not under the State! There are infinite possibilities—finance is the only difficulty; but not an insuperable one. I could give heart and brain and life to that.[320]

In another letter Russell made it clear he thought in terms of a movement which would continue and grow after the war, directed most specifically at the political education of the workers and financed in the first instance by Quakers and later partly by trade unions. What he hoped to see taught shows both the radical nature of his political thinking at this time and his determination to ensure a sound basis of knowledge: the movement, he said, was to differ from the Workers' Educational Association in having a political object:

It will try to teach men what they should know in order to be politically effective, and to give them a philosophy that will make their politics stable. History, economics, some psychology, a little ethics, are what is most wanted in the way of instruction—not ancient history, but very recent history . . . it would be ideal work for me. One would teach the abolition of the whole wages system—no more work for wages, no more slavery to capitalists or government officials. Freedom, growth unimpeded, free play for people's best energies. It is the essential preliminary to any successful movement of fundamental reform. [321]

Plans for the first series of lectures went ahead rapidly. Allen hoped they would be published as a book with a wide circulation, as well as given orally. In order to write, Russell was to be freed of NCF work except for two days a week. (Russell, who thought writing made him 'unhappy and odious', rather dreaded the prospect.) Manchester was the first town in which arrangements were confirmed, and here it was decided to rent a large hall and charge those who attended five shillings each for the course; the course might also be given in Glasgow, Birmingham and Leicester, and possibly Newcastle and Bristol. [322] Shortly after the end of his Welsh tour Russell settled in to write the lectures but, as he predicted, found little joy in doing so.

Meanwhile, the Government had found a use for the Cardiff speech of 6 July; the leisurely correspondence between Home Office officials and the Public Prosecutor as to what to do about it came to an end on 31 August, when Whiskard, a Home Office official with responsibility for the Home Office alternative service scheme, sounded the alarm; Russell, he had heard, was going to Haverhill the following day to address fifty conscientious objectors working under the scheme and must at all events be stopped. Blackwell promptly asked Colonel Kell of MI5 in the War Office to make use of a special wartime security power to ban Russell from entering all prohibited areas, which included most coastal districts. Kell complied, though at first doubtful of the appropriateness of using this restriction, specifically designed to deal with suspected enemy agents. When Samuel was informed, he thought the banning order would be hard to defend, and that it should be withdrawn in favour of a more limited one—as Blackwell also had thought possible—excluding Russell 'from certain areas such as South Wales and any places where our conscientious objectors are at work'. But the War Office attitude had hardened almost overnight, and MI5 could not so easily be persuaded to rescind the order. Kell wrote that he had consulted with senior officials in other branches (including the Director of Personal Services, Brigadier General Macready), and that the order should stand. Russell's view that there was no good reason to continue the war, he said, was very dangerous, and he must be prevented from airing 'his vicious tenets amongst dockers, miners and transport workers'. He went on to suggest that if Russell persisted, an even more stringent order might be enforced, confining him to one particular area.[323] At the time, no pretext was really necessary, as the order was not a judicial procedure and involved no hearing—an attractive feature from the official standpoint.

Certainly, the banning order was a shock. Russell gave Lady Ottoline a characteristic description, beginning with a seemingly unemotional factual account and only gradually allowing a small part of his feelings to show, before again pulling back, with an obvious effort, to a pretence of detachment. It is worth quoting in full.

I had a queer adventure today. About 12 o'clock, two men in plain-clothes from Scotland Yard appeared on behalf of the War Office, and served a notice on me ordering me not to go into any prohibited area. I was just going to Suffolk but I had to give it up. I have also had to give up going to Sussex on Monday. I shall also have to give up lecturing at Glasgow, Edinburgh and Newcastle as I had intended to do. I have no notion why they served the notice on me, or whether there is any hope of getting it rescinded. I spent the rest of the day seeing the Press. Massingham promised a leader; the D.N. and the M.G. were sympathetic; the Chronicle fairly hopeful; and the average newspaper is willing to take it to news. I am much more angry than over anything yet. It is a power conferred on them for dealing with spies, and they choose to suppose that I want to give military information to the Germans. It makes my blood boil. Fortunately Oxfordshire is not a prohibited area. Probably all my letters will be read by the Censor, so prudence in writing is desirable. I think it is utterly outrageous to put such an indignity upon me. But I had an amusing afternoon seeing journalists, from the Times to the Daily Sketch.[324]

At first Russell found the new blow depressing but hard to take seriously, and believed that if he set about it the right way he could get it rescinded. He arranged to lunch with Sir Francis Younghusband, the explorer, who was one of the few men he knew who were in touch with the War Office. He found him quite friendly but not in the least inclined to be indignant. Russell was at first wearily reluctant to get into yet another fight, but gradually his spirit reasserted itself and he began to find the situation stimulating. On 4 September he wrote:

I think the War Office action is due to a mistake. Probably they think I tried to stir up a strike among the miners in S. Wales when I was there. Of course I did nothing of the sort. The whole thing cheers me up. It is such a comfort to have something immediate and small to fuss about. Younghusband will probably discover why they have done it. I hear today that they have searched my flat from top to bottom, or more accurately, from end to end. There is lots of sport to be got out of this matter—I am enjoying it . . . last night I was tired but now I am full of fight. It is really *monstrous* of them. [325]

By the next day he had even decided that 'this business is more fun than anything they have done to me yet. I shall be sorry if it is all adjusted today—but I mustn't exasperate them unnecessarily'. [326]

Russell's expectation of an adjustment came from Younghusband's having arranged for him to meet on 5 September with General George Cockerill, director of special intelligence at the War Office, but the expected result did not follow. The General had in front of him the report of Russell's Cardiff speech; like Kell, he was particularly bothered by Russell's view that there was no reason why the war should continue another day. Such a statement, Cockerill said, was calculated to diminish the ardour of miners or munitions workers; Russell was also encouraging men to refuse to fight for their country. But the main purpose of granting the interview emerged when the General offered to withdraw the order forbidding Russell to enter prohibited areas if he would abandon political propaganda and return to mathematics.

A rather strange discussion followed regarding two human attributes, the conscience and the sense of humour. General Cockerill claimed to regard conscience as a still small voice, but said that when it became blatant and strident he suspected it of being no longer a conscience. Russell asked him whether he would not in fact feel less respect for him if he agreed to the bargain which was proposed. But the General replied, 'No, I should respect you more; I should think better of your sense of humour if you realised the uselessness of saying the same thing over and over again'. Russell was so indignant at Cockerill's apparent elevation of the exercise of 'a sense of humour' over the exercise of conscience that he refused for the rest of his life to lay claim to the quality. In 1932 he wrote:

Alas, I am that extremely rare being, a man without a sense of humour. I had not suspected this painful fact until the middle of the War, when the British War Office sent for me and officially informed me of it. I gathered that if I had had my proper share of the sense of the ludicrous, I should have been highly diverted at the thought of several thousand men a day being blown to bits, which, I confess to my shame, never caused me even to smile. [327]

The discussion moved to the lectures Russell was planning to give in Glasgow, Edinburgh and Newcastle on the general principles of politics. In reply to a question, Russell said that although the lectures would not directly involve the propaganda which was objected to, 'they would state the general principles out of which the propaganda has grown, and no doubt men with sufficient logical acumen would be able to draw inferences'. Cockerill declared such lectures could not be permitted, and appealed to Russell not to make the task of the soldiers more difficult. The interview concluded with Russell stating firmly that he could not possibly cease his propaganda as the result of a threat.[328] In the light of this interview it is hard to give credence to the Home Secretary's later statement that it was a coincidence that the War Office order interfered with the lectures, as it had only been intended to prevent him from making propaganda speeches—of the kind he gave in Wales—at the Home Office camps.[329]

Russell's first feeling was that he could not allow the order to interfere with his plans to lecture. He now thought it a near certainty that his activities would result in his imprisonment, believing he would be arrested by the end of the month and might well spend the rest of the war behind bars.[330] His anticipation of life in prison was made more vivid by the emergence of the National Committee from their spell in jail. Russell enjoyed seeing them again and reported that they seemed well and cheerful: 'They said the worst thing about prison was the lice. Chamberlain, who is rather a dandy, was given underclothes full of eggs which hatched; and he was not allowed to change them for a fortnight. It *almost* makes one wish to obey the law.'[331]

On the whole the Committee's experience seems, surprisingly, to have been reassuring. Fear of prison and its probable effects had haunted Russell in Wales, although he had been prepared to accept the risk; 'I had the feeling,' he wrote on one occasion, 'of a mouse walking into a trap', but now such fears receded before the excitement of the issue in hand. Russell confessed to being flattered by the authorities 'making such a dead set at me', and said it was the first thing that had persuaded him he was doing any good.[332] Until mid-September it seems he still planned to defy the order in some dramatic fashion and take the consequences, though what references there are are cryptic and almost conspiratorial. In a letter to Ottoline Morrell, he wrote that he heard a rumour was going around that he planned to resist the War Office; he supposed the source of this was Clive Bell. It was, he said, very important that no such impression should get abroad. 'I should be glad if you could lead Clive to think that tho' I contemplated such a course at first I have now abandoned it, as a result of wise advice. And I should like everybody to think so.'[333] Apparently some kind of double bluff was planned, but by the end of the month something must have occurred to change this, and Russell in fact made no attempt to defy the order.

Correspondence with the War Office meanwhile continued. On 7 September, Russell wrote to General Cockerill, thanking him for granting him the interview, but pointing out that the nature of the prohibition was leading people to infer 'that in the eyes of the authorities there is some reason to suppose me a person likely to seek and use dishonorably information which might be valuable to the enemy'. Russell asked if he might refute this imputation by repeating in public some of the content of the interview. Instead Cockerill, who recognized the force of Russell's complaint, provided him with an official letter from the Army Council expressly stating it was not the desire of the Council that any such imputation should rest upon Russell, and also repeating the offer to withdraw the order if he would give an undertaking not to continue propaganda. Russell also wrote to the Competent Military Authority (Lietutenant-Colonel the Honourable A. V. P. Russell), requesting permission to proceed to Glasgow to give the lecture on 'Political Ideals', the first of the planned course of six. He was asked to submit the lectures to General Cockerill for censorship, but replied that this was impossible as they would be spoken and not read. He sent the syllabus, but this was not considered sufficient; General Cockerill did, however, again express willingness to accept Russell's word if Russell would give the desired undertaking.

At length it became evident that all the negotiations had been based on a misunderstanding. In reply to a long letter in which Russell reiterated his reasons for refusing to give an undertaking (pointing out in particular the difficulty of knowing exactly what would seem subversive to the Government), General Cockerill wrote on 2 October: 'I think I must remind you that our correspondence originated in an interview which I accorded to you on being informed by a friend of yours that you were desirous to abstain in future from illegal propaganda, and to devote your attention to logic and philosophy, and that you would be prepared to give an honourable undertaking to this effect.' This impression must have been conveyed by Younghusband, but had certainly not been intended by Russell. However, as Russell admitted, it probably arose out of something he had said to Younghusband about his abortive American trip, and again one is left with the impression that Russell had been guilty of some whitewashing of his intentions for that tour. Explaining how he thought Young-husband's misapprehension might have arisen, Russell said:

The only thing I can think of is that I pointed out to him, what is the fact, that, if my passport to Harvard had not been refused, my whole time from October to June would have been taken up in the preparation and delivery of academic lectures on mathematical logic and ethics, and that nothing but official persecution had led to my continuing pacifist propaganda.

The War Office—or General Cockerill—was extremely anxious to have Russell's word that he would refrain from propaganda. What use they planned to make of it is not clear: it may have been intended merely to silence Russell; or it may have been hoped that the public could be made to see it as a recantation of heresy; or it may have been for use as an additional weapon should Russell again offend. The tone of Cockerill's letters suggests he saw it as something Russell could easily give, and could be trusted to adhere to, saving a lot of awkwardness all round. It seems likely that it was precisely in the hope of pulling off this coup that the War Office had decided to leave the ban in force, even against Samuel's recommendation. Russell's lunch meeting with Young-husband had been on Sunday, 3 September, and presumably the unintentionally misleading report to the War Office followed immediately by note or phone call. Kell's letter to Blackwell, stating that the order should stand, is dated 3 September, and may have been written on Sunday evening, or possibly this is a misdating for 4 September, Monday, a more likely day of the week to be dealing with such matters. In any event, the War Office probably felt itself in a strong position between what they thought was Russell's wish to withdraw and the stick-cum-carrot which the banning order seemed to have placed in their hands. But Russell ignored the stick, and refused to take the carrot.

Russell had explained that his lectures would be intended to influence opinion, not merely to convey information, but that what he planned to set forth was a general philosophy, 'out of which pacifism springs', rather than any particular conclusion. In spite of his repeated statement that he was not willing to give any undertaking, the General wrote that he would accept this as just such an undertaking. When Russell again refused to accept this position, the correspondence at last came to an end. Russell wrote once more for a specific answer to his request for permission to enter the prohibited area to lecture in Glasgow on 17 October, and drew a final official refusal. No comment was made on the fact, to which Russell drew attention, that he planned to give the same lecture in Manchester on 16 October, an activity with which the War Office was not able to interfere under the order.[334]

Both sides had kept their patience admirably; even a War Office spokesman admitted that Russell had conducted his negotiations throughout 'with courtesy and restraint'.[335] But Russell had controlled his caustic wit with difficulty, and had had to let off steam to Lady Ottoline on at least one occasion, sending her a letter to Cockerill, which he drafted but presumably never even intended to mail. The argument is the same as the one used in his published *Personal Statement*, but his examples are much more provocative. Discussing the difficulty of keeping to 'an honourable undertaking not to use my lectures for propaganda of the kind you dislike', he asked: 'Should I violate it if I expressed considerable respect for the teaching of Christ? Or would you prefer me to say that, while admitting the moral sincerity of the Sermon on the Mount, I considered it, from the standpoint of political sagacity, very inferior to "John Bull"?'[336]

Meanwhile, the utmost use for propaganda purposes was being made of the ban by Russell's supporters. From the outset the connection with work for the conscientious objectors was played down for fear of reducing 'the effectiveness of the case for agitation on the grounds of civil liberty'. This was logically appropriate enough: Russell's original trial, the refusal of a passport, his dismissal from Trinity, and the War Office ban could all be seen as threats to freedom of speech. Strategically, too, it was sound; the hope was to rouse dormant liberal feelings, already stirring uncomfortably under the operation of the Defence of the Realm Act and the increasing frequency of raids by the police, acting under order of the 'Competent Military Authority'.[337] Accordingly, the National Council for Civil Liberties (formerly the NCAC) handled and funded the public campaign, though the NCF reserved the right to supply information to Members of Parliament.[338]

The attempt to 'manage' the reaction to the Russell case does not negate the genuineness of the response. The War Office ban in particular was seen by many as ludicrously inappropriate. The Liberal press was united in condemnation and even *The Times* printed a letter from H. W. Massingham strongly condemning the ban and appealing to *The Times* to use its influence 'to discourage the persecution of an Englishman of whose accomplishments and character the nation may well be proud'.[339] Individuals, including such strange bed-fellows as Ramsay MacDonald and Sir Hugh Cecil, wrote privately to protest against one or other aspect of the Government's treatment of Russell.[340] Questions were asked in Parliament.

Plans for Russell's lectures were modified, but there was no thought of abandoning them, and he wrote them in whatever time he could snatch, although he was busy with NCF work all the time. In spite of the pressure the last lecture was dictated to Eva Kyle, the NCF secretary, on 17 September, and the syllabus was ready some time ahead of this.[341]

Russell gave the first lecture at Manchester, which was not in the prohibited area, on Monday, 16 October. In Glasgow the series was to begin on the following evening and, aware of the ban, 1000 people gathered in the hall for a protest meeting at which Robert Smillie was the principal speaker. The Glasgow *Herald* reported on the occasion:

Mr. Robert Smillie, President of the Miners Federation of Great Britain, sprang a dramatic surprise on the audience. He asked to be excused if he departed from his usual custom and read from a paper. After reading a long discourse he intimated that that was not his own speech but the lecture which Mr. Bertrand Russell was to have delivered. This announcement was received with laughter, followed by prolonged applause.[342]

At the end of the meeting a resolution was passed protesting the action of the War Office in prohibiting Russell from delivering his lectures in Glasgow. The War Office took no action against this demonstration—indeed would have been hard pressed to find any legal grounds for doing so—and the opponents of the government generally felt it to be a triumph for the cause of liberty. Certainly the War Office had given Russell all the advertisement he could need and good audiences were assured. In the end, the series was delivered in full only in Manchester and in Birmingham. Russell spent the six weeks commuting between these two centres and attending and addressing other gatherings as occasion served. He had become a very versatile speaker, as much at home addressing the Union Chapel Brotherhood in Manchester as he was in representing the National Committee at some of the divisional conventions being held around the country at this time.[343]

The lecture series was entitled 'The World as it can be Made', and the first lecture was called 'Political Ideals', the title under which the series was eventually published.[334] The first lecture came out as a pamphlet and circulated widely. Its theme was primarily inspirational. Russell spoke of the need for all men to live by conviction and ideals which would transcend immediate circumstances. He strongly stressed the value of individual differences and the importance of allowing room for the growth and use of creative impulses. Institutions were to be judged by the amount of security and liberty they gave for such development, but these conditions would not suffice without positive encouragement. Conceding the necessity for large organisations in modern society, Russell thought individual initiative could be promoted by subjecting every form of organisation, large or small, to democratic control. Turning to the function of force in government he summed up his views in an effective sentence: 'There is probably one purpose, and one only, for which the use of force by government is beneficent, and that is, to diminish the total amount of force used in the world.' He concluded with a call for a more hopeful attitude; belief in the power to improve world conditions was the first step towards bringing about the improvement.

The topics covered in the remaining lectures did not differ greatly from those with which he had dealt in the series on 'Principles of Social Reconstruction', but the tone throughout was more radical and the general direction in which he saw solutions to lie was more clearly pointed. In the economic system and in state institutions the emphasis, as he saw it, should be on devolution of power, to give the maximum of security, liberty, and personal initiative to the individual. Internationalism should be fostered not in order to do away with nations but in order to release people from the burden of fear caused by international tension and to free them to aim at higher development of civilisation together. In a final lecture on 'Education and Prejudice', Russell showed how important he felt the role of education to be in making the kind of people who could achieve the world which he hoped to see. Education must not be subject to rigid central control and should contribute to the growth of people who would be properly free, able to use their own inititive, and without prejudice. Since the war began Russell had again and again been disappointed in the slowness with which people responded to what seemed to him obvious injustices, illogicalities and criminal follies on the part of their rulers. More and more he was turning to education as the place at which all change must begin. Factual knowledge must improve but above all new habits of thought must be developed in the general populace if democracy was to be effective.

Between March and October 1916 Russell had turned, according to the viewpoint, from an irritating but respectable academic into 'one of the most mischievous cranks in the country'; or he had turned from a right-minded intellectual into a radical hero. The Government's decision to refuse him a passport was cheered in the House of Commons: and he himself was given an ovation at the end of the last of his lecture series in Manchester.[345] He could not be ignored both because he was already well-known and because he brought abilities to the field of agitation which were exceptional. The dilemma of the War Office over his lecture series was no coincidence. No one could deny his right and his competence to lecture on political ideals and ethics, but where could the line be drawn between the academic and the subversive? Was he to blame if his audience drew topical conclusions, or only if he himself used topical examples? The precipitating factor in Governmental alarm was probably that it was evident the principles he expounded were not academic to him, or intended to be accepted academically, and his close involvement with the NCF showed he meant to practise what he thought followed from what he preached. Russell seems to have relished the dilemma. He did not consider it subversive, but beneficial, to oblige people to question the actions of Government: if he could bring them to this point merely by clearly setting out certain general principles and encouraging logical thought, rather than by overt propaganda (such as he had used in Wales), so much the better.

Russell saw his work for peace very much as a whole. Helping in the NCF office, speaking to Welsh miners on the need for urging peace negotiations, writing against the sending of conscientious objectors to France, giving lectures to paying audiences in northern England—all these were part of a single-minded operation. And an equally important part of the activity was his challenge to the authorities and to liberal opinion. His work was furthered, not interrupted, by his trial in June, by the loss of his job, by the Foreign Office refusal to grant him a passport, by the War Office order banning him from prohibited areas. All these he saw as part of the struggle to defeat militarism, to bring the war to an end, and to establish peace on a firmer foundation.

CHAPTER 8
CONTROVERSY AND ATTRITION

Russell was moving into a major role in the National Committee of the No-Conscription Fellowship during the summer of 1916, in spite of the time taken up by his Welsh tour and his trial and its consequences. He seldom missed a meeting of the National Committee, and his public notoriety made him known and generally admired among the members as well as the leaders. For himself, he discovered what it was like to be part of a small group, working together with great intensity in a time of stress, with serious differences between them, but with mutual respect and an immense commitment to finding a solution that would further the goals they had in common. Throughout his personal campaign and his confrontations with the authorities he felt behind him the support of the group, and at the same time they began to place increasing reliance on his contributions to discussion and decision-making.

The measure of agreement reached at the National Convention in April regarding alternative service did not last long. By mid-June it was known that the Government was preparing another plan to offer civil work to some of the men in jail. Among the leaders, most anticipated—even assumed—that this would be just another unacceptable option, but there were a few who took seriously the charge that the Fellowship was simply committed to obstruction. At the end of June, just before the Government's Home Office scheme was introduced, the National Committee debated the possibility of devising a form of national service which could be offered voluntarily by the Fellowship. An exploratory outline was drawn up, probably by Marshall,[346] for an analytical examination of the whole question of alternative service from first principles to practical suggestions. At about the same time, the Rev. F. B. Meyer (a well-known Baptist sympathiser) fathered a scheme designed to improve the position of absolutists as well as of alternativists. The proposal obviated some of the features most objectionable to the NCF leaders by providing for a revision of the form of exemption given to each imprisoned man, not for a rejudging of the genuineness of his convictions. Full details are not known, although there seems to have been included some specific plan for a form of alternative service that would be free from direct Government control.[347]

Little is known of the fate of Marshall's planned re-evaluation, but it was she who sponsored Meyer's scheme in the National Committee, where it became the focus of fierce dissension. The controversy centred on the intrinsic merits and defects of the plan for only long enough to reveal almost irreconcilable differences, before opening the door to another whole area of serious disagreement, arising from the proposal that the Fellowship should give it open and official backing. Russell later summarised the grounds on which the scheme had been attacked:

A large section of the Committee objected to the proposal that the N.C.F. should advocate this course, on three different grounds: (1) That no scheme whatever ought to be put forward by the N.C.F., since if successful it would facilitate the work of the M.S.A.; (2) That the N.C.F. as a body could not take action on behalf of alternativists, in view of the resolution of the April Convention; (3) That we ought not to agitate at all about conditions whether in prison or elsewhere, but to accept hardships as an opportunity for testimony.[348]

Russell went on to point out that not all the opponents of the scheme adopted all three grounds, but in spite of this, one of the threatening features of the dissension in the Committee during the 'three-weeks' crisis'[349] was that alignment was similar on most issues, and two factions emerged.

One faction was led by Marshall and Allen and the other by Fletcher. It is tempting to say that those ranged on Allen's side were mainly socialist pacifists and those supporting Fletcher were Quaker or religious pacifists, but the statement needs some qualification. The terms 'socialist pacifist' or 'Quaker pacifist' are of use in identifying a person's primary affiliation, but there were few of the Quakers on the National Committee who had not been convinced socialists since before the war, while several of those who came in as ILP members joined the Society of Friends during or shortly after the war. Even more important in Russell's eyes was the recognition of a strong religious and mystical element in the make-up of most of the NCF socialist leaders. He believed the distinction 'between what are called "religious" and what are called "political" objectors' to be 'characteristic of politicians. . . . No one else would have supposed that it was impossible to be interested in the affairs of the world in a religious spirit'.[350] Russell felt at home in the counsels of the Fellowship just because beneath all the fine points of controversy which became so important to the disputants one thing was clear: these were all people trying to find the right solution, not serving their own interests, and motivated to a greater or lesser extent by what Russell defined as love of mankind. In this climate, although formal decisions were made by majority vote and feelings sometimes ran high, there could be no attempt to overpower or out-manoeuvre the other faction: all had to strive to understand conflicting points of view and to seek an outcome acceptable to the consciences of all. Paradoxically, it was in the company of so many to whom right and wrong were all-important that Russell received an education in the shades of grey which exist between black and white. Those who differed from him on the National Committee could not be dismissed as merely wicked: they had to be listened to and respect given to their convictions.

On the alternative service issue Russell gave strong support to Meyer's proposal, urging that the Fellowship had a duty to contribute something positive, and again putting forward the view that it was 'very wrong not to save men from the kind of thing that might break them'. At the meeting on 1 July, he analysed the position of the Fellowship carefully and in very practical terms, making a distinction between the action which the leaders should try to promote if they could, and the action which it was in their power to promote. In the long view, their objectives were to defeat conscription, to further pacifism and to secure freedom of conscience. While he admitted that the more uncompromising they were the more likely they were to promote these objects, he made an important proviso: if the Government pressed persecution beyond a certain point the breakdown and loss of some of the most valuable people might well result.

Support also came from Salter, who was a Quaker and active in the ILP (but not a member of the Friends' Service Committee), and Brockway. Allen is on record as having made the rather revealing remark, 'I've always felt that the one thing C.O.s could advocate is persecution'. In view of Allen's reputation as an inspiring and dominant chairman, it is surprising how often the evidence shows him as giving a mixed message; here he seems to have been torn again between an intellectual commitment to help the alternativists and an emotional attraction toward martyrdom. Russell shared many of Allen's views and admired him almost unreservedly: he never confessed to recognising the ambivalence of the chairman's message or claimed to foresee the difficulties to which it would contribute. His own stance was close to Allen's intellectually but was now leavened in practice by a more mature understanding of the limitations of human beings. Although at this time he could even share in some measure in Allen's personal desire for martyrdom, he could never wish martyrdom on others, especially those who might prove too weak to bear it without breaking.

The young Quakers were the ones who spoke out most strongly against what they held to be compromise. Fletcher declared that the Committee ought to make it plain that men who accepted alternative service were compromising the movement. The government would be greatly embarrassed by having thousands of men in civil custody and the Fellowship should do nothing to help it out of the dilemma. Fletcher was supported by his fellow-Quaker, Barratt Brown, and also by Walter Ayles, Will Chamberlain and J. H. Hudson (who joined the Committee at the beginning of July).[351] The last three were all socialists who became members of the Society of Friends around the end of the war. To the Committee members who favoured the new plan —and who were all, it should be remembered, personally committed to an absolutist stand—Fletcher's position seemed rigid and intolerant. It is not surprising to find Brockway complaining that Fletcher seemed to favour relief for the consciences of absolutists but not for those of alternativists. A much more powerful impression must have been made when Edward Grubb, the elderly Quaker treasurer, and possibly the only Quaker on the Committee who was not a socialist, broke his habitual silence to declare, in opposition to the younger Friends, that the crux of the matter was that some members of the Fellowship would not allow other members to say that they could conscientiously accept alternative service, and would not admit to the public that any were in this position, with the result that a true expression of the Fellowship was not being given.[352]

When Grubb made this remark the National Committee was already embroiled in a new controversy arising out of the alternative service question but going beyond it into an area closely concerning the work in which Russell had been assisting Marshall. A storm blew up over the nature of the Fellowship's engagement in political action, and of the policies followed by the Political Committee. The plans which had been worked out during Russell's first weeks in the Associates' Committee had led to the development of a network of contacts which had been put to very specific use in relation, for example, to the ill-treatment of Norman at Wandsworth and the case of the conscientious objectors sent to France, which were both recent issues during the crisis of June and July in the National Committee. It will be remembered that in the latter case Marshall had kept Asquith supplied with information and had made some commitments to confidentiality in return for the Prime Minister's active interest. She was still making sure that he was informed whenever resisting COs were included in drafts intended for France.[353] A similar and continuing liaison (also scarcely mentioned in the secondary sources) was formed with General Childs. He was, as we have seen, anything but sympathetic to the objectors, and resented the hours he had to spend dealing with complaints regarding their treatment. But use could be made even of this, and an important minor concession was gained on one occasion simply by undertaking to lay off the pressure which had been directed at his office.[354] More importantly, it early became apparent that Childs had a knowledge of and high regard for military law, which he would not see subverted. If firm evidence could be produced that an objector was being subjected to illegal treatment, Childs would intervene without hesitation. Later, there were to be some unexplained inconsistencies in his actions, attributable perhaps to the conflict between his legal rectitude and his view of political objection as totally unjustifiable, and of the NCF organisers as deserving to be dealt with under the Incitement to Mutiny Act. He also, like many people then and since, tended to identify absolutists with political objectors, whereas as we have seen the NCF's Quaker leaders were at least as uncompromising in their views. Yet by midsummer he had learnt some trust in the information given him by Marshall, and she on her side had found he could be relied on to listen to representation and to take the necessary action. She wrote to him on a number of occasions, and spoke to him frequently on the telephone, gradually building up a relationship of mutual respect in spite of a polarity of views and aims.[355]

While Russell and some others saw all this as a substantial achievement, some liked it less. Fletcher, though he claimed that he did not oppose political action as such, thought the Fellowship was devoting too much attention to trying to influence Parliament directly, and was not sufficiently concerned with public opinion. Though the Committee went on trying to wrestle with the question of the amount of support to be given to those who could acccept alternative service—an issue now further complicated by the announcement of the Home Office scheme—the heat which was generated at the meetings of 1 July and 9 July came mainly from this new slant. For once Allen was not at all ambivalent and made it plain that he held political action to be essential. Marshall hotly defended the kind of political work she had been doing, claiming that public opinion and political action should go hand in hand: to divorce them was to incur the responsibility of leading toward revolution. The effectiveness of all such work, she maintained, depended on the interaction between the two; she had always said she would not do political work without public opinion behind her; nor would she be prepared to rouse public opinion without bringing it to political action as its final expression. She would resign rather than continue on these terms. The threat of resignation was not an idle one. The Women's International League would have been very happy to have her full-time service again, and she had some justification for believing that if the NCF restricted itself to direct work for peace, she would be of most use in the WIL.[356] But she was also, naturally, deeply hurt at what seemed like an attack on her work, and Russell was probably right in his surmise that she felt the Committee was showing ingratitude, although she indignantly denied that any such thought had entered her mind.[357] Under pressure from Russell and Allen, both of whom sympathised with her view, she decided to wait out the crisis.

The trouble continued to escalate during the first two or three weeks of July. The committee met for long, tense sessions every weekend, and to these meetings Russell came faithfully, even when it meant making the long journey from Wales between his speaking engagements there. At times it seemed the Fellowship would break up, or at least that a special national convention would have to be held to enable the membership to break the deadlock.[358] There were many pressures on Russell and other leaders at the time. Five members of the National Committee were to go to jail on 17 July, to serve the sentence they had been given in connection with the publication of the *Repeal the Act* leaflet; Allen might be arrested at any time; Russell's appeal had just been dismissed and his dismissal from Trinity and the refusal to him of a passport had followed; Lloyd George became Secretary for War; raids and prosecutions under the Defence of the Realm Act multiplied; there were several episodes of personal violence against the anti-conscriptionists (one involving an assault on Brockway and another leaving Marshall lame for two weeks); NCF funds were running short; there were reports of more COs being sent to France; the new Home Office scheme, of which details were now available, promised to enmesh the Fellowship in further controversy.

When the Committee met on 14 July, all realised a decision had to be reached. Allen's faction now clearly had a (scant) majority, but it was obvious that forcing a majority decision in the Committee would not lay the matter to rest. At some point the membership would have to be consulted, although the idea of an immediate convention had been abandoned as impracticable. Every effort was made to accommodate as much of the minority viewpoint as possible, and in the outcome only Fletcher was completely unable to accept the policy decided upon. The meeting lasted until 2 a.m. on Saturday morning, and resumed later the same day. The idea of officially advocating the original scheme was dropped, but 'action of the same kind as that contemplated in the scheme was sanctioned'.[359] On 3 August, the matter was given cautious but honest publicity in a short article on the back page of *The Tribunal*, under the heading 'The N.-C.F. and Political Action', marking the end of the policy of giving only the majority view.

The National Committee of the N.-C.F. has recently been giving very careful consideration to its political policy. The Committee has decided that it cannot officially endorse any proposed solution of the problem of the Conscientious Objector which does not acknowledge the principle that a man should be given the form of exemption which he can conscientiously accept, and that a declaration by the man of what he can conscientiously accept should be accepted as final. After long discussion the Committee has agreed that the Fellowship should make the exposure of militarism and the spread of pacifist views its principal object, but that it should also endeavour to obtain for its members those forms of exemption which are acceptable to them. A minority on the Committee was opposed to taking any action to secure exemptions, and we much regret to announce that Mr. J. P. Fletcher, just before going to Pentonville Prison, resigned his membership of the National Committee on account of the decision stated above.

The resolution adopted by the Committee reads as follows:

"That, whilst the Fellowship should continue to make its principal object the exposure of Militarism and the spread of Pacifist views, it should make every possible effort, by political and other means, to secure for its members and other conscientious objectors those forms of exemption allowed by the Act which they applied for at the Tribunals, or can conscientiously accept."[360]

Russell was glad the crisis had been resolved, on the whole, as he thought best,[361] and there seems to have been general relief. Russell, Allen and Marshall spent the evening together, and Marshall, who was using Russell more and more as a confidant, wrote to him the following day. She addressed him as 'Dear Mephy', short for Mephistopheles, a nickname which he had been given by his NCF friends—reputedly 'because of his high cheek bones, narrow face, and the way he enjoyed all their plots and plans to hoodwink the police'.[362] She wrote:

I went to bed directly I got home last night and slept till 11.30! I don't know whether it is due to that fact, or to the relief of having arrived at a settlement after the strain and worry of the last few N. Com. meetings, but I am feeling perfectly exuberant today, and I must just write and tell you so. The horrible paralysis of the last few weeks has quite gone, and I am bursting with energy and ideas. . . .

This is a purely egotistical and unnecessary letter, but I am sure you will be glad to know that I am quite happy again. I have been miserable just lately, but was ashamed of myself for letting you discover it.[363]

Russell had held a unique position during the crisis. At no time did he assume a dominant role, but nor was he a silent attender. From the start he agreed with the policy advocated by Marshall, Brockway and Allen, but his reasons were, as before, neither religious nor political, but in part compassionate. His name was suggested as possible interim chairman, to serve when Allen should finally be arrested, but at this time Brockway agreed to take on the task.[364] In spite of his identification with one faction, Russell appears to have been respected and trusted by both sides: in fact, a high degree of mutual trust characterised the whole Committee even when disagreement was sharp.

The feeling of relief at emerging from the deadlock endured, but there were other anxieties. On 30 July, in a letter to Ottoline Morrell, Russell wrote:

> We had our Com^{ee} yesterday at Reigate. For the first time for ever so long it went off smoothly—Allen has conquered, as was to be desired, and has started a new policy which will continue in his absence. He is quite definitely to be arrested tomorrow. God only knows whether he will emerge undamaged—I don't expect it. I hope his case will force our friends to realise the necessity of absolute exemption in certain cases. It is obviously preposterous that he should be asked to grow cabbages.
>
> Fenner Brockway's fine has been paid, because C.A. is to go, and Brockway and I and Miss Marshall spent the night in the country not far from Reigate, and had much talk. . . .
>
> I hate having all the people on our National Com^{ee} whom I have got to love taken off—there will be only Brockway, and he won't be left long. There are new men, but they are very inferior—easy to work with, because they are not strong enough to disagree, but not inspiring. It is so difficult not to live in the mere longing for the war to stop—the whole thing is so oppressive and horrible. But after a little rest I shall feel more cheerful.[365]

Russell did not comment on the fact that, coincidentally, the four Committee members who now remained in prison on the *Repeal the Act* conviction comprised exactly that section which had been responsible for all the opposition in the previous few weeks: J. P. Fletcher, Barratt Brown, W. J. Chamberlain, and W. H. Ayles. In fact, it is a measure of the good faith of the leaders that, far from advantage being taken of this circumstance by those who were still on the outside, 'it was felt to be difficult to take energetic action on the resolution during their absence'.[366] Plans were made for canvassing the members to learn their opinions on the disputed questions, and meanwhile a great deal of emphasis was put on a vigorous peace campaign. The front page of *The Tribunal* was soon regularly devoted to peace propaganda, and the issue of 20 July carried an 'Urgent Call to Members' exhorting them 'to throw the full weight of the N.-C.F. into active, organised participation in the Peace movement'. Detailed suggestions for doing this were given, with stress being laid on local activities and upon the need to co-operate with other bodies. On 29 July, this was followed by a Political Committee circular of similar tone. Corder Catchpool, the well-known Quaker who had resigned from the Friends' Ambulance Unit on the advent of conscription, was active at the NCF head office for a time in this connection.[367]

As Russell had expected, Allen was arrested when he surrendered himself on 31 July, but his case was adjourned. When he again appeared at Lavender Hill police court on 2 August, the recruiting officer (who should have been warned) introduced his statement with the words, 'This is a very simple case. . . '. The record of the hearing runs to twenty pages, and it ended in an adjournment. Russell was present and the occasion later acquired an extra significance for him as it was here that he and Lady Constance Malleson met.[368] Finally, however, on 11 August, Allen was handed over to the military authorities and removed to Camberwell, where he refused medical examination. He was sent under escort to Warley barracks, was forcibly dressed in khaki, and was soon remanded for district court martial on a charge of refusing to obey an order.[369] Russell was extremely busy at the time—on the day before Allen's court martial he had lunch in London with E. D. Morel, was present for part of a meeting of the London members of the National Committee, travelled to Letchworth to address a meeting, and came back to London for the night, sleeping at the Liverpool Street station hotel in order to be able to reach Warley for the court martial on the following day, 18 August. But even the Army could not dispose of Clifford Allen in short order and once again he won an adjournment. At the weekend Russell was in Manchester, addressing a meeting of the Independent Labour party on 'N.C.F. Ideals'. By an oversight which made him very angry, he was not told the time of Allen's second court martial (on 23 August) until it was too late for him to get there. Allen was sentenced to one year's hard labour, later commuted to 112 days, as was the custom by this time. Four days later he was removed to Wormwood Scrubs.

During the fourteen days Allen had spent in the guardroom at Warley, Marshall and Russell were able to visit him.[370] On one such occasion Russell came up against the military machine. The date was 14 August, when the charge of disobedience had just been laid against Allen, and the incident can be told in Russell's own words. As was sometimes his way when deeply affected, he wrote nothing of his feelings, but in the jolting train on the way home he wrote a dry report, which he sent to Marshall:

Impossible achieve object of visit.

Sgt. R-H standing bareheaded at the gate, about to receive punishment for having shown so much leniency. Could do nothing.

C.A. put away for refusing to clean his own cell. To be tried tomorrow morning.[371]

Saw another Sergt., who refused access to C.A. I got him to ask the C.O., who refused. Then I saw the C.O. myself, but he said it was quite contrary to regulations, and refused, though quite politely. Sergt. (whose name I don't know) said he wd. let C.A. know I had come. Seeing nothing more to do, I went away.[372]

It was probably in fact quite in order to refuse visitors to Allen until he had been officially remanded for court martial, as he was by the commanding officer on the following morning, after which he received the normal privileges of a prisoner awaiting trial. His friends were again allowed to visit, but a sharp eye was kept on his guards in the hope of preventing further breaches of discipline. The offence of the delinquent sergeant, whose name was Ringer-Hewitt, had been to telephone Marshall on Allen's behalf. He was unrepentant and wrote cheerfully the next day to say that at least he had not been shot 'for the hideous crime of being a human being', and that he would continue to act as a go-between to the best of his ability, but with more circumspection. He not only did this, presumably at considerable personal risk, but he also escorted Marshall to the station after at least one of her visits, and sent her a box of heather to comfort her. The whole incident, which has not been recorded before, illustrates again the remarkable power and charm that Allen exercised over the people whom he met,[373] and is also a striking but not isolated example of sympathy shown to conscientious objectors by soldiers.

Russell was greatly moved by Allen's departure for prison.[374] Indeed, its effect throughout the NCF was not the less for the length of time for which it had been delayed. Carefully planned publicity was given to every stage of his progression through courts and court martial.[375] Plans had also been made to carry on Allen's work, but the National Committee and the Executive were badly depleted within a few weeks with the imprisonment of the members convicted under the Defence of the Realm Act, the chairman's arrest, and the gradual erosion caused by arrests under the Military Service Act.[376]

Publicly, Allen's arrest was seen by the National Committee as an opportunity for propaganda; organisationally, it was an additional but not unexpected burden; but personally, for Marshall and Russell at least, it was something of a tragedy. Marshall was by this time deeply attached to Allen. He was clearly fond of her, though possibly never as devoted to her as she to him. Russell, too, was helplessly conscious of the exceptional extent to which Allen's delicate health put him at risk. When Lloyd George said of the absolutists: 'I shall only consider the best means of making the path of that class a very hard one', it was of Allen that Russell thought, writing: 'Lloyd George the other day was abominable about the men who won't take alternative service—cruel and vindictive. To me they are personified in Allen, because I love him.' He also wrote an article for *The Tribunal*, the week after Allen was arrested, entitled 'Clifford Allen and Mr. Lloyd George'.[377] When H. W. Forster, Financial Secretary to the War Office, was reported to have said in the House of Commons that the men who refused alternative service under the Home Office would be returned to their units on completion of their sentences and would, he supposed, be sent to the Front, it was again of Allen that Russell first thought. By the time that he wrote, the War Office had 'given a private assurance'[378] that the men would not be shot, but would be returned to civil prisons. Russell foresaw that Allen would be in prison to the end of the war, as would almost all the Committee members; and he returned to his ever-present dread of the effect on the men of prolonged imprisonment: 'I am afraid almost all will be broken by it in health and vigour. It works on me till I see red. I hardly know how to keep a hold on myself—I am desperately tired, and very worried about work'.[379]

A quality of inspiration and excitement that had lit up the work of the NCF for Russell went out of it when Allen went, turning it from an adventure to a chore. In a letter to Ottoline Morrell on 1 September, he wrote: 'The N.C.F. does not have the joy in that it had, because all the vigorous and delightful people who used to be on the Com[ee] are in gaol. I miss Allen terribly. . . . There is no fire or enthusiasm left in me, only grim will. One must exist till the war stops, and then begin to live again.'[380]

Allen's departure influenced the NCF in another way and Russell, in common with Allen's other close friends, was slow to see an inherent danger. The National Committee, or at least Allen's followers on it, wanted to regard the imprisoned chairman as still in control, a position that was unrealistic. The work he and Marshall had done on policy and plans for the ensuing months[381] meant that for a while at least flexibility was diminished. In addition, Allen's last messages before imprisonment and those he was able to send from prison were in danger of being treated as pronouncements of an oracle rather than subjected to the kind of criticism and modification which would have occurred had they been part of a discussion within the Committee.

This problem particularly affected the area of alternative service, and specifically the National Committee's reaction to the
Home Office scheme. The fact was that the National Committee
had been too preoccupied with internal conflict during July to give
adequate depth of thought to the effect of this new Government
plan. This is not to say that no appropriate response had been
made; as soon as the outlines of the new scheme were known, the
Joint Advisory Committee of the conscientious objectors' organisations[382] had met to consider it and had made and publicised
criticisms that may have helped in getting some modifications
made in the plan. But in relation to the feelings of its own
members the NCF fell short.

The No-Conscription Fellowship leaders did not expect much
of the scheme, and doubted whether the Government was offering it in good faith, rather than as an expedient to divide the
objectors. If Russell could have known what a source of trouble it
was to prove, and how much of his time and energy were to go to
solving contingent problems, he might have had even more
reservations. The cases of all imprisoned men whose offences
might be the result of conscientious objection were to be reviewed
by the Central Tribunal appointed by the War Office, and those
who were pronounced genuine would be 'released from the civil
prison on their undertaking to perform work of national importance under civil control'. They were to be transferred to Section
W of the Army Reserve, and would not be subject to military
discipline as long as they continued 'to carry out satisfactorily the
duties imposed upon them'. A committee of the Home Office,
headed by William Brace, was appointed to oversee the work.
Those not accepted as genuine, or who refused to plead or to
accept the conditions, would be returned to civil prison.[383]

The scheme was very far from meeting the criteria which had
been seen as acceptable by a slim majority of the NCF National
Committee, and most of the features objected to by the Joint
Advisory Committee still remained. The consciences of objectors
were to be judged again, and this not on the grounds of their
demonstrated willingness to undergo imprisonment for their
convictions, but in relation to the records of their first tribunals
and to their backgrounds, where the critics of the scheme justly
held that the advantage might again lie with those whose principles could be seen to derive from specific religious upbringing and
affiliation. Russell commented gloomily: 'Those who are not
vouched for by Ministers of Religion are to be punished worse
than ever.'[394] The Central Tribunal was not empowered to grant
absolute exemption, in spite of the provision of the Military

Service Act for this form of exemption. Those accepting service under the new scheme, although under civil control, were not fully released from the Army, and could be returned to their units if the Home Office committee administering the scheme decided their performance was in any way unsatisfactory.

For convinced absolutists the scheme presented no personal problem. Neither it nor any other scheme for work imposed as an alternative to soldiering would have been acceptable, and to them this was clearly such a scheme. But the National Committee was placed again in a position which should have been familiar enough for them to take warning. Themselves predominantly absolutists, they had to respond on behalf on a membership which they well knew included many alternativists. But the form of the scheme, together with the promise to make the lot of those who refused it even harder, seemed to them manifestly so unacceptable that their condemnation began, as we have seen, before the details were known.

There was considerable pressure from those sympathisers who saw in the scheme an opportunity to end the persecution. If anything, this pressure seems to have helped to harden the National Committee's attitude, but at least they now allowed a voice to the alternativists and their influential friends. On 27 July, space was given in *The Tribunal* to the very sympathisers with whom Russell had earlier waxed indignant. A letter from Harvey was printed quoting from a statement by Murray. Both begged the COs to accept the new Government scheme. They believed the scheme was offered with no intent of dividing the pacifists, but in good faith, and claimed that it offered the COs, who had now amply established the rights of conscience and shown their courage, 'a chance to make a positive contribution to our national life which will have a permanent effect also in the wider world of international relationship'. The same issue carried on the front page an unsigned rebuttal of Harvey's letter, restating the absolutist claim that the rejection of all alternative service was not a negative refusal to help the nation, but a positive action in support of freedom: 'By doing this . . . we believe we are doing more for the community than by doing safe civil jobs as plain-clothes conscripts.' This was certainly closer to Russell's view, but he would not by this time have held out much hope that the members would unite against the Home Office scheme.

Allen continued to urge the unity of the Fellowship and the right of those whose conscience would permit them to accept alternative service. But now there was always a rider, implicit or explicit: surely members would not be prepared to accept such service unless it fulfilled certain conditions. In a letter to the Prime Minister on 2 August, the National Committee, still failing to see the writing on the wall, spelled out these conditions. The work must be that for which the individual was suited; it must have no association with the prosecution of the war; it must not render the COs liable to be used as 'black-leg' labour; the remuneration must not be such as to undercut trade union standards; pay and allowances should be equal to those of soldiers; the objectors must be free to express 'pacifist or other religious or political views'; prisoners should be fully informed before release what they were committing themselves to, and should not be required to sign anything until fully informed.[385] There was much reason in this list of desiderata. The Government was ostensibly offering the objectors a chance to do honourable national service; these requirements would ensure this and were not as unrealistic as some of the Fellowship's demands had been. But the Government, particularly now that Lloyd George was at the War Office, was in no mood to work towards satisfying the objectors. Harvey and Murray were deluded as to the nature of the scheme, and above all the fact—so hard for the leaders to grasp—was that a large number of NCF members were not prepared to argue, but would accept any form of civilian service that would get them out of prison. Russell's predictions were coming true.

Many men soon expressed their willingness to work under the new scheme, or at least to submit their cases for review by the Central Tribunal. On completion of their first sentences, some enjoyed a brief spell of furlough while awaiting a decision.[386] By the end of August the backlog was being cleared away and at the same time some of the projects planned under the Home Office committee were ready to receive the men. There was no lack of men although they went with mixed expectations. In private, Russell expressed great disappointment in the number of conscientious objectors who were accepting alternative service; it made him, he wrote, feel a failure.[387] Allen went much farther, writing from Warley:

Can you make them see . . . if they take work outside which is not part of ordinary prison routine and pretend to call it punishment they are no longer free – they are slaves playing with liberty and cease to count in the struggle for liberty, and thus in the efforts now making [sic] to prevent future war.[388]

Even in a letter written (on 21 August) 'To all men who have been released from prison to do civil work under the Government's new scheme', Allen reiterated the comparison with slavery. Yet he seems to have been unaware how harsh and offensive his wording sounded, and added a note to be circulated only to members of the National Committee and staff members, which read: 'I am convinced the way to influence the alternativists is not by storming at them or making them imagine they are considered foes and deserters, but a sympathetic spirit of understanding which my experience makes me confident arouses in them a spirit of emulation and special loyalty.'[389] For the first time, Allen's ability to arouse this spirit failed him—perhaps mercifully, as it was a quality which carried with it the risk (of which Russell was so conscious) of pushing men beyond the demands of their own consciences and their capacity for endurance. Allen perhaps came to view himself as having been particularly tender towards the Home Office men, but this does not stand up in the light either of his description of them as slaves or of his apparent intention to bring all his fierce moral pressure to bear on them. It is certainly true, as Kennedy suggests, that Allen was extremely concerned for the unity of the Fellowship, but the impression remains that in his heart he still hoped to preserve unity by inspiring all members to follow the harder path, not by allowing the consciences of alternativists equal honour with those of absolutists. As so often, the message given by Allen was ambivalent: he sincerely believed in freedom of conscience, but he could not credit that it could lead men so far astray. Nor can Brockway, now acting chairman, be justly accused of exceptional harshness towards the Home Office men, for which he had to be pulled into line by the conciliatory Allen.[390] Brockway's tone was similar to Allen's own, and no harsher. A letter to the branches, signed by Brockway and Marshall and dated 4 September, was in the same absolutist vein, and outlined reasons why 'members of the Fellowship, Absolutists and Alternativists alike, must be active in condemning this or any similar scheme'.[391]

In spite of his disappointment Russell did not join in public condemnation of the Home Office scheme or those who joined in it. The article he wrote shortly after Allen's arrest lacked a little of the balance he usually displayed in writing for publication, in that it tended to rejoice, in terms reminiscent of Allen himself, in the Government's reluctance to grant absolute exemption and in the resultant persecution, but although Russell's statement of the absolutist position on this occasion left little room for the acceptance of any form of alternative service, there was nothing in it that would be as personally wounding as Allen's and even Brockway's remarks. The fact that the Home Office men never seem to have lost faith in Russell's open-mindedness may have owed much to his moderation at this time.

All the efforts of the National Committee to exhort and shame the members into refusing the Home Office scheme failed, and by September many were established in work camps.[392] The released men found themselves under considerable restrictions and in many cases in physically severe conditions, but many managed to visit the NCF Head Office before being sent to their Home Office assignments, and some were still near enough to London to come in at intervals. One of the freedoms of which they made most use was that of writing letters, which poured in to the office, telling of their prison experiences, their reasons for accepting the scheme, the conditions they found, their doubts and hopes, and—not surprisingly—their reactions to the attitude of the National Committee. Very slowly it became possible to form some kind of picture of the men's needs and motivations.[393]

Evidently, men had accepted work under the new scheme for a variety of motives. The National Committee had been right in believing that the information given to the men while in prison would not always be full and accurate, and many came out uncertain what to expect. The War Office seems to have encouraged the release of as many men as possible under the scheme. Some had refused to sign the required undertakings and had been released nevertheless.[394] Many who came out were not wholeheartedly committed to the scheme, but had decided to take a look at it before assessing whether it met their needs and was acceptable to their consciences. Some believed they might be allowed to return to their own occupations, under some form of control;[395] a good many of these soon went back to prison. For a larger group it was the first time they had had the option of accepting alternative service, and it marked no change of purpose for some of them to accept the Home Office work, and settle down to it for the rest of the war.[396] There were others who still considered the absolutist position the better path, but who honestly admitted they were unable to face further prolonged imprisonment, which was undermining their health and sanity.

Still others were persuaded that the work was not in fact a form of alternative service to military service, but rather an alternative to prison and not inconsistent with absolutist principles. Much was made of this argument, as a counter to the condemnation coming from absolutist leaders. Norman, still a member of the National Committee, announced his acceptance of the scheme on 24 August, and came to a meeting of the Committee on 27 August aggressively prepared to defend his stand.[397] He had been sent to work on a Home Office project at Risbridge in Suffolk, where, to make matters worse, the men were employed on building a road which there was reason to suppose might be primarily intended for military use.

Russell was troubled by the meeting; he thought Norman's judgment might indeed be affected by the exceptionally harsh treatment he had suffered at the hands of the military at Wandsworth barracks. In a letter to Ottoline Morell, he wrote: 'Norman came yesterday and defended the road-making agreement, which we thought a mistake. I felt the whole question very difficult. He is rather the worse morally for his persecution: the fear of going back to it leads him a little to self-deception. But that is not surprising.'[398] Norman not only defended his immediate situation, but made a spirited defence of acceptance of the scheme, and asked for a statement regarding it from the National Committee. He also extended his argument that the Home Office work was an alternative to prison, not to military service, by claiming that if work under the Home Office should be refused, so should work in prison. On the latter point the Committee agreed to sound out the opinion of the members, but on the general principle their views were unchanged. Confronted with Norman's challenge, the Committee adopted a resolution 'reiterating its opposition to Alternative Service and expressing the view that the Home Office scheme is in its mind Alternative Service to military service'. Brockway wrote a strong editorial reaffirming this, and the letter to the branches condemning the scheme went out at about the same time.[399]

In spite of (or perhaps because of) his discomfort, Russell accepted the task of going down to visit Norman and the group at Risbridge House, near Haverhill. Norman was, as it were, fighting on two fronts. He was trying to challenge the Home Office on the question of the nature of the work and conditions of service; and he was attacking the official NCF attitude, circulating the National Committee's resolution as 'a vote of censure' and making capital of Allen's statements comparing the work to slavery, a comparison unwisely and insensitively used again in Brockway's editorial.[400] The Home Office knew a good deal about Norman's attitude and had been having some trouble with him already at Haverhill; but they totally misinterpreted the National Committee's position. Whiskard told Sir Ernley Blackwell 'that there is no doubt of deliberate intention on the part of the NCF to break down the scheme . . . and it seems to me that it would be very foolish to allow Russell to do down and harangue them with this object'.[401] Certainly the Committee disliked the Home Office scheme and hoped members would reject it, but they were almost as much at odds with Norman as was the

Government. Marshall stressed the importance of Russell's visit and especially the need to talk to the men individually or in small groups because of the varying points of view.[402]

It was at this point that the Home Office took fright and successfully sought the cooperation of the War Office in having Russell's movements restricted. On 31 August Norman cabled to Russell, presumably in response to news of the banning order, 'you have been refused access to Risbridge House so kindly come without fail Friday'.[403] But Russell, as we have seen, decided against an immediate confrontation on the issue, and stayed out of the banned areas. The survey of opinion continued though there were many camps now beyond Russell's reach. Gradually the National Committee moderated its tone, becoming more sensitive to the views and needs of the Home Office men, and to the fact that some men had been pushed to the brink of resignation from the Fellowship. By mid-September complaints from the camps of lack of support had lessened.[404]

Of the unsatisfactory conditions in the Home Office camps there is an enormous amount of evidence. Much of the work was either 'made work' and therefore hardly of national importance; or it was useful and therefore there was reason to fear it might be of assistance to the military. Although the men were supposed to have the running of the camps in their own hands, through an elected committee, the Home Office agent exercised absolute control of (and through) such vital matters as the supply of food, working hours, and pay, always with the ultimate sanction of having an offender returned to prison.[405] There was also much physical hardship. Like the Pelham Committee before it, the Brace Committee was bedevilled by ambivalence of purpose: the men had been promised 'work of national importance', but the authorities and a vocal section of the public were more concerned to see 'equality of sacrifice', with the result that conditions tended to be deliberately punitive and demoralising. So harsh were they in several of the camps that the health of the men, seriously impaired by the close confinement and inadequate diet of prison, was quite unable to withstand the strain. The most notorious of the centres was at Dyce, near Aberdeen, to which several hundred men were sent to work on road construction and to live in old army tents of rotten canvas. Here a young man called Walter Roberts died on 8 September: no more of a tragedy, as many people were quick to point out, than each of the far more numerous deaths which took place every day at the Front; but certainly one with no imagined purpose at all. The camp was soon closed, after operating for about three months.[406]

The NCF National Committee had no wish to get involved in publicising the complaints of the Home Office men regarding physical conditions, and continued to try to make a distinction between hardships and moral issues such as the nature of the work to which the men were sent. But by mid-September they seem at last to have conceded that the scheme was there to stay, and that a majority of the members would accept it rather than stay in prison. Reluctantly, fuller expression of the point of view of those who had thought it right to accept the scheme was allowed. The National Committe passed a resolution denying that they had intended any censure of those who did not share their views, and reaffirming the doctrine (of which they had recently rather lost sight) of the right of the individual conscience.[407]

In prison, Allen's health was breaking down. The two months of virtual solitary confinement and of total isolation from the outside world with which all sentences at hard labour began were an agony for him. In the first letter he was able to write from Wormwood Scrubs (dated 21 October 1916), he gave a vivid description of some of the bad times he had been through:

Cannot describe this experience; it has been a greater strain than even I thought. Solitude is a terrible thing when it is enforced. It is torture to receive thoughts and ideas that you cannot commit to paper, then to forget them and start chasing them; to know they were yours but have flitted. I have been the victim of sleeplessness and changing moods; it has been a desperate struggle.[408]

Although he still wrote, 'My mind is as unalterable as ever against civil work', he seems to have come to some recognition, in the face of his own 'desperate struggle', that men must not lightly be pushed to undertake more than they can manage, and he spoke of the alternativists in a tone resembling Russell's: 'Let me be remembered to the N.C.F. and the I.L.P., both to those who refuse and those who accept Alternative Service. Tell those who have yet to face the test, not to play at being strong, but above all things to be honest with themselves. Then whatever course they think it right to adopt, they will not be disappointed in the future.'[409] This marked a real change in Allen: his emotions and the direction of his influence were at last coming into line with his intellectual conviction, and he was showing more charity. Perhaps Russell's views had also played a part.

Rae has described the extent to which alternative service of one kind or another was accepted by members of the NCF as marking 'the collapse of its policy'.[410] This is an exaggerated view, but it does seem to have appeared in this light to Russell and the other members of the National Committee for a few weeks after the introduction of the Home Office scheme. In the early days, when acceptance of the rights of the alternativists had seemed the only way of preserving the unity and therefore the political strength of the Fellowship, those whose pacifism stemmed from socialism had urged this acceptance, while the young Quakers advocated that there should be no compromise whatever the cost to the Fellowship. But when the Home Office scheme threatened to reduce the absolutists to a numerically impotent handful, it was the political pacifists who tried in desperation to stop the tide. There was a paradox in the way in which Allen and Brockway appeared so unsympathetic to the alternativists during the early days of the scheme; but for the stand which they, together with Russell and Marshall, had made in the National Committee, the faction led by Fletcher might have excluded alternativists from the Fellowship altogether. In the event, while the absolutists did not win as much as they had hoped, neither did the less intransigent stand of those who took alternative service undermine them as much as they had feared. Over twelve hundred men remained in jail, some because they were absolutists, and a minority because they had been classified as 'ungenuine' by the Central Tribunal.[411] Allen, Brockway and Russell had been correct in predicting that it was on the absolutists that the success of the struggle would depend, but it is not certain that their number was the critical factor in what they did and did not achieve. In one way, the existence of the Home Office camps was a source of strength: in so far as acceptance of civil work could be seen as an easy option, then the men in prison must be seen as voluntarily accepting their harsh repeated sentences for conscience' sake. Their friends on the outside saw to it that they were not forgotten, and the jailed absolutists remained a painful thorn in the debilitated liberal conscience of the nation. But no one was more conscious than Russell that what had been a gladly-offered challenge was turning into a grim test of endurance.

CHAPTER 9
INCREASED RESPONSIBILITY

The turmoil of the summer of 1916 left Russell tired and a little discouraged. Many good men were in jail for their convictions, and the Government had, it seemed to him, amply shown forth the effects of militarism, yet the hoped-for consequences of resistance to compulsory service were as far off as ever. The articulate public did not seem as disturbed as it should have been, conscription continued, no end to the war was in sight, even the conscientious objectors' own ranks were weakened by the wide acceptance of the Home Office scheme. But Russell had no thought of withdrawing from the work: those left at liberty were committed to the imprisoned men. In spite of discouragement, there seemed no reason to despair: the No-Conscription Fellowship had scored significant success in focussing public opinion to good effect on cases of brutality and of the men sent to France, and the response of the authorities to Russell's outspokenness had made a number of liberals question what was becoming of the ideals that Britain was supposed to be defending. Surely the effectiveness of the protest must grow.

Shorthanded, the National Committee, and particularly those of the London members who also worked in the head office, had more to deal with besides the large problem of the Home Office scheme. Committee meetings were always held at the weekend for the convenience of out-of-town members. Although they were not as frequent as they had been during the July crisis, they were long, often lasting until the small hours.[412] Marshall was driving herself towards a breakdown, trying to do her own work and that of half a dozen others.[413] Brockway was expecting to be arrested at any time, and was trying to finish his book, *Socialism for Pacifists*, before he was taken.[414] Some attempt was made to give Russell the promised leisure to write but the two working days a week took no account of the long-drawn-out National Committee meetings, or of exceptional circumstances such as the need to visit Allen during his stay at Warley, and hardly surprisingly, the writing of the lectures did not go smoothly. Lady Ottoline was inclined to quarrel with Russell at this time on the grounds that he was secretive about his work. The correspondence between them was less frequent and regular than it had been, but in response to her criticism Russell did make an effort to list even those of his occupations which he had considered too tedious to tell her about. From these letters and from other correspondence we learn that he still had a handful of pupils in mathematical logic and that he was involved in a relationship with T. S. Eliot's wife, which for most of the time, at least, was platonic. Vivien Eliot had come to depend on Russell for help and understanding, and the help he was able to give her made him feel a sense of success.[415] He was also, of course, kept very busy at this time by the problems and excitements of the Government's refusal to give him a passport, and the restrictions placed on his movements. Final details for the publication of *Principles of Social Reconstruction* had to be arranged in early August. In addition to attending National Committee meetings, Russell sat on many of the other NCF committees, for example, a committee on maintenance of COs and their dependants, and the Literature Committee. What he described as the oddity of his days, with so many different occupations, was compounded by such occasions as the long visit one Sunday from a Serbian philosopher, of whom Russell wrote: 'he set to work to prove that the number of points in space is finite. . . . He is an amiable man, but without any brains'. It is not surprising that the day that Russell catalogued as typical began at 10 a.m. and that twelve hours later he was only beginning his final commitment, in this case attendance at the Literature Committee of the NCF, which he described as lasting from 10 p.m. to bedtime.[416]

Before the end of 1916 a relationship with Lady Constance Malleson (the actress, Colette O'Niel) enlivened but also complicated Russell's life. Ever since Ottoline Morrell had moved to Garsington, if not before, Russell's relationship with her had been strained. At times there had been some mutual recrimination. Lady Ottoline was apt to show possessiveness in the face not only of any friendship that Russell formed with another woman, but of his absorption in his work, whether academic or political, although she strove to support his work for the conscientious objectors in her way. Marshall and Allen were both guests at Garsington on separate occasions during the summer of 1916. On his part, Russell valued Ottoline as a confidante, but feared and resented her criticism. Both showed nostalgia for the intense closeness they had previously enjoyed, but in the main their relationship had cooled into friendship, sometimes supportive, sometimes merely uncomfortable. Russell was less than honest with Lady Ottoline about the extent of his involvement with Lady Constance.[417]

The concerns of the National Committee and the executive

during the last few months of the year included a reorganisation of the work at the head office, the return of those members who had been jailed on the *Repeal the Act* charge, discussions about the political activity of the organisation, some serious cases of ill-treatment of objectors, the holding of divisional conventions, and arrangements for an election of officers.

The main features of the reorganisation of the work at the head office which took place in mid-September 1916 are important. Fenner Brockway remained as secretary, Aylmer Rose as organising secretary. The Political Committee work which had become such an important part of the Fellowship's activity was now fully integrated structurally as it long had been in fact. The positions of honorary secretary to the Political Committee and of honorary secretary to the Fellowship were amalgamated and vested in Marshall. Seven departments were instituted, the secretary of each of which was to be responsible to Marshall. One of the purposes was clearly to free the honorary secretary from some of her load while enabling her to continue to co-ordinate and direct. In particular, Charles Ammon (later a noted member of the Labour Government) had undertaken some of the Parliamentary work, and now became secretary to the Parliamentary department. A young man, J. A. Harrop, was made secretary to the organising and propaganda department. Of these two, Marshall was able for a while at least to make very good use.[418]

Russell's position was not defined. He held no titular post on the staff or on the executive, but he was ready to serve in whatever capacity was needed, and to a great extent this meant being a personal assistant to Marshall. On 17 September, he finished writing his lectures, and two days later he expected to take over much of Marshall's work, but found that the extent to which he was able to do this was limited.[419] His inability to replace her, for instance, in 'dealing with Government people', is explicable in terms of his own unfortunate unacceptability at the time—his struggle with the Government on the banning issue was just then at its height, but he never seems to have liked this part of the work. Possibly the difficulty Marshall had in delegating work also played a part. Russell does seem to have had a little more spare time during the month between then and the beginning of his lectures in the north, but certainly did not lack occupation.

Besides the day-to-day work of the Fellowship, there was the ongoing problem of policy-making in the National Committee. The release of the four members from Pentonville jail in early September did not make a significant difference to the work load at head office. Of the four, Chamberlain was the only one who had been engaged on a full time basis in work at headquarters for the Fellowship. He originally planned to resume as editor of *The Tribunal*, but when it became apparent how short a spell of liberty he could expect, he decided to allow B. J. Boothroyd to carry on. His decision may also have owed something to some dissatisfaction with the policies being followed by the National Committee.[420] He was in fact arrested in the first week of January 1917, under the Military Service Act.

The return of the four absent members made the deliberations of the National Committee both more controversial and more valid. As before, the divisions within the Committee did not exactly correspond with the divisions within the Fellowship at large. Even while the head office and the executive were dealing with the flood of work arising from the Home Office scheme, and even while (as we have seen) they were finally coming to terms with the fact that a large number of members were irrevocably alternativists, the main topic under discussion in the National Committee was tangential to the whole issue of alternative service. The question of political action was renewed. The hard-won July decision to continue every possible effort to obtain the forms of exemption COs could accept had not really provided an answer to the all-important question of whether political pressure should also be used to save men from severe ill-treatment. Russell set out the problem:

When they [the four Committee members] returned from prison, it was found that the question had grown into a somewhat different form from that in which it had at first arisen. At first, it had been felt by almost all that we ought to work for absolute exemption, but there was division of opinion as to how far we could work for alternativists. During the autumn, the real question was found to be whether we should use political action to secure *any* form of exemption, or any mitigation of conditions. The minority were of the opinion that we should rely exclusively on publicity for such purposes, and on the effect of publicity in rousing public opinion.[421]

The young Quakers, who claimed to have an increasing following among the membership, were now arguing that direct politicking was unacceptable and that the Fellowship should have the faith to stand or fall by its pacifist witness.[422] The witness was appropriately expressed in two ways: primarily, by the sufferings of the men in prison; and secondarily, by direct pacifist propaganda. It is easy to see the appeal of such purist views to men like Barratt Brown and Fletcher, who were giving a strong lead within the Society of Friends in the same direction. But the older Quaker, Grubb, again dissociated himself from the views of the younger Friends, commenting that in the early days of the Society the Quakers did not take injustice lying down.[423]

When Marshall had withdrawn her resignation in July, it was on the understanding that she would be free to use the machinery of influence which the Political Committee had built up. She and Russell never doubted that the primary purpose was to work for major objectives, but for them urgent cases continued to take temporary precedence, and every effort would be made to protect men from excessive hardship or death. Just such an emergency was current at the time of the release from Pentonville of the four Committee members, and it well illustrates Marshall's methods, in which, no doubt, she had Russell's full concurrence (although it was seldom he who made direct contact with the officials). Cases were occurring of serious ill-treatment of COs at Birkenhead. The men most affected were all active trade unionists, who may have been victimised for this, or perhaps were simply the only objectors in the unit at the time, or possibly happened to be the only ones able to endure the systematic brutality long enough for the case to become public. They were refused the right to a court martial, by the usual device of refusing to allow them to disobey an order. They were instead physically forced into compliance with the orders given on the parade ground, and manhandled into marching and other exercises. They were literally thrown, dragged and kicked through a stiff obstacle course. On one occasion, much of the ill-treatment took place within sight of civilian onlookers, who included the wife and sister of the man concerned.[424]

On receipt of the news, Marshall immediately went into action. She telephoned Childs and went to see him. He said that if it were true (and he did not show much inclination to doubt her) 'someone would be sacked.' He showed her official correspondence and explicit instructions issued to prevent this kind of occurrence, which he said was due to the inexcusable ignorance of some of the wartime officers. When his letters did not produce an immediate effect, Marshall saw him again, to find him as annoyed as she was at the delay. Shortly, he arranged not only to have the objectors court-martialled but to hold an enquiry into the conduct of the officers involved.[425]

The contact with Childs had obviously been the most directly effective action that Marshall could take, but she had backed it up with every vehicle of pressure available to her. Letters were sent to prominent people, questions were asked in Parliament, people in the Birkenhead area were asked to write to the War Office, a statement of the facts was sent to all branches of the Gasworkers' Union (to which one of the men belonged), and his own branch was prompted to raise the question at the Trade Union Congress meeting then being held. The National Council of Civil Liberties, also meeting at the time of the Trade Union Congress, discussed the cases. Some of the distinguished people approached declined to have anything to do with it, but others, including G. Lowes Dickinson, H. G. Chancellor, MP, and Philip Snowden, took it up in their respective spheres of influence. Full details were sent to all the Labour Members of Parliament. All this was excellent propaganda, as well as enlisting public opinion in support of the victims.[426] In the course of a long conversation with Childs at about this time, Marshall also got him to clarify the whole position relating to the treatment of men under Army Order X and the Home Office scheme. She told Allen that General Childs had 'practically dictated' an article for *The Tribunal*, summing up the whole position.[427]

By early November, Marshall was able to write that the cleavage among the leaders over political action lacked the personal bitterness that had characterised it in July.[428] But until mid-October there was considerable hostility shown, and its dissipation owed a good deal to Russell. A meeting at which his influence proved crucial occurred on 14 October. It seemed that the very success of Marshall's intervention in the Birkenhead affair was reason for criticism. One of the most virulent attacks on the methods which had been developed came from Chamberlain, who claimed that the Fellowship had degenerated into a society for the entertainment of cabinet ministers and War Office officials, while Ayles complained that the NCF was now helping the Government to administer the Military Service Acts, and was even making conscripts by its aid to the alternativists, whom he saw as nothing else. None of the opponents of the policy is known to have said unequivocally that the men in France, or at Birkenhead, should have been left to their fate. To do them justice, they did not oppose publicity for such cases, and may have convinced themselves public opinion would have forced the rescue of the men, without direct representations to Government officials. Brown, who had led off the discussion at the National Committee meeting of 14 October, spoke more moderately than Chamberlain and Ayles, disclaiming the right to criticise action which had been taken in their absence. He believed the action not inconsistent with the resolution which had been passed in July endorsing some use of political action, but urged that the policy should now be given up. The main emphasis, he held, had been on seeking exemption and ameliorating conditions rather than on peace work. Both Brown and Brockway, who defended the political policy, called for a revival of the spirit of the Fellowship, and both referred to an article by Russell in the current issue of *The Tribunal*, which seemed to them admirably to express the essentials on which all were agreed and to which there was an urgent need to return.

At this time Russell was writing regularly for *The Tribunal*. The article referred to, entitled 'What We Stand For', appeared on the front page and was in line with the inspirational pacifist material to which that page was now usually dedicated, although Russell's article was specifically directed to the condition of the NCF. Admitting a tendency for the Fellowship to become bogged down on minor issues—in which he included the controversy about alternative service—Russell urged that the emphasis be placed on the positive aspects of their aims:

Some of us say our aim is to smash militarism–which was also the aim of the Government in the early days of the war.

Of course we wish to see militarism disappear. But our ultimate aim is not to *smash* anything; it is to build, not to destroy, to win over, not to defeat, or bring the Kingdom of Heaven on earth—nothing less.

He went on immediately to link this with an injunction not to regard the men who were opposing them as enemies. These two points were the core of the article: the need to work for the brotherhood of man, and the need to regard all as brothers, making no exception of those who were now ranged against them.[429]

Russell's attitude at the 14 October meeting was not conciliatory. He had no intention of allowing the minority to get away with paying lip-service to the general tone of his article while refusing to face the real intent of his message. The difference, he held, was not merely one of policy but also of spirit, and he again stressed the wrongness of setting up anyone as 'the enemy', with whom there could be no parley. Every opportunity should be taken to explain the objectors' viewpoint. Opponents should be given a chance to understand ('They don't all *want* to be wicked,' said Russell), and ought to be met on the basis of their intentions.[430] Russell liked to put those with whom he was arguing on the spot by using their own beliefs against them, and he was probably well aware that what he was saying was strikingly close to the Friends' belief in 'that of God in every man'. Unfortunately the response of the young Quakers is not recorded; they may have found the doctrine unpalatable from such an inconvenient and agnostic source. It must be admitted that while Russell himself could now (with an effort) seek for the spark in public servants, he was still apt to strain at allowing for the divine in some politicians. But the whole tone of the discussion shows how far he had come: strongly as he made his point, he patently strove to convince, not to demolish, his opponents, and his criticism was constructive in intent and effect.

Whether because of a fundamentally improved understanding of each other's point of view, or simply because full opportunity had been given for a frank discussion of the differences, the meeting marked a turning-point. The factions might still not agree on how it was fitting to treat their Government opponents, but at least their opponents within the Fellowship were once more treated with enough brotherly love to make possible a great increase in openness, and to lessen fears that this would lead to an irrevocable split. The practical decisions taken at the meeting reflected the new spirit. The July resolution would be laid before the Divisional Conventions and both factions would be free to defend their viewpoints. Account was also to be taken of the responses to a questionnaire to individual members which had been initiated already.

There are few detailed descriptions of the Divisional Conventions (of which two had already taken place) but of the six which remained three voted to rescind the July resolution, one was evenly divided, and two others did not take a vote. One, discussing related questions, but not the resolution itself, strongly favoured continued political action. It began to seem that the members were not behind the policy favoured by Russell and Marshall.[431]

Russell, whose northern lecture tour began on 16 October, was one of the National Committee representatives at the Manchester Convention on 21 October and at the Midlands Convention held in Birmingham on 4 November. Members found the issue regarding political action confusing. At the Leeds Convention, Fletcher explained that he would not feel free to stand for election to the National Committee (from which, it will be remembered, he had resigned before going to prison) if he was not supported in his attitude to political action. One of those present, a Mrs Wray, although sufficiently doubtful to refrain from voting on either side, noted afterwards that she had completely failed to understand the basis of his objection, although she knew and admired him. She wrote to Marshall that she had now come over to her side. Russell would have applauded her reasoning: 'I take a fact like Gen. Child ringing you up as a great victory for our work, and I can't see how we can best serve our cause by dropping political propaganda and merely appealing to a war-mad public led by a Northcliffe Press. . . . What of the 35 C.O.s in France if no action had been taken?'[432]

When the Conventions were over and the National Committee took stock, they found themselves obliged to share the confusion of the members. Although the Conventions had come down, by and large, against political action, the answers to the questionnaire overwhelmingly took the opposite view (but only ten per cent of the members had answered). The questions on this were not of course identical with those set before the Conventions, and made more reference to the alternative service question. The National Committee, at its meeting on 11 November, resolved to defer the matter until after the election of the new Committee which was to take place at the end of the year. Candidates were asked to prepare election addresses, to enable the members to know where they stood on important issues. There was a growing conviction that even to rescind the July resolution might be misleading: rather the new Committee should be left free to formulate policy which might supersede or develop from the previous policy.[433]

While the alternative service question was of moment to every man who had to make up his mind whether he would accept work under the Home Office scheme, or resign himself to spending the rest of the war or longer in prison, it seems clear the political action issue was not as important to the members as it was to the National Committee. The implications of the idealistic but rather less than compassionate policy advocated by the young Quakers were probably not fully recognised. Mrs Wray was not the only one who was puzzled. Many surviving letters attest to the simple faith that many of those going to prison had that those on the outside would continue to do their best for them, by whatever means were at their disposal. For most, the success with which the Fellowship had intervened in cases such as those of the men sent to France and the men subjected to illegal brutality greatly strengthened the morale of all members and was not seen as any compromise. Allen saw, too, the need of the men to know that the struggle to obtain absolute exemption—so long the declared goal—was being pursued.[434] Within the Society of Friends Fletcher's policy had a considerable following, though there was also some strong dissent; it represented from one viewpoint a high ideal, but it was unsuited to the NCF. Fortunately, the divisive potential of both issues —alternative service and political action—was partly defused by open discussion within the National Committee and the wise if somewhat belated decision to allow the whole membership to take part in the discussions, although some anxiety as to the future direction of the NCF remained among the leaders until the composition of the new Committee should be known, and relations with the FSC continued to grow cooler.

Circumstances enabled Allen to share in this anxiety, and to express to the Fellowship his views on the current policy issues. His first sentence ended on 25 November. He was released early that morning—at 6.30 instead of the usual 8.00, in order to avoid a demonstration—and taken under escort from Wormwood Scrubs to his unit, now at Newhaven. He enjoyed one day of liberty, and was then once more given an order, which he refused. He remained under arrest in the guardroom from then until his court martial on 12 December, when he was sentenced to a year's hard labour and removed to Maidstone prison. His release from Wormwood Scrubs had been eagerly anticipated, especially by Russell and Marshall. The state of Allen's health had earlier given them hope (apparently fostered or shared by Childs) that he would be forcibly subjected to medical examination and released. He had in fact been examined by the medical officer at Wormwood Scrubs, who had found 'no actual illness of consequence', but had admitted 'he would probably never become fit for military service'. General Childs passed this report to the director of recruiting (Lord Derby), who considered it insufficient grounds for discharge.[435]

During Allen's three-week stay at Newhaven, the physical conditions were appalling. He was held at first in an unheated, uninsulated wooden hut so cold he could scarcely hold a pencil until he bought a stove of his own; and was later transferred to Newhaven Fort, where he occupied what was quite literally a dungeon, dark and extremely damp.[436] Nevertheless, his health improved and his spirit was renewed. Catherine Marshall visited him frequently. As his official court martial friend, she had wide privileges, and was able to arrange visits from other people whenever she herself was not able to go. Allen particularly looked forward to seeing Russell, who was equally keen to visit, and after some delay and difficulty caused by the order banning him from coastal areas, Russell was issued with a permit and went to Newhaven at least once or twice, in addition to attending Allen's court martial as a witness, being escorted to and from the station by a guard.[437]

Allen's stay at Newhaven was a remarkable interlude. In spite of the harsh conditions, he met with universal kindness, and on his side he won the respect and admiration of those around him. His most pressing needs were for companionship, the opportunity to talk and to write, and the feeling that he was still in touch with the Fellowship and counted in its counsels. Marshall devotedly supplied endless material on all that had taken place since his arrest, and on the current controversies, and he gradually regained his assurance. The first term of imprisonment had hit Allen much harder than he had expected, and his sanity may even have been in jeopardy. The time at Newhaven greatly strengthened him. When he went back to prison he was no less likely to be broken physically but there was never the same danger of his mental disintegration. For Marshall, the strain had been very great, in spite of the relief of being able to discuss personal and Fellowship policies and plans at length with Allen. For Russell it had been an important opportunity to renew contact with what for him was the best element in the Fellowship, but he too was left desolate when Allen returned to prison. Of the court martial he wrote: 'C.A.'s Court Martial yesterday was very poignant. He was so brave and gallant, so calm and strong and able. The room was filled with officers, so that there were only 3 of the general public admitted—by law a Court Martial must be public. Allen made a very wonderful short statement explaining his position.'[438]

Allen's continuing influence is hard to assess. In a sense what Marshall had built up in him—the feeling that he was still the prime leader—was illusory. He was vitally important as a source of inspiration to Russell and the other leaders as well as to many a bewildered eighteen-year-old CO, and as chief among those who witnessed silently from prison, but he was not part of the decision-making body. One episode in particular brought this home to Marshall. Allen's time at Newhaven coincided with a mutiny (which has never been fully described) among those who had previously served without protest in the Non-Combatant Corps units stationed in the area. The issue was the handling of munitions, from which many of the non-combatants had considered themselves exempt, a view not shared by the War Office. Marshall, and even Allen himself on his one day of freedom, and later within the guardroom, had had long talks with the men who were resisting orders. Both held that the NCF should offer support to those now faced with court martial, belated and limited as their resistance might seem. But on 9 December the National Committee decided otherwise. Russell was absent from this meeting, having arranged to spend that weekend at Garsington with his philosophical pupils, an indulgence which Marshall regarded as quite unwarranted.[439] When the Committee refused to accept responsibility for the Non-Combatant Corps men unless they completely repudiated the Corps, Marshall said she would resign in order to continue work for them for at least the following few weeks of crisis, and the Committee agreed that she should feel free to act privately on their behalf, without resigning, but that the Fellowship would go no farther than in giving a certain amount of publicity to the struggle.[440]

The sense of being overwhelmed in the National Committee on that occasion increased the anxiety felt by Allen and his close supporters for a favourable outcome to the election, which would give Marshall and Russell a mandate to carry on with the type of political action all three felt to be of value. In a long message to the Fellowship, published as an editorial in *The Tribunal* of 14 December, Allen again outlined his views on policy, urging that peace propaganda should be only one of the means used by the Fellowship to gain its ends, which should continue to be the granting of whatever form of exemption a man could conscientiously accept.

There was an interim period between the arrest of Brockway, which finally occurred on 28 November, and the election of the new Committee and chairman. Dr Salter, who was standing as a Committee member but not for the chairmanship, agreed to fill the post temporarily, and plans for the election went ahead. They were complicated by the almost unavoidable decision to appoint full members to office regardless of whether or not they were in prison, and to appoint also substitute officers mostly from among those who had absolute exemption, had been discharged or were not liable for military service. Allen stood unopposed as chairman. Those nominated for the office of substitute chairman were Brown, Morgan Jones, Bryce Leicester, Marshall and Russell. In addition votes had to be cast for five national members, five substitute national members, a divisional representative, and a substitute divisional representative; the intricacies of the ballot were formidable since most candidates stood in several capacities.[441]

Although the post of substitute chairman was hardly an enviable one, and although the number of those still at liberty to hold it was diminishing, the recent controversies made of the election a real if subdued competition. No breakdown of the voting is extant, but probably the contest lay between Barratt Brown and Russell, both well known through their appearances at divisional conventions and meetings all over the country. Brown's support probably came mainly from the religious objectors, and he did not lack personal popularity; but the respect in which Russell was held had been greatly enhanced by his personal peace campaign and his tangles with the Government during the past six months, and was now mixed with a warm possessive affection. In addition, he had the advantage of identification with the policies of Allen, without the disadvantage of being so strongly tied to one faction that he could be considered divisive. Committee members and the Fellowship at large seem to have seen him as a leader who would go after essentials and keep the NCF on the right track.

There was however one area in which he was something of a

heretic, and his heresy had been the subject of unease just when the election was under way. It will be remembered that the NCF had based its opposition to military service on a belief in 'the sanctity of human life' without further defining the phrase. The tribunals had helped to ensure the most radical interpretation, arguing that no man could have a conscientious objection to military service if he did not also hold that it was wrong to kill another human being under any circumstances, and this had therefore come to be tacitly assumed to be the meaning of the basis for all members, as it certainly was in fact for many. Russell never had believed there were no circumstances in which it was necessary to take human life; in an essay, 'The Ethics of War', published in *Justice in War-time* (early 1916), he distinguished three kinds of wars he could support: those of colonisation, principle and self-defence, but declared that the present war belonged to a fourth category, wars of prestige, which he could never support.[442]

During the time of his close connection with the NCF, Russell, fully committed to the aims for which the Fellowship was working, did not go out of his way to advertise the fact that he was not an absolute pacifist, but neither did he avoid the issue when it was thrust upon him. Toward the end of 1916, amid the growing discussion of war aims and post-war objectives, he found himself obliged to state his views publicly. He did so without fanfare and the effect was minimal, but it did not pass completely unnoticed. The last of his northern lectures dealt with 'National Independence and Internationalism', and in it he stated his belief that the international authority he hoped to see established would need to possess an army and navy. These, he believed, should be the only military forces in existence, and would be temporary.[443]

At about the same time Russell was asked to take part in a Conference on International Sanctions, arranged by the Friends' Peace Committee at Devonshire House. After a day of discussion of general principles, attention was given to the programme of the League to Enforce Peace. Lowes Dickinson spoke strongly in favour of the League's proposals, and Russell spoke against them. Although, as he had made clear in his lectures, he was not opposed to underwriting international organisation with force, he saw the current proposal as one which would bolster the political *status quo*, rather as the Holy Alliance of the nineteenth century had done. Marshall, who had not been able to get to the meeting, wrote to both Russell and Lowes Dickinson shortly afterwards. Her interest did not arise from any fear of an implicit threat to the Fellowship but because the Women's International League Conference planned for

26 October was proposing to make a statement on the matter. In reply, Russell gave in capsule form the argument of his lecture on 'Internationalism', a concise statement of his thinking:

On the general principle, although I think that the ultimate goal should be the abolition of force, I do not think that that goal can be reached in international affairs, any more than within a single State, except by passing through the stage where such force as is used is subordinated to Law. I conceive the development of human affairs as passing through three phases:- (1) Anarchy, (2) Law, (3) Liberty. In international affairs we are still at the first stage, in national affairs at the second; and, in some rare cases of good personal relations, at the third. I do not think it possible to pass from the first to the third except through the second, and therefore, I believe that something like the League to enforce Peace will have to be formed, as soon as a majority of civilised Governments desire to preserve the peace more than to promote their own power.[444]

While Russell's views created no great stir among the NCF leaders, to whom they had presumably long been known, they caused discomfort to some of the members to whom they were new. On 26 October Russell 'had a fearful rumpus about it at an NCF meeting', and on 5 November the secretary of the Tottenham branch of the Fellowship wrote with obvious distress about the divergence, as he saw it, between the views expressed in Russell's lectures and the basic principle of the NCF. After a spirited debate, the branch had passed a resolution rescinding their nomination of Russell as vice-chairman. Some members had defended Russell, others had been fearful that their action would give offence, but the writer believed Russell would understand and accept the decision.[445] Unfortunately no reply from Russell is extant. Although the issue never became a major one and on the whole does not seem to have detracted from the loyalty of the members to Russell, there is a curious footnote. When the addresses given at the Conference on International Sanctions were published in a special issue of *War and Peace* in January 1917, the review and summary in *The Tribunal* was less than scrupulously honest in its report of Russell's contribution, laying stress on his opposition to the use of force as embodied in the proposals of the League to Enforce Peace ('He is, of course, opposed to the use of force in this connection') without making it plain that Russell had declared he saw force as temporarily necessary in even the most ideal international organisation, and objected only to its embodiment in this imperfect instrument.[446]

The ballot papers for the election to the National Committee were issued on 20 December and had to be returned by 1 January 1917. By mid-January the results were announced. Russell had been elected substitute chairman and also as one of the five national members, and faced a year of arduous work on behalf of the Fellowship.

CHAPTER 10
RELUCTANT ADMINISTRATOR

Neither Russell nor Marshall faced the new year cheerfully. Marshall, who had been ill, was at home in Keswick on holiday—but her holiday was marred by toothache. Russell, just back from Christmas at Garsington, wrote her a letter in which his effort to be encouraging made little headway against his own gloomy and bitter mood. She had asked him to recommend some reading, and he discoursed cynically on the lessons of history:

The thing to remember in reading history is that the mad extravagant things people did are exactly what people do now. The book about Napoleon . . . tells you how Ll. George became P.M.; the book about Russia will enable you to understand the position of Rasputin. Contemporaries know nothing. Nero was thought a saint: caricaturists alluded to his time as "a sweeter, simpler reign". Under his successor, an unknown hand daily put flowers on his tomb, though the penalty for doing so was death. There is hope for us all. Panegyrists to this day stick up for him, pointing out that the people he murdered were his mother and his aunt, which is rather an endearing trait, seeing what elderly relatives are apt to be.

However, this is irrelevant. I find myself constantly taking refuge from the present in more humane and kindly times, such as that of Nero. I wish the outlook for peace were brighter. I think we shall have peace in the autumn, after Ll. G. has drunk the blood of half a million young Englishmen in an offensive which he knows will effect nothing. I do not think Ll. G. worse than the rest of mankind—on the contrary I think he belongs to the best 10 per cent—it is the human race that is vile. It is a disgrace to belong to it. Being busy is like taking opium, it enables one to live in a land of golden dreams—I must get busy again. The truth is not the sort of thing one can live with.[447]

Marshall wrote off hastily, advising Russell, 'For goodness sake get busy again, quickly, and get rid of the distorted vision of Truth to which idleness—or plum pudding?—seems to have given rise'.[448]

Russell's letter need not be given serious consideration as a profound statement of his thinking on history; all the same, the war irrevocably changed his view of the past and the use of history. The letter invites comparison with an essay written in 1904, in which Russell had said of history:

It selects from past lives the elements which were significant and important; it fills our thoughts with splendid examples, and with the desire for greater ends than unaided reflection would have discovered. It relates the present to the past, and thereby the future to the present. It makes visible and living the growth and greatness of nations, enabling us to extend our hopes beyond the span of our own lives.[449]

Writing after the war, he admitted 'The intellectual optimism of a bygone age is no longer possible to the modern student of human nature', and linked this view to modern psychology which, he said, 'has dived much deeper into the ocean of insanity upon which the little barque of human reason insecurely floats'.[450] Later still he was to write that one of the most important things history ought to do for the reader was to enable him to understand why people did what they did,[451] but he never returned to the view he had held before 1914 that this motivation would be found to be substantially rational: rather he expected to find it in complex psychological processes and irrational impulses whose importance had been brought home to him so devastatingly by the war.

Russell, in whom a nostalgia for philosophy was stirring, sent a written contribution to a meeting of the Aristotelian Society on 8 January 1917, but did not attend.[452] A lacerating exchange took place with the Whiteheads just at this already low point. Alfred Whitehead refused to lend Russell some notes he wanted to borrow, and wrote savagely—in a separate letter written on the same day—to blame Russell as a pacifist for current atrocities (the deportation of Belgian and French labour to Germany), and by implication for the fact that his younger son Eric (very dear to Russell) was to leave with the Flying Corps in April. Evelyn Whitehead hardly improved Russell's feelings by writing that Alfred's irritation was not because of their differing views, but because all their pacifist friends had deserted her in her illness.[453] A week later she wrote again, but referred once more to almost irreconcilable differences.[454]

Since busyness was the only escape, it may have come as a relief when the votes were counted and the announcement made that Russell had been elected acting chairman, although the job was not something which he would have sought for his own sake. Tedious administrative duties were a far cry from his maverick peace activities of the summer of 1916. Responsibility of this kind, though he felt he could not shirk it, had little appeal for him, and it made matters worse that the goal seemed less clear and less close then when conscription had been introduced. Within the Fellowship unsolved problems had been bequeathed to the new Committee and it was clearly going to be impossible to please everyone. Relations between absolutists and alternativists had settled down, but each group had its own pressing problems: the Home Office men were restless under unsatisfactory conditions and still felt under-privileged in the Fellowship; the absolutists were feeling the effects of prolonged imprisonment and were divided among themselves as to what they wanted of the National Committee. There was no lack of work and no delay in setting to work.

When the Committee came together under Russell's chairmanship, the two policy questions to be decided were the outstanding one relating to political action and another, regarding the response to industrial conscription, which had surfaced in the last weeks of the old year. At the first meeting, held on 20 and 21 January, both were discussed. The political action question was settled quickly and easily: the election had in fact given the Committee a mandate to carry on with the kind of tactics previously used. The branches were sent a report of the decision:

> The issue was raised at the first meeting of the new Committee by a resolution in the following terms:-
> "That the Fellowship make a practice of giving full publicity through press, Parliament, public meetings, and the "Tribunal", to the witness of its members, but make no efforts, direct or indirect, to alleviate their conditions, or obtain for them exemptions of any kind, devoting its energies solely to arousing the public conscience on war and conscription of war."
> The defeat of this resolution by 8 votes to 3 left the Committee free to continue the general policy laid down in the July resolution, without specifying how far that policy should be applied to the alleviation of conditions—the point dealt with in the Questionnaire. A resolution was then proposed debarring the Fellowship from taking any steps to alleviate hardships imposed on C.O.s in Home Office Camps or in prison. With the addition of an important amendment the resolution was carried in the following terms nem. con. (8 members voting for it, 3 abstaining).
> "That the N-C.F. shall not as an organisation take steps for the alleviation of hardships, except in cases involving questions or principle or the undermining of health either in Home Office Camps or in prison."[455]

The second issue, that of industrial conscription, had boiled up as a result of Lloyd George's creation of a Department of National Service. The Cabinet crisis of early December 1916 had been watched by Russell and the other pacifist leaders with interest. When it culminated in Lloyd George's triumph they knew that they were in for 'a rough time' which would affect conscientious objectors to military service, and might also spread the net of compulsion much wider.[456] 'Industrial conscription' was a term (pejorative, but not really inaccurate) currently used by the Government's left-wing opponents to refer to proposals that labour should be directed into the occupations most needed for the prosecution of the war, and the direction legally enforced. The attempt to reorganise in order to make more efficient use of manpower was not unexpected.[457] The full measure of compulsion which the Fellowship feared and which Lloyd George desired was never implemented, because of the realisation that it might bring enormous labour unrest.[458] The NCF joined with the National Council for Civil Liberties and the labour organisations to resist the introduction of industrial conscription, but more crucial was the question of the stance to be adopted should it come. Since in fact the Government was forced to leave national service for those outside the scope of the Military Service Acts on a voluntary basis, resistance to this form of compulsion was not put to the test. But although the decisions made remained academic, they are of some interest, not least for the method by which they were reached.

The National Committee continued to show a greatly increased openness in its treatment of this and of the political action question. Lloyd George's original announcement had been made just before the final meeting of the old National Committee in December. It had seemed that an alteration in the basis of membership might be necessary, if only to forestall the development of a parallel organisation with much duplication of machinery and division of effort, but there were different views as to how this should be done. The committee had decided to publish articles in *The Tribunal* explaining two different approaches. Aylmer Rose suggested widening the basis of the Fellowship so that all persons liable for compulsory industrial service and prepared to resist might become full members. Barratt Brown urged that the basis should be altered to make the Fellowship open to 'all men and women who are liable for service of any kind for war purposes, and who declare their refusal to allow their occupations to be changed for such purposes'. Although Brown denied that this would exclude those who had already accepted the Home Office scheme, or other work of national importance, or that it would make it impossible for others to accept alternative service in the future—he based this denial on the freedom of the individual to define the phrase 'for war purposes' according to his or her own conscience—it clearly would have moved the Fellowship much closer to the exclusive absolutist position consistently advocated by himself and Fletcher.[459]

Comments from members were invited, and were considered by the new National Committee. The letter to divisional and branch secretaries gave a full account of the discussion:

The new National Committee when it met on January 20th had before it a considerable amount of correspondence on the subject, from which it was clear that there was opposition to both the possible changes of basis suggested in the "Tribunal" articles, though there was a general desire to alter the basis in some way so as to meet the new situation. It was felt that, in view of the fact that the Fellowship had always left members free to accept alternative service from the Tribunals or work in the Home Office Camps, it was impossible to impose a definite pledge on members to refuse to work under the new scheme. At the same time, it was felt that those associates who do refuse such work on conscientious grounds will have a right to full membership. After considerable discussion the Committee decided to recommend to the branches the following alteration of the conditions of membership:

The present Statement of Faith to remain unchanged.

Under "Application of principles to War Work", for the paragraph beginning: "The members of the Fellowship" substitute "Membership of the Fellowship shall for this purpose be open to all men and women who are liable to either Military or Industrial Conscription. Members will refuse to engage in any employment which necessitates taking the Military oath. Whilst leaving the decision open to the individual judgement of each member the Fellowship will support members who conscientiously resist compulsory alternatives to Military or Industrial Service involving a change of occupation which has for its object the prosecution of War."
Carried nem. con. 3 members abstained from voting.

The letter went on to outline the arguments which had been put forward for and against the adoption of Brown's suggestion that all members should pledge themselves to refuse to accept a change of occupation for war purposes. Finally, each branch was asked to send in its opinion as to whether it endorsed the proposed alteration, so that the National Committee could decide whether or not it would be necessary to call a convention on the issue. Almost all the branches which responded endorsed the suggestion and the basis was accordingly altered.[460]

Russell devoted two of his editorials in *The Tribunal* to the question of industrial conscription. In the first, he considered it in relation to the pacifist viewpoint, in the second in relation to liberty. The first article was a logical development of the absolutist stance. Russell declared that it would become impossible when industrial conscription had been fully established for those who believed that war was wrong to serve the community and the state at the same time, since all work ordered by the Government would have the sole purpose of increasing the intensity of the war effort and freeing men to fight. The one exception would be in the case of a man or a woman who continued in his or her previous work. Those women, and men over military age, who had agreed with the absolutists could, in Russell's view, hardly fail to feel committed to the same position if industrial conscription became law.[461]

In the second editorial, Russell discussed the whole question of liberty and obedience. He denied that the claims of conscience could not be recognised without plunging the nation into anarchy, pointing out that in the days of religious persecution it had been thought that all citizens must have the same religion. Russell claimed that obedience, although often classed among virtues, was 'a virtue very difficult for a conscientious citizen to practise' and that 'the pioneers of human progress had been conspicuous for their lack of obedience'. He stressed the absolute value of conscience:

The reason why the State ought to respect the claims of conscience and why the individual ought to follow its dictate, is not that conscience cannot err. I hope every conscientious objector recognises that very many among those who have gone to fight have been actuated by conscientious motives to exactly the same extent as the most sincere and ardent pacifists. It is not because conscience cannot err that it must be respected, but because the determination to live according to conscience is in itself a thing of infinite value.[462]

There is nothing unexpected in the first of these two articles, which gives the logical absolutist viewpoint. Russell did not discuss the appropriate stance to be taken by those who were able to accept alternative service, but neither did he condemn them. He simply addressed himself to those who had supported the absolutist position as far as military service was concerned. The argument of the second article has a wider interest because of its basis in liberalism and morality. Although in fact neither religious nor socialist, the concept that obedience to the State is not necessarily a virtue in a citizen may have sat more comfortably with the Quaker pacifists than it did with some socialist pacifists. Most of the leaders held views similar to Russell's in this, but, for some members, belief in the right of the State to command the citizen had been a stumbling-block to resistance and a barrier to absolutism.

Other questions of principle would arise to divide and trouble the National Committee, but these two which were current when Russell took office did not prove to be of great difficulty. The National Committee was again able to handle its business in one weekend a month as a general rule. Much more of Russell's attention was now centred on the work of the head office, where the leadership was shared between Marshall and himself.

By the time Russell became chairman at the beginning of 1917 there was probably no one else still at liberty who knew as much about the workings of the NCF, with the exception of Marshall, who had also shown a brilliant ability to assess needs and to adapt to circumstances.[463] As we have seen, the two had been working closely together, and held the same views on most policy questions. None of this ensured that the even closer working relationship demanded by Russell's acceptance of the chairmanship would be an easy one.

Marshall had some grave deficiencies, exacerbated at this time by tension and fatigue. Although she expected a great deal of dedication from all who worked with her, she found it difficult to allow them the satisfaction of handling a job without interference, and she was very defensive under criticism. She was also in a curious position, not uncommon among women of ability. For all the equality between the sexes which theoretically formed part of the philosophy of both socialists and Quakers, and for all her own modern upbringing,[464] she was culturally attuned to accepting or appearing to accept direction from men. She was also a woman working in a men's organisation. So she avoided attitudes of leadership while in fact trying to push and pull and drive others, including some of at least equal stature in the organisation, into doing what she was sure ought to be done. Like many people, she had found Allen's leadership easy to accept, and although less close, she and Brockway also managed well together. She had now worked with Russell for over six months, but a new dimension was added when he became chairman, and the success or failure of their relationship could make or break the organisation.

As we have seen, Russell had not previously emerged as a dynamic leader within the NCF. While his personal peace campaign had been dramatic and newsworthy, and had greatly added to his prestige among pacifists, his contributions within the National Committee had been generally low-key (although of value) and his service at head office had been given with remarkable humility. He was willing to remain for a long time a learner in the political milieu, and to perform the most unexciting of jobs if they were seen to be necessary.[465] He recognised Marshall's gifts and was prepared to accept direction from her where a lesser man, for sexist or other reasons, might have balked. He knew better than anyone how much the Fellowship owed to Marshall and he knew her need for warmth and support. During the previous autumn, when she had suddenly felt overwhelmed, it had been to Russell that she had turned. Heading her letter 'S.O.S.' she wrote, 'I am drowning in a sea of loneliness. . . . I want some help very badly'. Russell was already aware of the strain she was feeling and was on his way to visit her before her letter even reached him. His advice had been carefully prepared. She felt great relief that he took her appeal seriously, and added a postscript to her letter of thanks: 'I am tickled at the idea of your writing out notes, with sub-headings, for a talk with me, just as I do for an interview with General Child [*sic*] or Lloyd George!'[466]

Russell had cancelled an engagement to offer the support Marshall needed, and he followed up his advice by arranging a weekend of relaxation which she described in a letter to Allen: 'Had wonderful weekend with Mephy a month ago—his prescription for fatigue and bad attack of missing you. Sunshine, moonlight, wood fires; walks, talks, reading aloud (I hemmed 3 prs. curtains!); poetry, philosophy, fun. Thought and talked much of you. . . .'[467] Although Russell could extend a helping hand in such a situation, he could not change Marshall's personality or induce her to husband her resources. From October 1916 she suffered increasingly from headaches and undefined illness, forcing her for periods of a day or a week to cancel engagements or to go away to rest. Although she was certainly still carrying a fair share of the load at this time, she began to have irritating lapses, forgetting, for example, to answer important letters.[468]

Russell's accession to the chairmanship made a difference in the relationship between himself and Marshall. Where he had been up to that time to some extent under her tutelage in the administrative sphere, he now had primary responsibility, and he was rightly determined to accept it fully. He was acutely aware of his deficiencies as an administrator, and his greatest weakness seems to have been his tendency to exaggerate them.[469] There is little evidence that he in fact lacked the necessary qualities: he does not seem to have been generally inefficient; he was certainly not lacking in industry; he had served a long apprenticeship; he had a grasp of essentials and of the overall picture; he appears to have been well-accepted by most of the subordinate personnel; and, as we have seen, he was heard with attention by the members of the National Committee. Above and beyond this, some of his more brilliant qualities were applicable to the job: he had an instant grasp of arguments; he wrote letters and reports rapidly and lucidly and seldom with as much as an erasure or crossing-out; he had a wide historical background and a gift for restoring perspective when his fellow-workers slipped into hair-splitting controversy; he was decisive, and prepared to stand by his decisions. Although he lacked Allen's ambience and Brockway's political and administrative experience, the great admiration he had won by his exploits of 1916 stood him in good stead. He found the minor details of organisation difficult to keep in mind and needed to be well-supported by his staff. He hated administrating other people's work, far preferring to work on his own, and indeed had little taste for any aspect of the work now demanded of him. He did it only from duty, pushing himself all the time; it is absurd to believe it beyond his capacities, but a person seldom does a job well by sheer will power, and his feeling of inadequacy made him defensive. Marshall did her best to supply him with the help he needed to keep the work running smoothly, writing out almost daily lists headed 'For Mr. Russell', or 'B.R. to do'. This was, I think, an inappropriate function for her and would have been better done by a paid secretary with no stake in the leadership. Marshall's own insecurity (reflected in her impulse to control while accepting the appearance of subordination) combined with her formidable organising ability, was threatening indeed, to both parties, in juxtaposition to Russell's lack of self-confidence and loathing of the job he had taken on. Both tried to be open, but both found criticism hard to bear, so their struggles toward a better understanding met with only partial success.

Marshall's ill-health and the deterioration of the working relationship between her and Russell were not the only causes of tension in the head office at the outset of Russell's chairmanship. The financial condition of the Fellowship was poor. The staff was large and was dispersed uneconomically between three offices. The maintenance of the families of conscientious objectors had been taken over in July 1916 by a committee headed by J. R. MacDonald and Ada Salter; funds for this part of the work were now raised and held separately. The general fund-raising campaign initiated in August 1916 cannot have been over-successful, because it was decided to appoint a commission to study the structure with a view to economy and increased efficiency: those chosen were Russell, Salter and Francis Meynell (who represented London on the National Committee). Their most dramatic work was done at the end of January 1917, immediately after Russell took office as chairman. They not only collected opinions from the staff on various matters, but dismissed several workers and made the decision not to replace certain others who were leaving at the time. An exaggerated account of the action caused some disquiet among out-of-town members, and rightly or wrongly Marshall, who had been ill at home in Keswick when it occurred, felt that it had been precipitate and had left her too short-staffed for efficiency. The Commission did not at this time prepare the full report for the National Committee which seems to have been suggested, but gathered material which Marshall used in late spring when she was reviewing the whole head office operation again. The whole story of the Commission is poorly documented and does little more than hint at an uncomfortable situation, a shortage of funds much more acute than has previously been remarked, and perhaps a rather novel view of Russell in the role of an administrative new broom.[470]

Russell's responsibilities now included a great deal of routine work at head office, initiation of policy, response to political and external events, chairmanship of the National Committee, special care of the men in the Home Office camps and the writing of a weekly editorial for *The Tribunal* and of other articles when appropriate. He also had a general responsibility for the content of *The Tribunal*. His later recollection was that he had edited it for a period of time,[471] but this was never his official position. B. J. Boothroyd, a young Quaker member of the staff, remained as editor from the time of W. J. Chamberlain's imprisonment (under the Defence of the Realm Act) in July 1916 until some weeks before his own arrest in October 1917, when Lydia Smith, a Quaker school teacher, took over. As well as writing the weekly chairman's article, Russell revised the proofs with Boothroyd and was responsible on behalf of the National Committee for all that appeared.[472]

An exchange of letters between Russell and Marshall early in March 1917 well illustrates the kind of pressure that they were under and the friction that inevitably resulted. The occasion was a visit that Russell paid to the Home Office settlement at Wakefield. Marshall's letter began, 'I like you fleeing to your funk hole!' and went on to accuse Russell of leaving a great deal of extra work to be done by Boothroyd, who was not well, and by herself, who had just got back to work after two days in bed. Boothroyd had come to her for information for a newsletter to be prepared for Brockway, awaiting his second court martial, and there had been the proofs of *The Tribunal* to be read, including extra material since there happened to be a special double issue that week. She continued:

And then you tell me to delegate things to you and not to overwork myself!
. . . I know this is not your fault, because you are performing a still more urgent duty at Warwick; but could you not have arranged for someone other than me to be responsible for this? Mr. Grubb for instance? I should have been glad not to have had it to do—or at any rate to have had warning before yesterday that I must make time for it somehow. I have already—yesterday and Monday night—been through the survey with B.J.B., which occupies about ½ the Trib. this week.
   I enclose the promised—or rather threatened—report of the first week or work with the reduced staff according to the Commission's arrangements.
   I am sorry that I have to write you such a wholly nasty letter. I wish I could think of just one nice thing to say, but there is not one I have in my mind at present, and I have no time to hunt.

Russell was not used to such open criticism and replied with some irritation, trying to point the moral:

You really must not write me letters such as the one I got from you this morning. If I did not realize that you are so tired as to be hardly responsible, I should be seriously annoyed.

(1) Wakefield is not a "funk-hole".

(2) The arrangement that Boothroyd should write to Brockway was made on your suggestion after consultation with you. I gave him all the information he asked for, and would have given him more if I had known he wanted it.

(3) I arranged with Boothroyd that he should come here with Tribunal proofs Monday night after my Chelsea meeting. He never turned up, and when I asked him why he hadn't come, he replied that it had occurred to him that you would do equally well.

In general, it is not from laziness that I do not do more work. I do as much as I can without doing it badly and becoming ill. Every one must judge for himself or herself in such matters. It seems to me that you make a mistake in wearing yourself out, and that you ought to go away for a month's holiday; but you think otherwise, and I don't feel it my business to find fault with you. But I do think that if you are treating other people as you are treating me, it is a further proof how much you need a rest. Do *please* consider it. One can't work *well* when one is so tired.

Russell added a postscript:

You do not enclose the threatened report. P.S. I am not a *bit* cross really, only I want you to realize how much you need a complete rest. The N.C.F. would not shut up shop, much as it would miss you.[473]

Too much should not be made of such a petty exchange, but it was symptomatic of real difficulties. Russell's diagnosis of Marshall's problem cannot be faulted. Whatever the reason may have been, she was pushing herself into illness. Throughout March she was, in her own words, 'alternatively laid up and overwhelmed with work'.[474] Although much of the work she did continued to be well and thoroughly done, she became increasingly critical of others. On his part, Russell fell prey to a crippling sense of failure, purposelessness and inadequacy. Whether or not he was guilty of using this manipulatively, it undoubtedly made him sometimes hard to work with: not all the fault was on Marshall's side, and few people either at that time or later seem to have found her as difficult a colleague as Russell did. There may well have been a kind of passive aggression in his behaviour at this time, a use of any real or fancied shortcomings on his part as a stick to beat other people's consciences with—how could Marshall criticise him when he was trying so hard and so much against his nature and inclination? In one of his now much less frequent letters. to Ottoline Morell, probably written within a few days of the above exchange with Marshall, he wrote:

You ask about me—but there is nothing to tell about myself—I am not overworking—on the contrary, the moment I am not busy I get much more tired than when I am. I have no vivid feelings at all except constantly increasing horror of the war—I have to fight it down by being busy, because it is an obsession and perfectly useless and rather insane.

I am speaking a good deal, and I enjoy that—I was at Leicester the night before last—600 people or more—they cheered and cheered till I thought they would never stop. But that sort of thing no longer gives me any real encouragement because the people who are with us remain impotent. My *feeling* is that the war may go on for many years, though that doesn't seem to be the view of people who ought to know. Apart from the war, nothing really interests me, but I fill my days with work and trivialities. The disappointment after our hopes at Christmas was too much. . . .

It is quite impossible for me to give you any idea how weary and hopeless I feel—I go on doing things, in order to be occupied, but not because I think them useful—they seem quite futile. One just waits for the end of the war—after that I suppose some sort of life may be possible again—if one can live till then. . . .

The N.C.F. no longer interests me—all the best people are in prison and there seems no way of getting them out. Those who remain are full of petty quarrels and sordidnesses.[475]

CHAPTER 11

PACIFISM AND REVOLUTION

Russell never lost sight—even when immersed in the tedious and demanding detail of the NCF chairmanship—of the relationship between the resistance of the conscientious objectors and the larger objective of a peace which should come soon and endure long. The continuation of the war had long seemed to him the great primary evil. Caused by hatred and militarism, much more hatred and militarism followed in its train. The restoration of civilisation could only begin when the fighting ended, and then only if the peace was the product of negotiation, not of conquest; and if possible the common people should be brought into the settlement in some new way. But in late 1916 Russell would have settled for a peace negotiated by statesmen if nothing better were offered.

The possibility of peace negotiations had shown signs in late 1916 of becoming for the first time something more than a pacifist's pipe dream. Unknown to the public, Lord Lansdowne had actually declared to the Cabinet in November his belief that it might be impossible to win the war, but that a reasonable peace might be obtained on the basis of a return to the *status quo ante bellum*.[476] The Cabinet had discussed his memorandum, but had decided, largely on the optimistic advice of the military leaders, to press the war through to victory. Lansdowne was not without support within the Government, and it is possible that the seed he had planted might have begun a slow growth, had it not been for Lloyd George's accession to power on 5 December. War-weariness was at the root both of the increased acceptance of the idea of a negotiated peace and of the growing clamour for effective prosecution of the war. The latter was more articulate and influential, and settled Lloyd George firmly in the saddle. But there was also international pressure for the opening of peace negotiations.

Russell's belief in the role that America could play in bringing the war to an end revived and early in December he decided that the time was ripe to urge President Wilson to intervene. He had welcomed Wilson's re-election in November by a country apparently grateful to him for having kept it out of the war. On 4

December Russell wrote an open letter to the President, an action to which he attached great significance at the time, and which attracted considerable attention in the United States. The letter was smuggled out of the country and into the States by Katherine Dudley,[477] Helen Dudley's sister, and was taken by her to the American Neutral Conference Committee, who arranged to have her deliver it to them more publicly (but without revealing her name) at a dinner at the Hotel Astor in New York which had coincidentally been arranged for that evening. This ensured it instant publicity, and the whole dramatic story together with the text was in many papers, from the *New York Times* to the *Los Angeles Times*, on the following morning, 23 December. A small committee took the letter to the White House where the President is reported to have listened with 'polite aloofness'. A meeting in Madison Square Garden was also organised, at which the speaker was mobbed, apparently by over-enthusiastic supporters.[478]

Russell's open letter was an eloquent plea for active mediation on the part of the United States. He pointed out that the military situation made victory impossible for either side, but that great as was the damage that was being inflicted, it was not such as would prevent the war from going on for a long time yet. Prolonged warfare, in addition to killing thousands, had already destroyed hard-won liberties and now threatened the very existence of civilisation. Public opinion was generally represented as supporting the continuance of the war, but Russell thought this deceptive. He believed the desire for peace almost universal 'not only among the soldiers, but throughout the wage-earning classes'. The fear which kept hostilities going could be allayed only by the United States, which had the power both to compel the belligerents to make peace, and also, by becoming the guarantor of the peace, to remove the mutual distrust which might otherwise lead to renewed war. Admitting he had no formal right to address the President, Russell wrote in conclusion that he spoke because he must:

> Above all, I see that none of the issues in the war are as important as peace; the harm done by a peace which does not concede all that we desire is as nothing in comparison to the harm done by the continuance of the fighting. While all who have power in Europe speak for what they falsely believe to be the interests of their separate nations, I am compelled by a profound conviction to speak for all the nations in the name of Europe. In the name of Europe I appeal to you to bring us peace.[479]

Even before the letter reached the President, there had been the first signs of an international interest in peace negotiations. On 12 December, Germany issued a Note to the Allies proposing a conference to discuss peace terms. Wilson followed this up on 18 December with a Note inviting belligerents to define their war aims. A flurry of international Notes ensued, from neutrals backing the President's initiative, and from belligerents.[480] On 1 January 1917 the Allies rejected the German Note, declaring that a statement of aims must precede any meeting, and on 10 January they issued a declaration of their own aims. These included an enunciation of the principle of self-determination, involving a wholesale redrawing of the boundaries of southeastern Europe. The principle was perhaps calculated to appeal to liberal opinion in the United States, but the threatened application was anathema to Germany's allies.

It is easy to see all this as pointless diplomatic fencing, the more so as it proved unproductive: yet such ritual dancing was also bound to precede any serious peace negotiations. The attitude taken by the pacifists combined elements of realism with a fundamental naivety. Deeply suspicious of the men in power in Britain, Russell yet believed the German authorities were prepared to negotiate in good faith and to make large concessions to obtain peace.[481] He possibly did not overestimate the deep desire for peace among the common people on both sides, but the pacifists never did succeed in making the desire articulate. As Russell saw, all the advantages of what he called the momentum of war were on the side of the war leaders, which again was why the prospect of American mediation seemed to offer such hope. On 22 January 1917 President Wilson spoke to the Senate in terms that were almost all that the advocates of a negotiated peace could have wished. He declared that the aim must be a peace without victory, and foreshadowed the creation of a League of Nations. Russell wrote a front-page article for *The Tribunal*, welcoming the statement: 'The truth of what he says is evident to all who are not caught up in the madness of war, as a study of neutral opinion shows. But during war it is difficult for either side to believe that there is anything more important than victory.'[482] This was the crux. At the beginning of 1917, the military stalemate was almost total. Late in 1916, there had been some reluctant recognition of this, even in high political places—it had led to the opening of the ritual dance—but so great was the wish for victory, especially among the military leaders, that they had persuaded themselves that a new offensive would succeed where previous ones had failed. Lloyd George's rise to power marked the political triumph of this view and the dance came to an abrupt end after a few purely ceremonial gestures used mostly to justify continuing the fighting. On the Allied side the drive for victory led to the immense tragedies of the Nivelle offensive and of Passchendaele, exactly as Russell predicted at the beginning of 1917. On the German side it led to the resumption of unrestricted submarine warfare, an action which broke the stalemate and made victory possible, although, as it turned out, the fruit did not fall to Germany but to her enemies. At first it seemed that it would turn the scale in Germany's favour: British shipping losses rose to the level of one in four and went uncontrolled until May 1917, when Lloyd George instituted the convoy system. But more significant in the long run was the effect on the United States. Germany's announcement of full-scale U-boat warfare was made on 31 January. On 2 February the United States broke off diplomatic relations with Germany, and on April 6 she declared war.

Russell weighed the pros and cons of America's entry into the war in a front-page *Tribunal* article. His standpoint was not that of absolute pacifism, since he admitted that if it could be shown that American intervention would shorten the war, he would welcome it. But he doubted that this would be the effect. He accurately predicted that participation in the war would soon bring the United States to a much more bellicose and militaristic frame of mind. True, it might make ultimate victory possible, but he did not see this as a desirable conclusion, and he thought it might not come until Europe was 'so weak and exhausted as to have lost all importance for mankind'. There was only one hope of improvement—and Russell hardly sounded confident as he wrote of it:

The war may help the weary populations of the world to see that force is not the road to a secure peace or to friendly relations between the nations. If so, good may come out of it in the end. But it will come through revulsion against war, not through continued belief in punishment, destruction and death.[483]

Seven years later, Russell offered his retrospective judgment on America's entry into the war, in a lecture before the League for Industrial Democracy in New York. His view then had not changed radically since 1917, but he was now prepared to be somewhat more specific in assigning blame. He said that the Germans, by their folly in returning to unrestricted submarine warfare, had given American high finance the excuse it had been waiting for to bring the States into the war. He believed that had the Germans held their hands, all the belligerents would have come to accept the Kerensky formula of 'no annexations and no indemnities'. Only the great corporations—Russell named Morgan and Standard Oil—stood to gain by American intervention, but it had taken the emotional and practical impact of U-boat warfare to bring public opinion and liberal Government thinking into line with the wishes of big business.[484]

For good reason, we have seen, the gloom which had settled over the pacifists by the end of 1916 had not been materially affected by what they had briefly hoped was the opening of peace negotiations. The metamorphosis of the anticipated American intervention on behalf of a negotiated peace into American military intervention, where Wilson's ideals were to be sought only after Lloyd George's objective of unconditional victory had been attained, was a heavy blow to Russell. In spite of his revulsion from the Liberal Party, which had been almost instant and complete at Britain's entry into the war, he still had an ingrained belief in liberal idealism, but the American declaration of war eroded another portion of this faith. For all his tendency at times to appear cynical, and his usual capacity for a disciplined rationalism, Russell was always an idealist: he needed a belief in at least the possibility of progress. Fortunately renewed hope had come from another source just a few weeks before American intervention.

To Russell, the news of the Russian revolution which reached England in early March 1917 sounded like the harbinger of the fulfilment of all his hopes. Indeed, the first response on all sides was one of welcome. Imperialists hoped it might presage an end to the rival Russian expansionist tradition. For liberals it meant an end to the embarrassment of the alliance with the oppressive Tsarist regime. The Government welcomed it mainly (I suspect) because it was politic to praise what was clearly an accomplished fact and was popular in Britain. The official message brought to the House of Commons congratulated the Russian people on the establishment of free institutions and expressed the hope that the revolution would lead to 'the prosecution with renewed steadfastness and vigour of the war against the stronghold of an autocratic militarism which threatens the liberty of Europe'.[485] But Bonar Law, the Leader of the House of Commons and Chancellor of the Exchequer, in presenting the statement, expressed also his compassion for the fallen Tsar who had been until recently, he said, 'Britain's loyal ally'.

The most wholehearted welcome came from some of the workers and from the pacifists, and, together with a considerable section of liberal opinion, they continued unreservedly to support and praise the new regime throughout the spring and summer of 1917. The warmth of their enthusiasm did nothing to make the British Government more comfortable with the new situation in Russia. If the alliance with the notorious Tsarist state had been an embarrassment to the Liberal Government at the outset of the war, the alliance with anti-monarchical revolutionaries was no less embarrasing to a British Government which seemed to have grown increasingly authoritarian by 1917.

Russell was not only delighted by the turn of events, but claimed to have predicted it. In accepting a request from Morel for an article on the revolution for his magazine, the *U.D.C.*, he wrote that in his last one he had prophesied 'that revolution was going to sweep over Europe beginning in Russia. . . . You compelled me to cut out this prophecy and robbed me of just fame as a prophet'.[486] He wrote to an American friend on 23 March: 'The Russian Revolution is a stupendous event. Although one can't tell yet how it will work out, it can hardly fail to do great good. It has been more cheering than anything that has happened since the war began.'[487] So little violence accompanied the initial stages of the revolution that it could be freely praised by religious as well as political pacifists. Harvey is reputed to have 'literally jumped for joy'; and in May, London Yearly Meeting of the Society of Friends met the change with enthusiasm.[488] The pacifists, and particularly the core leadership of the NCF, played a much larger part than has previously been realised in organising the first mass expression of public rejoicing, and in attempting to initiate a more far-reaching response.

By 17 March, Russell was working with a Committee for Anglo-Russian Co-Operation which was operating out of 4 Duke Street, Adelphi, the address of the Parliamentary department of the No-Conscription Fellowship. The group appears to have been the same as, or else a sub-group of, the one referred to in most sources as the Anglo-Russian Democratic Alliance. Possibly they began simultaneously and merged almost immediately.[489] George Lansbury and the *Herald* sponsored the organisation, which was also supported by Robert Williams, Robert Smillie and W. C. Anderson. Whoever initiated this Committee, those most actively engaged on its business from the outset included Russell, Marshall, Ammon, Miles Malleson and Meynell. Of these Meynell is the only one whose connection with the work at this juncture is noted by Lansbury's biographer.[490] (Meynell worked for Lansbury's *Herald* and for the associated Pelican Press.) All, with the exception of Malleson, were among the most active officers of the No-Conscription Fellowship at the time. They constituted themselves a sub-committee to deal with propaganda and literature, which in fact encompassed a large part of the business of the organisation, and they set to work with vigour.

Given the pacifist bias, the focal point of the campaign was obvious and logical. One of the first actions of the Russian Provisional Government had been to issue a statement of the principles by which it would be guided. The first three of these were as follows:

> 1. An immediate general amnesty for all political and religious offenses, including terrorist acts, military revolts, agrarian offenses, etc.
> 2. Freedom of speech and press; freedom to form labour unions and to strike. These political liberties should be extended to the army in so far as war conditions permit.
> 3. The abolition of all social, religious and national restrictions.

The statement further delighted liberal opinion by concluding: 'The Provisional Government wishes to add that it has no intention of taking advantage of the existence of war conditions to delay the realisation of the above-mentioned measures of reform.'[491] Since the document did not as much as refer to Russia's two most pressing problems—the distribution of land and the prosecution of the war—there were grounds on which its significance could be questioned, but not by the British socialists and pacifists. Their concern was frankly less with its relevance in the Russian situation—of which many of them knew little—but with its supposed relevance in the British situation. These first three points of the Russian 'Charter of Freedom' invited comparison with what the anti-war groups had long pointed to as the decline of civil liberty in wartime Britain. Other principles on the list, particularly one declaring for the adoption of universal suffrage, seemed to promise a measure of democracy beyond that which had prevailed even in pre-war Britain. A British 'Charter of Freedom' was drawn up, whose points parararalleled the new Russian liberties:

> We demand equal liberties for Britons! This demand involves
> (1) Release of Irish prisoners, and of Conscientious Objectors.
> (2) Cessation of prosecutions under Defence of Realm Act and Munition Act; suppression of *agents provocateurs*.
> (3) Home Rule; also the right of asylum.
> (4) Adult Suffrage.

Russell believed the revolution in Russia opened up immense strategic possibilities in Britain, provided the opportunity was seized at once. The earliest document in which the above list appears, which was probably of Russell's authorship, continued:

> In an immediate demand for the above four points we shall have on our side
> (a) The Irish.
> (b) Those who favour a democratic form of suffrage.
> (c) Those who favour peace by negotiation.

(d) The Civil Liberties Group and all those Liberals who are tired of Ll[oyd] G[eorge].

(e) All Labour discontent, especially the Clyde workers and S. Wales.

(f) Perhaps more important than all these, the sense of unrest and hope generated by the overthrow of an ancient tyranny which has been one of the chief causes of German militarism.

(g) All the horror of war and fear of universal disaster which has been gradually growing up, but has hitherto found no sufficient expression.

The Russian Revolution has stirred men's imaginations everywhere and has made things possible which would have been quite impossible a week ago. It is vital to seize the moment while the effect is at its height. A dramatic action now may decide hundreds of thousands of waverers and alter the whole course of future history.[492]

The organisers of the British 'Charter of Freedom' campaign concentrated on three main activities: the preparation of literature, the canvassing of influential persons who might be sympathetic, and the holding of a mass meeting. Marshall quickly drew up plans for a formidable amount of work, which had all to be done in addition to the ongoing work of the Fellowship. An effective handbill was produced: the left-hand column listed the new Russian freedoms, the right-hand column, headed 'In Britain', was blank except for the words 'In deference to the Censorship the items for this column are omitted'. The members of the Committee for Anglo-Russian Co-Operation wrote a letter for wide circulation, drawing attention to the complete amnesty in Russia for political and religious offenders. Among those to whom they sent the letter were themselves, in their alternate capacity as members of the National Committee of the NCF. The National Committee duly endorsed it and Russell, as chairman, sent it on to branch secretaries, with a plea that they would do all in their power 'to promote the agitation for the introduction of the newly won liberties of Russia into this country'.[493]

The list of people to be approached for support was long, and was divided up among the active workers of the Committee. Some of these potential sympathisers were asked specifically to appear or speak at the planned mass meeting, others simply for a general commitment to the aims of the organisation. Russell and Marshall worked closely together and did much of their canvassing jointly, mostly within a period of one week, from 17 to 24 March. Among those whom they visited were Lord Parmoor, who promised to speak to Lord Bryce and Lord Loreburn; H. W. Massingham, who undertook to see Lord Courtney; J. A. Hobson; Leonard Woolf; Helena Swanwick; and Sir S. Olivier. All of these were sympathetic.[494] The Committee was particularly anxious to secure the support of the old Parliamentarian, John Burns, and to persuade him to chair the public meeting. Marshall's first visit to him, at which

Burns declared that the time was not ripe, was followed by another the next day from Marshall and Russell, and later Norman went to see him. Although the latter reported that he thought he had shaken Burns in his refusal, nothing came of it.

In spite of this disappointment, plans for the public meeting went ahead and grew in scope. The date was set for 31 March. On 24 March, when it was apparent Burns would not agree, Marshall wrote to Lord Parmoor asking him if he would take the chair. By this time the Albert Hall had been booked, though Marshall confessed it might be difficult to fill; she had thought more in terms of a place the size of the Central Hall, Westminster. Lord Parmoor had shown considerable interest in the campaign, but he did not agree to chair the meeting (his reasons are not known), and that office was finally filled by Lansbury.[495] Admission was by ticket, but there was no charge. In spite of the shortness of the time, the Pelican Press turned out a beautifully-produced twelve-page programme which included the words of songs to be sung by the audience. An organist was engaged to give a recital while the auditorium was filling. The speakers included H. W. Nevinson, Robert Smillie, Robert Williams, Israel Zangwill, Maude Royden, Josiah Wedgwood, Albert Bellamy, Dr Lynch and W. C. Anderson. In the interval Clara Butt, then at the height of her career, sang 'Give to us peace in our time' alternately with the audience, and other inspirational songs were sung while a collection was being taken. A resolution was passed sending 'joyful congratulations to Russia and calling upon the Government of Great Britain and other countries to follow the Russian example by establishing the same freedoms'. The meeting concluded with the singing of the 'Red Flag'. None of the small group which had done so much of the organising took an active part; Russell and Marshall were supposed to sit on the platform[496] with some of the distinguished supporters whom they had drawn in, but Russell, it seems, stood on the floor among the crowd with Lady Constance Malleson.

Next day Russell wrote an enthusiastic letter to Ottoline Morrell, which is worth quoting at length:

> I feel I must tell you about the Albert Hall meeting last night, because it was a really wonderful occasion, and you can find out nothing about it from the papers. The Albert Hall was absolutely packed, and 20,000 people had to be refused tickets. Every person there was wanting a real absolute change in everything—not the sort of piecemeal niggling reforms that one is used to, but the sort of thing the Russians have done. There was *no* opposition. The C.O.s came in for their share of applause—that one had expected. But besides that people cheered for a republic, for freedom in India, for all the things one never hears mentioned. Jos. Wedgwood, who represented moderation, suggested that

it was possible to believe that some good objects could not be obtained without war, but he could only get a hearing after an urgent appeal from the Chairman. The whole atmosphere was electric. I longed to shout at them at the end to come with me and pull down Wormwood Scrubs. They would have done it. The Reporters applauded, but did not take notes. A meeting of the kind would have been utterly impossible a month ago. Smillie and Williams were admirable as regards Labour. The regular pacifist gang were not speaking, and the general public did not know what sort of meeting it was going to be. "To cheer the Russian Revolution" sounded quite respectable. But the speakers one and all urged that we should do likewise. The audience was largely Russian Jews. I saw my little friend Tchitcherene (the Sec. of one their organizations) afterwards, beaming like a cherub. There was a lot said about Ireland—the Sinn Fein martyrs were enthusiastically cheered—the Russians have really put a new spirit into the world, and it is going to be worth while to be alive.[497]

One of the most noteworthy features of the Albert Hall meeting was the extent of the response. Whether Russell's estimate of the number of people refused tickets was accurate there is no means of knowing, but Ammon had reported some days before that tickets had run out and that there was a long line-up, and other accounts indicate that 5000 were turned away from the doors. The hall held 12000 people.[498] Tickets had been issued through left-wing organisations (the *Herald*, the National Union of Railwaymen, the ILP), but to all comers. Russell's comment that the audience did not know what to expect was shrewd: in fact, it turned out that a few felt they had been tricked into coming by false advertising. A friend of Marshall's claimed that she had gone because she was interested in freedom in Russia, only to find it was all about lack of freedom in Britain.[499] The enthusiasm of the audience suggests her resentment was not general, and the reception given to every mention of anti-war activity was impressive. Not only were the conscientious objectors cheered, but Russell was warmly applauded when Anderson referred to the ban which had prevented him from giving his lecture in Glasgow.[500]

Obviously it was an emotional occasion, but it should not be discounted on this ground: the audience brought much of the emotion with them. Indeed, what is surprising is the spontaneity and openness of this mass demonstration against the war and against the restrictions to which the war had given rise. It might be said that the holding of the Albert Hall meeting gave the lie to the claims of its sponsors that freedom of speech had disappeared in wartime Britain, but the Government was of course in a cleft stick and could hardly interfere with a meeting to celebrate the revolution to which it had itself extended decorous greeting. Presumably the *Daily Express*, always so keen to encourage disturbance at pacifist meetings, felt itself to be in the same

ambivalent position at this juncture. In March 1917 criticising the
Russian revolution was akin to criticising motherhood.

Like the local response to Russell's Welsh tour, the Albert Hall
meeting gives a remarkable glimpse of a section of public opinion
apparently quite disaffected from the Government's civil policies
and the continuation of the war, but normally inarticulate and not
prepared to take political or direct action to change the situation.
One wonders in what lasting ways the meeting affected the
thought and action of the mass of people who attended it and
whether more capital could have been made of it. There was little
direct follow-up. The sub-committee on which Russell and
Marshall had worked did not remain active, and the 'Charter of
Freedom' campaign was little heard of after the Albert Hall
meeting, probably because it was felt to have served its purpose,
and because other, more far-reaching plans were afoot, in which
the initiative passed on the one hand to the Labour Party and on
the other to a group generally described as the United Socialist
Council.

The activities of the Labour Party throughout the summer in
connection with the abortive Stockholm conference need not
concern us here. The NCF warmly welcomed the attempt to send
British representatives to an international socialist meeting on war
aims which would include belligerents on both sides, but took no
active part aside from making sure delegates to the crucial Labour
Party conferences of 10 and 21 August were supplied with
material on the NCF position and the stand of the conscientious
objectors.[501]

The main activity of the Labour movement's left wing during
the early summer was the calling of the Leeds Convention of 3
June. Francis Johnson of the Independent Labour Party and Albert
Inkpin of the British Socialist Party were responsible for making
the arrangements, but they acted on behalf of a committee of
thirteen, representing quite a wide spectrum. Although neither
the NCF as a body nor Russell and Marshall as individuals appear
to have played any part in organising the Leeds Convention—
indeed, they apparently failed to get official representation for the
Fellowship at that gathering[502]—Ammon was one of the conve-
nors, and 4 Duke Street was still the address used by the group.[503]
Lansbury was also on the organising committee, as were Smillie,
Williams and Anderson, suggesting continuity between this and
the Anglo-Russian Democratic Alliance.[504]

Although Russell was not engaged in preparations for the Leeds
Convention, he watched events throughout the spring with acute
attention. His interest was twofold. Unlike some of those who

welcomed the revolution, he wanted to know exactly what was going on in Russia. Secondly, he believed in its relevance to problems in Britain and he hoped to have a part in what reforms could be initiated by the people. In both of these, his judgment was somewhat coloured by his desires; or perhaps it is fairer to say he shared some of the innocence of most of those who watched the beginnings of the Russian experiment in hope. Information was hard to come by, and even harder to interpret. On 2 April Russell wrote to Lady Ottoline:

> I think the Russian Revolution has brought peace much nearer. It seems clear that the Army is on the side of the extremists, and that therefore they can't be suppressed. The "Committee of Soldiers and Workmen" seems to be the supreme power. Also the Army internally is being democratized, with Committees of officers and men in equal numbers to look after discipline. It seems that during the war the Revolutionaries have carried out a secret propaganda which has completely altered the views of peasant soldiers, and made them agree with the urban industrial workers. It is all *wonderful*.[505]

There was little wrong with Russell's factual information, except that the location of supreme power had not been so readily settled, but his belief that everything had been so simply (and presumably permanently) set to rights would seem extraordinary, had it not been shared by such a large proportion of the British liberals and leftists.[506]

In 1915, Russell had denied being a socialist, although he leaned to syndicalism.[507] By early 1916, it will be remembered, this rather fine distinction had disappeared: the ILP conference of April of that year had found him more radical than the official leaders. *Principles of Social Reconstruction* indicated that his belief was still in a decentralised form of socialism, and his antipathy to a too-powerful state was shared by many of his fellow socialists, and particularly by the socialist pacifists who were defying the state. It may be debated whether this dislike of centralised socialism should be seen as simply an untenable residue of liberalism—a failure to come to grips with the real meaning of socialism—or whether a system such as guild socialism represented a plausible alternative form which might have proved viable had it been seriously pursued by enough people. The latter was and continued to be Russell's own view. For him, socialism was unacceptable if it could not be divorced from strong centralised power. In an interview given just before the Russian revolution he had stressed that if the war had done one thing for him it was to make him afraid of the power of the state, and he refused to concede that state socialism, however great a concept, would live up to its promise in actuality. He saw guild socialism, which he linked with the ILP, as combining political and industrial methods and being compatible with individual liberty: sound education of the people's critical faculties would prevent them from being the dupes of the cheap press.[508]

The Russian revolution led Russell to renewed study of various forms of socialism—or, more loosely, of alternatives to the capitalist society. In April 1918, shortly before going to prison, he completed *Roads to Freedom,* a small book in which he described and evaluated state socialism, anarchism, and syndicalism.[509] The views expressed shed light on Russell's reactions to the events of the summer of 1917, and particularly to the Leeds Conference.

In *Roads to Freedom* Russell reiterated his fear that state socialism would lead to a corrupting concentration of power; he spoke of anarchism as the ultimate aim, but not yet within reach; and he recognised that while syndicalism, with its stress on industrial unionism and the class war, had much to contribute, its spirit was too revolutionary for Britain and its ultimate aims too indefinable. Russell declared himself in favour of guild socialism, which he described succinctly:

The Guild Socialists, though some persons in this country regard them as extremists, really represent the English love of compromise. The Syndicalist arguments as to the dangers inherent in the power of the State have made them dissatisfied with old State Socialism, but they are unable to accept the Anarchist view that society can dispense altogether with a central authority. Accordingly they propose that there should be two co-equal instruments of Government in a community, the one geographically representing the consumers, and essentially the continuation of the democratic State;.the other representing the producers, organized, not geographically, but in guilds after the manner of industrial unionism. These two authorities will deal with different classes of questions. Guild Socialists do not regard the industrial authority as forming part of the State, for they contend that it is the essence of the State to be geographical; but the industrial authority will resemble the present State in the fact that it will have coercive powers, and that its decrees will be enforced, when necessary.[510]

Meanwhile, in early 1917, Russell made it his business to keep members of the NCF in touch with what was going on in Russia; for example, at a conference of divisional secretaries with members of the National Committee, held on 20 May, he gave an address on the international situation, dealing at some length with the state of affairs in Russia, and stressing the importance of the revolution to those who stood for liberty as much as for peace.[511] He naturally also welcomed the statement of war aims issued by the Russian Provisional Government in May, under pressure from the Soviet, and the dismissal of Miliukov. The commitment to 'no indemnities, no annexations' was exactly what the pacifists were urging.[512]

At the same time the No-Conscription Fellowship, and particularly Russell, hoped to see energetic action taken by British labour in emulation of the Russian example. The high point for these hopes was the Leeds Convention, called for 3 June 1917. Although its official purpose, like that of the Albert Hall meeting, was simply to welcome the revolution, the resolutions prepared went beyond this, and no one took the event more seriously than Russell. Even if the NCF had no official representation at the gathering, there was no bar to the attendance of Russell and Marshall. Ammon was there as one of the organising committee, and Meynell, who had assisted with the arrangements, was present. Salter was a delegate from the Bermondsey ILP. Constance and Miles Malleson travelled to Leeds with Russell. Delegates came from local Labour Parties (209), trade union organisations (371), ILP branches (294), British Socialist Party branches (88), women's organisations (54), other socialist groups (16), peace societies, UDC branches and other bodies (118).[513]

And so often when he had been deeply stirred, Russell wrote to Ottoline Morrell:

I got back from Leeds yesterday. It was a wonderful occasion, but a little disappointing from the point of view of practical outcomes. Snowden and Macdonald and Anderson are not the right men—they have not the sense for swift dramatic action—the right man would be Williams (of the Transport Workers), but he is not yet sufficiently prominent. Smillie is perfect except that he is old. The enthusiasm and all-but unanimity were wonderful—out of 2500, there were only about three dissentients. Nothing was lacking except leaders.

To my great surprise, they gave me about the greatest ovation that was given to anybody. I got up to speak, and they shouted for me to go on the platform, and when I got there they cheered endlessly. They applauded everything that had to do with C.O.s—Allen's name came up often, and always produced a great cheer. It was a good beginning, but a very great deal remains to be done—Macdonald, whom I travelled down with, was persuaded we should be broken up by soldiers—he has lost his nerve—he does the things, but expects disaster.[514]

Four resolutions were passed at the Conference. The first, moved by Ramsay MacDonald, acclaimed the revolution. The second pledged those present to work for peace without annexations or indemnities, and called upon the British Government to announce its agreement with the war aims and foreign policy announced by the new Russian Government. The third, moved by Ammon, dealt with civil liberties and was exactly on the lines of the 'Charter of Freedom' campaign, urging that Britain should follow Russia's example by introducing universal suffrage, freedom of speech and of the press, freedom from all restrictive labour laws, and a general amnesty for political and religious prisoners. Russell had come determined to speak in support of this resolution,[515] but was one of several to rise at the same time. The

Chairman, Smillie, gave him the floor on the ground that, having once stolen one of Russell's speeches, he needed to make amends. Russell's account of the outstanding reception he received is confirmed by several other accounts. In his short speech, he limited himself strictly to speaking on behalf of the conscientious objectors, stressing the part he considered them to have played in bringing about the 'new state of opinion in this country and the world'.[516] His concern for the conscientious objectors was deep—he had, as he mentioned in his speech, seen Clifford Allen only a few days previously—and as chairman of the NCF he used the few minutes at his disposal to speak to the resolution that concerned them. But he saw their struggle as part of something bigger, and even the Russian revolution as only the beginning of something global. At this time he thought the revolution had restored relevance to the stand of the objectors, though later he came to suspect it had left them behind.

The fourth resolution went far beyond the first three. It was, and has been since, subject to such differences in interpretation that it should be quoted in full:

This conference calls upon the constituent bodies at once to establish in every town, urban and rural district Councils of Workmen's and Soldiers' Delegates for initiating and co-ordinating working-class activity in support of the policy set out in the foregoing resolutions, and to work strenuously for a peace made by the peoples of the various countries, and for the complete political and economic emancipation of international labour. Such Councils shall also watch diligently for and resist every encroachment upon industrial and civil liberty; shall give special attention to the position of women employed in industry, and generally support the work of the trade unions; shall take active steps to stop the exploitation of food and all other necessaries of life, and shall concern themselves with questions affecting the pensions of wounded and disabled soldiers, and for suitable and remunerative work for the men on their return to civil life. And, further, that the conveners of this conference be appointed to a provisional committee, whose duty shall be to assist the formation of local Workmen's and Soldiers' Councils, and generally to give effect to the policy determined by this conference.[517]

The first people to disagree on the meaning of the resolution were its mover and seconder, although in the euphoria of the occasion little attention was drawn to this. Anderson, introducing it, claimed that it was not intended to be subversive or unconstitutional and would not be so unless the attitude of the authorities made it so. Some of the audience apparently felt this a faint-hearted approach. When Russell mentioned his support for Robert Williams of the Transport Workers' Union, who was the seconder of the resolution, he presumably endorsed the latter's far more radical interpretation; Williams declared roundly that if it meant anything, it meant 'the dictatorship of the proletariat'. Parliament, Williams said, had done nothing for the working masses, and never would. The British had to be prepared to revolutionise their constitution just as the Russians had. Still more significantly, he referred to the 'hundreds and thousands' who were represented by the delegates, and he added: 'We want these men to go back to their constituents and convince them to use the power that lies in their hands to give or to withhold their labour in the place where wealth is produced. . . . We want to assert our right to the ownership and control of the country.'[518]

The delegates were in no mood to haggle over words, and it was the more revolutionary utterances which received the loudest applause. No statement was too extreme to be accepted—Sylvia Pankhurst declared that the Provisional Committee appointed at Leeds might one day be the Provisional Government of Great Britain—but there is no doubt that some of those present hugged quietly to themselves a less radical interpretation of the proposals. The fiery but vague wording of the resolution went unchallenged, although few were clear as to how it should be implemented. Russell's recognition that the revolutionary fervour of the day would not be sufficient to ensure action was shrewd.[519]

Secondary accounts of the Leeds Convention have stressed the anomaly of finding Parliamentary constitutionalists of long standing, notably MacDonald, Snowden and Anderson, supporting the final resolution. The anomaly was not as great as it may seem, even without the plausible option of Anderson's interpretation. In the first place, it is an exaggeration to say, as Graubard does, that the resolution created 'extra-parliamentary Soviets with sovereign powers'.[520] It did nothing of the sort. The terms used were revolutionary and were borrowed from the nomenclature in use in Russia, but the proposed Workers' and Soldiers' Councils had no inherent power, and no strategy to bring them any was outlined. Secondly, and in close relation to this, is the curious fact that for all the Marxist and revolutionary rhetoric, not one of the four resolutions demanded more than basic liberal reforms, or foreshadowed any major economic change: there was no formalisation of Williams' suggestion that the workers should go back and take control of the industries in which they worked. This was all the more remarkable in view of the major industrial unrest which had prevailed throughout the preceding month.[521] Thirdly—and this too has been almost totally ignored—there was a sense in which the delegates could fantasise power to their newly-created Soviets without envisaging the total destruction of Parliament. Russell's exposition of guild socialism in *Roads to*

Freedom (quoted on p. 160), makes the concept of dual instruments of government quite clear. It should be remembered too that during this period a comparable duality did in fact exist in Russia between the Duma and the Soviet; and their incompatibility as bedfellows was not yet visible to the eyes of outsiders.

None of this should be interpreted as denying the existence of an out-and-out revolutionary element at Leeds. There were those who wanted the overthrow of the whole system of government and were not particular about the means to be used. And a number of stable and solid citizens, people who had long worked within the existing system, now declared themselves openly in favour of radical change in the whole political and social structure. Russell would certainly have counted himself among these, and his support of Williams indicates that he saw a need for economic change. A few days later he confessed to an interesting dichotomy in his attitude, but only as the extent of desirable change. Writing to accept an invitation to speak to the National Guilds League, he briefly outlined his views and confessed that all his bias and sympathies were with the syndicalists. It was only 'reluctant reason' that compelled him to adopt the milder position of the guild socialist.[522]

Russell's revolutionary mood during the summer of 1917 will bear further examination. In part, it was undoubtedly a reaction from the mood of helplessness and despair in which he had entered the new year. But there was more to it than emotional release. The Russians appeared to have found a way to do all those things that Russell had been crying in the wilderness since the war began. He believed that the revolution not only brought peace nearer but made a totally different kind of peace—a 'people's peace'—possible. At the same time, a complete change in the political, social and economic structure would remove the causes of war and make possible a much more creative and fulfilling life for all. At the end of June, he wrote: 'There seems every hope of a real international spirit throughout Europe, combined with a far more humane economic system. This country and Germany are the most backward, but both show signs of hope.'[523] What was essential was that the revolution should be international and this lent it urgency: if the people of England and Germany did not at once follow the lead of the Russians the opportunity would pass and might not come again for a long time. Russell's revolutionary fervour and also its fading within a few months are both explained by this. When the floodtide passed without advantage being taken of it, the revolutionary approach became no longer possible or relevant, and in March 1918, he wrote:

If the Russian Revolution had been accompanied by a revolution in Germany, the dramatic suddenness of the change might have shaken Europe, for the moment, out of its habits of thought: the idea of fraternity might have seemed, in the twinkling of an eye, to have entered the world of practical politics; and no idea is so practical as the idea of the brotherhood of man, if only people can be startled into believing in it. If once the idea of fraternity between nations were inaugurated with the faith and vigour belonging to a new revolution, all the difficulties surrounding it would melt away, for all of them are due to suspicion and the tyranny of ancient prejudice. Those who (as is common in the English-speaking world) reject revolution as a method, and praise the gradual piece-meal development which (we are told) constitutes solid progress, overlook the effect of dramatic events in changing the mood and the beliefs of whole populations. A simultaneous revolution in Germany and Russia would no doubt have had such an effect, and would have made the creation of a new world possible here and now.

Dis aliter visum: The Millennium is not for our time. The great moment has passed, and for ourselves it is again the distant hope that must inspire us, not the immediate breathless looking for the deliverance. But we have seen what *might* have been, and we know that great possibilities do arise in times of crisis. In some such sense as this, it may well be true that the Socialist revolution is the road to universal peace, and that when it has been traversed all the other conditions for the cessation of wars will grow of themselves out of the changed mental and moral atmosphere.[524]

The sense of urgency that Russell felt in the summer of 1917 must have caused him to set great store by a vigorous pursuit of what had been begun at Leeds. The extent of the follow-up is hard to assess. The facts about what took place at Leeds are well-documented, although, as we have seen, interpretations varied. But when we come to what happened after Leeds, even the facts are in dispute. Graubard says that the people who had 'in a sudden moment of excitement . . . voted to create Soviets in their midst, . . . then promptly forgot to do anything more about it'.[525] Snowden made the remarkable statement that the fourth resolution had been harmless and that nothing had come of it because 'when the Committee which had organised the Conference met afterwards, we considered it was unnecessary to carry out the proposal'.[526] Attributing the failure largely to Lansbury's illness at this time and to the supposed dissolution at Leeds of the Anglo-Russian Democratic Alliance, Postgate claims that although the *Herald* spent yet more of its resources in advertising the programme worked out after the Conference,

there was no organisation behind these demands. No Workers' and Soldiers' Councils were founded, few soldiers even heard of the "Workers' Charter" that was produced, and what action the workers at home took was directed by shop stewards on the Clyde and elsewhere, or by unofficial miners' committees in South Wales.[527]

Postgate is probably correct in his statement that some of the post-Leeds activity merged with the shop stewards' movement, although he is in error in suggesting that the group which had convened the Leeds meeting—whatever name it went by—lost all opportunity for control at that point. And, while the movement projected at Leeds did not last long, some further conferences were held and even a few local Councils or Soviets were formed. It was even claimed that eight battalions of soliders had joined the Council by August.[528] The relationship between the Leeds Conference and the Shop Stewards' and Worker's Committee Movement, with which it might be thought to have so much in common ideologically, and which in fact represented the only hard-core industrial revolutionary element in the country, is of interest, but it need not concern us except in one negative direction: Russell was curiously silent on the subject.

What we shall deal with here is some evidence that the Provisional Committee was not still-born, and with the response made by Russell and the NCF to the attempt to implement the fourth resolution. The Committee was in fact quite active during the weeks following the Convention. By early July, in addition to issuing the finely-produced account of the Leeds meeting, they had divided the country into twelve regions and had planned a divisional conference for each region, to take place between 28 July and 18 August. A local secretary was named for each division; a basis for representation was drawn up; circular letters were sent out; nominations and applications for credentials were called for; and a 'Manifesto to District Conferences' was prepared. These materials bore the signatures of the original thirteen conveners of the Leeds gathering, who of course included Lansbury and Snowden. The address used was again 4 Duke Street, Adelphi.[529]

Russell was involved in furthering the scheme both within the NCF and as an individual. After Leeds he worked at least for a short time on drawing up an outline of the policy they hoped to see adopted, and copies of this were distributed in leaflet form. He was also naturally very concerned to have the NCF adopt an official relationship. There is no evidence as to whether the National Committee had even discussed the Leeds Convention in advance, but once the fourth resolution had been passed the question had to be decided of whether the NCF would seek formal representation on the Workers' and Soldiers' Councils. The National Committee met a few days after Leeds, on 15 and 16 June. Curiously, *The Tribunal* report of this meeting[531] makes no reference to Leeds, although it is reasonable to suppose that those who had been present gave their impressions of the event. If so, the reaction cannot have been discouraging. Even before the next National Committee meeting Russell drafted a letter to branch secretaries encouraging them to be prepared to send delegates to the district conferences, although suggesting they delay final arrangements until after the National Committee meeting, at which the relationship of the Fellowship to the new movement would be considered. The letter, which also included Russell's arguments in favour of the involvement of the NCF, was probably never sent.[532] Instead Russell gave his views in an editorial called 'Pacifism and Economic Revolution' in *The Tribunal* of 5 July. He wrote of the likelihood that the war would not end without revolutionary changes in the structure of society. While violent revolution was unlikely in Britain, he thought there would be profound economic changes. He faced the problem of the pacifist in this situation:

Those who believe at once in pacifism and in a radical change of our economic system are sometimes in doubt as to how far they can co-operate in a movement which, though it is in favour of bringing the war to an end, does not adopt an out-and-out pacifist position, and sometimes allows itself to use language suggesting a spirit of revenge against those who have hitherto been the more fortunate in a worldly sense.

He himself held that belief in the brotherhood of man must lead to a desire for a more just economic system as well as for peace: 'It is impossible to doubt that the abolition of the capitalist would be a tremendous step towards the abolition of war, and ought therefore to be supported, if it becomes feasible, by those who aim at establishing a secure peace throughout the world.' He did not think pacifists should be deterred from participation by the fear that such movements might lead to class war and violence. Rather, they should exert all their influence on the side of a peaceful approach. The methods of ordinary industrial disputes would suffice.[533]

By the time the National Committee met again, on 13 to 15 July, the Provisional Committee appointed at Leeds had already issued its call to the district conferences, and these were due to begin before the end of July. Arguments for and against NCF participation were canvassed and the decision to recommend branches to appoint delegates was reached by only the narrowest possible margin—the resolution in favour of representation, moved by Neil McLean and seconded by Ernest Hunter, a young man now working at the head office, was passed by six votes to five. The argument against it—summarised in an amendment moved by Jones, seconded by Alexander Wilson (a northern Quaker), and defeated by the same margin—was that the NCF had a particular function, and should not identify itself with a movement whose programme 'must involve proposals of an economic, political and social character to which the organisation as such does not necessarily subscribe'.534 Unfortunately there is no record of the names of those voting for and against. Russell may have been disappointed that he could not carry the whole Committee with him, but that the resolution passed at all is a reminder of the extent to which it was still possible to believe that revolution throughout the civilised world could be carried out without violence. Within a few days of the meeting, a circular was sent to the branches recommending them to support the movement and appoint delegates to the coming Workers' and Soldiers' Councils.535

On the same weekend, the Executive Committees of the Friends' Service Committee and the No-Conscription Fellowship, and the Conscription Committee of the Fellowship of Reconciliation met, 'to consider their relation to Internationalist movements for freedom'. Rather than issuing a joint manifesto, the committees put forth together individual statements by four of the leaders. The approach suggests that agreement was hard to reach on anything but general principle, and yet that they were close enough together to be anxious to avoid anything giving the appearance of controversy or discouraging to the frail nascent international movement. No concrete proposals were made, and the statements differ mainly in emphasis. Barratt Brown, for the Friends' Service Committee, wrote on 'Revolution and Non-Resistance: An Appeal for an Unarmed Revolution'. He directed his appeal to the possessors of power and property, calling on them to 'help to prepare a bloodless revolution by not resisting the people's aspirations', and he appealed to the soldiers and workers to unite and organise to achieve a revolution by the methods of non-resistance. Edith M. Ellis, also of the FSC, wrote on the contribution of the conscientious objectors to the movement for freedom. Henry Hodgkin of the Fellowship of Reconciliation wrote of the need for a peace based on freedom and brotherhood, and resting on the will of the peoples. He stressed that the war had shown that armed force was no way of achieving ideals, and that there was a need to unite with all those in all lands whose goal was the same. Russell's contribution on behalf of the NCF was entitled 'Pacifism and Revolution'. His argument was similar to that contained in his editorial of 5 July, but he laid still more emphasis on the positive outcome to be hoped for, stressing that the essence of the new spirit was the demand for liberty and life, and full development. This, he wrote, was exactly what the pacifists stood for:

Those who have the love of what is living will wish to see others develop freely, according to the capacities of their nature; they will suffer when they see others treated as parts of a great machine, in which the individual human spirit counts for nothing, or when they see the life of a slave made subservient to the power or glory of a master. And so they will be led to oppose all forms of tyranny, whether that of armies and navies, or that of the rich over the poor, or that of men over women, or even that of the criminal law, except where it can clearly be proved that the law is necessary and the punishment not harmful to the "criminal".

He spoke again of the need to oppose the power of the landowner and the capitalist, but in an un-Marxian climax he claimed that 'the success of revolution depends always on the power of new ideas over men's minds'. He claimed the pacifists had a particular task in 'keeping the spirit of the new movement creative of good rather than merely destructive of evil'.

The pamphlet containing these statements was issued as a supplement to *The Tribunal* of 19 July 1917, and although stocks were quite rapidly exhausted, efforts were made to have it taken to as many as possible of the district conferences of the Workers' and Soldiers' Councils.[536]

Little further comment on Russell's views is needed here, except to draw attention to the unity of thought between writing such as this and his earlier intellectual analysis of the principles on which a better world could be built, given in *Principles of Social Reconstruction* and *Political Ideals*. Perhaps it is in the more emotional journalistic appeals that we can most clearly see a kind of dualism in Russell's attitude. Intellectually, he was an international socialist, seeing as essential the abolition of capitalism and the redistribution of economic power, together with the destruction of militarism and bureaucracy. Emotionally and methodologically, however, he was still—or again—a liberal, believing in progress, in the maximum of personal liberty, in the power of ideas, and that reason will prevail.

July and August 1917 marked the peak of revolutionary fervour. The district conferences were eagerly anticipated in some circles. Russell cherished a hope of being elected to the Council of Workers. Hopes of a pacifist international revolutionary movement were still high at the time of the Inter-Allied Socialist Conference in London on 28 August. The NCF prepared a budget of material for the delegates and a special letter of greeting for those from Russia. Russell, together with Smillie, Marshall and Hunter, attended a small private meeting with the delegates from Russia—which was described as 'fruitful' (but unfortunately the fruit was not specified).[537]

Probably the response to the workers' conferences was dissappointing.[538] The difference, papered over at Leeds, became apparent between the aims of the extreme left (represented by the British Socialist Party), who really willed power to the Workers' Council, and the aims of the established leaders of the Independent Labour Party, who were content to have the movement cool into just another propaganda organisation.[539] But the Councils were seen as enough of a threat to meet with organised opposition from right-wing groups on some occasions. The riot at the Southgate Brotherhood Church on 28 July, which Russell described in his autobiography, was preceded by the posting of notices in local public houses inciting the violence. It was often difficult to obtain a hall for such a meeting because of the danger of having it wrecked, which the National Council of Civil Liberties claimed was part of the deliberate policy of the right-wing British Workers' League and the Anti-German Union. These groups were also reputed to keep 'a perfectly well-known band of bullies for the purpose of breaking up meetings and wrecking halls', and to make use of anonymous leaflets, threats over the telephone and forged tickets for the same purposes. The NCCL claimed that although this activity was well-known, few arrests were made. In a letter to Lady Ottoline, Russell gave an account of his experience at the Brotherhood Church, even more vivid than the story in his autobiography. Russell's description of the effect of the incident on him differs—he does not seem, as he claimed in the later version, to have gone home 'in a mood of deep dejection'. On the contrary, he wrote to Lady Ottoline:

I got shaken out of the mood of doubt and depression I was in by the events at our meeting this afternoon which was broken up. A vast crowd of roughs and criminals (paid) led, or rather guided from behind, by a few merely foolish soldiers (Colonials) broke in—it was only due to great self-restraint on the part of the delegates that there was no bloodshed. There were two utterly bestial women with knotted clubs, who set to work to thwack all the women of our lot that they could get at—the roughs had horrible degraded faces. The crowd outside as we were leaving was very fierce—several women had almost all their clothes torn off their backs. But absolutely no one showed the faintest trace of fear. Most women would have been terrified, but ours were not even flustered.

I realized vividly how ghastly the spirit of violence is, and how utterly I repudiate it, on whatever side it may be. The mob is a terrible thing when it wants blood.

The young soldiers were pathetic, thinking we were their enemies. They all believed we were in the pay of the Kaiser.

At one moment they all made a rush at me, and I was in considerable danger—but a woman (I don't know who) hurled herself between me and them—they hesitated to attack her—and then the police appeared. She showed wonderful courage.

I found the whole thing bracing. I realized that there are things I believe in and that it is worth living for—love, gentleness, and understanding.[540]

A few days later Frank Russell wrote that he had met Marshall, who had recounted 'with great glee' the story Russell later used in the autobiography of how the police had rescued him not because of his own fame and distinction, but because he was the brother of an earl. Frank, as the earl who so often found himself in the shadow of his younger brother, described it with relish as 'a very humiliating story' and added, 'The story is deliciously grotesque, and I can quite imagine it to be true; at any rate I intend to believe it'.[541]

Instead of being a step to greater things, as Russell so much hoped, the conferences to set up the Workers' and Soldiers' Councils seem to have marked the beginning of the end, and within a few months the whole movement faded from existence, except where, as suggested above, some elements of it merged into the stronger Workers' and Shop Stewards' movement. Russell is not known to have commented on the passing of something of which he had had such high hopes, but in a sense the more moderate and evolutionary approach of *Roads to Freedom* was his epitaph for it. He had been a revolutionary only for those few heady months when it seemed that revolution might overturn the world and make a new beginning possible.

CHAPTER 12

TROUBLE AT THE DARTMOOR HOME OFFICE CAMP

Once the National Committee had come to terms with the fact that a large majority of the members of the Fellowship were accepting the Home Office scheme, they strove loyally to give them the support they needed,[542] although the new Committee of 1917 was almost as overwhelmingly absolutist in the personal convictions of its members as had been the earlier one: alternativists must have continued to vote for absolutist leaders. The exceptions were few. C. H. Norman not only accepted work under the scheme, but was as militant about it as he was about everything else he did. Morgan Jones described himself as having evolved from being an absolutist to being an alternativist, but he specifically dissociated himself from Norman's views, and does not appear to have taken much part in any controversy, although he was anxious to explain himself.[543] These two were the only members of the National Committee who were themselves working under the scheme, and possibly the only Committee members who felt this would have been the right choice for themselves.

The position of the Home Office men was psychologically uncomfortable. The fact was that few people respected them. Although many were completely sincere in their acceptance of this form of service, and all were doing what the Government had proposed for them and had encouraged them to do, they were officially treated as something between criminals and badly-behaved soldiers. A trade union leader who met with William Brace, chairman of the Government committee supervising the work, reported that Brace 'showed . . . hatred and contempt for the men who accepted the scheme', an attitude which Marshall also found in other officials connected with the work.[544] The whole tone of the Brace Committee's final official report reflected the same feeling.[545] Within their own organisation the men were often defensive; some clearly found it difficult even to like themselves, and these were always painfully seeking self-justification or adopting an aggressive stance.

In this difficult situation, the National Committee under Russell's chairmanship made itself carefully sensitive to what was going on in the camps, although full communication was not always easy. There was an obvious danger in relying on unofficial personal letters, which continued to arrive in some volume. A plan to hold a conference with members of the National Committee and camp secretaries on 10 December 1916 had fallen through because of a ban on weekend leave imposed by the Home Office.[546] The new Committee set out instead to go to the camps, and a successful series of visits was made during the first few months of 1917, in which Russell took an active part.[547] As a result of his journey to Wakefield on 7 March, the National Committee discussed other ways of getting into closer touch with the Home Office men. It was decided that *The Tribunal* would give publicity to serious grievances, that is, 'to such as involve questions of principle or grave injury to health'. Such matters would also be further publicised by questions in Parliament and releases to the press. Russell felt a personal responsibility towards the members in the camps, and sought to establish a correspondence with the camp secretaries, on a weekly basis if possible, 'so as himself to be informed of events in Camps, and to be able to give advice if desired; also to submit questions of principle to the National Committee when asked to do so'.[548] Although Russell undertook this in his capacity as acting chairman, he himself was to do the work involved. In the event the response was less than had been hoped for.

The wide general decision as to the kind of grievances in which the men could be supported had of course to be followed by a number of minor decisions. For example, men sent out from the Home Office settlements to work under private employers often concluded they were being used to free other men for military service. The National Committee, which agreed with the need to avoid this, accordingly upheld those who might resist this type of service, and also was prepared to 'do all in its power to induce the Home Office not to send men back to prison or the Army for refusing private employment'.[549] Action was also taken on behalf of individuals, where their complaints seemed to be justified: this covered a wide range of different cases.

The question of most concern to Russell and the National Committee was that of 'slacking' in the Home Office camps. From the outset there had been talk in some quarters of a deliberate policy of working inefficiently and as little as possible as a way of sabotaging the whole scheme: proponents mostly regarded the scheme as in no way a release from military service,

but as an alternative form of imprisonment. The policy was hard
to justify on pacifist grounds, since it made no appeal to the public
conscience. Its avowed purpose of wrecking the Military Service
Acts was consistent with a revolutionary ideology, but not,
strictly speaking, with the non-violent revolutionary concept
adopted by most of the anti-militarist leaders, and it was anathema
to all the National Committee, with the exception of Norman.
The Committee had anxiously discussed the question during
1916, but had delayed issuing a letter on the subject. On 3 March
1917, after further discussion, Russell finally sent out a statement
from the National Committee. Several policy questions were
covered, but by far the most important was 'the question as to
what obligations are created by the undertaking which is signed,
or understood to be accepted, before release from prison'. From a
legal point of view, the memorandum declared that it could
hardly be maintained that any obligation was created, because the
men were not free when they signed, and because the authorities
retained the power to send a man back to prison if they were not
satisfied he was fulfilling the conditions laid down. The moral
question, however, was more complex, and the argument for
rejecting this form of resistance was developed at some length:

There are some men in the Home Office Camps, who, believing the whole
scheme to be bad, advocate the policy of defeating it by evading work as far as
possible. This policy appears to the National Committee to be open to objections
of the same kind as those which we should feel against a policy of joining the
Army with a view to undermining discipline. We feel that, in signing the
undertaking, men subject themselves to an honourable obligation either to carry
out its provisions to the best of their ability, or to announce to the authorities that
they no longer intend to carry out its provisions and are prepared to accept the
consequences. Part of the undertaking is "to serve the Committee . . . [*sic*] with
diligence and fidelity on such work of National Importance as the Committee
shall prescribe for me." It seems to us that, since they are granted release from
prison as a result of giving this promise, a man binds himself to work as well as
he would work for an ordinary employer. Those who wish to defeat the whole
scheme, if they are to act in the same spirit in which the N-C.F. has acted as
regards military service, will be bound—so it seems to us—to regard the
undertaking in the same light in which we regard the Military Oath, as
something which must be refused just because it creates an obligation which we
are not prepared to fulfil. Apart from the question of the moral justification of
giving an undertaking without intending to fulfil it, we feel that the effect upon
public opinion of a policy of evading work would be so bad as to cause serious
damage to the whole movement.[550]

There is no means of knowing how widespread was the
deliberate slacking abhorred by Russell, or whether those who
shirked were members of the NCF or not. But immediately after
the memorandum was issued, the tension surrounding the ques-

tion was greatly heightened by two occurrences. The first of these was the concentration of a large number of men at the prison at Princetown, on Dartmoor; and the second was a virulent series of attacks against the Home Office men made in the local and national press.

For the Government, the appeal of the Dartmoor settlement must surely have been that it would account for a large number of the men who had accepted the Home Office scheme and who were proving so difficult to place in situations which they would accept and which would not be objectionable to one or other influential body of public opinion. In the last two weeks of March 1917, nearly 1000 men were sent to Princetown, mostly from Wakefield and Warwick, where they had already had experience under the scheme, or direct from Wormwood Scrubs.

Letters arriving at head office gradually enabled Russell to form a picture of the setting and conditions. On arrival, the men found themselves the occupants of a huge convict prison, standing in a village set high in the middle of the moor and seven hilly miles from even the small market town of Tavistock. In the other direction a narrow-gauge railway wound through the hills to the village of Yelverton, where connections could be made for Plymouth. Apart from chores within the prison, and a few indoor industries such as bootmaking, the work was mainly agricultural. Many welcomed the opportunity to work outdoors. Initially, a certain amount of self-government was encouraged: this at once raised a question of principle. While many felt the measure of self-control removed what had been one of the major objections to the scheme, and would make it much less demoralising, others, among them Norman, claimed such co-operation would simply be helping to administer the Military Service Acts.[551] Before this had time to become a real issue, Home Office policy changed and the men found themselves doing all their work under the direction of prison warders, so that they were back with the former question of whether to work well or to slack.

It was even more interesting to Russell to learn how the men were responding to the new situation. As they came in, they fell into different groups. Those described by one NCF correspondent as 'the members of the "strange religions"' kept themselves to themselves and did their work; they were mostly convinced alternativists and in many instances averse to playing any part in self-government. Few of these were members of the NCF. Other convinced alternativists such as the Quaker, Howard C. Marten, were not apolitical and were willing to take an active part on the Men's Committee, and in organising whatever activities would make for the most satisfying life as long as they should have to stay there.[552] Then there was a group, with leadership mainly from men who had been previously at the Warwick settlement, who opposed co-operation. Their policy was not precisely defined, but it was closer to a 'go-slow' or 'work-to-rule' movement than to an overt work-strike, which would of course have quickly put them back in prison. Norman led this faction. However well he could justify his position ideologically, it can hardly be doubted that among his following were found, in addition to some sincere men, those whose integrity was weakest and those who had been rendered desperate or cynical by imprisonment or by their previous experience under the Home Office scheme. Aylmer Rose believed the scheme itself was the greatest corrupter:

> To my observation the Warwick faction is composed of political wreckers, professed alternativists who have become so cynical in their outlook as to startle me by their unlikeness to the C.O.s they once were, and slackers of all varieties and grades. ... The Scrubs men are all—or almost all—genuinely desirous of doing real work and earning the alleviations granted them from prison by abiding by the terms of their contract. But this wretched scheme seems to have as terrible a power of corrupting men as the Army itself, and the contrast as regards cynicism between a "Scrubs man" and a "Warwick man" is scarcely less noticeable than that between a new recruit and an old soldier as regards language. It seems to me that the attitude taken up towards the work under the scheme by a large section of the men here, and by the Warwick leaders, must result in permanent injury to character.[553]

Rose, the former organising secretary of the NCF, was in a different position from any of the main groups. He was a convinced absolutist, but his short stay in Wormwood Scrubs—he had only been arrested in January 1917—had, he thought, completely broken him up. He went back to prison later, when he had regained his health and equilibrium, and he began his third sentence as late as 23 February 1919.[554] But meanwhile he felt obligated to do the best he could in what was for him a very painful position.

Russell, to whom Marshall showed this letter, responded to it with great warmth:

> I should like to say how fully I agree with your point of view. I think the point of view of Norman and those who try to wreck the scheme by not working lamentable, very bad for them, and very damaging to the cause of the C.O. generally. This is, as you know, the opinion of the Committee, and we are glad it should be known in the Camps. ... Perhaps Norman's influence may wane after a time. Wakefield seems now fairly satisfactory. I rather believe in the usefulness of study circles to keep alive the interest in general politics and the wider problems of pacifism. I deplore the cynicism of the men, which has struck me in the Camps I have visited. No doubt it comes of having no opportunity of doing anything that they feel to be worth doing. This is one point of view from which a

study of pacifist literature might do good. I think we are conscious of the different currents of opinion in the Camps, but it is difficult to do much, because we are suspect both to the men and to the authorities. Let us know if you see anything we can do.

Russell concluded his letter with a reassurance that must have been important to Rose: 'I was very sorry indeed that your health broke down; I did not feel critical under the circumstances.'[555]

Russell made several attempts to make arrangements to visit the Dartmoor settlement, but throughout April Norman found reasons to delay the visit.[556] Meanwhile, the situation became worse. Conditions were harsh, with long hours of work and a scant diet: food was scarce, as indeed it was for all Britain in that spring and early summer of 1917. But most seriously, the work proved to be anything but work of national importance. The prison farm was organised and equipped with the sole purpose of keeping men occupied at hard and heavy penal labour. The maximum of work for the minimum of production was the criterion, rather than the other way around. Men spent three weeks digging a field (with overweight spades) which might have been ploughed in three days, and sixteen men occupied in crushing oats with antiquated machinery produced six bags a day.[557]

The situation of the Dartmoor men was exacerbated by a wave of public feeling against them. Locally, this seems to have begun spontaneously. Within a few days of their arrival, a group of COs were attacked in Tavistock, and later others were waylaid at Yelverton.[558] Marines took part in the attack in Tavistock, and two of the COs were hospitalised for several days. Naturally there were problems in assimilating a thousand unorthodox young men at a time when young men out of uniform were seldom seen. But the hostility was fanned and perpetuated by wide publicity in an influential section of the national and local press. During the early days some of the men had been issued with free railway passes, and this and the lack of organised occupation during the first few weeks of the settlement formed the basis for some of the early complaints. But the attack soon widened to take in every aspect of their treatment and behaviour. The following were typical of the headlines: 'Princetown's Pampered Pets'; 'Objector's Holiday: Concert, Moor Walks and Rides, and Refreshments'; 'C.Os at Princetown: Laziness and Deliberate Slackness the Rule'; 'Pampered Conscientious Objectors'; 'Shirkers of Work and Duty: the Egoists and Idlers of Princetown'; 'C.Os Cosy Club'; 'Coddled Conscience Men'.[559]

The amount of space devoted to the attack throughout the month of April suggests a planned campaign on the part of the press. Whether there was any motivation behind it other than general newsworthiness and the acceptability of a scapegoat during those months of food shortages, heavy casualty lists, and the final comb-out of men who had previously held exemption, is hard to establish. The whole position of the conscientious objector was under discussion by the Government at the time, and there were those who were anxious to see that this did not result in further leniency. Norman at the time, and Graham later, held that a deliberate effort was even made to goad or to trick the objectors into a violent outbreak that would morally vitiate their cause as well as making reprisals possible.[560]

The practical hardships suffered by the men as a result of the press campaign were both direct and indirect. The vicar of Walkhampton, a small hamlet some five miles from Princetown, was among those whose letters in the local press could be described as a deliberate incitement to violence against the Dartmoor men, and when five of the conscientious objectors attended evening service there, his flock showed their discipleship by attacking them after the service.[561] Within a few weeks many of the privileges originally granted had been withdrawn. The men were forbidden to travel by railway, or indeed to visit any of the towns and villages on the moor outside of Princetown itself. How rigidly these rules were enforced is hard to tell: certainly they were circumvented at times. Norman managed to be in London for a meeting of the National Committee on 15 June and (perhaps understandably) wrote angrily to Russell when *The Tribunal* of 21 June published his name in a list of those present.[562]

The press attacks were of course linked with the whole question of deliberate shirking, and made the National Committee even more anxious to have the men in the camps adopt a firm stand against this policy. In addition to issuing the letter of 3 March giving their views, Russell and other Committee members had particularly directed their attention to the question on their visits to the camps, and believed they had made some progress in sounding out and influencing opinion wherever they had been able to go; but at the end of April, relations between Dartmoor and the National Committee took a sharp turn for the worse. On 26 April Marshall was told by General Childs over the telephone that the authorities had some incriminating documents which might prove very dangerous to the NCF. He said he thought she should know the facts, but he could not discuss them over the telephone, so Marshall went to see him at the War Office in the afternoon. After she had made it clear she must be free to take what action she thought necessary as a result of whatever information he might see fit to give her, he read part of a letter from a Dartmoor man claiming that his part of the fight was to do his utmost to make the scheme a farce and to cost the Home Office as much as possible by systematic slacking.[563] General Childs said he did not know whether this policy was advocated by the No-Conscription Fellowship, but he considered it dishonourable, and he pointed out that it afforded considerable justification for the attacks being made in the press and in Parliament.

Marshall was aware that the treatment of conscientious objectors was under review, and she knew also, of course, that the accusations about slacking were not unfounded.

She felt that under the circumstances, whilst it was taking a great responsibility to inform Gen. Childs of the views of the National Committee, it would be a still greater responsibility to leave him in any doubt as to what the National Committee's view was on the point, which had been fully discussed and deliberately decided on by them. She felt sure that the National Committee would wish to state the facts. To wait to do this until after the next meeting of the Committee would have looked as if the Committee were criticising the "slacking" policy *as a result of the Home Office and Press attacks*—an unfortunate impression to create.

Miss Marshall therefore told Gen. Childs (1) that the National Committee did not support the policy described in the letter he quoted; (2) that they had told their Camp members so some time ago; (3) that she believed that only a small minority of men in the camps advocated that policy, and that most of those who did were not members of the N.-C.F. or the F.S.C. or the F.O.R.[564]

Although it was not widely known at the time (and seemed improbable to some who heard the rumour) the Cabinet member who was particularly interested in finding a new solution to the problem of the conscientious objectors was Lord Milner (whose godson, Stephen Hobhouse, had inconveniently turned Quaker and pacifist), and Marshall was in communication with his secretary, Major Thornton. She had seen him on 26 April, before her visit to the War Office. After her talk with Childs, she considered it wise to write to Thornton in order to clear up in his mind any doubt as to the attitude of the National Committee towards deliberate slacking in the Home Office camps.[565]

Because of their discomfort about the situation at Dartmoor, Russell and Marshall may indeed have welcomed the opportunity to make the official NCF position known to the Government. The new development seemed to them sufficiently serious that they called a special meeting of the London members of the National Committee on 1 May,[566] to discuss all aspects of the question: conditions in the camps; the attacks of the press; the policy of slacking; and Marshall's statements to the authorities, which they unanimously endorsed.[567]

Although the meeting seems to have gone smoothly, it was a time of tension for the executive. Russell and Marshall quarrelled seriously later the same day, apparently about what seemed to him her fault-finding and nagging in the office. Russell found Marshall at this time intolerably carping and critical, but he does not seem to have been able to respond with open anger. Instead, he became more and more convinced of his own inadequacy, and in his turn increasingly critical—but in the main silently so—of her faults. After their quarrel on 1 May she wrote him a letter of apology,[568] and he replied with a long, thoughtful and highly critical letter, which he did not mail but did not throw away. It might have been helpful to both of them for her to have received it. Russell put his finger on Marshall's contribution to the state of tension, and also revealed unconsciously a great deal about the nature of his own response.

> I agree entirely that we *must* learn to work together without mutual irritation.
> I am painfully conscious of my own shortcomings. It is difficult in middle age to take up work requiring wholly different habits of mind from those that one has practised hitherto. I dislike the work so much that I should be overjoyed if I could have a painful and dangerous illness from now till the end of the war. But that is neither here nor there.
> I do not think you are equally conscious of your shortcomings, and I think if you were it would be a good thing. You seem to me to have a wrong conception of how to get work out of people. You try to do it by fault-finding, which is really a militarist method. My chief trouble is forgetfulness, which is entirely due to mental fatigue. Repeatedly, after you have been scolding me, I have hardly slept a wink all night (that happened again the night before last), which makes me more tired and therefore more forgetful. Also your manner of fault-finding fills one with despair, which simply makes one want to give up the work altogether. It is not only I who feel this: every one at the office feels the same, except Miss Rinder. After you have been criticising, I have to go round consoling, and persuading people that they are not so incompetent that they ought to retire. I know this way of treating people is against your principles, and if you can become conscious of it you will amend. Your present way of treating us all is paralyzing, and is one of the reasons we are not more full of initiative. . . .
> We all have faults; you yourself have a good deal of the faults you mind in us. . . .
> But I am saying all this because I think it is only hurry and anxiety that has led you into these habits, not anything deep-seated and incurable.
> I will give you an illustration of what I mean. Your way of treating General Childs has obviously been very successful: you knew you had no *power* over him, and you gradually led him on by gentle steps. Now he has developed further than any one would have thought possible. But your method of treating us is quite different, because instinctively you regard us as subject to your authority. The feeling of authority is one which a pacifist should root out from his instincts. I feel your answer, which will be to point out the need of efficiency. But that seems to me in essence the same as the argument that "we must get on with the war". Many ways of getting efficiency are incompatible with respect for human beings.[569]

The point about pacifism and the nature of authority is a problem inherent in pacifist idealism and practice, and returns to bedevil peace movements wherever they occur. The question of authority continued to exercise Russell.[570] But of more relevance to the conflict between Russell and Marshall is the rest of the quoted passage which shows him as responding with feelings of inadequacy and depression to a situation that could perhaps have been more appropriately handled with anger or outspokenness. He was in error in believing all found her as difficult to work with as he did,[571] and almost certainly he was wrong in thinking his chief trouble was forgetfulness; more probably, far more difficulty was caused by his willingness to believe himself inadequate and by his inability to face the confrontations called for. His letters to Lady Constance Malleson[572] also reveal that during this time he was much preoccupied with his relationship with her, and subject to intense swings of mood as it alternately prospered and faltered.

The misery of the conflict between Russell and Marshall was in some ways increased by the fact that the two seldom differed on major policy issues and continued to share a clear concept of what they wanted the Fellowship to be. Allen, aware of the problem, wrote begging Russell to make Marshall successful by bearing with the things that angered him, because he believed that she could do for the movement what very few others could.[573] How far their differences were resolved on this occasion is not known, but on about 4 May Marshall left for a few days' much needed break, although she took work with her.

On the day after the special meeting of the London Committee members, Russell wrote a letter to the full National Committee, which read in part:

> You will have seen the attacks which have occurred in the Press, of which a brief summary is enclosed. It was felt [at the special meeting of the London members of the National Committee] that there is a difficulty in defending the men under the Home Office against these attacks so long as the policy of deliberate slacking is pursued, and that it would be desirable to issue at once to the Camps a letter reiterating in stronger language our previous advice against this policy.

Russell went on to mention Marshall's response to Childs' inquiry, and the Committee's support of it. With no attempt to explain the relevance, the letter then gave an account, derived from the camp *News Sheet* (no. 6), of the meeting between a group of Home Office officials and the men's representatives at Dartmoor. The purpose of including this description is not quite clear, but the grievances listed on that occasion seemed decidedly picayune. The first was 'That the jam is not good'. Only four of the thirteen points could, by the most generous stretch of the imagination, be considered matters of principle.

A draft of the new letter to the camps was also enclosed, for the approval and comment of the members of the National Committee, although Russell was careful to make it plain that no final decision to send such a letter had been arrived at. He also pointed out that the question as to whether the content of the letter, or its general purport, should be allowed to become public would have to be discussed at the next meeting of the National Committee. The draft letter took a firm line, reiterating and reinforcing the arguments which had been made in the 3 March letter and repeatedly by Russell in correspondence with men at the camps.[574]

The material on the Committee meeting of 1 May was sent out with dispatch. As Norman was a member of the National Committee, it was in his hands by 3 May, and there was an immediate uproar. It is difficult to do justice to Norman's position in the dispute. He was not unprincipled, though he may have been disillusioned and sometimes self-deceived. A letter of 29 April to Marshall, written before he had knowledge of her interview with Childs, shows that he sincerely believed a move was a foot to take away all exemptions from the conscientious objectors.[575] He believed that by denying there was any essential difference between those who remained in prison as absolutists and those who continued their resistance under what he regarded as the penal system of the Home Office camps, he was strengthening the unity of the movement for the renewed struggle. Ideologically, also, he was a Marxist revolutionary, and his vision of the struggle for a better world was much more stark than that of such a man as Russell.[576]

But even if one makes an effort to understand Norman's motivation, his methods were hard to justify and his manner aggressive and provocative. Immediately Russell's letter came, he called a meeting of NCF men at the Dartmoor settlement, and read aloud to them parts of it and of the draft letter. He wrote angrily to Marshall and to Russell, and, despite a telegram from Russell pointing out that the documents were confidential, he referred to them again in an extremely critical article, 'The NCF Executive and the Home Office Men', which appeared in issue number seven of the *News Sheet*, which was probably just going to press. In all these statements Norman misunderstood or wilfully misrepresented the actions of Marshall and the Committee. It was true that he had opposed the circulation of the letter of 3 March, but he now claimed that his objection had been to its publication only and not to its content:

As there is practically no deliberate slacking in the Camps, certainly not among members of the N.C.F., the present writer objected vigorously to the issue of any such letter as the letter of the 3rd March. . . . One motive in protesting against the letter . . . being issued was a certain belief that it would come to the knowledge of the authorities or the Press, and might be the means of damaging the whole movement.

This claim, suggesting—although not explicitly stating—that Norman had no quarrel with the intent of the letter, is quite inconsistent with what is known of his position, and even with the tone of his statement in the same article that: 'Certain members of the Executive went careering round the Home Office Camps preaching the doctrine of submission to the Home Office.' Norman went on to criticise the indiscretion of the National Committee at camp meetings and much more specifically that of Marshall in her dealings with the authorities, laying the blame on these indiscretions for the entire press campaign against the Home Office men.[577]

Norman's polemics aroused great indignation against the National Committee, with Russell and Marshall being the main butts. A letter from an objector called Wood to a member of his NCF branch well illustrates the distortion:

The position is rather critical just now, we now know for certain that the Government is behind this Press campaign, and that Lord Milner has been deputed to bring out a fresh scheme. I am afraid it will not be very favourable from such a man as that. . . . You know no doubt that all our leave is stopped and that we are confined to Princetown. We had a meeting here last evening of the N.-C.F. and our members are very indignant at the action of the National Committee in attacking us down here. It seems that information against us has been supplied to General Childs by Miss Marshall and Bertrand Russell and that it is intended to make public a letter accusing us of not acting fair to the Scheme. We passed a resolution condemning their action and inviting them down here to see things for themselves before they take any further action in the matter and wreck the whole movement. It is distinctly unfair of the National Committee to take the step they have without hearing our side; there is a bias in favour of the absolutists we know, but seeing that the majority of the men have accepted the Scheme, the Committee ought at least to give us fair play. We have enough to put up with without the N.-C.F. turning against us. The general charge of slacking as laid down by the National Committee is absolutely untrue: I admitted to you weeks ago, that a few men are trying to wreck the Scheme but most of these men have been shifted and there is no slacking worth talking about now. . . . It is rather strange, but it appears that this Press campaign was started almost immediately after Miss Marshall's statement to General Childs. I can assure you there is a strong feeling here about it.[578]

The NCF secretary at Dartmoor also wrote to Russell and to Marshall, telling of the resolution passed at the meeting, which deplored the communication to the Government and declared the men's belief that the National Committee was not only misinformed but had made little effort to find out. Russell, Marshall and Salter were urged to visit Dartmoor at once, and it was hoped that the Committee would meanwhile refrain from making any more such statements. Russell, with justification, found the imputation of lack of interest particularly irritating, and wrote back coldly: 'You have evidently forgotten that ever since Princetown camp was formed, I have been endeavouring to arrange a meeting there, at which I could get in touch with you.'[579] The crisis kept Russell busy answering the letters from Dartmoor, and with the greatest reluctance, he also decided he must break into Marshall's short holiday, which she was spending at Kynance Cove, Cornwall. He wrote to her:

I cannot say how sorry I am to interrupt your holiday, but a situation has arisen which only you can deal with. Norman has fastened on the fact that you told the authorities our attitude about slacking (as to which I don't see how you could have done otherwise), has magnified and distorted it, and has set the whole of Princetown ablaze. Only you can state authoritatively what really occurrred, and prove to the men that they have not been sold.[580]

He enclosed a dossier of relevant documents, forwarded by express the letter that Norman had written to her, and urged her to spend the night of 9 May at Princetown on her way back to London. He also sent her a cable, but by the time all this reached her it was too late for her to make the visit, since she had to be back the next day to meet Clifford Allen, once more between prison sentences. Although she wrote at once to Norman, and promised to visit as soon as she could, Russell considered the matter too urgent to wait and left immediately for Dartmoor himself, in time to hold a meeting on the evening of 9 May.

The meeting of 9 May was crucial, and was a remarkable achievement on Russell's part, for which he has never been given credit.[581] It turned out to be in fact a confrontation with Norman on his own ground, from which Russell emerged the clear victor, and able to suggest a positive solution which led to improved understanding between the National Committee and the men. The only account of the meeting is one written by Russell and circulated presumably to members of the National Committee.

On arrival at Dartmoor, Russell had about an hour's conversation with Norman, Rose, Smith and Mayers, who were all members of the executive of the Dartmoor branch of the NCF. Later about twenty men gathered, who appeared to Russell to be fairly representative of all factions. What followed is best given in Russell's own words:

I made a statement justifying the Committee, and (in particular) Miss Marshall's communications to the authorities. As Norman had been suggesting that these were of a nefarious character, I read Miss Marshall's extracts from her letter to Major Thornton. I argued that the authorities know that there has been some slacking, and do not know of any friction between the National Committee and the H.O. Camps, and that her statement was calculated to make the authorities think C.O.s as a rule are opposed to slacking, which, according to Norman, is the fact, and is what he wishes the authorities to think, since his charge against Miss Marshall was that her action was likely to have the opposite effect.

I then said that those who live in an isolated community are not in a good position for judging questions of policy depending on public opinion. I said I would not enter upon the question of principle in relation to slacking, since they repudiated the practice; but I would ask them to take some definite step, such as a resolution in Camp meeting, to express definitely their rejection of the policy of slacking. This, I said, would make it much easier for us to help them, as we were most anxious to do. Finally, I begged them to believe in our sincerity, and to dismiss utterly from their minds the notion that we wished to benefit absolutists at their expense.

Norman spoke next. He repeated old charges of the unfairness of the Tribunal. He said that but for his opposition the autumn letter to the Camps would have gone out; and but for him this new letter would have gone out. He pointed out that the National Committee think acceptance of the H.O. Scheme has let down absolutists, and that Rose had said so in the Tribunal. He repeated the charge that the H.O. men had been given away by us to officials. He said he objected to our assuming jurisdiction over private morals.

I made the obvious replies.

A general discussion followed, with a heated argument as to the amount of slacking, and about the merits of the letter of 3 March, to which most of those present seemed to be opposed.

Some of those present were vehemently with Norman, many were critical of the National Committee, but most grew more friendly as the discussion proceeded. They regretted that none of us had come sooner, and I said, under pressure, that this was due to Norman in a great measure. He replied that he understood we wanted a big meeting, and that had proved impossible.

With the immediate subjects of conflict cleared out of the way, the discussion turned in a more positive direction, and Russell was quick to seize the opportunity.

The general view . . . was that the way the N.C.F. could help most would be by trying to get a decent H.O. scheme, with real work not under penal conditions. I said that I could not tell what line the National Committee would take as to our promoting such a scheme, but that, on one condition, I personally was prepared to advocate our doing so: the condition I made was that they should pass a resolution, which could be quoted as evidence, against the policy of slacking. Norman and some others at first opposed this, but the general feeling, at the end of the dicussion, was in favour of it. If they pass this resolution, I shall urge the National Committee to take up the question of improving the H.O. Scheme. I was urged that, if we do so, we should point out that no trouble has arisen with men who got work from the Pelham Committee.

Russell gave a sympathetic hearing to certain other of the men's concerns, and the meeting concluded on a cordial note. Russell summed up his impressions:

I am clear that the visit was very useful; I think it has done a great deal to diminish suspicion of the N.C.F. *It must be followed up.* I am also clear that the proposed letter ought not to go out, at any rate at present. If they themselves pass a motion against deliberate slacking, that is in every way preferable to an attempt on our part to do what appears to some of them like dictation. They think our line is that whoever dislikes the H.O. Scheme ought to go back to prison. I denied this; and we must avoid any action that would lend colour to it. Dislike is a different thing from conscientious objection.[582]

Russell had not overestimated the effect of his visit to Dartmoor. A general meeting of the men at the settlement (not, it should be noted, of the NCF branch only) was held on 17 May, and the following resolution was passed:

This meeting repudiates the charge that a policy of slacking is, or has been pursued at this Settlement, and declares that the men here are prepared to perform the work provided, in a reasonable spirit; but protests against the penal character of the work imposed by the Home Office Committee, and demands civil work of real importance with full civil rights.[583]

The National Committee had a meeting scheduled for only two days later so was able to make an immediate response, resolving to institute a vigorous campaign exposing the penal character of the work, and demanding work of real social utility and freedom from the threat of return to the Army.[584] The campaign was duly launched and gained increasing support throughout 1917. With the help of the National Council for Civil Liberties, the appeal was particularly directed at organised labour, and a large number of trade union groups passed resolutions protesting the type of work and the degrading conditions offered to the men in the Home Office scheme.[585] Although by the end of 1917 vocal public opinion was less hostile to conscientious objectors, the NCF campaign was probably only one of a number of factors contributing to this. Sporadic episodes of vilification continued to occur, the most spectacular accusations being those made by the Bishop of Exeter in a letter to *The Times* of 8 October 1917, in which he claimed that the settlement at Dartmoor was nothing less than a centre for the planning of violent revolution, to which Russell offered a mordant reply in *The Tribunal.*[586]

Even though public opinion appeared to be becoming gradually more sympathetic to the conscientious objectors, it was a long time before conditions under the Home Office scheme were ameliorated, and they were in fact to get worse before they got better. Although the original Brace Committee can hardly be accused of being too sympathetic, a reconstitution of the Committee which took place in July 1917 made this charge even more unlikely. Only Brace, the chairman, was left of the original

Committee; the other two were replaced by ex-Army officers. In addition, one of these had served as a prison governor. For full-time inspector of the camps and work centres, the deputy-governor of Wormwood Scrubs was appointed. At the same time a more stringent code of rules was introduced.[587] Not until November 1917 was the door opened cautiously to the possibility of some improvement for the more fortunate of the Home Office men. Those who had behaved well for twelve months were permitted to accept employment under private employers, and the country was at least enabled to make use of some of the special skills of these men, who included many university graduates and other skilled and trained persons; but it was a slow and discriminatory way out.[588]

Discontent and sporadic outbreaks of trouble at the Home Office centres continued. For instance, the early months of 1918 brought a one-day strike at Dartmoor (resulting from the death of a CO) and further physical violence against objectors in Knutsford and Wakefield.[589] Reports of slacking continued intermittently[590] and there were also still occasions on which the Home Office men felt that they were second-class citizens in the No-Conscription Fellowship, but there was never again the degree of misunderstanding and distrust that had prevailed in the early days of the Dartmoor settlement. The removal of some ringleaders may have had an effect, but if so, they are curiously faceless: only Norman's name comes up repeatedly in connection with the policy of deliberate slacking, and he remained at the settlement until February 1918. In other respects, the stricter rules merely added to the men's frustration. Remarkably, there is no direct evidence to convict Norman of advocating shirking, but he was certainly anxious not to have the policy openly condemned by the NCF, and in any event the kind of mischief and misunderstanding between the Home Office men and the National Committee which he was fomenting in the first week of May must have led to further trouble if it had gone unchecked. Trouble was prevented not by any action on the part of the Home Office but by the stand of the National Committee, and specifically by Russell's firm and tactful intervention. No Home Secretary would have believed that the NCF's chairman could have had anything but a disruptive influence: six months earlier Samuel had declared that the reason why Russell's movements had had to be restricted by the War Office was to keep him out of the areas in which most of the camps were to be found, since the Home Office had learnt at that time that he planned to go to them 'with a view to creating agitation and disturbance . . . and to upset . . . the work of the Brace Committee'.[591]

There is a curious postscript to this chapter. Within a few days of what can only be seen as his triumph at Dartmoor, Russell sat down and composed a four-page letter of resignation from the position of chairman of the NCF. The first reason he gave was that he found himself even more incapable in administrative and executive matters than he had expected to be.

It is difficult to alter habits in middle life, and my habits are those of a writer. Remembering a large number of details is impossible to me, and the attempt deprives me of ideas and initiative in the direction in which I might be effective. Writing and speaking are easy to me, but administration is impossible. I had hoped to alter this by an effort, but I now know that it is beyond my power.

Secondly, Russell thought that although the work of the conscientious objectors was still of great importance, there was now work to be done on wider lines as well. Work that might hasten the coming of peace was more important than anything else, 'particularly if peace comes in the spirit advocated by the Russian Revolutionaries'. The NCF was not the best organ for this work because although thousands now wanted an end to the war, very few would accept the pacifist position; so a wider base was needed for effective pressure for peace. Finally, Russell pointed out—what the National Committee knew very well—that he could not condemn the use of force in all circumstances. He felt the Russian revolution had given this matter of principle a practical relevance.

If the "sacredness of human life" means that force must *never* be used to upset bad systems of government, to put an end to wars and despotisms, and to bring liberty to the oppressed, then I cannot honestly subscribe to it. I have hitherto interpreted it differently; but perhaps the Nat. Com. will feel that I have been wrong in so doing. [592]

What comes through is a sense of deep discouragement. The letter has been folded and is soiled on the outside as if it was carried around for some time, perhaps while Russell tried to make up his mind whether to show it to the National Committee. Probably he decided against the step—there is no record of discussion or reaction. In part, it was probably the reflection of one of those transient moods of despair to which we know he was subject, but which he seldom showed openly to his colleagues. His mood may even have been a direct result of the unresolved dispute with Marshall, showing the depression and self-depreciation which so often follow on the suppression of anger.

But there is no doubt that by mid-1917 Russell had ceased to find the NCF work wholly satisfying and could hardly wait until he could resign with a good conscience. Nevertheless, May was too soon. Although the tenor of the abortive letter of resignation suggests he thought the NCF had by this time little to say in the wider movement for peace, we have seen that in fact he continued to work assiduously for several more months to tie the work of the Fellowship in with the response to the Russian revolution, which he saw as central to the drive for a people's peace. In any case, for a variety of reasons it was extremely difficult to leave the NCF at this time. Russell put away the temptation to resign before the year was out, and settled down to do all he could to secure the release of the absolutists.

CHAPTER 13
THE ABSOLUTISTS

In early 1917, the absolutists were still to Russell the spearhead of the conscientious objectors' movement, and his work for them the most important part of the job for the No-Conscription Fellowship. Although his hope of a successful outcome to the struggle was much less than it had been, he still thought that a great victory would be won if the Government could only be induced to grant absolute exemption to the men who had proved their sincerity by staying in jail. At the beginning of the year there were over a thousand COs in prison, of whom many were serving their second sentence and a handful were in for third and even fourth sentences.[593] Besides the principle involved, there was the grim fact of the physical and mental deterioration of the imprisoned men, and the growing feeling among some of them that passive acceptance of punishment should not be continued indefinitely.

When Russell discussed the prospects of the No-Conscription Fellowship in an editorial at the beginning of 1917,[594] he emphasised the need to agitate vigorously on behalf of the absolutists. The National Committee, and of course the Propaganda and Literature Committee, on which Russell and Marshall were also active, gave attention to this from the beginning of February. A new series of leaflets was issued, each of which described the case of some particular man as well as giving a summary of the numbers imprisoned. Branches were encouraged to develop similar leaflets dealing with men who were well-known locally. A renewed attempt was made to influence the churches, relatives of men in prison were canvassed for active support, trade unions were approached, letters were written to influential persons, and in particular every effort was made to interest MPs in the plight of the men still in jail. At the beginning of March Russell urged the members and the branches to play a full part in the campaign, which was actively continued in the following weeks.[595]

The main objective continued to be to obtain absolute exemption for those who could not accept alternative service. The NCF had always claimed that the weakness of the Military Service Acts lay in the demand that the tribunals judge conscience. From a more common point of view, it was the position of the absolutists that had a fundamental weakness: their claim to be unable to accept any form of compulsory service was not susceptible of objective proof, and since absolute exemption was obviously a desirable thing to have, it was subject to abuse. Some of those in authority were now prepared to admit that the tribunals had done a poor job of judging conscience, and a poorer job still in assigning the type of exemption a man might receive. Nevertheless, the strength of a conscientious objection could not easily be proved by words and in the atmosphere of 1916 it had hardly been surprising that the word of the absolutist had seldom been considered sufficient. But by the beginning of 1917, there were essential differences in the position. Many of the men in prison had now been twice recognised as genuine: first, by their local tribunals, which had recognised them as conscientious objectors but had given them a form of exemption which they could not accept; and secondly, by the Central Tribunal, which had offered them work under the Home Office scheme, which they had refused. A few others had declined to appear before one or both of these tribunals, and some 200 were classified as 'ungenuine'.[596] But nearly 1000 men were in prison because they would not accept the Home Office scheme, which, whatever its faults and hardships, was unquestionably less grim than serving repeated sentences at hard labour. Russell felt the case was proved:

The authorities know, by this time, that the claim for absolute exemptions is a genuine conscientious claim; they know that hundreds are now in prison for this reason alone, that they cannot accept alternative service. . . . There can no longer be the faintest doubt in the minds of the authorities that, in refusing absolute exemption to these men, they are punishing them for a proved and tested conscientious conviction. There may have been some excuse for the Tribunals in the early days, since at that time the kind of evidence of genuineness which is convincing to an unsympathetic sceptic did not yet exist. But what excuse can there be . . . now, when abundant evidence of the most conclusive kind exists to show that there are many men whose conscientious conviction cannot be met by anything less?[597]

The campaign for absolute exemption involved no change of principle, but concern for the well-being of the imprisoned men lent it a new urgency. Statistically, the lives, health and sanity of the men in jail were still at much less risk than those of the soldiers in the trenches, and the Fellowship was reluctant to press for any alleviation of conditions. But the inhumanity of the prison system was revealed as it had never been while it inflicted suffering only on the inarticulate, and in a few respects the evils were even exacerbated by the peculiar circumstances of the conscientious objectors.

With few exceptions, the objectors served their sentences at hard labour. 'Hard labour' is a misleading term referring to a whole punitive system, of which the enforced work was only a part. While the hours of work were long and tedious, especially at first, it was seldom heavy manual labour. The most common of tasks was the stitching by hand of heavy canvas mailbags (one wonders how the demand ever kept pace with the supply). The real harshness of the sentence lay elsewhere: in the initial period of solitary confinement and deliberately debilitating diet; in the inadequacy of the exercise periods; in the denial of all but the most limited communication with the outside world; in the restrictions on reading and writing; in the close and often harsh supervision and punishment; and above all in the almost total deprivation of ordinary human interaction. The silence rule denied the prisoners the right to any speech with each other or with the warders. After the first two months some of the day was supposed to be spent working 'in association', that is in the corridor or with the cell doors open, but without the right to speak. Visits from the chaplain were permitted, and there was a weekly church service, but some chaplains were abusive to the COs and many offered little comfort or humanity.[598]

The practice of commuting the sentences of most conscientious objectors to 112 days, which had been adopted in mid-1916, worked both to their advantage and to their disadvantage. The break between sentences could be an enormous source of strength, especially for any man who was fortunate enough to spend some time at liberty within his unit before being again charged with disobedience, or even for those who spent several weeks in the guardroom awaiting court martial. But it was inevitably followed by a repetition of the debilitating first stage of a new prison sentence. More menacing still was the fact that there need be no end to the imposition of repeated short sentences. Conditions at hard labour were so severe that the maximum sentence which could be imposed for any crime was two years, since it was officially recognised that life or sanity would be threatened by a longer term. Yet objectors might be sent back again and again until the total far exceeded two years.[599]

The winter of 1916–17, the first winter in which the COs were in jail, exposed them to the added hardship of cold, presumably the common lot of all prisoners, and very severe in some prisons. In Dorchester prison the temperature was reported to be 40°F; in Wormwood Scrubs the men were docked of one of their regulation three thin blankets just before the cold weather began, on the ground that there were not enough to go round. Allen wrote from Maidstone that the cold had given him a new idea of suffering.[600]

The spring of 1917 brought the peak of the U-boat blockade. Unable or unwilling to enforce effective rationing on the free and particularly on the affluent, Lord Devonport, the food controller, cut back prison food allowances which had been designed in the first instance to do no more than sustain life.[601] The quality and even the quantity of food varied from prison to prison and from time to time, but most prisoners were constantly short of food from early 1917 on. The conscientious objectors were doubly exposed to the dangers of this semi-starvation. As we have noted, they repeatedly endured the initial period of extra deprivation. Secondly, serious weight loss was supposed to be taken note of by the prison doctor, who could order supplementary rations if necessary; but the standard procedure was to take the man's weight at the beginning of his sentence as the norm, and so an objector who began his third or fourth sentence already emaciated from the effects of imprisonment must suffer further severe weight loss before notice would be taken of his condition.[620]

What Russell seems always most to have dreaded was the destruction of men—their moral or mental breaking (not always separable from physical deterioration)—and this was now beginning to happen. As a result of the prolonged inhuman treatment in the jails, a small file of mental cases began to grow, more deaths occurred, there were suicides. Men could also be broken by intense short-term cruelty, which again became a threat to the absolutists in the summer of 1917. A number of men who were returned to their units on the completion of their first or second prison sentences were denied the right to court martial and were subjected to pressure to force them to conform to orders. In two notorious instances—those of James Brightmore at Cleethorpes and of John Gray at Hornsea—the men were subjected to direct brutality. Others were sent to France: one of these received the maximum sentence at Field Punishment No. 1, being tied up (within range of shell-fire, but not right in the front line) for two hours a day, while the others were subjected to a variety of minor brutalities. Several were ordered to put on respirators, under threat of being forced into a gas chamber without them, but the threat was not carried out.[603]

John Gray, the man tortured at Hornsea, finally gave in and obeyed orders in circumstances which Russell must have found an intolerable demonstration of what war could lead to. Gray had served one sentence and had been deemed genuine by the Central Tribunal, but had refused to accept the Home Office scheme. He was returned on 5 May 1917 to Hornsea, but to a different unit from his original one. Here he was subjected to a systematic attempt to break his resistance. The bombing officer removed the pin from a Mills bomb and threw it at Gray's feet when he refused an order to throw it. Gray continued to stand still, and it is not clear who removed the bomb, since the officer is reported to have run for cover. For a number of days Gray was given the attention of the physical training staff, who knocked him into the positions he refused to take, becoming more brutal as their efforts failed. He was pulled round the field, with his arms behind his back, by a rope tied around his waist. On another day, he was stripped and had a rope tightly fastened round his abdomen: he was then thrown eight or nine times in a filthy pond and dragged out by the shrinking rope. Although there is evidence that more than one officer and NCO who took part in these efforts to make a soldier out of Gray seemed to enjoy it, eight men ultimately refused to carry out orders to inflict the treatment.

When news reached the NCF of Gray's case, General Childs was at once informed of the irregularities, and before long the commanding officer was relieved of his command and placed on half pay, but it was too late to save John Gray, who had finally given in and was accepting orders. The case was exactly the kind dreaded by Russell, and it is of tragic interest that once Gray, who had stood up to so much, had been broken in will, he was not able to renew the effort. Rae writes: 'Gray's fate remains a mystery. Although he had accepted military service only under duress, he does not appear to have gone back on this decision.'[604] Had Gray again refused orders, the probability is that his court martial would have gone through at once and with as little attention drawn to it as possible. But he would then have had to face prolonged imprisonment, for which perhaps he was no longer morally strong enough. An undated letter among Marshall's papers[605] clears up some of the mystery as to what became of him, confirming that he remained a reluctant soldier, who continued to read *The Tribunal*, made converts among his fellow soldiers, and looked ahead to the time when he could again work for socialism. But he despised his own weakness:

I reprove myself for being so weak, and having to bow down to militarism, and hold I am partly responsible for the continued abuse of the C.O.s still in prison. When I was offered the Home Office Scheme I never wavered, but refused same point blank, and can you imagine me agreeing to become a soldier, after refusing to compromise with the authorities. ... I think of our former chairman Clifford Allen, and Fenner Brockway, and others too numerous to mention, and I envy them, and you will forgive me when I say there are times when I feel my position keenly.

The letter made painful reading for Russell and his colleagues.

The attitude adopted by the NCF to the new wave of brutalities had been to make them public as an example of the inevitable result of prolonged militarism. Russell wrote an editorial on 'The Renewed Ill-Treatment of "CO's"', in which he stressed this aspect while claiming (with some justice) that reaction to such cruelty was growing stronger, especially among the Army rank and file.[606] The editorial was not one of Russell's most convincing. He showed none of the spontaneous indignation and deep personal feeling that one expects from him in the face of such brutality, and when he calls on friends of peace to feel 'above and beyond all their sympathy . . . a stern rejoicing that militarism is showing its true nature', one wonders what had become of the Russell who had been so moved by Chappelow's ordeal in a blanket a year earlier. No private correspondence referring to these episodes is available which would make possible a comparison between Russell's public utterances and his private feelings, but the explanation is probably to be found primarily in the limitations imposed by NCF policy. Care had to be taken at all times to avoid the appearance of mere complaining at hardship.

The NCF executive found it increasingly difficult to care for the interests of the conscientious objectors while honouring this principle. Such incidents of overt brutality remained rare (a fact for which some credit must go to the vigilance of the Fellowship and to the rectitude of General Childs), but the long-drawn-out ordeal of the absolutists in prison went on. There was some renewed polarisation within the Fellowship. While the worsening condition of the men in prison seemed to some to reinforce the argument on principle for pressing for the release of the absolutists, the minority became more extreme in its opposition to all agitation on behalf of the jailed men.

The controversy was subserved by an unfortunate disagreement concerning the extent to which men were or should be adversely affected by imprisonment. Several of those who had been involved in the National Committee dispute which had led to the resignation of J. P. Fletcher in the summer of 1916 were now in jail. Some of those who believed the NCF should devote all its attention to the peace campaign and allow the men in prison to await the transformation of public opinion, however long that might take, tended to make light of the prison hardships. Between sentences, W. H. Ayles wrote a letter to the press[607] in which he extolled the clarity of mind which he claimed came to all in prison, and linked this euphoric attitude with the demand that the COs' friends work for peace rather than for the release of the absolutists. His view was supported by

W. J. Chamberlain (who, ironically, was to suffer a breakdown in prison a year later),[608] but not surprisingly Russell and Marshall saw it as unrealistic and dangerous. They were committed on principle to working for the release of the absolutists and they well knew from the reports they were receiving that many men were indeed damaged by prolonged imprisonment. Among others, Allen's letters continued to stress the torment of incessant thinking combined with enforced inaction, and he never made light of the ordeal.[609] Brockway, psychologically strong and physically healthy, was as little affected by jail as any man, but he observed the effects on others and was convinced irrevocable damage could be done.[610] Russell gave his opinion unequivocally in an editorial at the end of March,[611] declaring that for him and for the majority on the National Committee the harm to the imprisoned and to the community made it essential to work for release. There is ample evidence in the correspondence that he was probably right when he claimed that the majority of the men in prison supported this view.

During the summer, however, the attitude of the young Quakers became even more uncompromising. From March on, Edward Grubb had hoped to move the Meeting for Sufferings[612] towards a protest to the Government against the repeated sentences imposed on the absolutists, but the Friends' Service Committee, under the leadership of Fletcher and Brown, led the Meeting to adopt their position and to keep silent on the issue. Even Wilfred Littleboy, a committed FSC member who supported the decision, had to admit that among his fellow-prisoners, the decision 'caused considerable disappointment'. In effect this remained the official Quaker stand for the rest of the war. To some extent it marked a separation of Quaker policy from that of the No-Conscription Fellowship, at least while Russell and Marshall remained active,[613] although neither Grubb nor Salter, the other Quaker members of the NCF National Committee, associated themselves with the position taken by the Service Committee. To do the FSC justice, one very real concern continued to be to avoid any discrimination in their favour as Quakers. Edith Ellis wrote to Allen: 'This [release for Friends only] is of course an added danger for us. Woe betide us if we got out, and left you in.'[614] Brown followed the example set by Fletcher a year earlier and resigned from the National Committee, but he remained active in the Birmingham branch and the Midland division, and was at pains to explain to Allen, Marshall, Russell, the National Committee and *The Tribunal* that he had no hard feelings about the break. In his note to Russell he spoke with regret of leaving when things were so difficult and when he knew Russell himself would have liked to be free.[615]

Russell's standpoint remained unchanged, and was expressed in a letter written later that year:

I wish I could make you feel the problem in the way I do. I think very likely the F.S.C. attitude is right in dealing with Friends, but I am sure it is not right for our membership. Take the question of H.O. Camps; if we had followed B.B.'s policy, we should have thrown men into the arms of Norman and they would have become utterly cynical. This applies to quite two thirds of the H.O. men. As it is, this has not happened. I think the question of visitation is similar in essence. To my mind, a duty of human kindness is involved, and it is essential to remember that many of our people have come with difficulty to pacifism, through the insight of their best moments; many of them really need friendly support, or else they will feel deserted. I feel we are in some way developing the cruelty of fanaticism, which is the very spirit that supports the war.

Russell's remark about 'visitation' (meant, I think, only as an illustration) confused some Friends who read the letter. But by that time, in any case, Friends were having difficulty in understanding Russell's point of view, and Ellis thought his lack of understanding of theirs 'rather pathetic'.[616]

The increasing commitment to passivity on the part of the FSC was one end of a spectrum of response to the serious position of the absolutists in the summer of 1917. At the other end of the spectrum some of the prisoners desperately sought a more active resistance. Allen in particular looked for a way in which those in prison could play a larger part in the struggle. Russell thought the Home Office scheme had allowed the public to forget the thousand absolutists still in jail.[617] He suffered above all for Allen, knowing him to have both an extremely active nature and a compulsive introspectiveness, a combination which made solitary confinement and the repressive silence rule an agony.[618] But it was for public as well as personal reasons that the idea of being forgotten in prison was anathema to a man like Allen. It is not to belittle his spiritual strength to say that his was an intensely political nature and that his actions were always at least in part political. For him acceptance of imprisonment must be a means to an end, not merely the consequence of a moral stand. Essentially, Russell shared this view, which was why he had welcomed the prospect of going to prison in 1916, yet was to serve his sentence so reluctantly in 1918, when it seemed no longer to have a purpose. But however much he sympathised with Allen's objectives, Russell deplored the plans to which they now gave rise, and did not agree that the logic was sound.

Allen first proposed that men should hunger-strike while in the hands of the military following their second or subsequent sentences. He argued the need to counter 'the belief of most people that COs are either cowards, or have a mania for being imprisoned'. Marshall[619], to whom it seemed 'an essentially and profoundly wrong thing to do', paid an urgent visit to Maidstone and was able to dissuade him, largely because he came to realise his health might gain him rapid release, but those following his lead might have to suffer forcible feeding for a long period.[620]

Alternatively, Allen began to think of a work strike, and managed to discuss the idea in secret with all of the twenty-five COs who were imprisoned at Maidstone with him. At the start all opposed it, but he claimed that all except one (Scott Duckers, a lawyer of strong character) shortly came to agree that it was necessary. The primary argument at this point was the propaganda value of the step, and Allen said plainly that he saw it as desirable only if the National Committee overwhelmingly endorsed its value for publicity and agreed to organise it on a national scale. Between sentences, just before his third court martial, he wrote a long and careful letter to the National Committee to this effect. But when the Committee refused to adopt the policy, Allen became convinced that it was a moral issue for him, no longer merely one of an effective propaganda gesture, and although he now loyally expressed his support of the decision not to sanction a general work strike, he declared that he had to proceed with it alone as a matter of principle. He issued an open letter to Lloyd George on 31 May, just before going back to prison.

After a brief statement of his purpose, and of the penalties to which he expected to be subjected, Allen devoted almost half of this long and rather rambling document to refuting the charges of cowardice and a desire for martyrdom. He then gave as his main reason for deciding to stop work his conviction that Lloyd George's motive in refusing absolute exemption and continuing the persecution of the imprisoned men must be 'a secret determination to retain some form of Conscription in this country after the War'. The letter concluded with a reaffirmation of the personal worth of the stand for freedom of conscience, which conveyed a sense of dignity and strength beyond that carried by the body of the letter.[621] Not brought out in the open letter, but present in Allen's statement to the National Committee, was also a logically defensible argument that work for the Government, whether done in prison or under the Home Office scheme, was inevitably work to assist the Government directly or indirectly in the prosecution of the war.[622]

Even had the logic of Allen's final position been more complete, the way in which he shifted ground, and finally justified going ahead when he did not receive the support he at first declared to be essential, suggests that his decision, however successfully rationalised, had a strong emotional component and was, as Robbins surmises, 'in part a bid to regain lost prestige'. Kennedy claims that 'the national committee's rejection of Allen's carefully formulated strategy placed him in an awkward position'.[623] True as this may be, it is certain that Allen's proposals put the Committee in a very awkward position—and especially Russell, who held office after all as a substitute for Allen, as well as being one of his two closest friends. The plans in fact came as a bombshell, the more so as Allen had earlier declared he could see no grounds for refusing work in civil prison.[624] In 1917, almost all the leaders still held that to recommend a general stoppage would be irresponsible and detrimental to the cause of the absolutists. A strike by Allen alone promised to be divisive and damaging to the Fellowship and disastrous to himself. Far from believing that either form of action would assist propaganda, the leaders feared it would further alienate public sympathy and understanding just when the Government was known, by Allen as well as by the executive, to be considering a new solution. Russell also felt keenly his responsibility for the health of the imprisoned men, which would inevitably be seriously at risk, and there was again the fear of pushing men beyond what they could endure.

Later, Allen claimed that the National Committee had been motivated by Quaker passivity, and was out of touch with the revolutionary spirit of the time.[625] But the argument does not stand up as far as it refers to the summer of 1917, although it may have had relevance later. The influence of the more passive among the Quakers was no longer strong in the National Committee, whatever lead they might be giving within their own Society, or in certain local branches of the NCF. As for the revolutionary spirit, we have seen the involvement of the executive, and particularly of Russell, in trying to extend the virtues of the Russian revolution to Britain. It is hard to see how Allen's proposal could have met with any other response at that time. The instinctive—and perhaps psychologically sound—reaction of most of the Committee was far from academic. One senses that they felt something unhealthy about it, and something horrifying about Allen's condemnation of himself in all probability to a slow death.

As Allen's close friends, Russell and Marshall must have felt the horror acutely. They had consulted with him before he went back to prison, had failed to dissuade him, and were now committed to getting a fair hearing for the plan. So clear was the general perception of the unwisdom of the course, that the division was not between those who supported and those who opposed the work strike, but simply between those who wished to avoid giving it any publicity whatever and those who contended that the view of the absent chairman must at least be taken seriously and put before the Fellowship. Marshall at length—but almost alone—came to believe in the rightness of the step Allen was taking.[626] Salter was the chief proponent for ignoring Allen's letter altogether. Russell remained completely opposed to work-striking; before Allen's plans were generally known, he had written an editorial counselling patient endurance as the best means of working a slow but sure change in public opinion.[627] But he supported Marshall in her insistence that Allen must be given the publicity he had expected.

Marshall was away when Allen's open letter came before the Propaganda Committee, which not only disapproved of the planned action but also complained with some justice that it was 'a very poor document', that it repeated itself, and that it entirely failed to make clear the argument of principle in favour of a work strike. Salter, with a strong following, was able to overrule Russell and delay publication.[628] Marshall wrote urgently to point out that they had no authority to do this except as far as publication in *The Tribunal* was concerned, and even there they might delay but could hardly suppress what was intended as the chairman's message to the Fellowship.[629] Her argument was unanswerable: Allen in fact had forced the hand of the National Committee and he was now back in jail and could not be argued with. Less justifiable and less politically sound, perhaps, was Marshall's demand for twenty copies to circulate privately to influential people. Allen's plan met with disapproval almost wherever it went outside the Fellowship, mixed in some instances with embarrassment or pity. With few exceptions, the response of the members (as far as it is on record) was similar, although a number conceded that it might later become good strategy. After Marshall's letter came, Russell saw to it that the open letter reached Lloyd George and went to the sympathetic press. An emergency meeting of the London members of the National Committee agreed that *The Tribunal* should print it in full, together with a supporting statement, one on the other side by Salter, and the National Committee's decision, all of which accordingly appeared in the issue of 14 June. The Committee declared itself opposed to the organisation of work-striking in prison, but declared (using a well-tried formula) that it would support those who adopted the practice as a matter of conscience. The central argument used by the physician Salter in defence of the Committee's decision related neither to the principle nor to the propaganda value, but to the effects which a strike would have in depriving the men in prison of work which, however grimly tedious, gave them a hold on health and sanity. To Russell, this was a telling argument, though not perhaps primary.

After this publicity, some controversy inevitably ensued, but there was not sufficient support in the Fellowship for Allen's view for it to become a really divisive matter during 1917. *The Tribunal* opened its columns to letters on the subject, individuals expressed opinions to the members of the National Committee, the topic came up a number of times at meetings of the Committee, and care was taken to make use of any opportunity to discover the views of those members of the National Committee who were in prison—which in itself extended the discussion over a number of months. In mid-July J. H. Hudson, in Carnarvon prison, smuggled out a letter, a remarkable document in more than one way. Addressed to the members of the NCF in Lancashire, it was nearly 1500 words long, written in a tiny but legible handwriting on both sides of a scrap of paper barely five inches by seven and a half inches. A lucid exposition of the case against the work strike, it was read by Alexander Wilson at a meeting of the National Committee on 9 November 1917.[630] In early September, when Brockway was in Chester Castle between sentences, Marshall took the opportunity to discuss the issue very fully with him, and he wrote to Russell at some length. He saw, he said, no ground of principle to lead him to stop work, but he believed that a nationally organised strike would be good when a real revolutionary feeling had arisen in the country; he was not hopeful that this would be soon.[631] Chamberlain wrote so strongly in *The Tribunal* of 19 July against the proposal to strike that Marshall felt compelled to defend the sincerity of those who supported it.[632]

Russell's anxiety was renewed for a short while when the work strike question showed signs of taking a new turn in August. Some of the prisoners in Wormwood Scrubs proposed to stop work and possibly to go on a hunger strike in order to draw attention to the severe shortage of food from which they were suffering, and in order to 'make the fight more absolute'. An unusual feature was that there were other prisoners involved in the plans as well as the conscientious objectors.[633] Using one of the mysterious channels of communication that always seemed to be open to the NCF when they were needed, the men concerned submitted the plan to the executive, requesting that approval or disapproval should be conveyed by means of a red or white signal displayed in a certain tree outside the prison, within twelve days. The senders of the message seem to have had every confidence that they would have their reply in plenty of time, but communication on this occasion was roundabout. Not until the last moment was Marshall able to make arrangements to signify disapproval by sending out a party of children whose white kites conveniently became stuck in a tree. Because news of the plan reached head office so late that a reply had to be made at once, Russell and Marshall had made the decision, but it was not a difficult one, and they were rightly confident of the support of the rest of the National Committee. Marshall wrote a careful letter to her correspondent (who was in the Dartmoor Home Office settlement and whose information evidently came from a recent arrival there from Wormwood Scrubs). She sent a copy of the National Committee's earlier resolutions, which clearly stated the objection both to the organisation of work-striking and to any work strike not based on grounds of pure principle, and enclosed a statement which she and Russell had drawn up to explain their own views:

We would urge our Comrades to consider very carefully before taking the step they propose, and in any case, if they do take it to take it on the ground of principle alone and not from a mixed motive of "wanting to make the fight more absolute" and "wanting to obtain better food". This combination of principle and expediency inevitably lessens the effect of the protest made on behalf of the principle. This has been proved by experience in the case of some of the complaints made by men in the Home Office Camps.

The statement went on to explain that those outside were vigorously pressing for improved food—it was admitted that Wormwood Scrubs was 'one of the worst "hotels" in this respect'—and to ask for as much detailed information as could be supplied to help in this campaign. In conclusion, Russell and Marshall had this to say:

One reason which weighed with the National Committee in passing the attached resolution was that the results of refusing work in prison are so serious from the point of view of men's future health and they felt that such a course should only be adopted by those who feel under a moral obligation to do so on grounds of principle. The Committee will, of course, support those who do feel so bound but they strongly depreciate [sic] any organisation of such a policy on grounds of expediency.[634]

For the last time during Russell's chairmanship, the National Committee again discussed the matter of work strikes and hunger strikes in October and November, giving lengthy consideration to opinions canvassed in and out of the prisons. Russell was still adamant in his view that all reasons put forward for such forms of protest were invalid, and urged the Committee to 'take a very strong line against any kind of strike'. By nine votes against four abstentions, the Committee reaffirmed its policy, and declared that such action was not likely to secure release and was undesirable as a policy.[635]

There, for the time being, rested the question of protest action from within the prisons, and the National Committee's attitude to them. Allen's was not the first work strike, and both work and hunger strikes had been used intermittently and were to occur more frequently as the war dragged on, and to multiply (perhaps justifiably) when the war was over and release still not in sight.[636] A third type of protest, the refusal to hold to the restrictive day-to-day prison discipline, and in particular the inhuman silence rule, was to be more effective; it is curious that this form of protest was not developed earlier and used more widely. Adopted by an individual, it resulted only in solitary confinement and constant punishment, but agreed upon by any large body of prisoners it was extraordinarily hard to control, and, unlike the other forms of protest it often proved psychologically rehabilitative in itself.[637]

Allen may have been right that the National Committee clung overlong to a policy outdated by changed circumstances, but I am left with a strong feeling that 1917 would have been too early to gain support or success for resistance within the prisons. Accordingly, Russell seems to have been justified in exerting his influence against work and hunger strikes while his chairmanship lasted. As we have seen, even Brockway, always on the alert to make resistance more effective, felt that the time was not ripe in 1917.

All this took place against a background of rumours of impending Government action to offer relief of some kind to the absolutists.

CHAPTER 14
NEW DIRECTIONS AND DISAPPOINTMENTS

Persistent rumours began in May 1917 that the Cabinet was considering a new solution to the conscientious objectors' problem, and these rumours were not unfounded. The initiative owed little or nothing at the outset to the efforts of the NCF, and a great deal to the efforts of the mother of one particular absolutist. In a memorandum to the War Cabinet on 9 May, Milner admitted his interest had first been engaged by his knowledge of the circumstances of one man. The case, which Milner described but did not name, was that of his godson, Stephen Hobhouse.[638] Stephen Hobhouse was a member of a wellknown west-country family, who had given up his inheritance some years before the war, become a Quaker, and gone to live and work in the east end of London. His mother was Margaret Hobhouse, sister of Beatrice Webb and of Lady Courtney. She supported the war, but was determined that her son should not remain in prison, the more so as his health was not good, and was worsening under prison conditions. The story of her campaign, as it directly affected Government officials, has been told by Rae,[639] who was, however, ignorant of the extent to which Margaret Hobhouse was advised and informed by the NCF executive and who did not have access to recently-discovered evidence linking Russell with her efforts. Stephen himself made only the briefest possible reference in his autobiography to the circumstances of his release, and his biographer implies that Margaret's activity on her son's behalf was confined to the arousal of public opinion.[640] Every one of the parties to the several negotiations wanted confidentiality preserved—and so it has been, for sixty years.

Probably, as has been suggested, Margaret Hobhouse acted independently in her first approach to Milner to persuade him to take up the cause of the conscientious objectors. But the NCF was at once involved in the situation, since Milner sought information from the Fellowship to support his case. Marshall met with Major Thornton, Milner's private secretary, on 26 April, and corresponded with him while the memorandum to the Cabinet was being prepared.[641] Mrs Hobhouse was equally willing to accept help privately, and she sought out Russell and Marshall. Throughout the summer of 1917, she was kept supplied with information, and in her turn, she shared with them her knowledge of the discussions and decisions of the Cabinet. She had a strong ally, or convert, in Philip Kerr, one of Lloyd George's private secretaries, who was instructed by the Prime Minister to examine the position of the absolutists and to make recommendations on policy. Lloyd George may not have known that the source of most of Kerr's information was the NCF, although he must have known that Kerr's previous association with Lord Milner in South Africa might dispose him favourably to Milner's cause. Kerr's arguments and conclusions were all the Fellowship could have wished. On the grounds that the Military Service Act had been defective, and the tribunals often in error, he claimed the absolutists were being imprisoned contrary to the intent of the law, and concluded there was no other course open to the Government except to let the men go.[642]

The reaction of the War Office brought this first move within the Cabinet to an abrupt halt. At the beginning of May, when Mrs Hobhouse was just beginning her private campaign on Stephen's behalf, Childs telephoned Marshall, and referred to this pressure on behalf of one man with indignation. Marshall had given Childs copies of Allen's letters from prison, and the General claimed to have been so much impressed by them that he was sending them on to a member of the War Cabinet with a covering letter. What Marshall recollected of this letter, which Childs had read to her over the telephone, was that he had said:

S[tephen] H[obhouse] has influential relations, C[lifford] A[llen] has none; S.H. is a C.O. as a result of definite religious beliefs, C.A. is a C.O. because of his mentality; S.H. is well known for good works, C.A. is one of the most dangerous men in the kingdom; but I will not be a party to any action which releases S.H. but not C.A. The day S.H. comes out of prison C.A. will too. There is nothing to choose between the genuineness of the two men.

Marshall had also asked Childs his opinion of a long 'psychological' letter of Allen's (presumably that of 24 March 1917, in which Allen described the mental torture of imprisonment), and she reported that Childs had described it as 'extraordinarily interesting and a fine and honest utterance'.[643] Marshall was immensely cheered by this sign of grace in a man whom she recalled as having said he wanted to shoot all conscientious objectors, and as having, even in his more moderate moods, made a big distinction between the religious and the socialist objectors. Russell, too, was encouraged: it was clearly to this conversation that he referred in his letter to her of 3 May. He wrote to Ottoline Morrell that much was happening, some of it very good, as regards the men in prison, and added, 'This is Miss Marshall's achievement'.[644]

The reported conversation with Childs has the ring of sincerity and he was, it seems, developing a reluctant respect for some COs—but they still were, in his view, enemies of their country. Less than three weeks later, it was Childs whose strong reaction to Milner's and Kerr's proposals ensured their dismissal.[645] At a meeting of the War Cabinet on 22 May, at which Milner's memorandum came up for discussion, Childs' description of the absolutists was damning. He said that:

The absolutists . . . presented two types: those who adopted an attitude of resistance to every attempt to make them work, and those who not only refused to undertake any service for the State, but were increasingly busy in their endeavours to induce their fellow-citizens to defy the Government. This latter class were working in close co-operation with the Union of Democratic Control, the No Conscription Fellowship, and other bodies whose activities, in time of war, were unpatriotic and dangerous. Such men, if they were released by the Military Authorities, would have immediately to be imprisoned under the Defence of the Realm Act.

He went on to dismiss even the proposal that some might be let out on grounds of ill-health, backing this with a view of prison that seemed to show that so far, at least, Marshall's efforts to educate him were incomplete.

With reference to the suggestion that really genuine cases should be released on medical grounds, as otherwise, should any objector die in prison, he might be regarded as a martyr and public opinion be stirred in a high degree against the Government, General Childs said that in the existing "low category" of physical fitness for Military Service this would not be feasible; while it was further suggested that, in the present admirable conditions of prison life, there was no reason to apprehend any such fatality.

Later in the same meeting, when the Home Secretary described the conduct of political objectors in the Home Office work centres as constituting a grave scandal, Childs is not on record as having reported what he knew from Marshall of the strong official condemnation by the NCF of any policy of shirking in the camps. Within a few weeks he persuaded Derby to abandon the practice of commuting the long sentences given to objectors to 112 days, although Marshall had previously understood him to be opposed to the change. Describing the absolutists as 'unworthy of consideration', Childs claimed this would enable the War Office to 'defeat the absolutist movement fully and finally'.[646] The move made sense from the military point of view. There was a belief initially that a short prison sentence would lead to a willingness to serve, but this rarely happened, and the repeated court martials were disruptive, expensive, bad for discipline and an opportunity for pacifist propaganda.

Childs may not have been insincere with Marshall, but possibly something happened at about this time to harden his attitude. He does seem, in spite of his tendency to believe religious objectors more likely to be sincere than political ones, to have found the influential agitation on behalf of Stephen Hobhouse distasteful; or maybe he reacted unfavourably to Allen's decision to refuse to work in prison. War Office files contain Kerr's memorandum, Kerr's covering letter to Childs (16 June), and a copy of Allen's open letter to Lloyd George, all marked with underlinings and exclamation marks in the same green pencil by an obviously hostile hand, which is most likely that of Childs.[647] But Allen's letter was not in circulation before the beginning of June, and Childs condemned the absolutists to the Cabinet as early as 22 May. Perhaps Marshall was merely over-optimistic about the General's increased understanding; the letter which Childs had read out over the telephone can legitimately be interpreted as meaning only that he was as determined to keep Hobhouse in jail as he was to keep Allen, but his motives for reading the letter to Marshall remain inexplicable.[648]

The criticism that Marshall had met with from the men in the Home Office camps for her discussions with Childs regarding the situation at Dartmoor had led her to consider resigning the political work, but during May she had received sufficient endorsement of her efforts from the National Committee, and perhaps particularly from Russell (in spite of the personal friction between them) to feel able to continue with it. When it turned out that her trust in Childs had been, from an NCF standpoint, misplaced, the closeness of the liaison which she had formed again came under criticism. Barratt Brown, to do him justice, resigned not because of the apparent failure of Marshall's work, but because he disliked the whole political approach, and particularly the quasi-cordial relations with War Office officials—'the Official Unofficial touch with the Government'. It is hard to tell from what direction the pressure on Marshall to resign the political work was renewed, but by July Russell was adding his voice to it. Marshall had planned to take most of June and the whole of July off, but she did not stay away. Russell described her reappearance in mid-July as 'very worrying'.[649] He believed that cutting down her work might make her more efficient and more tolerable, and he thought also that a change in the nature of the political work might save the Fellowship's relationship with the Quakers. What most of the Committee saw as Childs' bad faith was much used as an argument (which prevailed) for giving up the relationship with the War Office, although Marshall reminded them that Childs had unfailingly put a stop to illegal brutalities when they had been brought to his attention, and had in other ways contributed to the just administration of the Military Service Acts. Other aspects of the political work were to continue, particularly those which involved working with any senior official who had shown any interest in the plight of the conscientious objectors. After lengthy discussion in the June and July meetings of the National Committee, Marshall resigned her responsibility for the political work, and tried to settle down to giving the administrative work her undivided attention; branches, members, and the National Committee had all recently been critical of lapses in efficiency at head office.

The failure in June of Milner's first effort to do something for the absolutists, and the condemnation by the National Committee of Marshall's liaison with the War Office, led to a lull in any direct action to obtain absolute exemption for the men in prison. Russell was meanwhile busy with two pieces of work, neither of which he shared officially with his colleagues in the NCF. One had to do with the protest of Siegfried Sassoon, the other was an under-cover use of his talents on behalf of the absolutists.

Siegfried Sassoon had entered the war with no qualms, believing it to be a war of defence and liberation. He had fought as an officer at the front, earned the Distinguished Service Order, and been wounded. He had expressed the horror of the war in his poetry, and he was one of those for whom custom did not dull the impact. In hospital in London in April 1917, recovering from a light wound, he read one of Russell's books (probably *Principles of Social Reconstruction*); he read what he described as the lies of the newspapers about the battle he had just come from; he read of aborted peace feelers; and his outrage crystallised into a conviction that the war was now being needlessly and deliberately prolonged by the politicians. He planned to take no further part in it, but to do what he could to end it, and in July he drew up a public statement of his intention.

Sassoon, on the advice of Ottoline Morrell, came to Russell, who warmly supported him, helping him plan his strategy and write a public statement. Sassoon was far from being a pacifist, so there was no official involvement with the NCF, although they did publicise his statement. Such a connection, as well as being inappropriate for the Fellowship, would have damned his cause and made it less effective than it was hoped the revolt of a distinguished officer would prove to be. Russell admired

Sassoon's courageous stand, and Sassoon developed a respect for Russell amounting almost to hero-worship. When he issued his statement, he wrote to Morrell, 'I would like above all to know that B.R. is satisfied that I've done something toward destroying the Beast of War.'[650] Partly at Russell's instigation, the statement was read in the House of Commons on 30 July, and the next day it appeared in *The Times*. On the following day the NCF office was raided and 100 copies of the document were removed.[651]

The outcome of the venture, which Sassoon and Russell hoped would be so dramatic and far-reaching, was discouraging. The War Office and Sassoon's regiment acted with unusual subtlety. He was not court-martialled or harshly treated in any way. Instead, with the connivance of some of his officer friends (notably Robert Graves) he was judged by a medical board to be suffering from shell-shock and was exiled to a comfortable hospital for mild cases in Midlothian, Scotland. Above all else, Sassoon's protest had been on behalf of his fellow-soldiers, dead and alive: his letters and his poetry reflect the profound bonding of the shared experience of the trenches. Three months of comfort and safety and helpless obscurity—he realised the War Office would never consent to court-martial him—made him feel that instead he had deserted his comrades. He did not change his views, but in November he agreed to rejoin his unit.[652] Russell does not, however, seem to have been greatly disappointed in Sassoon and while in prison in 1918 published a defence of his war poetry.

The need to keep any new avenue of protest from being associated with the contaminating name of the NCF also underlay another of Russell's activities in the summer of 1917. He had begun to believe, with frustration, that it was difficult for the pacifists to be heard outside their own limited circle. In early June, just when Marshall's political efforts for the absolutists were being brought to a standstill, a chance came his way to do an effective piece of ghost-writing and to reach a new audience. When Milner failed to carry Margaret Hobhouse's first attack to a successful conclusion in the Cabinet, she decided to broaden the basis of her campaign and to enlist public opinion in her support. How she came to solicit Russell's help is not clear. Although the NCF were glad to have her on their side, Marshall initially distrusted her at least as much as Russell distrusted Childs. Russell later summed up his view of her: 'Her son persuaded her that Christianity and War are incompatible, so she gave up Christianity.' He added that she worked assiduously for the conscientious objectors.[653] Limited as her sympathy was with her son's motivation, she had come to understand enough of his principles to know that he would not want to accept release except on terms consistent with his conscience.[654] And she was honestly appalled by what had been revealed to her of prison conditions: she continued to work in this cause after Stephen's release and even after the war.

Russell may have already known Margaret Hobhouse through his friendship with the Webbs. In any event, the NCF gladly accepted her as a fellow-traveller as soon as they became aware of her efforts to influence the Cabinet in May 1917. The executive evidently felt the alliance had to be exploited all the more because it was unusual and offered the possibility of opening new doors. Early in June Russell gave Mrs Hobhouse some information for a letter to the *New Statesman*.[655] At about the same time, she began to plan a pamphlet to urge the case of the absolutists. Russell was soon supplying her with material from the NCF files and with advice, and the project quickly grew in scope. The outcome was a small book, published in August 1917 under the title '*I Appeal Unto Caesar*'.[656] It is now clear that the body of it was written by Russell.

The greatest secrecy was preserved regarding Russell's authorship. Probably Marshall and perhaps one or two others knew at the time, but there were very good reasons why as few as possible should be in on the secret. Margaret Hobhouse was most appreciative of Russell's assistance, but most apprehensive of having it discovered. If Russell had obeyed her wishes, the evidence of her letters would not now be available. She wrote: 'By the way, is my correspondence with you safe from molestation in the post? Perhaps when you have finished with it you will kindly destroy— and I should rather it was not known to others—as you are not supposed to be helping me and I am not saying a word to anyone.'[657] Both Hobhouse and Russell knew that the book would lose all its special effectiveness if it were known to emanate from the NCF. Besides its supposed authorship, it had features which an NCF publication could never have aspired to. Mrs Hobhouse had approached a number of distinguished people who, though for the most part strongly pro-war, might be persuaded to make a guarded statement on the unsatisfactory nature of the treatment of the absolutists. The book boasts not only an introduction by Gilbert Murray, but 'Notes' (actually passages excerpted, with permission, from letters written to Mrs Hobhouse) by the Earl of Selbourne, Lord Parmoor, Lord Hugh Cecil and Lord Henry Bentinck (Ottoline Morrell's brother). The little publication was calculated to reach an influential audience with whom the NCF had little credibility.

Margaret Hobhouse wrote a four-page foreword. Her correspondence with Russell shows that substantially the whole of the rest was written or compiled by him, although he was careful to consult her and to conform to some extent to her wishes, making use of the arguments she was in the practice of using. But he refused to smooth over the awkward and unpopular opinions of the absolutists. He wrote to her:

I feel also a certain scruple in agitating for the release of these men without letting it be known what it is that they really believe. They care more about their beliefs than about themselves, and they think, rightly or wrongly, that they help the spread of their beliefs by being in prison for them. It is hardly fair to them, or even really kind, to minimise their opposition to the views of the majority of mankind. I feel sure this is what your son himself would think.[658]

The bulk of the book was largely in the words of the objectors themselves. One chapter dealt with the careers and views of representative men, and made use of many court-martial statements. Another described prison conditions and their effects, mostly as they were revealed in letters written from prison. The compilation of these chapters offered little scope for Russell's distinctive style. As for the selection of material, some might have accused him of leaning too far towards softening the tone of the political objectors. There is a piquancy in finding Lilla Brockway disgusted with Mrs Hobhouse for the description of Fenner, which leant heavily on his missionary parentage. 'It sounds,' she wrote to Marshall, 'as though he were a wretched little Sunday-school prig.'[659]

In the first chapter, a short general statement of the problem, Russell's authorship can clearly be recognised. It begins with a lucid outline of the position of the absolutists, and then moves into the argument for their release. When Russell came to present this ostensibly from the point of view of the pro-war Mrs Hobhouse, and for an audience of the like-minded or even less liberal, he was not able to prevent (or to resist) a suggestion of satire, or at the very least of double meaning. He wrote severely of the absolutists that although their numbers were negligible as far as the Army was concerned, 'there is no doubt that the treatment of them has caused criticism abroad, and has tended in this country to rouse sympathy for the very class which, of all others, right-minded people would least wish to invest with the halo of heroic endurance'. In another passage he purports to explain the wrong-headed beliefs of the men:

They will say in all sincerity that they yield to none in anxiety to save their country, and many of them in support of this can point to a past record of self-sacrificing social service. But they maintain, paradoxical as it may appear, that victory in war is not so important to the nation's welfare as many other things. It must be confessed that in this contention they are supported by certain sayings of our Lord, such as, 'What shall it profit a man if he gain the whole world and lose his own soul?' Doubtless such statements are to be understood figuratively, but the history of religion shows that founders of religions are always apt to be understood literally by some of their more slavish followers. These men believe that the greatest goods are spiritual goods. They believe, like Spinoza, that hatred can be overcome by love, a view which appears to derive support from a somewhat hasty reading of the Sermon on the Mount.[660]

One wonders how much closer Russell could have got to mocking his readers or even the nominal author. Such a passage could hardly have been written by Margaret Hobhouse, but fortunately for the cause, no contemporary reader seems to have questioned the authorship. The book was of course hailed by the anti-war press and praised by the liberal papers, but also earned favourable reviews in *The Times Literary Supplement* and in the *Observer*. Even the *Spectator* admitted that the little book deserved 'the attention of the Government and of the public generally'. Four editions were printed between July and October 1917, a total of 18000 copies. Mrs Hobhouse gave all her profits to the cause of prison reform, and there is no reason to suppose that Russell received a penny for his work. The NCF distributed copies to all who attended the Inter-Allied Socialist Conference at the end of August; Milner gave one to the King;[661] 100 were placed in libraries by the Fellowship at Mrs Hobhouse's expense. Well pleased with the circulation, Mrs Hobhouse gave a donation of £6 anonymously to the NCF.[662]

Russell's venture into ghost-writing must be judged a success. '*I Appeal Unto Caesar*' was the most prestigious of several publications which appeared in mid-1917, designed to take advantage of and to feed the mellowing feeling towards the absolutists which was beginning to appear particularly in religious circles, and which was even affecting the fringes of Government. Russell himself seems to have had no doubt of its effectiveness, writing complacently in November in an article in *The Tribunal*:

As a result largely of Mrs. Hobhouse's "I Appeal Unto Caesar", many influential people who formerly had only contempt and derision for the C.O. have now come to believe that the policy of indefinitely prolonged imprisonment is not the wisest in the case of men whose sincerity and earnestness are sufficiently patent to arouse public sympathy.[663]

Margaret Hobhouse's name (which she always gave as 'Mrs Henry Hobhouse') and her capacity for making a nuisance of herself, carried weight, and what Russell had done was to ensure that that weight was thrown into the scale on behalf of all the absolutists and not merely for her son and perhaps other religious objectors. Possibly Russell chuckled inwardly when the FSC, in a letter to the *Friend* to explain their opposition to an appeal to the Government for release, innocently made a comment directly in line with Russell's own thinking. 'Any action,' they wrote, 'in support of alleviation, exemption, or release comes better from those who do not themselves hold our position. Hence the value of books like, "I Appeal Unto Caesar".'[664] But some Friends thought it all led to 'exaggerated hopes', causing the imprisoned men 'to become self-centred' instead of filling 'their minds with the greatness of the cause'.[665]

'*I Appeal Unto Caesar*' was Russell's most spectacular piece of ghost-writing in the summer of 1917, but it was probably not his only one. The Rev. F. B. Meyer published a substantial pamphlet, *The Majesty of Conscience*.[666] Meyer was the Baptist minister who had frequently shown concern for the conscientious objectors, although himself a supporter of the war. He was not greatly trusted or liked by Russell and his colleagues, and his judgment was sometimes poor: Russell, in the throes of the crisis over the banning order, had reported in disgust that Meyer had written that he was glad to see the matter satisfactorily settled by the Government's offer to withdraw the order 'if I hold my tongue'. ('Meyer,' said Russell, 'is a worm.')[667] The evidence connecting Russell with *The Majesty of Conscience* is less conclusive than for Mrs Hobhouse's book, but some passages in it bear the hallmark of his style, though they are interspersed with others which do not seem likely to be by Russell. The NCF was certainly active in encouraging Meyer and was supplying him with information. After an interview with General Childs, 'who was obviously very much perturbed about the Mrs. Hobhouse book', Meyer had wondered whether it was wise to go on with his planned pamphlet, and it was only after a long talk with Hunter (from the NCF head office) that 'he consented for publication of his book to be continued with'. Childs had questioned the accuracy of the portrait of the religious character of the COs in the Hobhouse book, so Hunter fortified Meyer with more specific data about those of the men who could be described as 'truly religious people'. Reporting to Marshall, who was away ill at the time, Hunter added, 'I think that the pamphlet is so important that there is no objection to Meyer stressing the religious side', a comment which drew an approving checkmark in the margin from Marshall.[668]

Anonymity is not the same as ghost-writing; but Russell and the *Herald* seem to have taken advantage of the fact that leaders were unsigned to put some of Russell's opinions before the public in July 1917 without the controversy and opprobrium which now attached to his name. Russell commented on the assignment in letters to both Constance Malleson and to Ottoline Morrell. The two articles which have been identified were published on 21 July and 28 July. Both deal with the situation in Germany, then experiencing a government crisis which lead to great hopes—affecting even Lloyd George—of a more democratic government in Germany with which it might be possible to negotiate. In the second article, Russell (if indeed he was the author) ingeniously turns the situation back on the Prime Minister by constructing 'the speech which Mr. Lloyd George would have delivered if he had adopted the same term as was adopted by the German Chancellor'. Russell clearly felt that there was a real hope of a changing Germany, but doubted whether the British Government was sufficiently open to respond in a way which would move a negotiated peace nearer.[669]

Less satisfying than his career in concealed authorship were Russell's efforts to replace Marshall in the political sphere. After her resignation in July it proved extremely difficult to find a successor who would undertake such of the work as the National Committee had decided should continue. Several memoranda which Marshall drew up during these months show how extensive this field of her work had been, and the restrictions now placed on it still left a very large area of responsibility. Presumably it was almost in desperation that Russell, at the July Committee meeting, provisionally agreed to take it on. If Marshall's judgment was impaired by tension and overwork, this incident suggests that Russell's was also faltering. Rumours, later substantiated, were again rife of a renewed attempt from within the Cabinet to obtain the release of the absolutists, and there were many important people whose influence might be enlisted. On 17 August, for example, when Russell returned from a short holiday, one of a number of items on a list of work which Marshall had drawn up for him read, '*Political work*. All important interviews are waiting for you to deal with them—Smuts, Milner, Parmoor, Bryce, Asquith, Salisbury, and Gilbert Murray'.[670] Russell was too much aware of the disfavour in which he was held to feel competent to take on this kind of thing, and too busy—he was soon to begin giving a lecture course on mathematical logic—but no one else came forward. No wonder, too, that Marshall resented handing over work she did so well and enjoyed so much to someone who so little wanted to take it on. By September Russell had decided that he could not possibly handle the extra load, and this side of the work was virtually laid down for a few months, while attempts were made to find someone suitable to take it on. In November Marshall agreed to resume the responsibility, although, by the wish of the National Committee, the close contact with the War Office was not renewed.[671]

By that time Marshall felt keenly that opportunities for influencing the Government had been allowed to slip by—but in fact it is doubtful whether any NCF action would significantly have changed events. Even all the sympathy aroused by the Hobhouse supporters did not suffice to win release for the absolutists, partly because of their own intransigent attitude, and partly because of that of the authorities. Allen and others expressed a categorical resistance to the idea of non-punitive internment which was mooted at about this time, and the Fellowship did not welcome a scheme for jail delivery to be based on the King's pardon following on the judgment of yet another tribunal. The latter suggestion came from Lord Parmoor—a respected ally of the conscientious objectors—but with some justification Russell thought it would be used only to free the most notable cases, for whom public sympathy could easily be aroused.[672] On the other side, the War Office resolutely blocked any suggestion of release on terms that might have been acceptable to most absolutists. Possibly the attitude originated with Lord Derby or General Macready, but all the evidence suggests that Childs, more than any other single man, was responsible for stonewalling the attempts to get the men out of prison. He continued to insist on legal treatment for conscientious objectors in the hands of the military—and he also facilitated the release of a number of unfortunates who had become mentally deranged, but any who thought he would further the release of the absolutists were mistaken. In the interview with Meyer, as reported by Hunter, Childs certainly seems to have represented himself as one of 'those who were endeavouring to get the "Absolutists" out', and had told Meyer that the Hobhouse book made it more difficult. Hunter had had to reassure Meyer that 'the only thing that is likely to strengthen Childs' position in endeavouring to do something for the "Absolutists" was to change public opinion'.[673] But Childs surely must have known very well whose cause would be furthered by the book, and at almost the same time, upon hearing that a copy had gone to the King, he wrote to the King's Assistant Private Secretary. He again said, as he had to Meyer, that the absolutists were being represented as a body of dedicated Christians, which he judged was far from being the case. He added bluntly that 'the day that absolute exemption is granted to anybody whether his objection be based on religious or on other grounds we are beaten'.[674]

After all the earlier hopes, little progress was made. Russell and Marshall were kept informed when Milner tried twice more, in August and in October, to get the Cabinet to agree to release, but he failed again.[675] Good grounds to hope for the release of the absolutists as a class never recurred while the war lasted.[676] But public opinion had been aroused to some extent, and the Government, thinking it advisable to offer some palliative, promised certain concessions for men who had served twelve months with hard labour, whether the period was made up of one or more sentences. To Russell, most of the mitigations seemed more insulting than helpful. Some, such as the privilege of paying a fellow-prisoner to clean one's cell, were clearly class-oriented and economically discriminatory. Others were niggardly in the extreme, granting permission, for example, for the prisoner to write and to receive once a fortnight a letter about one-third of the length of that previously allowed once a month, and to be visited for fifteen minutes once a month instead of for half an hour every two months. The only concession of real value allowed the men to have two exercise periods a day, and to converse during these times. Russell wrote an indignant editorial, and Marshall expressed the opinion strongly (but unofficially) that the objectors would do well to reject the supposed mitigations outright, except for the one concerning exercise and conversation.[677]

Russell found more to welcome in the Government's announcement, made at the same time, that seriously ill objectors might be released from prison, a concession that owed a good deal to the Hobhouse lobby and to the impact of '*I Appeal Unto Caesar*'. When Milner failed to gain release for the absolutists, Margaret Hobhouse separated their cause as such from her efforts on behalf of her son. Although the public and Parliamentary lobby was still demanding release for all (influential churchmen submitted a memorandum in late November), the letter which Mr and Mrs Henry Hobhouse wrote to the Home Secretary petitioned for the release of Stephen only, and urged the Government to consider 'that the cause of Stephen Hobhouse stands somewhat alone.' The grounds given were that he was unfit for service, should have been granted absolute exemption, and was now in deteriorating health. The letter must have caused great distress to Stephen if he ever read it.[678] There had been too much publicity for such special favouritism to be shown: but it was still possible to make a distinction between the sick and the intransigent. Hobhouse and Allen were released at almost the same time, but only on the basis of their illness.

Permitting the release of prisoners who might otherwise have died in prison does not seem an enormous concession, and indeed was one which was likely to save the Government a great deal of adverse publicity and embarrassment. Yet, as Rae has shown, even this seems to have had to be politically bought by an agreement on the part of the Government to withdraw its opposition to the five-year disfranchisement of conscientious objectors,[679] which accordingly went through as part of the 1918 Suffrage Act.

Margaret Hobhouse's campaign, together with the political uses to which it could be put, had certainly played a large part in gaining the release of her son. To some extent Allen rode to freedom on Stephen's coat-tails, aided by his own notoriety and the fact that, unlike Hobhouse, he was now so ill that fears for his life were well-founded. A few days later a prisoner, Arthur Butler, who was neither well-connected nor notorious, died of tuberculosis in Preston prison: his mother had been allowed one brief visit the day before his death, but there had been no talk of his release.[680] Interestingly too, when Hobhouse was released he was immediately transferred to Army Reserve W (which rendered him free of fear of rearrest unless he misbehaved), while Allen and the other handful of sick men who were shortly to gain their freedom were let out under the 'Cat and Mouse' provisions which had been introduced in 1913 to deal with hunger-striking suf-fragettes, and which permitted re-arrest as soon as the prisoner's health was restored. Later all were transferred to Army Reserve W, and few of these sick men seem to have been sent back to prison, although later, when hunger strikes became common, rearrests were not infrequent.[681]

Russell was immensely relieved when Allen's release ended the saga of his work strike. Predictably, constant punishment had caused his health to worsen rapidly. He had entered Winchester prison on 1 June 1917, and had been removed to the prison hospital a month later. He was allowed no communication with the outside (although scraps of news leaked out) until November, when Marshall's first visit was aborted by the prison authorities, without explanation, after four minutes, an act of gross and seemingly meaningless brutality (unless, of course, Marshall committed a breach of regulations).[682] Within a few days he was released and removed directly to a Quaker nursing home in Hampstead to begin his long and incomplete convalescence. The tangible outcome of his suffering and of the permanent damage he had allowed to be inflicted on him had been no more than to win his own freedom and that of others in like condition. It brought the release of the absolutists no nearer, and indeed it could be argued that it made it less likely, by giving the Government the excuse it needed to get the Hobhouse lobby off its back. Allen as we saw had become convinced that the work strike was for him a moral issue, and with this one cannot argue. But any strategic value it might have had was negated when he decided to go ahead on his own in the face of the National Committee's opposition and the evident unreadiness of the Fellowship at large.

To have Allen finally out of jail lifted a heavy weight from Russell. After his first visit to the nursing home, which Allen was too ill to receive until mid-December, Russell wrote to Ottoline Morrell, rather over-optimistically:

He is terribly worn out, and his heart is gone wrong, but I think he only needs rest—there is nothing really serious if he is allowed to remain at liberty. . . . It was a very very great joy seeing him again. He has had a most terrible time—he sleeps very little, and when he does, he has ghastly nightmares about what he has gone through.[683]

The effect on Marshall was more complex. Russell had underestimated the seriousness of Allen's illness, and the tension of waiting out his long and uncertain recovery was forced on her. Just at the time of his release, her own health became a matter of urgent concern. A lengthy illness in September had been followed by a state of health even worse than her usual one, and her friends began to fear she was in danger of a mental breakdown.[684] Russell concurred and was himself so desperate about the position that he momentarily gave approval to a plan which did all concerned no credit either for humanity or good sense. Details have not come to light, but Marshall's suggestion, made shortly before the news of Allen's release, seems to have been that she would deliberately expose herself to prosecution (cause would not have been hard to find) and would combine testimony for the anti-conscriptionists with a period of enforced rest in jail. Swanwick begged Marshall to give up the idea and took Russell severely to task for in any way countenancing it: reason soon prevailed and the idea was dropped.[685] But by the time Allen was released, Marshall was ready, although not without bitterness and reluctance, to withdraw from active involvement in the Fellowship. Later, after the intervening period of great anxiety while Allen was in a Quaker convalescent home and she with her parents in Keswick, they spent some months together in the north of England and in Scotland. Allen, of course, remained nominally chairman of the NCF. Both kept in touch with the organisation, but Allen was not well enough to resume any kind of work until after the war, and although Marshall occasionally entered into correspondence with members of the executive and of the office staff, she played no active role beyond appearing at the closing Convention in November 1919.

As for Russell, his decision to give up active leadership in the NCF had been taken some weeks before. Allen's release had made him more comfortable in the decision. 'It was,' he wrote, 'very largely for his sake that I kept on with it so long.'[686] His year as chairman had been extremely busy, but he had not found it altogether fulfilling. On the positive side, the year had held the glorious optimism engendered by the Russian revolution, and a long period of hope for the release of the absolutists. In November, Russell had been 'immensely cheered' by Lord Lansdowne's letter to the *Daily Telegraph* in favour of opening peace negotiations.[687] But the first two faded by the end of the year, and the Lansdowne letter could promise nothing substantial or immediate. Russell's personal life has not been discussed in any detail here, but during the course of 1917 his relationship with Lady Constance Malleson was the source of intermittent happiness, but also of pain. At least it had enabled him to redefine his relationship with Lady Ottoline Morrell, who had shown a desire to run his life even after their intimacy had ended. They remained friends, and the friendship was of value to Russell, but there was not unnaturally an underlying tension. Russell protected his developing relationship with Constance Malleson by an increased reserve towards Ottoline Morrell, which she resented at the time, and even by lies, which hurt and angered her later, when she knew more of what had taken place.[688] The whole range of Russell's correspondence with Lady Ottoline reveals, as nothing else does, how subject he was to changing moods and to deep periods of depression. During 1917, these became even more frequent. The pattern seems to have been that whenever Russell was not engaged in some active project which he could directly connect with his vision for the future, he sank into despair. The letters to Ottoline are heavily weighted with this despair, maybe disproportionately so; he had a great need to share his pain with her, and perhaps did not equally share his times of joy. If he had anything gloomy to say, it was to her that he said it. On new year's day, 1918, again discouraged about what work there was to do for peace, he added: 'The year that is just over is the first since I grew up during which I have written nothing to speak of.'[689] The phrase 'nothing to speak of', in one sense, served to continue his deliberate concealment of his highly successful ghost-writing.

As chairman of the NCF, Russell had had successes and failures. The absolutists were still in prison, trouble still occasionally threatened in the Home Office camps, the affiliation with the

Quakers had weakened, but the essential unity of the Fellowship had survived the stresses imposed on it, and the men in jail remained steadfast. In spite of his tendency to criticise himself as an administrator, Russell must have recognised that he had done what had to be done. He does not seem to have been able to take great satisfaction in it, but he remained committed to the job until the end of the year, although (as we have seen) he would have been glad to be free of it sooner.[690] Significantly, when the time came, he was able to hand over without guilt or regret.

By Autumn 1917 many elements combined to make Russell feel that the time had come for him to retire. Once his mind was made up, his mood lightened, and he wrote to Ottoline Morrell outlining his plans and his reasons:

> I give up all pacifist work at Xmas, except an occasional committee. I have undertaken to write a book for an American publisher by April, on "Socialism, Syndicalism and Anarchism", which involves a good deal of reading. After that, I want to get back to philosophy, and later on I want to make a bigger and more solid book on the lines of "Social Reconstruction" if I can. Pacifist work, except by those who were *not* pacifists from the start, seems to me now quite useless, and the sense of futility drives one mad. But since I decided to give it up, I have grown sane again, but rather sober and drab. . . .
>
> Until Xmas I am still terribly busy—but now that the end is in sight I don't mind.[691]

The letter probably gives a fair picture of Russell's state of mind. The struggle of the conscientious objectors seemed to him still worth while, but he was disillusioned about prospects for their release, and if passive endurance was to be the only way for them, he thought there were others who could better support them than he. Further, as he said, only new voices against war could make an impression.[692] He felt the need to change his angle of attack. He would not give up all political writing, but he would move back one stage from the front line and work again on the underlying principles of politics, and on educating the public. Although he said he accepted the commission to write *Roads to Freedom: Socialism, Syndicalism and Anarchism* 'solely for the sake of the filthy lucre',[693] he welcomed the chance to organise and expound his thinking on matters which the Russian revolution had made him see as so vitally relevant. The expansion of *Principles of Social Reconstruction* was never carried out, but the plan shows he thought there was still a message to give.

Of all Russell's reasons for retiring, the two strongest were probably a kind of battle-fatigue and the pull of philosophy. Of his inability to continue the struggle, he wrote:

I think very good things will happen after the war (not so much in this country), but I have no longer any wish to have a part in them. I see Macdonald and Snowden and Morel, and the others who have done the fighting against the war all through, are in similar mood, though they are less self-conscious. Public resistance to one's community seems somehow to sever one's roots, so that one gradually perishes.[694]

For Russell, the desire for renewal was not separable from the need to return to philosophy: three years of what seemed to him unsuccessful wrestling with the temporal had made him long for what he regarded as the infinite. He needed to put himself in touch again with the abstract values which were the justification for the whole devoted effort and which, to continue his metaphor, would nourish his roots again. The civilisation which Russell had seen going up in flames in 1914 was for him an abstract concept—and one which depended on the highest intellectual endeavour as much as it did on the preservation of individual integrity against the demands of militarism. In spite of his exile from Cambridge, he knew the return to philosophy would not be hard: he had never left it as completely as he had expected to. While the Government and the pacifists saw him as a rebel, he was still the world's most eminent logician, and students and scholars sought him out.[695] In 1916, when Russell was excited by the prospect of 'endless work on political theory', he had recognised that some day he might be 'suddenly overwhelmed by the passion for things that are eternal and perfect, like mathematics'. He added that even the most abstract political theory 'is terribly mundane and temporary'. By the end of 1917 the time had come (although not suddenly), and he looked forward keenly to getting back to philosophy in the spring of 1918.[696] He had even taken some first steps. While he was arranging to give his lectures in the north of England on 'Political Ideals', he also planned two courses of lectures on mathematical logic and on philosophical logic in London—one in the late autumn of 1917 and the other early in the new year.[697] The latter course proved to be one of Russell's seminal works in philosophy, when it was published as 'The Philosophy of Logical Atomism'.[698] He had also begun again to contribute reviews of philosophical books to periodicals like the *Nation* and *English Review*.[699] There was another factor drawing Russell back to philosophy: somehow in the course of the war, a block which had descended on his philosophical thought as a result of severe—and, he thought, justified—criticism by his most outstanding student, Ludwig Wittgenstein, in 1913[700] had at last dissipated, probably through Wittgenstein's prolonged absence in the Austrian army. He felt free again to move forward—free, and very eager.[701]

Russell gave up the chairmanship of the NCF at the end of 1917.[702] The elections to the National Committee were delayed by the removal of the ballot-papers in a police raid,[703] and votes would not be counted until the second week in January. The form and tone of the election differed from that of December 1916—mainly because the job of chairman of the NCF was now one that no one wanted, and indeed it was hard to find people with the health and the time to spare to make up the National Committee. Members were not asked to choose an acting chairman or acting honorary secretary, but only to cast their votes for four 'national members' and for divisional representatives who would then choose officers from among themselves.[704] Meanwhile—and well into the new year, even after the new officers were appointed—Russell conti-nued to attend and to chair a great many meetings of various committees.[705] Continuity would have been difficult without his help, especially as Marshall's illness forced her from the scene at just the same time. But once he was officially free, enjoying reading for his book on *Roads to Freedom* and looking forward to the still greater happiness of returning to philosophy, his mind began to put the turmoil of the last months in perspective. On 23 December 1917, he wrote to Morrell: 'Today I went to the Westminster Cathedral and sat there some time—I always think it very beautiful—and listening to the chanting one's mind gets gradually to permanent things, away from exasperation and despair. Mankind are terribly tragic, but there is a splendour through all their blindness.'[706] But Russell had one last ordeal to face before his wartime exasperations were over.

CHAPTER 15
PHILOSOPHER IN PRISON

During a large part of 1916 and 1917 it is no exaggeration to say that a spell in prison was something Russell had included in his plans for the immediate future. He had been sure his opposition to the war and his support of the conscientious objectors would sooner or later result in a prison sentence. But as he entered 1918, the likelihood seemed remote. His withdrawal from leadership in the No-Conscription Fellowship was almost completed, and although he had been re-elected as a member of the National Committee both his public statements and his private correspondence make it plain he did not intend active involvement.

On the other hand, he was not as detached from the concerns of the NCF at the beginning of 1918 as he had perhaps hoped to be. He was not finding it easy to drop completely something to which he had given himself so totally, and he not only attended the National Committee meeting of 11 and 12 January but took part in the discussion on almost every issue that arose. A final attempt was made by Alexander Wilson to persuade him to continue as acting chairman, but on this Russell was firm, saying he had quite decided not to serve again and not to undertake any executive work beyond attendance at National Committee meetings. Russell nominated Salter instead, and the latter finally agreed, although clearly with great reluctance.[707] Russell stayed on a special *ad hoc* committee concerning militarism in schools, an issue in which the NCF was interested especially since the Government's decision to register boys at age fifteen and call them up before their eighteenth birthday. He also agreed to serve as one of the NCF representatives on the National Peace Council, but he stuck to his decision not to take any executive responsibility.

One of the last assignments Russell accepted for the No-Conscription Fellowship was to write a front-page article for *The Tribunal* of 3 January 1918, and an editorial the following week. He later recalled doing this only to help out the editor, who was ill.[708] Russell had written editorials or articles for *The Tribunal* almost weekly since 7 December 1916 (a total of fifty-five articles), and that of 3 January, entitled 'The German Peace Offer',[709] is far from being one of his better ones in style or content. The Bolsheviks, who had come to power in Russia in November 1917, knew that Russia must have peace. Lenin had called for a general armistice, followed by a peace with no annexations and no indemnities. Not surprisingly, the Allied governments showed no sign of falling meekly in line behind the new and uncongenial Russian leader, but the move was welcomed by German statesmen whose hope from the Russian revolution all along had been an end to the need to fight on the Eastern front; and it was also greeted by socialists in France and Britain. While it was perhaps logical from the pacifist point of view to hope the move would hasten the coming of peace, with or without social revolution, it seems in retrospect naïve to have thought that Germany's leaders were any more sincere or disinterested than the Allied leaders whom the pacifists now so much distrusted. Yet Russell's article seemed to imply this, and was less well thought-out than his anonymous *Herald* leaders of July 1917. But the main thrust was that prolonging the war would reduce Europe to starvation and ensure that when the revolution came—as he was sure it ultimately would—it would be so violent as to bring all that was best in Western civilisation to an end. Russell called on Labour to use its power to bring about a just and lasting peace, on the lines of the war aims which had been drawn up at the Labour Party conference just a few days previously.

None of this, it may be imagined, was welcome to the Government—which of course monitored *The Tribunal* every week[710]—but the remark for which they decided to prosecute Russell was peripheral to the main theme of the article. In the passage on the expected effects of starvation throughout Europe, Russell had turned his attention briefly to the part that the Americans might be expected to play, and had written: 'The American Garrison which will by that time be occupying England and France, whether or not they will prove efficient against the Germans, will no doubt be capable of intimidating strikers, an occupation to which the American Army is accustomed when at home.' Russell was always most bitter when he was attacking a fallen idol, and now that America had moved away from the role of neutral peacemaker in which he had earlier hoped she would be cast, her faults were very apparent to Russell. For good measure, he threw in a few remarks, insulting—and not at a very elevated level—but seemingly not subversive,[711] about the British Government: 'I do not say that these thoughts are in the mind of the Government. All the evidence tends to show that there are no thoughts whatever in their mind, and that they live from hand to mouth consoling themselves with ignorance and sentimental twaddle.'

On 1 February two police detectives called on Russell while he was in his bath, asked him to confirm that he was the author of 'The German Peace Offer', and mentioned the sentence about strike-breaking. They asked him whether he edited *The Tribunal*, but when he answered that he did not, they did not enquire further.[712] Russell and Joan Beauchamp, the publisher of *The Tribunal*, received summonses a few days later to appear at Bow Street court on Saturday, 9 February.[713] When the summons came Russell wrote to Ottoline Morrell: 'It was some remarks about America that they chiefly disliked.[714] It is very annoying, particularly as the remarks were rather foolish and not good for propaganda.' At this point he expected a fine, and planned to refuse to pay it or have it paid for him. In a depressed mood he wrote: 'I am so little good for work just now that I would just as soon be in prison; it is the only way to be useful when one is so slack.'[715]

The contrast between this trial and Russell's earlier one is marked, although the NCF did its best to make an occasion of the event, which was described in a front-page article in *The Tribunal*:

There was a crowded court at Bow Street on Saturday afternoon last, when the *Tribunal* prosecutions were heard. The National Committee of the N.-C.F., which was sitting at this time, adjourned to the court and many other people well known in the movement were to be seen there.

Mr. Bertrand Russell received many congratulatory handshakes on his entry, and the atmosphere was tense with interest and enthusiasm.[716]

The Crown prosecutor (Mr Travers Humphreys) read out the offending passage, and declared that it would have a 'diabolical effect' if published without contradiction, and also that it was 'difficult to overstate the effect which that passage would have in all probability upon the soldiers of this country and their Allies'. General Childs was in court in case his support should be needed to back this statement. Russell's Bloomsbury friends laughed appreciatively when the magistrate (Sir John Dickinson) read out Russell's comments on the Government, and the mood of the magistrate doubtless deteriorated.[717] He convicted and sentenced Russell to six months in the second division, without the option of a fine. Beauchamp was sentenced to a fine of £60 and £15-15s costs. The penalties were unexpectedly heavy, and a number of those present were startled by the extraordinary bitterness with which Dickinson pronounced the sentences, declaring that 'Mr. Russell seems to have lost all sense of decency and fairness, and has gone out of his way to insult by deliberate and designed sneer the army of a great nation which is closely allied to us. . . . The offence is a very despicable one'.[718] Russell wrote that he never 'felt anything equal to the concentrated venom of the magistrate' in sentencing him. 'It was a blast of hatred, quite astonishing.'[719] Ammon said he found it extremely difficult to restrain himself from contempt of court 'at the obvious bias and spite of the magistrate'. Lytton and James Strachey came away with their 'teeth chattering with fury'.[720] There had been a second charge against Beauchamp on the grounds of publishing 'false statements', in a letter from a conscientious objector who described the respect in which the resisters now seemed to be held in the Army, but the hearing was adjourned and the charge later dropped when the defence offered to call witnesses to support the truth of the statement. The Crown prosecutor asked for the adjournment *sine die* after consulting with General Childs (who knew only too well the NCF's capacity for backing up its statements). The charge had been unwisely worded in that it made the truth and not the effect of the statements the issue.[721]

Russell and Beauchamp 'were conducted with all solemnity to the cells' while bail was arranged.[722] As the court emptied, an incident occurred which has not previously been recorded, and which showed something of the tensions between the officials and the anti-militarists. Ammon wrote to Marshall that as General Childs left the courtroom a young man asked him if he was proud of his work:

At first the gallant General thought he meant his ordinary work but after reflection it dawned that possibly it meant getting B.R. six months. Whereupon he wrote to me that if I knew the young man I might tell him that he might get "a punch under the jaw" from someone not quite so equably tempered as himself . . . he had no more to do with it than myself and was only summoned as a witness in case evidence should be needed as to the probable effect of B.R.'s article on the troops, also he was disturbed by the thought that he shook hands with me outside the Court which might be the cause of internecine trouble.[723]

The meaning of the passage is not completely clear, but it is likely that Childs knew of the criticism Marshall had suffered for her dealings with him, and possible that he had had similar criticism. If so, he would find it wounding. He, Marshall, and Russell all knew that the exchanges had been conducted according to an implicit protocol—in effect, that of the gentry of 'liberal England'; both Marshall and he are likely to have felt their honour impugned by what they saw as the unwillingness of colleagues to trust them to negotiate with respect and good faith according to these understood rules and regulations. Years later (in 1935) Childs and Lord Allen corresponded and both spoke of the mutual trust and respect which had existed between them.[724]

Meanwhile the friends of the offenders waited outside for their

release on bail pending the hearing of their appeals. *The Tribunal*
reported: 'The crowd waited patiently for their appearance, and a
hearty cheer went up as they came down the steps. The enthusiasm displayed reminded us of the prosecutions in the early days of
the Fellowship, and it was good to see the high spirits of both
"criminals".'[725]

Russell had put on a good act, but he was really in anything but
high spirits. He wrote to Ottoline Morrell that evening: 'The
whole business is hateful to me—the charge is not one that is any
good for propaganda—and I profoundly dislike the prospect of six
months in prison. Besides, I had meant to have done with that sort
of work, and to get back to philosophy. However, it is the fortune
of war, and one mustn't take it too seriously'.[726] As he thought
about it, his case seemed to him after all 'not a bad one for
propaganda' and he began to plan his defence for the appeal,
although later he decided to leave this in the hands of the
lawyers.[727] But the whole business remained a chore, something
that had been forced on him and had to be gone through as
creditably as possible, a far cry from the challenge that had been
the essence of the 1916 trial. His friends and acquaintances offered
him a great deal of sympathy and support, although a number
agreed with him that the passage at issue was a poor one to have to
defend. F. M. Cornford wrote:

I must say first that I am sorry you wrote that about the American army, because
it seems to me fantastically untrue (the sort of thing you say at a dinner table, but
ought not to print). Also (though you cd. hardly foresee this) it has given this
base and cowardly government a chance of manoeuvring you on to ground
which is indefensible. ... Of course everything the judge said was canting
humbug—but all this injures your power of standing up for the really noble and
important things you have stood for. ... I care more for you than I ever did. ...
Will you let me know if there is anything I can do?[728]

Immediately after he heard the outcome of the Bow Street trial
Allen wrote perceptively: 'If I can read you aright, I surmise you
are bothered with the result and wish to goodness there was some
way, especially just now, by which you could be unmolested with
prison and politics. ... I know you rejoice fearlessly in the fight,
but you don't want to fight just now.'[729] The day after the trial
Gilbert Murray offered warm and generous support, writing:

I am filled with soreness and indignation at this further persecution of you. Of
course, as you know, I do not agree with your views of American policy, but I
am perfectly sure that neither Wilson nor Page nor the American Army, so far as
it has a means of expressing itself, wants people sent to prison for lèse majesté
when they use insulting language about them. ... I have just read your article in
the Tribunal of Jan. 3 and cannot understand how any honest magistrate can have

persuaded himself that there was anything in it to deserve punishment. . . . If I can be any use please let me know. I am doing what I can on my own.[730]

Russell wrote back appreciatively, taking the trouble to explain his position and letting Murray know that the cause of the persecution, as far as he could discover, was the fact that he had given up pacifist work almost entirely and 'the authorities realized that if they wished to punish me they must act at once, as I should not be committing any further crimes'. Russell added, with some bravado, that he did not much dislike the prospect of prison, provided he was allowed plenty of books to read.[731] The question Russell raised here of the Government's motivation in prosecuting him at this time and on such a picayune charge is still of interest—but still unanswerable. Possibly the Government felt Russell's influence in the United States would be weakened by giving publicity to such an anti-American utterance. Alternatively, perhaps Russell was only one part of a broader target—*The Tribunal* was subject to a series of attacks at this time, ranging from prosecutions to the breaking-up by the police of the presses on which it was printed. *The Tribunal* article had certainly been ill-timed: Home Office files indicate that it arrived on the desks of officials at the Home Office, the War Office and the Foreign Office at almost exactly the same time as the minute carrying the decision, made jointly by all these departments, to rescind the banning order because Russell was supposedly severing his connections with the pacifist organisations and ceasing his pacifist propaganda.[732]

If Russell had wanted any assurance of the affection in which he was held by those whose views were similar to his it was provided fortuitously just a week after his trial, when he agreed to go with Ottoline Morrell to a *Herald* League social (she referred to it as a reception, but the plebian term applied to it by Gladys Rinder appears to fit it much better). Rinder, a long-time worker in the NCF head office, wrote a vivid description in a letter to Marshall:

On Sat. even. I was at the Herald League Social where there were at least three times as many people as the Hall would hold to begin with. . . . The first diversion was caused by Lansbury's reference to B.R., who—unknown to the platform—was standing in the middle of the audience (we *all* had to stand for over an hour!) There were the usual cheers, then the audience by screaming and pointing opened the platform's eyes and next one saw the comic and interesting sight of B.R. carried by four undersized and rather feeble looking youths up the hall. He looked pallid but pleased and at the same time as if he was seriously wondering how soon he would be dropped with a thud on the floor, finally he had to climb over the balustrade and he never seems cut out for a gymnast!![733]

Another social occasion, which Russell contemplated with

horror, was planned for a month later—a dinner sponsored by the NCF officers to bid him farewell. Hunter, the good-hearted and energetic young man who was now doing much of the work at the head office, was the chief mover and would probably take the chair, where Russell thought he would be *'quite intolerable'* and would make him squirm to a degree which he could not contemplate calmly. Hunter was even threatening to recite an ode of his own composition. Russell's dread was not assumed: he added 'I hate being made a laughing-stock, much more than prison', and begged Allen to come out of retirement and rescue him by offering to take the chair.[734] Allen did not agree to come and no account of the occasion remains, but apparently it passed off much better than Russell had expected—anything would surely have been an improvement on his imaginings—and he confessed to Marshall that it had not been painful.[735]

Most of Russell's time between trial and appeal was taken up with more serious matters. He was 'working day and night' to finish *Roads to Freedom* before he went to prison, and in fact completed the book by mid-April;[736] he was still giving his second course of philosophical lectures, which came to an end on 12 March; and he became determined, on thinking it over, to do the most he honourably could to secure a mitigation of the sentence. There was little hope the length would be reduced, much less of a commutation to a fine, but perhaps the sentence could be served in the first division. Here an important question must be faced. What was Russell's justification for seeking and accepting the privilege of imprisonment in the first division instead of allowing himself to be subjected to the hardships faced by the young men with whom he had been working?

There is scarcely a need to deal with less than honourable motives.[737] No one who knew Russell believed him to be motivated by a desire to avoid discomfort or hardship or danger except of a very special sort: irreparable damage to his mind. And all who knew him well realised that his request for privileged treatment was conditional—that he would far rather accept any kind of punishment than be dishonoured. His notion of honour was simple and traditional: he must neither do nor seem to do anything in conflict with the principles he was known to stand for. It was important that his opponents should see him as honest and a man of his word, as well as that his friends should know him to be so.

Substantially, the reasons why Russell sought first division treatment grew from those which had motivated his withdrawal from active peace work at the end of 1917. Russell saw the NCF, through no fault of the conscientious objectors, as no longer playing the leading part in opposition to the continuation of the war, or in furthering the values he held dearest; and he was convinced that his part was to return to philosophy. 1918 was not 1916. In 1916 Russell had been no less conscious of the effect imprisonment might have on his intellectual powers, but prison then had seemed a vital form of service, part of a campaign whose success he still believed possible, and therefore (if it came) something to be welcomed whatever the consequences. In 1918, he still respected the stand of the conscientious objectors but it no longer seemed to him the growing edge of the fight for a better world. Since he had to go to jail, he would do so as a last ungrudged service to the No-Conscription Fellowship, but not believing that his imprisonment was helping any cause.

The signing, on 3 March 1918, of the treaty of Brest-Litovsk greatly discouraged Russell. He is not known to have commented at length on this treaty, by which Germany imposed crushing losses on the new Soviet state and ensured her own long-sought freedom to turn her undivided attention to the western front. But at about this time he wrote down some of his thoughts on political action, and it is apparent that Brest-Litovsk had reinforced his view of the changed position of the NCF. While he still applauded the individual decision to refuse to participate in the work of destruction, he made a distinction between this and 'the duty of preaching'. 'The attempt to persuade others,' he wrote, 'belongs to politics: it is a duty if it has a chance of being successful, not otherwise. ... I believe that since Brest-Litovsk our duty to preach has ceased, because our chance of success has ceased. The end will come—might come tomorrow—but not through us.' The relevance to Russell's own case and to that of the men still in prison becomes clear as we read on:

If we have any effect on posterity, it will be owing to what we have done together with what we shall do after the war. At present, the thing for us is, so far as is compatible with not helping them, to avoid their ruining our capacity for work afterwards. If we coud get the men out on condition they promised to abstain from propaganda, I should advise them to promise. Those momentarily free, who could do useful work if they evaded arrest, I should say, ought *now* to do so. I have long said the time would come for this policy, and I think it has come. That is to say, the part of our policy that was *political* (aimed at affecting public opinion) should be altered. It is a duty to attempt to stop a run-away horse, at whatever personal risk, but not a run-away express train.[738]

Russell did not publicise the statement, nor is he known to have made any attempt to have the NCF adopt the policy reversal adumbrated here, which might have caused a furore as great as that over the work strike, and might indeed have shattered morale among the imprisoned men. Much more important at this juncture is his view of what there was to be done. A sacrifice that could no longer be seen as bringing nearer the overthrow of militarism and the end of the war was of no use in itself. The time would come when there would again be essential work to be done by those to whom the cause of peace was important, and meanwhile Russell concluded the statement with the claim that their political duty was 'to be in readiness for after the war, and efficient when that time comes (if ever)'.

Nevertheless, Russell at first tried to make the best of the prospect of prison, as he had to Murray: it was a relief that he was not to serve at hard labour; he would not be in prison during the cold weather;[739] in second-division, he found prisoners were allowed a certain number of books (but not writing materials).[740] As he learnt more about second-division imprisonment—where conditions in fact did not differ substantially from those in the third division—he was not reassured, but on the whole he continued to think that the effects of his prison term could not be too severe, until an occurrence in late March brought him up with a sharp jolt and renewed all his fears. On 26 March Russell met E. D. Morel, who had been released at the end of January after serving five months in the second division.[741] Morel, like Russell, had been convicted of an offence under the Defence of the Realm Act and all the representations of his influential friends had failed to get him transferred to the first division. Russell was shocked by his appearance and his account of prison life and wrote to Murray:

I saw E. D. Morel yesterday for the first time since he came out, and was impressed by the seriousness of a six months sentence. His hair is completely white (there was hardly a tinge of white before)—when he first came out, he collapsed completely, physically and mentally, largely as the result of insufficient food. He says one only gets three quarters of an hour for reading in the whole day—the rest of the time is spent on prison work etc.[742]

Swartz dimisses Morel's sufferings in prison as 'malnutrition of the ego' followed by physical complications, and discounts the story that his hair turned white as a result of imprisonment.[743] Evidence scattered through Morel's papers justifies Swartz's estimate of him as 'a vain man' (with an underlying lack of self-confidence), and it is true that Russell, who deeply admired him for his pre-war work in the Congo Reform Association as well as for his service to the Union of Democratic Control, was blind to his weaker side.[744] He did not entertain the thought that Morel's sufferings may have been partly the outcome of deficiencies in his personality. If he had recognised this he might have dismissed it as irrelevant, for Russell was no stranger to the idea that prison was to every man his own special form of martyrdom: and he knew where his own vulnerability lay.[745] Soberly, he concluded his letter to Murray: 'It seems highly probable that if the sentence is not mitigated my mind will not remain as competent as it has been. I should regret this, as I still have a lot of philosophy that I wish to do.'[746]

Before his meeting with Morel on 26 March, Russell had been content to await the outcome of his appeal and leave it to his friends to do what they thought fit. He knew that Murray was doing what he could for him, speaking to Asquith and Lord Fisher and attempting to put pressure on the Home Secretary, George Cave.[747] Murray had hoped to influence Arthur Balfour, but this channel had closed to him in mid-March when Murray's plan to visit America, and to speak at a conference of the League to Enforce Peace, had found disfavour with 'the Northcliffe people in America', leading Balfour to withdraw his hoped-for support. Murray wrote that he had been attacked by the press 'as a Pacifist and Bolshevist and Potsdammer—almost as if I was you', and promised to look for other 'more blameless patriots' to speak to Balfour on Russell's behalf.[748]

After seeing Morel, Russell was no longer content to remain passive, and got in touch with the friends who had offered to help him. He had already begun to think out a plan of campaign to press for first division if the sentence should be confirmed and wrote to Murray:

Hirst is willing to approach Morley, Loreburn, Buckmaster and Lansdowne, asking them to write to Cave. It seems to me that Asquith and Grey might be willing to; also a certain number of un-political learned men. If you were willing, you could probably do this better than anyone else. If private representations fail (as they probably will) letters to the Press will be necessary. All this will have to be done quickly if it is to be effective.[749]

Murray wrote reassuringly that he had already approached several politicians. He was less hopeful about philosophers, whom he seems to have regarded as prone to prejudice, so Russell asked H. Wildon Carr (the president of the Aristotelian Society) to undertake this side of the campaign. Good Friday (29 March) found Russell near despair. A new blow had fallen—the age for compulsory military service was to be raised to fifty-one,[750] which meant he might be in prison until the war ended, 'which may be many years'. To Lady Ottoline he confessed it was hard 'to keep up any sort of courage'. There was a possibililty he might be able to get exemption, but he was not sure whether it would be in a form he could accept: 'Possibly I could get off, like Norton,[751] by having my philosophical work recognized as of national importance, but my duty to the Absolutists seems to make that impossible. It is a pity. . . . Still, I have done the bulk of my work—it is not comparable to the waste of a young man.'752

At the weekend Allen arrived to spend the next two days at T. S. Eliot's house at Marlow with Russell.753 Allen was living testimony of the ravages that could be wrought by prison—he was still appallingly thin, subject to insomnia, unable to stand much strain or excitement without a relapse, and it seemed to Russell he no longer had the smile that 'used to be so lovable'. But it was reassuring to find him 'morally . . . even better than he was' and with a very active mind,754 and it was a great relief that he was able to appreciate Russell's concern over the effects of imprisonment and to discuss fully with him what could be done to obtain exemption without compromise and without letting down the absolutists. Allen also gave Russell 'a great number of hints on prison life', some of which seem to have afforded amusement to both of them. Allen's high regard for him as an inspiration to the younger men both by his teaching and his example offered strength to Russell, yet some of Allen's old ambivalence can be detected—perhaps understandably. He sincerely hated the idea of Russell's suffering in prison, but he could not help thinking such suffering would be good for the cause, and in their discussion of the extension of the Military Service Act he even urged again the merits of the work strike.755

Russell's appeal hearing had been fixed for 12 April, but was not held until three weeks later—perhaps the delay was one of the first fruits of Murray's efforts. The latter continued very active in Russell's cause, and on Russell's drawing his attention to the new hazard under the Military Service Act, he added this to his concern over the sentence already passed. He did, however, reassure Russell that he thought that if the Home Secretary saw reason at all he would not relieve him with one hand and knock him down with the other.756 Russell was glad to have the help of his friends, especially Murray and Carr, but he was most anxious that they should not seem to commit him to any compromise with his principles. In a statement drawn up on 30 March (but whose use is unknown), Russell laid stress on the fact that he had been prosecuted just when he was known to be withdrawing from pacifist work, concluding: 'The authorities know that my present desire is to devote myself wholly to philosophy, to the exclusion of pacifist agitation, on the grounds that my efforts in such agitation are fruitless.'757 Soon, however, Russell became alarmed at the possible use that might be made of this approach by his friends. He had explained his position very carefully in a letter to Murray on 2 April:

I will not give an undertaking to avoid propaganda, but you may state that, *of your own knowledge*, my intention to return to technical philosophy was formed last autumn, and carried out at the New Year—*before there was any thought of prosecution*. (I want this to be quite clear; Carr can confirm it.) But although I see no present likelihood of altering this intention, I will not be under any honourable obligation not to alter it.[758]

Murray drew up a petition, to be used if the appeal failed, which also mentioned Russell's having given up pacifist work. But when Russell thought it over, he found that the phrasing might seem to commit him for the future, and wrote to Murray to ask him to omit anything which suggested this.[759] A rapid exchange of letters followed. Both Carr and Murray thought Russell was 'confusing the point at issue'.[760] Carr indeed told Murray he feared Russell was 'in a very dangerous condition of strain', and said Miss Wrinch (one of Russell's pupils) reported him as being in 'a great state of excitement'.[761] To Ottoline Morrell Russell wrote that the crisis in his affairs necessitated his staying by the telephone, and to Allen he wrote, 'I am having some difficulty in restraining my philosophical friends from committing me behind my back'.[762] But fortunately no breach developed. Murray wrote painstakingly to explain his view:

To plead at your trial that you had ceased, or intended to cease, or were willing to cease, from political propaganda would be a course requiring great care and exposed to all the dangers of misunderstanding which you speak of. But, when the trial is over and done with, I do not see that any statement made by other persons about your past history is open to the same objection.[763]

Few of the philosophers approached condoned Russell's position—Samuel Alexander described the offence as 'this incredible folly (and I must say wickedness) of his'—but most agreed to sign a petition.[764]

Russell seems to have found Murray's argument convincing although not wholly satisfying—he still thought 'people would feel it a little "slim" if, after obtaining advantages by means of it', he were to return to pacifist work.[765] But he had found a solution. He instructed his legal counsel not to mention his retirement from pacifist work, and wrote out 'an authorized statement' 'to be used if necessary'.[766] He sent a copy to Murray, explaining that he would like best to have it shown to the authorities whenever anything was asked on his behalf. If Murray thought that undesirable, Russell would rely on him not to do anything inconsistent with it, or that would lay him open to 'the charge of slimness' if he later returned to pacifism. If anything like this did happen, the statement could be made public. Russell concluded his letter. 'Probably it is best that I should not know henceforth what you do'. The accompanying statement, dated 8 April 1918, briefly recapitulated (in much the same terms as the statement of 30 March) the circumstances of Russell's retirement, mentioned that the War Office had been informed of the decision before the article complained of was written, and stressed that the retirement was only due to the fact that Russell saw nothing effective that he could do in pacifist work. He concluded with this reservation: 'If the situation were to change in such a way as to make me alter my judgment on this point, I should perhaps alter my decision. I will not give any undertaking, express or implied, which would remove my liberty to do so, or place me under any honourable obligation.'[767]

Russell's philosophical friends may have wished as much as the Government did that he would make a commitment to stay away from pacifist activity and devote himself to what seemed to them his real work, but it is safe to assume that they honourably observed his wishes and were careful to avoid giving the impression that he was willing to give any undertaking. He susbstantiated his intention to do serious philosophical work by sending Carr an outline of the work he planned for the near future, and which he would begin in prison if he was put in the first division.[768] In spite of the awkwardness of their protégé, Russell's friends made progress, and he had reason to face his delayed appeal hearing with some confidence, although he continued to assume that he would spend the next five months in prison.[769]

The appeal of Russell and Beauchamp was heard at the Sessions House, Clerkenwell, on 1 May, before Mr Lawrie, who was altogether more civil to both defendants than the Bow Street magistrate, Sir John Dickinson, had been. General Childs was called upon to give evidence as to whether in his opinion the passage quoted 'was likely to prejudice His Majesty's relations with a foreign power', but an objection to this evidence by Mr Tindal Atkinson, KC, appearing for Russell and Beauchamp, was upheld. Russell had collected for his defence material from an American government publication supporting the truth of his statement that troops had been used in strike-breaking in the States. He later said that it had not been admitted as evidence, but he may have been referring to the original trial, since at the appeal Atkinson quoted without hindrance from what was presumably the same US government publication.[770] Atkinson also referred to a recent letter from Sidney Low in *The Times* which had criticised the US for the paucity of her contribution so far to the Allied war effort, and pointed out that no charges had been laid against *The Times*. 'It appeared,' he said, 'like a case of catching the minnow and letting the whale go free. He thought perhaps the word "minnow" was hardly the right one—he might almost have said "stickleback"'. Many of those present greeted this with laughter, taking it to be a complimentary description of Russell, although it was probably meant to refer to *The Tribunal*.[771]

Finally, both appeals were dismissed, but Mr Lawrie stated 'that the bench felt that it would be a great loss to the country if Mr Russell, a man of great distinction, were confined in such a form that his abilities would not [have] full scope and the sentence would [be] served in the first division'. Mr Lawrie was also clearly reluctant to send Beauchamp to jail at all, but when she refused to pay the fine, she received one month in the first division.[772]

The immediate objective of Russell and his friends had been achieved and he went to serve his term in the first division. No clear picture emerges from all the extant correspondence as to how this had been accomplished. In his autobiography,[773] Russell said he owed it to the intervention of Arthur Balfour (who was Foreign Secretary, and a philosopher in his own right). The link between this and the efforts of Murray and Carr is missing, although it will be remembered that Murray had planned to find advocates in that quarter. A more intriguing suggestion is that the Home Secretary, Cave, was obliged to obey Frank Russell's demands because he had been the latter's fag at Winchester.[774] However it came about, the difference that it made to Russell—as he stresses in his autobiography and as he recalled with relief for the rest of his life—was immense. Prisoners in the second division worked eight or nine hours a day, usually at sewing mailbags, seated on a small backless stool. They had a very poor diet, no privacy, no conversation, no writing materials, and although they had a few more books than third division prisoners only the briskest workers could gain time to read for an hour a day. Russell later described his first-division imprisonment, Wood adds other details, and there is a wealth of detail in letters to and from Russell in prison.[775] He had an extra-large cell, for which he paid a rent of 2/6 a week; his room was cleaned by another prisoner for 6d a day; special furniture was brought in by order of his sister-in-law; he was not allowed to smoke, but was sent chocolates instead; he was permitted to write and to receive one letter a week; a visit once a week by three visitors was allowed; he had flowers in his cell and most if not all of his meals were sent in; most important, he had *The Times* daily, unlimited books (though they had to have the governor's approval) and writing materials. None of these privileges seem to have been peculiar to Russell (as Wood implies), but could all be countenanced by a reasonably liberal reading of the conditions for first-division prisoners.[776] It took a few anxious days before Russell began to receive all the books and writing materials he wished; indeed if the chairman of the Visiting Committee had had his way, Russell would have been denied them.[777] They were justified under a provision which exempted first-division prisoners from compulsory work and allowed them to have the tools of their trade, if it happened to be one which could be pursued in jail. The whole experience had a remarkable eighteenth-century aristocratic flavour to it, and although there is ample evidence to confirm Wood's suspicion that 'for all his levity, Russell felt his imprisonment deeply',[778] he settled down good-humouredly to make the most of the possibilities of the situation. Russell's relationship with Lady Constance Malleson, a source both of pleasure and pain to him during his imprisonment, provides an example. Just before he had gone in, she had apparently fallen in love with someone else as well, and Russell was extremely jealous. Lady Constance was acting out of London at the time, so could seldom visit, but she was anxious to reassure him and they had arranged not one but several code names by which he could send messages to her—in the portmanteau letters to Rinder, the NCF secretary who was fully in Russell's confidence and who sent the messages on to the various addresses. Russell describes how he also smuggled out letters inside the uncut pages of books, and how he persuaded the governor that love-letters to Colette, written in French, were historical letters copied from a book he was reading.[779] It has recently come to light that she, on her part, sent him additional messages via the personal column of *The Times*, using the code name 'G.J.' which was one of those which occurred in letters to and from Rinder. Several of the messages tactfully stress her loneliness.[780]

Anticipating Russell's sentence, Marshall had suggested—remembering the full laugh for which he was well-known—that he should start a 'laughter strike' in prison,[781] and indeed (in spite of his boast that he had no sense of humour) he found enough to laugh at to provoke a reproof from a warder on one occasion.[782] But there was a more serious side. It had not been simply to ensure the survival of Russell's wit that he had sought the relative comfort of the first division, and when we look at how he spent his time in prison it is clear that he had meant what he had said about being ready to return to the life of the mind. All his success in injecting humour into his imprisonment, all the anecdotes that can be told, must not be allowed to conceal the reality of up to eight hours of serious work a day (four for philosophical writing, four for philosophical reading) with an added four hours of general reading[783] which included a voracious consumption of novels.[784] Two of his pupils, Wrinch and Demos, helped to keep him supplied with the philosophical books he needed (although there were frustrating interruptions in the flow from time to time[785]), and Demos later recalled that Russell claimed he had read over 200 books and written two during the five months of his imprisonment.[786] The first book was his *Introduction to Mathematical Philosophy*, which was in the hands of Eva Kyle by early July.[787] Based on the lectures he had given in autumn 1917, its writing had not been difficult. The second 'book' can only refer to the preparatory work he did for the important *The Analysis of Mind*, towards which a great deal of his prison reading was directed. He also wrote a long review of Dewey's *Essays in Experimental Logic*,[788] and upon reading an unappreciative review of a collection of Sassoon's poetry he managed to smuggle out a reply which was published pseudonymously in the *Nation*.[789]

If evidence were needed that Russell had resigned from the NCF because of an overwhelming personal desire to return to philosophy, the work of his several months in prison surely supplies it. But it was more than a personal desire. Russell, with neither pride nor humility, knew the power of his own mind and felt himself often on the frontier of what he saw as civilisation: the reaching of man's intellectual capacity toward new abstract concepts. This was not divorced from the world; in a sense it was just part of the world's work. In 1917, writing of his longing to get back to philosophy, he had said: 'I used to live with a sense of some kind of cooperation with the community—even the most abstract work always appealed to me instinctively as part of the life of the world.'[790]

Russell's letters from prison have little to say about his fellow-prisoners, but presumably he met some of them during exercise periods, and he later described his wartime criminal acquaintance in some detail.

There was a period during the war when I associated habitually with criminals. I cannot say that I found anything peculiarly dislikeable about them. They fell into various classes. There were debtors who had been ordered by a judge to pay more than they possessed and had therefore been sent to prison for contempt of court. There was a rich, blind lawyer, seventy years of age, who had gone to gaol for bigamy. There was a fine, upstanding soldier who had been sentenced with what he thought undue severity for returning five minutes late from leave and had thereupon vowed that he would not do another hand's turn of fighting for the authorities: in order to keep this vow, he had made a point of stealing whisky whenever he was released from prison, which, however, occurred with increasing rarity. Then there was a fat, cheerful, good-natured fellow, who was a connoisseur in prisons and always chose his gaol with care; his reason for a criminal career was that only in prison could he escape from his wife. Then there was a man who had been for seventeen years an officer of the Salvation Army, whose boy had been fined for coming late to school; the Salvationist considered that the fine had been inflicted from malice and therefore refused to pay it; he was, however, persuaded that the Lord had led him to that place for a wise purpose. In addition to these desperate ruffians, there were three members of the Soviet Government and a large number of men who considered it their duty to obey the precepts of the Sermon on the Mount. On the whole, the people I met in prison seemed to me more agreeable companions than the members of the best clubs.[791]

Despite this pleasant company, and well as Russell's work had gone at the beginning of his prison stay, he was not immune to the demoralising effects of incarceration, and long before his six months were up he was suffering from severe headaches, anxiety, restlessness and an inability to work well.[792] At times he became almost obsessed with the thought of release, even briefly considering a hunger-strike to obtain this end.[793]

The practical details of how Russell escaped conscription under the new Act which raised the age limit are even more obscure than the process which led to his transfer to the first division. The justification was of course the same. When he first entered prison, the matter was causing him anxiety, and his financial situation was also poor—he calculated his income at about £100 a year—and at one time he suggested to Lady Ottoline that if his friends wanted to establish a research fellowship for him this might help with both problems.[794] Carr and Whitehead did not at first think it would help with his position under the Military Service Act,[795] but they seem to have changed their minds, and with a good deal of unobtrusive management from Gladys Rinder a considerable sum was raised and arrangements made to secure Russell a respectable philosophical occupation. The proposal was for a lectureship at £150 to £200 a year for three years, and his friends contributed generously; Sassoon sent £50, declaring that he 'would be glad to burn at the same stake as B.R.! (and probably would have done so had we all lived a few hundred years ago)'.[796] Murray was also playing an important part.[797] A number of influential people were alert to the need to avoid a confrontation between Russell and a tribunal (let alone the Army) if possible and were planning to do what they could when the time for Russell's release drew near. One must infer that the Government was also not anxious for a confrontation, because shortly after Russell came out of prison he had assurance that he would not be imprisoned as a conscientious objector, and it is plain that this did not depend on 'Murray's lectureship scheme'.[798]

Shortly before his release Russell sent a letter of resignation to the NCF National Committee and at about the same time he resigned from the Executive Committee of the Union of Democratic Control. He remained as one of the many vice-presidents of the National Council for Civil Liberties, and he served on the Council of the UDC, attending meetings with some regularity. Such low-key activities fitted with his views of peace work at the time. Had he seen a good reason he would have become active again: but the war came to an end in November 1918 without presenting such a cause.

As for Russell's actual release, he was let out, in the end, some days before his most optimistic expectations, for reasons which are not clear. Clark says he was released on 18 September and went immediately to Colette, with whom he then quarrelled. But in fact he came out on 14 September and went to Gladys Rinder's house for dinner, with other guests. She wrote to him the same night:

I was *so* excited to night that I never said how perfectly *lovely* it was of you to come to dinner with me your first evening, I shall always feel very proud to think of it and it was just gorgeous. It was *so* good to see you again in freedom, and to think of you as very happy indeed, not only with that high sort of happiness that comes with a triumph over outside things but just jollily, humanly happy.

The anticlimax described by Clark followed within a few days,[799] but need not be detailed here.

CHAPTER 16
A SADDER WORLD, A WISER MAN

Had the hope to end the war in 1916 or early 1917 by a negotiated peace been fulfilled, we might all have been living in a very different world today. I think too that a shorter war, ending in such a peace, would have left a substantially different Russell from the one we know of. Perhaps such speculation is unprofitable, and I easily resist the temptation to enlarge on the wider theme; but Russell cannot be understood without recognition that while the war ended in victory for the Allies, for him the end was the defeat of his hopes for a better world in the near future—not, of course, because it was the Allies who were victorious, but because he saw the seeds of trouble in the postures of victor and vanquished which might have been absent in a negotiated peace.

Each year of the war had made its own imprint on Russell. The events of late 1914 had shocked him violently, had shaken the roots of his liberal optimism, had reinforced his personal pessimism, had disillusioned him (permanently) with the Liberal Party while confirming an already cynical view of politicians in general, and had made him feel almost completely isolated. But he had gone on working in whatever ways he thought appropriate to counter the disaster, and 1915 had been a year of painful learning and growth. Association with the Union of Democratic Control did little to mitigate his sense of aloneness, because of his impatience with opponents of the war who did not share his sense of urgency.

In mid-war, curiously, Russell had found much of what he had been seeking; but at immense cost. In 1916 he found people as dedicated as himself to ending the war; he found men and women he could whole-heartedly admire; he experienced the heightened intimacy of working closely and in trust with a small group of people doing exciting and risky work; and he began a new relationship that would be important to him for many years. Much of this adds up to an increased vulnerability, and it was a painfully sensitive Russell who saw inadequate heroes breaking or failing under stress, who suffered—as did all Europe in one way or another—with those who were killed in battle, and who endured the anomaly of having, in the eyes of the world, abrogated his right to share this grief. He took consolation in an overwhelming belief in the rightness of his cause, and in hope for its success.

Russell's hopes for a new world reached a peak with the coming of the Russian revolution of March 1917; and so did his renewed belief in the fundamental rightmindedness of humanity. When events forced him to recognise that the millennium was not just around the corner, and even peace was still far off, something important came to an end for him. He became aware of his own weariness, and of the seeming futility of the short-term struggle against militarism. He did not, I think, become cynical, but he was deeply disillusioned; the sense of purpose and excitement in opposing the war were long gone, and there was nothing to help those still out of prison to sustain more than a shadow of the comradeship which had been the oxygen of the early days.

The last year of the war was an interval in Russell's life. His belief in the efficacy of what he had given himself to for three years was gone. All sense of purpose might have gone too had he not been able, with an effort, to turn back toward a wider vision. When he took refuge in a return to philosophical thought and writing, more was involved than a mere escape, desperately as Russell needed escape and healing at this time. He was returning, as another person might to conventional religion, to the values he held eternal (and for which he had been struggling) and looking to them for reaffirmation. Despite his tendency to despair, Russell had other sources of strength, and some of these owed a great deal to his experiences of the war years. The simplistic conviction of 1916 and early 1917 that the world could be turned around in short order by the will of the people and the example of the courageous was replaced by a belief that it must indeed be turned around, but that this would take a lifetime, perhaps many lifetimes. Although he was able to verbalise this kind of faith even in 1918, he was personally unable for many months to settle down to acting on it. After he came out of prison in September 1918 he wandered aimlessly, almost neurotically, for a period of time, unable to settle in any one place, with any one person, or in any one job, before he stabilised himself once more by an effort of will.

Writing in 1931, Russell summed up his view of the part he had played in the war, and its effect on him.

When the War was over, I saw that all I had done had been totally useless except to myself. I had not saved a single life or shortened the War by a minute. I had not succeeded in doing anything to diminish the bitterness which caused the Treaty of Versailles. But at any rate I had not been an accomplice in the crime of all the belligerent nations, and for myself I had acquired a new philosophy and a new youth. I had got rid of the don and the Puritan. I had learned an understanding of instinctive processes which I had not possessed before, and I had acquired a certain poise from having stood so long alone.[800]

I quarrel with the extent to which Russell here belittles his contribution. The work of the No-Conscription Fellowship and his part in it had probably prevented the shooting of some conscientious objectors, the influence of '*I Appeal Unto Caesar*' had certainly helped save the lives of Allen and others who had fallen ill in prison. Russell's championship of the alternativists had increased understanding in and out of pacifist circles, and later may have contributed to a more compassionate and rational official approach during the Second World War. Within the NCF he had helped preserve the unity which was, despite its tenuousness, one of its most remarkable achievements. No less important was the preservation of individual integrity, not only Russell's own, but that of the young men who resisted conscription. Whether or not a personal refusal to fight was justified, it arose for many of the members from a deeply-held conviction, and the communal support of the Fellowship gave them the strength to hold to it.

The larger objectives of the organisations Russell had been serving were not accomplished. The principles advocated by the UDC had influenced public opinion on both sides of the Atlantic, but had been shelved by the entry of the United States into the war. Some would say the ideals and a number of the leaders of the Union were to have too great an influence between the wars, while some would wish they had more; but Russell cannot be faulted for making no extravagant claims for it or for his part in it at this time. The NCF, to which Russell was much more committed, had failed in one after another of its declared goals and the objectives of its leaders: the Military Service Act was passed, retained in force and extended; large numbers of conscientious objectors accepted some form of alternative service; absolute exemption was never won for those who had refused orders in the Army and been imprisoned; objectors remained in prison long after the war ended and recruitment was suspended; the endurance of the COs did not cause a sickened public to demand abolition of the system; the wartime resistance did not father a post-war pacifist socialist international movement of the kind envisaged by the leaders in 1916. But neither did the conscientious objectors give up what they stood for, and—as far as one can tell—they ended the war better understood and more respected among the general public than they had been in 1916.[801]

While Russell's judgment of his effectiveness during the war may be unduly harsh, his evaluation of what the period had done to him is perceptive. I would fault it only in that I think he exaggerated the extent to which he stood alone. When he accurately described himself as having acquired a new philosophy and a new youth, as having got rid of the don and the puritan, and as having learned an understanding of instinctive processes which he had not had before, not one of these was something he could have done alone. He remembered with clarity the hostility of his academic colleagues, but he did not give sufficient credit to the warmth and support and—equally formative—the friction he had found among those into whose company his convictions drove him. The life of a Cambridge don was a somewhat isolated one, or at the very least one which afforded all the opportunities for privacy that anyone could wish, and to exchange this milieu for the daily turmoil of the No-Conscription Fellowship for two years was a remarkable thing to do, and bound to have lasting effects.

Now that the scope of Russell's contribution in 1916 and 1917 is known, it is apparent that the direction and effect of the NCF, if not its survival, were dependent on the practical, political and administrative work undertaken by Russell and Marshall. His abilities also informed in a special way his extensive speaking campaigns and the written material he willingly turned out in journalistic fashion, meeting weekly deadlines and writing for the need of the moment. Russell recollected ten years later: 'It was obvious also that nothing could be achieved by writings addressed exclusively to specialists. Thus throughout the years of the war I was endeavouring, however unsuccessfully, to write so as to be read by the general public.'[802] Few activist organisations have had a hack writer of such distinction, and Russell on his part had acquired an invaluable facility.

More important still was Russell's direct influence on people, and particularly on the other leaders of the No-Conscription Fellowship, who had all the problems of any group of convinced idealists. The NCF had been a forcing-house for learning about human nature, for the growth of toleration of personal vagaries and the recognition of differences of opinion even among those who shared the highest ideals and integrity. Russell's penchant for scoring off his acquaintance by his caustic brilliance had given way to a genuine desire to understand and as far as possible accommodate those who differed from him. Gradually his new ability to see both good and bad in the same individual had extended to those more radically opposed to him; although he retained his incisive ability to pronounce on the morality of an action he was no longer so quick to label its perpetrator good or bad once and for all. He had gained a much more complex view of life, in which people could do good things with bad intentions and bad things with good intentions, and he developed a remarkable ability to give loving counsel to his fellow-members of the National Committee. This seems to me pre-eminently a gift which the pre-war Russell would not have laid claim to, nor have been credited with by his friends. He had failures; although he offered immense support to Marshall for over a year, the unresolved tensions of their working relationship (for which both must share the blame) were mutually destructive by the end of 1917, and contributed to her breakdown. But she confided in him during her worst times, and when he was facing his trial she wrote, 'Whatever befalls, you have my admiration and sympathy and affection.'[803]

Two other of the many affectionate letters written to Russell early in 1918 bring out the special quality of his contribution to the leaders of the No-Conscription Fellowship. Allen wrote on 10 April:

I almost wish I had the capacity to write you an old-fashioned letter—such as would commence "Master". But I think you must be taking to prison a very sure knowledge of how you have inspired us younger men during the last 2 years not so much with the willingness to suffer as with the right reasons and motives for suffering. . . . If ever I contribute anything of value to the world, it will be in great measure due to the fact that you were willing to help me understand my own mind without patronising with yours.[804]

Joan Mary Fry sent an even more striking and perceptive tribute. Fry was a member of the National Committee during 1917 and an active Quaker chaplain. She does not seem to have taken a large part in the controversies within the Committee, but her bias may be assumed to be primarily Quaker rather than socialist. After Russell's trial she wrote:

This is not a letter to be answered. . . . Still I have no better means for telling you that you have my admiration in your criminality! . . . What I want to say is that your work at the N.C.F. as far as I know it, seems to have been a beautiful thing from an artistic point of view: you have shewn us what it is to appeal to the best in everyone, and to work with a true sense of a unity deeper than our differences, strongly marked as they have been. Personally, I should like to thank you for something—I hardly know how to name it, which you have made visible to me, whilst I have had the great privilege of working with you.

To the cause of truth and freedom you have given of your best, and how good that best is may be measured by the hostility now shewn to you. We dare not pity you, however sad we may be at what lies before you, since you could not but be a mark for enmity by the very nobility of your service. That there is a fair solution for the terrible problem which we have to solve, I firmly believe, but if you cannot take this comfort yourself, you can, at least, find some consolation in knowing that you have given others the strength to go on trying to solve it.[805]

I have described Russell's ability to value his colleagues and have written of his seeming faith in the potential good judgment of the common people, and at the same time I am well aware of his own bitter declaration in the *Autobiography* that what the coming of war had taught him was the realisation 'that the anticipation of carnage was delightful to something like ninety per cent of the population'.[806] The clause has to be read as part of one of the most cynical and savage passages in the book; nevertheless, it does reflect something of what he had felt in 1914, when it seemed to him impossible that such folly could stem from pure motives. Nothing serves better as an example of Russell's changing attitudes—his feelings as much as his thought—than his views of the human race (though one must do him the justice of not putting too much weight on any single exaggerated statement thrown out, especially in private). Before the war Russell had, without much apparent thought, assumed a liberal view of humanity (combined at times with a jaundiced view of his friends); the populace was essentially reasonable, often sound in its views, and to be expected to develop well with the benefits of education. The educated classes were more consciously rational, though often corrupted by self-interest. Politicians were among the least trustworthy of the species, but could be kept under control in a democracy. The outbreak of the war had destroyed this vision, causing Russell to find his fellow humans hateful and even himself subject to red rage, directed mainly against those of his close acquaintances, friends and colleagues who supported Britain's intervention. He disbelieved the purity of their motives and loathed what seemed to him their complacency. He did not bother at first to make distinction between the decision-making ruling class and the flag-waving populace, but gradually he came to believe hope lay in the people. In late 1916 and early 1917 the rulers seemed to him even more sinister and untrustworthy, but now he believed the people to be glorious and rightminded, and he lived in expectation of their laying down their arms and refusing any longer to be part of the ghastly absurdity of war. By the end of the war, he had come to a more sober and realistic view. Rulers, though still not greatly to be trusted, were human like everyone else, neither completely good nor completely bad. From the people no immediate miracle could be expected; yet he was not cynical.

To the end of his life he acted on the belief that humans could be brought to a recognition of their own highest interest, which was also the highest morality—the impulse to life—and he never lost hope that they would save the world. The war had not greatly changed his vision of the future he would like to look forward to, but his picture of the route by which it might be reached was altered. There was no certainty of the direction in which the world was moving: whether it would advance to new heights or fall back into chaos would depend on the efforts of individual men and women. Statesmen had chosen the wrong path in 1914, he believed, and the danger in which they had placed civilisation would not be over for many years: in fact, Russell was to see it escalate throughout the remainder of his life—and was to be unshaken in his conviction that the blame could be laid at the door of those who had gone into war so easily in August 1914. In 1918 he could fortunately not see so far ahead, but he knew now that things would not be set to rights merely by intellectual arguments and logical systems. There were destructive impulses to be overcome, and constructive ones to be nurtured and taken advantage of as well as reason to be brought into play. To free the people to be a force for sanity and peace could only be the outcome of a long slow process, and Russell dwelt increasingly on the need for a new concept of education, which he saw as liberation, freeing the individual to reach his highest potential. Russell did not mean this in any vague sense: the potential he hoped to see released would embrace (according to the abilities of the individual) disciplined intellectual endeavour and a high degree of political and social consciousness as well as personal fulfilment. He had thought often during the war of entering the field of popular education, and although the specific schemes he considered did not come to fruition, both the Beacon Hill School experiment and much of his post-war writing were in part the product of his interest.

Pre-war liberal England had been less a man's world than a gentleman's world. August 1914 showed that differences between conservatives and liberals were not as significant as they had seemed; it showed, too, that men not of the ruling class would still accept leadership and march to the beat of the drum. The young gentlemen fought bravely and were killed in tragic numbers; the working classes also fought and died; and many survivors were educated into a new, tougher, more egalitarian frame of mind. Liberal England was buried with its dead; it had been a beautiful place to live if you were of the right class and the right sex and an exciting place of possibilities even if you were not, providing you had either great ability or great luck. Many of its qualities were extraordinarily attractive. The leisured class could (and some —Russell for one—did) pursue excellence singlemindedly. They enjoyed a community of values which was comfortable and at times could be productive; I have commented on the relationship of good faith built up between General Childs and Catherine Marshall—the more remarkable because she was of the wrong sex (though of the right class) to be accepted into such a gentleman's agreement. Perhaps such relationships of mutual trust between political opponents are a luxury we can no longer afford: but depersonalisation has not ensured greater honesty. Liberal England was attacked when Russell was placed under a ban supposed to apply to a person capable of spying, and was, as Russell saw clearly, made a mockery of by the suggestion that he should release himself from this invidious position by giving his word to refrain from subversive speaking (and this in order that he might not be convicted of lacking a sense of humour).

Russell, a beneficiary of pre-war liberal England, had never been blind to its faults. Still less had his support of the Liberal Party been uncritical, and when, as he saw it, the Party parted company with the values of which he had thought it the guardian, he stayed with the values and let the Party go. Politically, however, the values needed a context. During the early days of the war he had decided that no one except the socialists cared for internationalism (although he had previously believed this to be a plank in the Liberal platform), and so he was forced to re-examine socialism. His former reservations had been primarily because any increase of the power of the central state was anathema to him, a view he held more strongly with every minute the war went on. The solution lay in a form of guild socialism, and in *Principles of Social Reconstruction* he laid the stress on decentralisation and full intelligent participation at every level of government. He found it unnecessary—as he would have found it impossible—to abandon any of his liberal ideals: indeed his hope was that this new kind of democracy would enable all to practise the virtues and enjoy the benefits previously the prerogative of the privileged few. The informed and creative individual was the key ingredient of the participatory socialist democracy Russell now envisaged, and here is the strong link between his political and educational thought.

Like most of his wartime colleagues, Russell had looked to Russia to set an example, a delusion more easily preserved because of the Allied war against the struggling Soviet state. Not until his visit to the USSR in 1920 did Russell realise the discrepancy between his vision and the land which had been expected, in spite of difficulties, to be moving towards becoming the prototypical Utopia. Visionaries handled the disillusionment in many different ways, many continuing to hope against hope. Russell met it head on, quarrelling with his socialist friends over what he had experienced in Russia, and publishing his findings in *The Practice and Theory of Bolshevism*.[807] Perhaps Russell had too much liberal baggage to travel far on the socialist tram, but it can also be argued that the destination of the socialist tram—the ever-stronger centralised state—was not the one Russell had bought a ticket for, but that the institutions he had envisaged in *Principles of Social Reconstruction* might have been as legitimate a destination.

Russell was right in thinking he had taken enormous strides during the war. If his fellow-philosophers saw his peace work as a temporary 'aberration'[808] from which he fortunately recovered at the end of 1917, they were to discover that they had welcomed back a changeling. He had never been an apolitical academic, but before the war there had been an implicit tension between his political and his philosophical interests. At best, he had felt he had lived 'an odd double life between mathematics and suffrage',[809] with one form of activity affording relief from the other. A parallel tension between intellect and emotion was still imperfectly resolved. Irrationally, I find it disappointing that one who had been so warmly appreciated as a friend and counsellor in the NCF continued for so many years to mismanage his own life. The story has been too much told and too little understood of his search through all his middle years for a satisfying human relationship, and of the hurt he was sometimes guilty of inflicting. The war years had freed him in a number of ways, but he still had to strive towards a balance between instinct, mind, and spirit, the three components he described as 'all essential to a full life'.[810]

Russell emerged from the experiences of 1914 to 1918 more mature, more flexible, disillusioned to some extent but not cynical, better aware of his own capacity, more tolerant, politically more knowledgeable and much less naïve. He was shocked by the changes in his world, but thought he knew now what his contribution should be. He had formulated a political philosophy and defined to his own satisfaction the relationship between politics, civilisation and personal fulfilment. He faced the future without delight but with determination, and may be given the last word in a passage which shows much of what had happened both to Russell and to his world in the war years:

Despair in regard to the world is difficult to ward off in these days. All our previous hopes, one by one, have proved delusions. Our views as to human nature were superficial. But despair is always due to a narrow outlook: there is always a better and a worse, even though both may be bad. I have never felt more strongly than now the determination to be of use, if possible, in building up the world after the war—not so much (as regards my own part) in material or political ways as in ways that concern the life of the mind. The world after the war will be a hard utilitarian world. It will be difficult to preserve, in such a

ABBREVIATIONS USED IN NOTES AND BIBLIOGRAPHY

AP	Clifford Allen (Lord Allen of Hurtwood) papers, University of South Carolina
BRA	Bertrand Russell Archives, McMaster University. Special groupings indicated as BRA/NCF, BRA/1916 trial, etc
EDMP	E. D. Morel papers, British Library of Economic and Political Science, University of London
CEMP	Catherine Marshall Papers, Cumbria Record Office, Carlisle
OMP	Lady Ottoline Morrell papers, Humanities Research Center, University of Texas. OMP/1132 indicates letter numbered in OMP as 1132 from Russell to Ottoline Morrell. The number is essential as a finding aid, since numbering corresponds poorly to date order, and dates are often lacking. Letters from other correspondents are identified by file, e.g., OMP/Strachey
FH	Friends House, Euston Road, London
PRO	Public Record Office, London
SCPC	Swarthmore College Peace Collection, Swarthmore, Pennsylvania
WILPF/Col.	Archives of Women's International League for Peace and Freedom, University of Colorado, Boulder, Colorado
WIL/Br.	Archives of the Woman's International League, British section, in the British Library of Political and Economic Science, London
A.F.B.	A. Fenner Brockway (Lord Brockway)
B.R.	Bertrand Russell
C.A.	Clifford Allen
C.E.M.	Catherine E. Marshall
O.M.	Ottoline Morrell
G.M.	Gilbert Murray
Autobiog.	Bertrand Russell's *Autobiography* (1967–9, in three volumes)

LL	*Labour Leader*
MG	*Manchester Guardian*
Souvenir	*No-Conscription Fellowship. A Souvenir of its work during the Years 1914–1919*
Trib.	*The Tribunal*
Times	*The Times*, London
Parl. Pubs.	Parliamentary Publications
H.C. Deb.	House of Commons debate
H.L. Deb.	House of Lords debate
p/	postmarked—as in p/5 October 1916
n.d.	no date
n.s.	not signed
ts.	typescript
ms.	manuscript

NOTES

1 Kenneth Blackwell, 'Wittgenstein's Impact on Russell's Theory of Belief' (unpublished MA thesis, McMaster University 1974).
2 'Journal' (November 1902–April 1905) in OMP, transcription by Kadriin Timusk in BRA.
3 *Our Partnership* (Longmans, Green, London, 1948), p. 243.
4 The most understanding account of Lady Ottoline, and of her relationship with B.R. is to be found in Andrew Brink, 'Russell to Lady Ottoline Morrell', in *Russell*, no. 21–22, spring-summer 1976, pp. 3–15.
5 *The Autobiography of Bertrand Russell*, 3 vols. (Allen & Unwin, London 1967–9), I, p. 146.
6 'A Free Man's Worship' in *Independent Review*, December 1903, reprinted in *The Basic Writings of Bertrand Russell*, ed. R. E. Egner and L. E. Denonn (Allen & Unwin, London 1961), pp. 66–72.
7 See Richard Rempel, 'From Imperialism to Free Trade: Couturat, Halévy, and the Development of Russell's First Crusade', in *Journal of the History of Ideas*, July 1979.
8 See Thomas C. Kennedy, 'The Women's Man for Wimbledon, 1907' in *Russell*, no. 14, summer 1974, pp. 19–26. For B.R.'s suffrage activities, see also Newberry, 'Voteless Women of No Degree' in *Lucely Speaking* (privately published by Lucy Cavendish College, Cambridge, March 1977).
9 For example, p/6 March 1912, OMP/368.
10 For example, p/4 March 1912, OMP/366.
11 B.R.'s first book was a study of *German Social Democracy* (Longmans, Green, London 1896).
12 Negative evidence for this exists in the lack of contemporary comment; positive evidence will be found when we examine the background to the writing of *The Policy of the Entente,* (Manchester and London, n.d. [1915]), which seems to have been something of a late atonement.
13 Irene Cooper Willis, *England's Holy War* (Garland Library of War and Peace, New York 1971, first published in 3 parts, 1919–21), p. 5.
14 G. M. Trevelyan to B.R., 17 July 1904, BRA. The correspondence arose out of Tolstoy's manifesto on the occasion of the Russo-Japanese War, (*Times*, 27 June 1904, pp. 4–5).
15 *Cambridge Review*, 16 November 1911, p. 118; *Autobiog.*, II, p. 16.
16 OMP/1059; p/25 July 1914, OMP/1058.
17 *Times* and *Daily Mail*, which supported intervention, showed more awareness of the immediacy of the crisis—which they were at the same time fomenting. For an interesting study of press attitudes (especially of the Liberal press), see Cooper Willis, especially part I, 'Going into the War'.
18 *Autobiog.*, I, p. 146.
19 B.R. to Lucy Martin Donnelly, 22 August 1914, BRA.
20 B.R. to M. Llewelyn Davies, 'August 1914', BRA.
21 Ms., BRA.

22 Here B.R. crossed out the words 'or the bulk of the Liberal Members of Parliament', apparently realising he was damning an important part of his hoped-for constituency. For B.R. and the Liberal Party, see also correspondence between G. W. Turner and B.R. in April 1915, when the occasion was Russell's refusal to renew his subscription to the Cambridge Liberal Association. BRA.

23 *Autobiog.*, II, p. 16.

24 p/5 August 1914, OMP/1066; Evelyn Whitehead to B.R., 4 August 1914, BRA.

25 *Correspondence Respecting the European Crisis*, Parl. Pubs. 1914, vol. 101 (Misc, no. 6), Cd. 7467 (HMSO, London 1914). The document which so incensed Russell was no. 123, Sir Edward Grey to Sir Edward Goschen, 1 August 1914, describing a conversation with the German ambassador.

26 See, for an example of the former position, A. N. Whitehead to B.R., 28 August 1914, BRA; and for the latter an entry in Kathleen Courtney, 'Extracts from a Diary during the War' (printed for private circulation, 1927).

27 *Nation*, 15 August 1914, pp. 737–8; *Autobiog.*, II, pp. 16, 42–3.

28 B.R. to Donnelly, 22 August 1914, BRA.

29 B.R. to Donnelly, BRA.

30 *Daily News*, 5 August 1914 (cited by Cooper Willis, p. 85). This left that part of the former clientele of the Liberal press who could not so rapidly turn around and support the war without any paper representative of their views.

31 'Thursday mg.', OMP/1095. This letter is difficult to date precisely, but in it B.R. refers to the diminution in the number of undergraduates, so it must be placed after the beginning of the Cambridge term in mid-October 1914. B.R. to Charles Trevelyan, 2 October 1914 (xerox copy in BRA) refers to the need not to alienate public opinion by publishing 'explicit criticism of Grey or of the immediate causes of the war'.

32 For a fuller discussion of the alternatives open to the radical Liberal press, see Cooper Willis, and Introduction by Jo Newberry (Vellacott) to the Garland edition.

33 B.R. 'Will this War End War?', *LL*, 10 September 1914, p. 2. B.R. had intended his reply for *Nation*, but on learning that Angell was also replying, he withdrew it. p/22 August 1914, OMP/1083; B.R. to J. L. Hammond, 5 September 1914, BRA; *Autobiog.*, II, pp. 45–6.

34 'Sat. night' [near end of August 1914], OMP/1089.

35 Smith, Elder, London 1912.

36 p/14 October 1914, OMP/1128; p/3 October 1914, OMP/1119; *Report of the International Commission to Inquire into the Causes and Conduct of the Balkan Wars* (Carnegie Endowment for International Peace, Washington 1914). Other reading included H.N. Brailsford's *War of Steel and Gold* (Bell, London 1914), which Russell praised highly; 24 and 27 December 1914, OMP/1171, 1172.

37 p/14 October 1914, OMP/1128.

38 As early as September he had wanted such a book written, but had judged himself 'too ignorant of the economic and business aspects' to write it himself (p/17 September 1914, OMP/1109). By December, however, he was enthusiastic. He had partly made up for his ignorance by contact with F. W. Hirst, editor of *The Economist* (p/11 November 1914, OMP/1144), and by his reading.

39 O.M., *Ottoline: The Early Memoirs of Lady Ottoline Morrell*, ed. Robert Gathorne-Hardy (Faber & Faber, London 1963), p. 278; *Autobiog.*, II, p. 19; several references in October 1914 (e.g. OMP/1132, 1134, 1135) and in

December (OMP/1169, 1171, 1176); Marwick, *The Deluge: British Society and the First World War* (Oliver & Boyd, Edinburgh and London 1964), pp. 37–8, 51–2. See also M. E. Hirst, *Quakers in Peace and War* (Swarthmore Press, London 1923), pp. 494–6.

40 n.d. 1914, OMP/1118.

41 Letters from Elizabeth Perkins to B.R., BRA. 13 October 1914, OMP/1126 refers.

42 p/29 October 1914, OMP/1141.

43 10 August 1914, OMP/1069. See also 'Wed. night', probably 12 August, OMP/1081; p/4 September, OMP/1100; p/24 September, OMP/1115, OMP/1101; 9 September 1914, *Autobiog.*, II, p. 17; Angell, *After All* (Hamish Hamilton, London 1952), p. 191; A. J. P. Taylor, *The Trouble Makers* (Hamish Hamilton, London 1957), p. 16; H. M. Swanwick, *Builders of Peace* (Swarthmore Press, London 1924), pp. 31–5; Marvin Swartz, *The Union of Democratic Control in British Politics during the First World War* (Oxford University Press, London 1971), p. 31.

44 There are copies of this letter in BRA/UDC and in CEMP.

45 Swartz, pp. 28–45. On the issue of secrecy, see also H. M. Swanwick to E. D. Morel, n.d. [misdated in pencil '21 Sep. 1917'], EDMP.

46 Swartz, pp. 37, 45. Correspondence in EDMP refers.

47 p/24 September 1914, OMP/1115. See also entries in B.R., 'Diary' (1914–15), BRA; p/6 December 1914, OMP/1165; Swartz, p. 49; H. Hanak, 'The Union of Democratic Control during the First World War' in *Bulletin of the Institute of Historical Research*, 36, November 1963, pp. 168–180; Reports of honorary secretary (E. D. Morel) on 2nd and 3rd Council Meetings, SCPC/UDC.

48 Intended as an article for the *Contemporary Review*, but rejected, it was published as no. 3 of the UDC series of pamphlets; reprinted in P. Stansky (ed.), *The Left and War: The British Labour Party and World War I* (Oxford, New York 1969). p/10 September 1914, OMP/1103; B.R. to Donnelly, 14 December 1914, BRA; E. D. Morel to Charles Trevelyan, 17 September 1914, EDMP.

49 'Go to Germany', *Suffragette*, 14 May 1915. Swanwick, p. 90.

50 *Autobiog.*, I, pp. 213–14. The letter B.R. later chose to print shows only a very small part of what the young woman suffered and indicates an acceptance of her rejection which in fact it took her weeks to reach. *Ibid.* II, p. 47. Original, n.d. [1914] in BRA. Also *ibid.* II, pp. 56, 61; and Dudley to B.R., three letters, n.d. [1914]; 19 August [1918], BRA; numerous references in correspondence with O.M. Ronald W. Clark, *The Life of Bertrand Russell* (Jonathan Cape and Weidenfeld & Nicholson, London 1975), pp. 234–41, gives a full account of this affair.

51 Open Court, Chicago and London 1914. B.R. to Carr, 22 September, 22 October 1914, copies in BRA, originals in the Hoose Library of Philosophy, University of Southern California; in Thompson, cited in n. 523.

52 p/29 October 1914, OMP/1141; also p/18 November 1914, OMP/1149. The lecture was published as *On Scientific Method in Philosophy* (Clarendon Press, Oxford 1914); reprinted in B.R., *Mysticism and Logic* (Longmans, Green, London 1918).

53 p/4 December 1914, OMP/1160. This total seems to have been an improvement on initial attendance. p/14 October 1914, OMP/1128, refers to a total of two (both Americans). See also p/28 October 1914, OMP/1139; p/22 May 1915, OMP/1279.

54 OMP/1147.

55 26 December 1914, OMP/1174.

56 p/5 January 1915, OMP/1187. See also 27 December 1914, OMP/1172.

57 p/2 January 1915, OMP/1206. See also 25-page outline in BRA.

58 Clarendon Press, Oxford 1915.

59 National Labour Press, Manchester and London n.d. [1915].

60 B.R. and G.M. also had some private correspondence on the subject; G.M. to B.R., and copies of B.R. to G.M., in BRA.

61 *Inter alia*, p/18 September 1914, OMP/1110; p/30 March 1915, OMP/1230.

62 See below, Chapter 15.

63 B.R., 'A Fifty-Six Year Friendship', in G.M., *An Unfinished Autobiography: with Contributions by his Friends* (Allen & Unwin, London 1960), p. 208.

64 *Atlantic Monthly*, March 1915, pp. 367–76. See also Ellery Sedgwick (the editor) to B.R., 25 February 1915, BRA.

65 Correspondence on this article with the Harvard philosopher R.B. Perry, including some that appeared in *Atlantic Monthly*, is collected in the Garland Library reprint of *Justice in War-Time*, i.e. *The Ethics of War*, appendices.

66 The three published articles were reprinted in *Justice in War-Time*. Ts. and proof of the withdrawn article are in BRA. It had been intended for the July issue, with 'The Future of Anglo-German Rivalry' going into another magazine, but Sedgwick made the substitution at the last moment. Sedgwick to B.R., 3 June 1915, BRA.

67 3 February 1915, OMP/1219.

68 Gertrude Bussey and Margaret Tims, *The Women's International League for Peace and Freedom* (Allen & Unwin, London 1965); Jane Addams, *Peace and Bread in Time of War* (King's Crown Press, New York 1945); Mercedes Randall, *Improper Bostonian* (New York 1964), ch. 6; Jane Addams, E. Balch and A. Hamilton, *Women at the Hague* (Macmillan, New York 1915); 'Sat. mg. 20 June 1915' [actually 19 June], OMP/1292; *LL*, 24 June, 1 July 1915. Extensive material in WILPF/Col., CEMP, WIL/Br and SCPC refers. For B.R.'s first impressions of Jane Addams at the Representative Peace Conference, see p/13 April 1915, OMP/1247.

69 p/25 June 1915, OMP/1295. The American was Albert Jay Nock. The following letters from B.R. to O.M. refer to these plans: [21 June 1915], OMP/1291; p/24 June, OMP/1294; [24 June], OMP/1298; p/25 June, OMP/1295.

70 p/25 June 1915, OMP/1295. Lowes Dickinson had also planned to go to the States with Jane Addams, but did not go until January 1916. E. M. Forster, *Goldsworthy Lowes Dickinson* (Arnold, London 1934), p. 166.

71 See below, Chapter 4.

72 Notations in B.R.'s diary sometimes include a brief indication of the topic on which he was to speak. *LL* had a monthly column on UDC activities, usually summarising meetings which had been held and occasionally mentioning a speaker by name (see, e.g. *LL*, 22 April 1915, where 62 lectures are said to have taken place, and Russell is named as having spoken to the Croydon Brotherhood). The National Peace Council *Circular* announced some forthcoming meetings until July 1915, when the practice was stopped, probably because of the attacks which were occurring by that time. References to this work occur frequently in letters from B.R. to O.M., including the following: p/14 February 1915, OMP/1223; p/17 February, OMP/1224; p/2 March, OMP/1239; [12 April], OMP/1248; n.d., OMP/1283; p/7 June, OMP/1284. See also A. Ponsonby to B.R., 15 October 1914, BRA.

73 W. E. Armstrong to B.R., 1 December 1914, BRA; p/24 November 1914, OMP/1156, and 6 December, OMP/1165; Swartz, p. 64.

74 30 August 1914, OMP/1094. See also p/7 August 1914, OMP/1068; B.R. to Donnelly, 23 February 1915, BRA.
75 p/14 February 1915, OMP/1223.
76 p/5 March 1915, OMP/1232; p/4 March, OMP/1231; Cooper Willis to B.R., 'Saturday evening' [probably 6 March 1915], BRA; *LL*, 4 March 1915.
77 20 February 1915, OMP/1225.
78 Armstrong to B.R., 12 June 1915, BRA.
79 p/11 May 1915, OMP/1265.
80 Letters from Arnold Abraham to B.R., December 1914 to May 1915, BRA; 18 May 1915, OMP/unnumbered; Armstrong to B.R., 11 December 1915, BRA. In a letter to the *Cambridge Magazine*, 27 November 1915, G. E. Moore suggested that if Trinity College Council found it necessary to ban UDC meetings as they did in late 1915, they should also ban the Moral Science Club and services in the college chapel, on the ground that these bodies also discussed and taught principles which might prove 'dangerous to the patriotism' of students.
81 p/14 August 1915, OMP/1072; p/30 August, OMP/1094; p/24 October, OMP/1136.
82 p/18 January 1915, OMP/1201.
83 p/13 February 1915, OMP/1222.
84 B.R. to H. McLeod Innes, Secretary of Trinity College Council, 22 May 1915, BRA/Trinity College.
85 p/27 May 1915, OMP/1279 (the second letter so numbered, though the first is p/22 May). Extensive correspondence BRA/Trinity College and from E. W. Barnes and D. A. Winstanley to B.R. refers. See also G. H. Hardy, *Bertrand Russell and Trinity* (University Press, Cambridge 1970; first printed 1942), pp. 26–31.
86 p/27 May 1915, OMP/1279; this passage in *Autobiog.*, II, 52.
87 10 May 1915, OMP/1265; n.d., OMP/1260.
88 18 May 1915, OMP/unnumbered; see 'Thursday mg.' [probably 22 April], OMP/1252, re German successes. See also *Autobiog.*, II, p. 19.
89 'Friday' [probably 28 May 1915], OMP/1268.
90 'Thursday evg.' [probably 27 May 1915], OMP/1267.
91 'Friday' [probably 28 May 1915], OMP/1268.
92 *Ibid.*; Committee on Alleged German Outrages, *Report of the Committee on Alleged German Outrages*, Parl. Pubs., 1914–16, vol. 23, Cd. 7894 (HMSO, London 1915). In a letter of 17 September 1914, B.R. had used the well-known story of the Russian army to illustrate the deficiencies of evidence: 'thousands of people saw it passing through England, Swedes were terrified by its concentration in Archangel, its landing instantly transformed the military situation, and the *Daily News* war correspondent in Belgium saw it with his own eyes—yet it never existed! No atrocity is anything like so well attested as this myth.' OMP/1109.
93 To these were later added an 'open door' (or free trade) policy.
94 Swartz, pp. 70–2; Swanwick, p. 79.
95 p/14 June 1915, OMP/1288. For the UDC and the conscription issue, see Swartz, Appendix F, pp. 235–7. The executive in June 1915, with E. D. Morel absent, drafted a resolution which, if passed by the General Council, would have pledged the Union 'to oppose to the utmost any attempt to impose compulsory service'; but on his return, Morel wrote a memo to C. Trevelyan opposing the resolution, which was quashed. Draft and memo in EDMP. Many UDC supporters would certainly not have been

happy with it. B.R. wrote to O.M.: 'Goldie [G. Lowes Dickinson] says he will leave the UDC if it goes in for opposing conscription! Doesn't that seem extraordinary?' p/18 June 1915, OMP/1290.

96 They were particularly sensitive to charges of being pro-German, or, worse still, not of wholly British stock. This may have owed a good deal to a personal quirk of Morel, who was half-French and even before the war had initiated a genealogical search of his ancestry. Papers in EDMP refer. H. M. Swanwick took a more robust attitude to her half-German parentage. In 1916 the UDC published 'Notes on the Careers of Members of the Executive Committee' largely to counter such imputations. Morel to J. W. Graham, [24 August 1915?], speaks of a *need* to examine the antecedents of UDC members with foreign names. EDMP. See also *U.D.C. Motives, Object, Policy* (UDC pamphlet, n.d.), SCPC.

97 p/25 June 1915, OMP/1295, with letter from Agatha Russell to B.R. enclosed. She was distressed that he was thinking of spreading his unpatriotic ideas in the USA. See also p/28 October 1914, OMP/1139; p/6 December, OMP/1165.

98 Meetings on 21 July and 29 November 1915 were broken up and there were other occasional disturbances. Swanwick, pp. 92–4; Henry R. Winkler, *The League of Nations Movement in Great Britain: 1914–1919* (Scarecrow Reprint Corp., Metuchen, N.J. 1967; first published 1952), p. 23. For a fully documented account of the opposition to the UDC, see Swartz, ch. 6.

99 p/25 June 1915, OMP/1295. See also: B.R. to Jane Addams, 19 June 1915, SCPC/Jane Addams; extensive material in CEMP; *Friend,* 9 July 1915; *LL,* 15 July 1915. Swartz, pp. 93–4, misinterprets the nature of the Representative Peace Conference and of the relationship between the UDC and the Society of Friends. The meeting was not a 'Quaker conference' but was convened and hosted by the Friends for the free exchange of opinions among many non-Quakers who were known to be concerned with peace from different points of view, among whom the UDC formed only one element, and the resolutions passed, including one which embodied all four points of the UDC platform, were not issued in the name of the Society of Friends but of the conference itself.

100 [8 July 1915], OMP/1302. *LL,* 15 July 1915, contains a report of the conference and of Russell's speech, which is printed in full as *The Philosophy of Pacifism* (League of Peace and Freedom, London 1915), League of Peace and Freedom Pamphlets, no. 1; B.R.'s speech is also in *Towards Ultimate Harmony: Report of Conference on Pacifist Philosophy of Life, Caxton Hall, London, July 8th and 9th, 1915* (Headley Bros., for League of Peace and Freedom, London [1915]).

101 B.R. to O.M., dated Thursday, 13 April 1915 (but probably actually 15 April: 13 April was a Tuesday), OMP/1247. *LL,* 22 April, refers to a Women's Conference on 15 April, but there were several at about this time. See also Swanwick to Morel, 15 April 1915, EDMP. Jo Vellacott Newberry, 'Anti-War Suffragists', *History,* October 1977, refers.

102 [Probably 8 June 1915], OMP/1240.

103 p/8 March 1915, OMP/1234. Also D. H. Lawrence, *Letters to Bertrand Russell,* ed. Harry T. Moore (Gotham Book Mart, New York 1948) (hereafter referred to as Moore), letter no. 3, pp. 39–40. (Originals seen in OMP/DHL.) Moore, no. 5, p. 42, 'Friday' 19 March 1915; p/8 March, OMP/1234; *Autobiog.,* II; *Portraits from Memory* (Simon & Schuster, New York 1963), p. 115.

104 p/8 March 1915, OMP/1234; p/3 April, OMP/1244; p/10 June, OMP/1287. See also Moore, no. 9, p. 49, 8 June 1915.

105 Allen & Unwin, London 1916. The US edition was published as *Why Men Fight* (Century Co., New York 1917) and has been reprinted by Garland Library of War and Peace (New York 1971).

106 In *Autobiog.*, II, p. 21, B.R. gives the impression that he was already working on these lectures before the discussions with Lawrence took place, but this letter definitely suggests that the idea emerged from the June weekend.

107 p/3 July 1915, OMP/1299.

108 *Ibid.*; Lawrence to O.M., n.d. [probably 12 July 1915], OMP/DHL.

109 8 July 1915, OMP/1302.

110 See Moore, no. 15, pp. 59–60, 14 September 1915; *Autobiog.*, II, p. 22.

111 See Bennett and Nancy Simon, 'The Pacifist Turn: An Episode of Mystic Illumination in the Life of Bertrand Russell', *Russell*, no. 13, spring 1974, which is an interesting psychoanalytical study (based only on secondary sources) of the roots of B.R.'s pacifism.

112 p/28 July 1915, OMP/1307; p/29 July, OMP/1308.

113 [11 July 1915], OMP/1302.

114 p/15 October 1915, OMP/1323; 'Sunday' [12 December 1915], OMP/1271.

115 *Autobiog.*, II, pp. 19–20.

116 p/3 January 1916, OMP/1345.

117 p/[15 March] 1915, OMP/1237; p/10 June, OMP 1286, 1287; [21 June], OMP/1306.

118 *Principles of Social Reconstruction*, p. 208.

119 B.R. to Donnelly, 10 February 1916, BRA; also in *Autobiog.*, II, pp. 59–60.

120 For a discussion of some individual responses, see Newberry (Vellacott), Introduction to *Why Men Fight* (Garland edition), pp. 9–10. See also letters of Dorothy Mackenzie (later Cousens) to B.R., in BRA; *Autobiog.*, II, pp. 71–2; Michael Holroyd, *Lytton Strachey, a Critical Biography* (Heinemann, London 1967–8), II, p. 173.

121 p/3 March 1916, OMP/1356.

122 *Principles of Social Reconstruction*, p. 247.

123 LL, 12 November, 3 December 1914; A.F.B., *Inside the Left* (Allen & Unwin, London 1942), p. 66.

124 At the planning meeting held in late November 1914, two other socialists, Clifford Allen and C. H. Norman, were present, while Christian pacifism was represented by the Rev. Leyton Richards, a Congregational minister active in the Fellowship of Reconciliation (he became a Quaker near the end of his life). Walter Ayles and J. H. Hudson, who were also there, both joined the Society of Friends after the war, and both entered Parliament as Labour members in 1923, a nice illustration of the importance of not trying to make the distinction between socialist and Christian pacifists a sharp one. Clark's statement that the NCF was for men 'who were outside bodies such as the Society of Friends . . . or the Independent Labour Party' shows a total lack of understanding of the nature, composition and problems of the organisation to which Russell gave two vital years. Clark, p. 273.

125 *Portraits from Memory*, p. 36. *Autobiog.*, II, p. 38.

126 NCF circular letter, 24 May 1915, copy in SCPC/NCF; LL, 20 May 1915.

127 'Chairman's Address to N.C.F. Convention, November 27, 1915', reprinted in J. W. Graham, *Conscription and Conscience* (Allen & Unwin, London 1922), pp. 176–82. See also LL, 18 March, 26 May 1915; C.A., 'Pacifism', in Julian Bell (ed.), *We Did Not Fight* (Cobden-Sanderson, London 1935), p. 2; Martin Gilbert, *Plough My Own Furrow: The Story of Lord Allen of Hurtwood as told through his writings and correspondence* (Longmans, Green, London

1965), pp. 44–6; Thomas C. Kennedy, 'The Hound of Conscience: A History of the No-Conscription Fellowship, 1914–1919' (unpublished PhD dissertation, University of South Carolina 1967), pp. 67–74; David Boulton, *Objection Overruled* (MacGibbon & Kee, London 1967), pp. 115–6.

128 C.A., ms. on 'Conscientious Objectors and Conscription', ch. 5, p. 22, AP; C.A., 'The Faith of the N.C.F.', in *Souvenir* (NCF, London 1920), pp. 8–10; Graham, pp. 172–5; Kennedy, pp. 68–75; Robert and Barbara Donington, *The Citizen Faces War* (Gollancz, London 1936), ch. 3.

129 The term 'London Yearly Meeting' is used both for the annual gathering for worship and business of Friends from all over Britain, and for the corporate body of British Friends. Any member of the constituent Meeting is a member of London Yearly Meeting.

Edward Milligan, in ch. 12 of the ts. draft of his biography of T. E. Harvey, discusses the tension that had been growing on the subject of the treatment of Quakers who had voluntarily enlisted. See also *Friend*, correspondence, especially April–May 1915. Some Friends thought the issue so divisive that it should be avoided at the coming Yearly Meeting (May 1915), but in the event it was faced and openly discussed. What emerged was charity towards enlisters, who were not disowned by the Society, and a new commitment to the support of those who decided to resist conscription. See also *LL*, 10 June 1915; *Friend*, 4 June 1915; Kennedy, p. 69. For the genesis and early history of the FSC, see Hirst, p. 507; L. R. Tucker, 'The English Quakers and World War I, 1914–1920' (unpublished PhD dissertation, University of North Carolina 1972), pp. 62–4; Kennedy, p. 89; Graham, p. 160–1. A great deal of uncatalogued material in FH refers.

130 Undated leaflets (early and late 1915) show the basis before and after this amendment, AP; *Souvenir*, p. 8; Kennedy, pp. 75–7; Boulton, pp. 111–2; Graham, pp. 174–5; *LL*, 6 May, 17 June, 2 December, 9 December 1915.

131 The case for and against conscription had been canvassed since the Boer War. The fullest history is given by Denis Hayes, *Conscription Conflict* (Sheppard Press, London 1949). See also Kennedy, ch. 1; E. Halévy, *History of the English People*, VI: *The Rule of Democracy (1905–1914)* (Benn, London 1961), pp. 154–5; Boulton, ch. 3; C. Playne, *The Pre-War Mind in Britain* (Allen & Unwin, London 1928), ch. 3 and *passim*.

132 'Friday mg.' [28? January 1916], OMP/1332.

133 C.A. to Peet, 3 November 1915, FH/FSC. John Rae, *Conscience and Politics* (Oxford University Press, London 1970), pp. 49–51, compares the British provision with those made elsewhere during the First World War. See also *Compulsory Military Service and Resistance to It* (War Resisters International, London 1968).

134 Earlier drafts of the Bill permitted claims on grounds of work of national importance, a need to make provision for dependants, or ill-health. For a full discussion of the drafting and passage of the Bill, see Rae, pp. 22–48.

135 Although Rae explains that Harvey and Rowntree 'were in touch with members of the Society of Friends of military age', they were in fact always more inclined towards forms of alternative service than were the young men of the FSC. However, as has been pointed out, the FSC did not represent all Friends of military age. Further, the Quaker MPs spoke for other objectors as well as those of their own Society; they had, for example, agreed to act as spokesmen for the Christadelphians to the Government long before the actual introduction of conscription: the need of this sect was exactly met by this additional clause, although more work was needed before they could enjoy its fruits. Rae, pp. 45, 12; Frank G. Jannaway, *Without the Camp: Being*

the Story of Why and How the Christadelphians were Exempted from Military Service (privately published, London 1917), pp. 32–5 and *passim*; Graham, pp. 347–8; Boulton, p. 91.

136 Rae, p. 30.

137 Wyndham, Childs, *Episodes and Reflections* (Cassell, London 1930), p. 148.

138 H. C. Deb., (5), 77 (1915–16), cols.949–60, 5 January 1916; Rae, p. 50; n.d., OMP/1392.

139 'Report of Proceedings', NCCL Annual Meeting, 19 January, CEMP/ NCAC. The secretary's report includes the most coherent account known to me of the early months, although the story can be pieced together from other papers in CEMP, and other sources. See also C.A., 'The Conscientious Objectors' Struggle', *LL*, 10 July 1916; Kennedy, pp. 138–9; Hayes, pp. 247–8; S. Pankhurst, *The Home Front* (Hutchinson, London [1932]), p. 285; Boulton, pp. 119–20; B. N. Langdon-Davies, in *We Did Not Fight*, pp. 186–7. In July 1916, after raids under the Defence of the Realm Act began to multiply, the NCAC changed its name to the National Council for Civil Liberties, and concentrated on this aspect, and on resistance to industrial conscription, a matter of close concern to many of its constituent bodies. The Council continued to publish and distribute anti-conscription material.

140 'Sat. evg.', OMP/1350 (this can be dated 15 January 1916 with some certainty because of a reference to B.R.'s first lecture, but it bears a pencilled date '29th Jan. 1916'); 5 February 1916, OMP/1352.

141 [25 January 1916], OMP/1273; n.d., OMP/1270.

142 24 February 1916, OMP/1354.

143 It is important to note that the NCF did not represent all types of objectors to the taking of arms. There were many religious objectors whose stand was based on a strict interpretation of the Ten Commandments, or less directly on an apocalyptic faith which forbade them to take part in the wars of the worldly. The needs of many of these had been met by the conscience clause. About 5000 men were granted the right to find alternative work of national importance, approximately 3000 served in the Non-Combatant Corps (formed early in 1916 expressly to provide a place for those who were granted exemption from combatant service only), a few found their way into the Royal Army Medical Corps, and 1200 served in the Friends' Ambulance Unit. The alternativists included the bulk of objectors from such sects as the Plymouth Brethren and the Jehovah's Witnesses. The Christadelphians made a special arrangement with the Army Council, the details of which remain a mystery (Jannaway, *passim*; Rae, pp. 113–5). Such sects not only did not need the NCF but were generally antipathetic to its political orientation and methods. The Quakers seem to have been the only religious group whose official gathering went on record against the acceptance of alternative service, and the non-authoritarian nature of the Society meant that this was far from being a generally accepted position among Friends. There were people of numerous denominations in the NCF, many of whom were at variance with the official position of their churches.
    The only published work which gives attention to the sources from which came the alternativist COs is Rae, pp. 72–81. Graham, p. 34, makes only brief reference and is misleading as regards the Christadelphians, who did not accept service in the Army except possibly in rare cases. The NCF took a fraternal if somewhat condescending interest in the non-combatants.
    For the religious origins of NCF members, see C.A., 'A Word to General Child', *Trib.*, 29 June 1916, and 'Conscience and Character', 21 June 1916, a study of the background of 127 members of the Manchester branch, CEMP.

144 p/13 March 1916, OMP/1357. Nicod, a young Swiss philosopher who died in

1924 (*Autobiog.*, II, p. 96), and Desmond MacCarthy accompanied him on parts of his holiday. Letters in OMP which were written during this vacation include nos. 1357–63, 1376 and 1379.

145 Another argument put forward by B.R. in favour of accepting Harvard's offer was that it would enable him to postpone a decision about Trinity, which suggests he was considering resigning his lectureship or at least further prolonging the leave of absence he had taken. All the pros and cons are discussed in 17 January 1916, OMP/1346. See also James H. Woods to B.R., 5 January, 25 January, 21 February, 21 March 1916, BRA; n.d., OMP/1334. This letter is printed in *Autobiog.*, II, p. 56, with a suggested date '1915', but it clearly belongs to 1916 (probably February) because of reference to B.R.'s lectures as nearly over and to the need to start work on the Harvard courses. See also B.R. to Donnelly, 10 February 1916, BRA; and in *Autobiog.*, II, pp. 59–60.

146 See Newberry, 'Anti-War Suffragists'. I am currently working on a biography of Marshall.

147 'Wed. evg.' [probably 29 March 1916], OMP/1376.

148 Although B.R. had not had time to do much towards this part of the NCF's work, he had attended and probably addressed at least one meeting, at an Adult School (Whitefield's Tabernacle) held to give advice to the young men facing the tribunals. 'Sunday night', OMP/1324; 24 February 1916, OMP/1354.

149 *LL* reported NCF activities and also carried an advice column for a few weeks after the Act was passed, but the latter was dropped when *Trib.* (the NCF's own paper) began publication on 8 March 1916. Much other material, especially in CEMP, refers to these activities, notably notes in C.E.M.'s writing on a meeting held by the Birmingham branch of the NCF, 5 February 1916 (addressed by C.A. and A.F.B.) and for a speech which she herself gave the next day to an ILP meeting at Clapham. Letters from the West Central London branch of the NCF to its members, 22 February, 6 March, 18 March 1916, also illustrate the range of topics with which the organisation now had to concern itself. CEMP. See also Graham, p. 75; Boulton, pp. 138–9. The youth of some of the conscripts, many of whom were only 18, should be borne in mind. C.A., 'COs and Conscription', ch. 1, pp. 6–7.

150 This was certainly a new group, although there is some evidence that the NCF had an active political committee before this (see *Souvenir*, p. 24; C.A. in *LL*, 20 July 1916). See also NCF circular letter, 9 January 1916, AP; *Trib.*, 8 March 1917, p. 3; Kennedy, p. 137; Graham, p. 183. For activities of other groups of associates concerning themselves, for example, with the maintenance of COs' dependants, see Kennedy, pp. 130–1. The principal source for the membership and activities of the Associates Political Committee from 17 March to 9 April 1916, is a large quantity of material, ms., ts., and annotated ts., much of it very rough, in CEMP. It includes notes, agenda and minutes relating to meetings of this Committee on 17 March, 27 March and 4 April, and of the National Committee on 2 April, together with a lengthy rough draft entitled 'Agitation on behalf of Prisoners' and marked 'Report to Nat. Convention': this was evidently used by C.E.M. as an outline from which to speak on that occasion. There is also assorted correspondence in BRA, OMP and FH.

151 From the outset the NCF, radical as it was, had favoured conversion over confrontation, legal over illegal means, constitutional over militant tactics. Before the Act had begun to take effect, the leaders had made policy

decisions enabling the members to stay within the law as far as possible. Although a case could be made for the logic of refusing to appear before the tribunals, the National Committee (by a bare majority) recommended men to take this legitimate opportunity of a public witness. C.E.M., ms. notes on a speech by C.A., 5 February 1916, CEMP; C.A. in *LL*, 10 February 1916, NCF circular letter, 31 January 1916; Kennedy, p. 167; Robert and Barbara Donington, p. 56. See C. H. Norman, *A Searchlight on the European War* (Labour Publishing Co., London 1924), pp. 92–4, for a strongly-worded argument that the objectors should *not* have gone before the tribunals.

152 'General Scheme for Agitation', 4 April 1916, CEMP. No description of the individual contribution of any member of the Political Committee can hope to be complete, and each probably did more than can be documented.

153 C.E.M. to Gilbert Cannan, 20 April 1916, copy in CEMP.

154 'General Scheme for Agitation', 4 April 1916, CEMP.

155 *Ibid.*; B.R., 'Diary' (1915–1916) 4 and 5 April 1916, BRA.

156 *H. C. Deb.*, (5), 81(1916), cols.261–8. In his 5 April speech Snowden referred to having received 2600 letters during the past five weeks 'dealing mostly with administration of this Act and other matters arising out of it'. He later claimed that during 1917 he received over 30,000 letters about problems arising from the MSA. *Autobiog.*, (Nicholson and Watson, London 1934), I, p. 406.

157 *H. C. Deb*, (5), 81(1916), cols.1443–52. *British Prussianism* (National Labour Press, London 1916). 'Report to National Convention', 8 April 1916, refers.

158 'Summary of conversation between Lord and Lady Courtney and Clifford Allen', n.d. [c. 17–27 March 1916], CEMP.

159 C.E.M. had seen Parmoor, but gave an oral report of which no notes remain. 'Notes', 17 March 1916, refer. CEMP.

160 On an occasion on which the Russells' Aunt Agatha was bemoaning the fact that Bertrand was doing nothing to help the war, Frank is reported to have 'burst out and said "Bertie is great and glorious and I won't hear anything said against him".' Russell was 'touched' when the report of this conversation reached him. In the letter in which he described the incident he also said that Frank was against conscription. n.d. [probably 15 Jan. 1916], OMP/1350.

161 F. Russell, *My Life and Adventures* (Cassell, London, 1923), pp. 328–9; *Trib.*, 13 July 1916; *LL*, 13 July 1916. The debates took place 4 July. The wording of Earl Russell's motion was: 'That in the opinion of this House it is undesirable to subject military prisoners to punishments not authorised by law.' *H. L. Deb*, (5), 22(1916), cols.521–31.

162 'Report to National Convention', CEMP.

163 *Times*, 14 March 1916; *Trib.*, 30 March 1916. The letter criticised the lack of respect being shown by tribunals to sincere COs, while expressing the Bishop's personal lack of agreement with the latter.

164 n.d. [probably 13 April 1916], OMP/1368; 8 May, OMP/1374; Bishop of Oxford to C.E.M., 6 April, BRA; 'Minutes', 17 March, 4 April, CEMP. The Bishop also spoke in the House of Lords on the COs' behalf on 4 May: *H. L. Deb*, (5), 21(1916), cols.904–13; *Trib.*, 11 May 1916.

165 'General Scheme for Agitation', 4 April 1916, CEMP.

166 Sir Oliver Lodge to F. E. Marshall, 1 April 1916; [Professor] Michael Sadler to Mr Marshall, 3 April 1916; draft replies in B.R.'s handwriting (with additions by C.E.M. as noted), all in CEMP. Correspondence with

the custodians of papers left by these two men has unfortunately not brought to light any of the original exchanges.

167 Kennedy, p. 129, thinks much of the NCF's propaganda was so remote and Olympian that it must have infuriated most people.

168 n.d. [probably 4 April 1916], OMP/1370; n.d. [probably 2 April 1916], OMP/1377, [25 January 1916], OMP/1273. Even in mid-April B.R. confessed that he still did not exactly like Allen, whom he found 'solemn and portentous'; [14 April 1916], OMP/1367. But by July he had 'come to love him', although he thought O.M. might still find him 'too farouche'; [9 July 1916], OMP/1394.

169 n.d. [probably 2 April 1916], OMP/1377; 9 April, OMP/1364. See also n.d., OMP/1368; p/25 April 1916, OMP/1371.

170 n.d., OMP/1270.

171 C.A., 'C.O.s and Conscription', ch. 4, pp. 9–12.

172 See *Trib.*, 30 March 1916. The first arrests under the Act were reported in *Trib.* 6 April and the names listed on 20 April. One member had been arrested as early as 17 March, but arrests only began in earnest at the beginning of April. Few men were court-martialled before mid-April.

173 For a discussion of some of the problems relating to the definition of the categories, see Kennedy, ch. 4.

174 Printed in *Trib.*, 15 March 1916; copy in FH. See also Gilbert, pp. 46–7.

175 C.A., 'C.O.s and Conscription', ch. 24, pp. 13–14; Kennedy, p. 123. Rae points out (p. 88 n. 5) that under the MSA a man was deemed to have enlisted and did not in fact have to take an oath. But under the Army Act of 1881 an oath had been required, and for the NCF the objection was to military service of any kind and the oath was never the real issue.

176 Boulton, p. 111; and 'Notes', 5 February 1916, in C.E.M.'s handwriting, on a meeting in Birmingham, which show C.A. to have been speaking out even then against acceptance of any forced change of occupation. CEMP.

177 Snowden, *H. C. Deb.*, (5), 81(1916), col.270. 22 March 1916; *British Prussianism*, p. 9; Kennedy, p. 179; *Trib.*, 30 March 1916; Graham, p. 89.

178 Rae, pp. 125–6, 195–200. Using the Pelham Committee records in FH, Rae gives the best description of the work of this body. See also *Daily Express*, 15 May 1916; *Trib.*, 25 May, 1916; C.A., 'C.O.s and Conscription', ch. 2, pp. 26–7, AP; Kennedy, p. 160.

179 For the views of branches, expressed in resolutions, see 'Agenda', CEMP, BRA. For C.A.'s views see editorials in *Trib.*, 23 March, when he said of the coming Convention, 'This occasion will be used to announce our future policy'; and 6 April, when he wrote less autocratically that delegates would 'declare their intentions regarding the penalties that await them, and upon the various schemes under discussion to impose civil alternative service'. The use of the pejorative term 'impose' should be noted, and the assumption that there would be no acceptance of a Government solution remained; indeed the editorial was titled 'No Compromise'.

180 p/10 April 1916, OMP/1364.

181 *Daily Express*, 8 April 1916. Some change of plans does seem to have taken place, since the printed agenda gives the place of meeting as 'Memorial Hall'. It is (barely) possible that this was all part of an elaborate double blind. Correspondence in FH also suggests that the Society of Friends had hesitated before allowing the meeting to be held at Devonshire House.

182 Copy of letter in AP.

183 There is a transcript of a shorthand report of the Saturday afternoon session in AP, and a full account of the whole Convention is to be found in *LL*,

which published a special supplement on 13 April, 1916 (hereafter referred
to as *LL Supp.*, 13 April). Other accounts are found in Kennedy, pp. 119–23;
Graham, pp. 188–90; A. Marwick, *Clifford Allen: The Open Conspirator*
(Oliver and Boyd, Edinburgh and London 1964), pp. 31–2; Gilbert,
pp. 51–3; Boulton, pp. 120–1; B. Webb, *Beatrice Webb's Diaries (1912–1924)*
pp. 59–61; Pankhurst, p. 297; 'Extract from the diary of Anna Barlow', AP.
See also *Daily Express,* 10 April 1916. There is an interesting account of
press reaction in T. C. Kennedy, 'Public Opinion and the Conscientious
Objector, 1915–1919', *Journal of British Studies,* 12 (May 1973), p. 112.

184 p/10 April 1916, OMP/1364.
185 Copy of the agenda in AP, proof copy in BRA, annotated copy in CEMP.
  For the first notice of the Convention, see 'Stop Press', *Trib.,* 15 March
  1916.
186 Snowden had recently spoken in Parliament urging peace negotiations. *H.
  C. Deb.,* (5), 80(1916), col.714, 23 February 1916; C. Cross, *Philip Snowden*
  (Barrie and Rockliff, London 1966), p. 150.
187 *LL Supp,* 13 April.
188 I am indebted to Conrad Russell for pointing out the exactness with which
  the resolution as finally passed achieved this, and for his suggestion that it
  was skilfully drafted. I hold to my view that it was nevertheless drafted
  during a struggle: the final wording may be inspired, but the English is
  clumsy (especially the repeated use of 'it').
189 From one of several memoirs of C.A., collected by Barratt Brown at the
  time of Allen's death in 1939, but never published. AP. Sylvia Pankhurst
  described C.A. on this occasion as 'a frail young man . . . regarded almost as
  a saint by thousands of followers', and Anna Barlow wrote in her diary that
  he had an 'amazing flow of language, lovely voice and a manner quietly
  impressive. He looks worn and nearly transparent. The men evidently
  would follow him'. Pankhurst, p. 297; 'Extract from the diary of Anna
  Barlow', AP. For a more critical view, see Webb, p. 59.
190 p/10 April, 1916, OMP/1364. The incident is also mentioned in the
  transcript report in AP. See also A.F.B., *Inside the Left,* p. 70.
191 Anna Barlow recorded in her diary (ms. extracts in AP): 'I have no faith in
  him.' But he showed courage in agreeing to speak on this occasion and he
  also served as a vice-president of the NCCL, a fact not mentioned by his
  biographer. James Marchant, *Dr. John Clifford: Life, Letters and Reminiscences*
  (Cassell, London 1924), pp. 153–4. *Concise Dictionary of National Biography,*
  II, p. 89; Gilbert, p. 52; NCCL letterheads in CEMP.
192 'Agenda'. For all these speeches, see transcribed report, AP.
193 *LL Supp.,* 13 April. A session on Saturday evening made some Quakers
  'sad' because of the 'war spirit' shown. Unfortunately, no more is known of
  this evening meeting. E. Ellis to Mennell, 11 April 1916, FH.
194 Ms. notes, CEMP.
195 Ms. notes on back of agenda, CEMP; *LL Supp.,* 13 April; p/10 April 1916,
  OMP/1364.
196 *Ibid.* 'The whole cttee. slept at a hotel in the city so as to be together and near
  the meeting.'
197 Dated 16 April. The last two words are added in ms., the rest typed. Both
  sides of this correspondence are in the Gilbert Murray papers, Bodleian;
  copies in BRA.
198 Extensive material in FH. Childs, p. 150; Graham, pp. 157–9; William R.
  Hughes, *Indomitable Friend. Corder Catchpool, 1883–1952* (Housmans,
  London 1964), pp. 32–3; Corder Catchpool, *On Two Fronts: Letters of a*

Conscientious Objector (Headley, London 1918), *passim*; Meaburn Tatham and
James E. Miles, *The Friends' Ambulance Unit, 1914–1919* (Swarthmore Press,
London [1919]), *passim*; Olaf Stapledon, 'Experiences in the Friends' Ambu-
lance Unit', in *We Did Not Fight*; Tucker, pp. 55, 105 n. 11; Margaret E.
Hirst, *Quakers in Peace and War* (Swarthmore Press, London 1923),
pp. 501–3.

All these sources, except Catchpool, avoid full discussion of the controversies surrounding the FAU. The official history (Tatham and Miles) is
particularly disappointing in this respect, bordering on the dishonest in its
failure to touch on the important issues at stake. Tucker ignores the FAU
almost completely. The columns of *Friend* remain the best printed source.
See *Trib.*, 30 March 1916, for a letter on 'The Friends' Ambulance Unit',
issued by the FSC to Friends of military age to warn them of the impending
expansion. The rumour was confirmed on 31 March by Snowden, who
reported to the NCF a conversation he had had with Sir George Newman,
Chairman of the FAU. The plan was wide and was never implemented in
full although there was some expansion. 'Interview with Mr Snowden at
Merton House, March 31 1916', CEMP.

199 For example, by Snowden in the speech for which B.R. had coached him,
and by C.A. on the occasion of a deputation to the anti-conscription group
in the Commons (see 'A Deputation', tss., two versions, n.d. [probably
25 April 1916], CEMP).

200 P. Morrell to B.R., 27 April 1916, BRA.

201 BRA.

202 By Kenneth Blackwell in *Russell*, no. 2 (summer 1971), p. 10. See also no. 6
(summer 1972), p. 5, for A.F.B.'s confirmatory comment on the suggestion.

203 It is unlikely that Whitehead (also an F.R.S.) saw *LL*, but B.R. may have
hoped that the signature would lead to speculation and discussion.

204 Corder Catchpool found himself critical of Allen 'when his clever brain
devised a legal loophole through which the proceedings could be quashed
and postponed for some months. Intellectual brilliance seemed a doubtful
element in a stand for conscience'. Account written after C.A.'s death, AP.
The fullest account of C.A.'s progress is in Marwick, *Clifford Allen: The
Open Conspirator*.

205 B.R. draft introduction to a proposed booklet, *On Active Service*, by C.A.
(ms., AP). The pamphlet was planned some time in 1917 as a collection of
extracts from C.A.'s court statements and appeals, but was never published.
Further material relating to it has been found in the WILPF archives,
presumably left at the Geneva office by C.E.M. after the war.

206 Longer sentences could be served at penal servitude, but the punitive
conditions of hard labour were so severe that no crime was punishable by
more than two years of this type of imprisonment.

207 B.R. made a note in his 'Diary', 1915–1916, of the date on which he wrote
the leaflet. BRA.

208 [14 April 1916], OMP/1367; 'Case history: Eric Chappelow', CEMP. See
also *Daily Express*, 21 April 1916.

209 Capt. Archer Shee, *H. C. Deb.*, (5), 81(1916), cols.2236–44; P. Morrell to
B.R., n.d., BRA.

210 Chappelow to Sanger, 13 April 1916, mimeographed copies; 26 April, faint
pencil original and transcription in B.R.'s hand; G.M. to B.R., 15 April;
B.R. to G.M., 17 April (all in BRA); G. B. Shaw to B.R., 18 April, BRA
and *Autobiog.*, II, pp. 62–3, and 20 April, BRA; Sanger to B.R., 27 April,

BRA; Chappelow to Winifred Helsby (his cousin), 15 April, CEMP; other correspondence in CEMP also refers. See also P. Morrell, letter to editor, *Nation*, 29 April 1916.

211 Correspondence in CEMP. A letter from C.E.M. to 'Dear Comrade', dated 30 April, is probably her returned letter. There is also an abrupt covering note from 'Reginald Brooke, Colonel, Commandant, Detention Barracks, Wandsworth'. It seems clear that the two belong together, although the disorder in which the papers were found makes certainty impossible. The Commandant was within his rights in refusing her permission to visit Chappelow. For Chappelow's later history, see S. Pankhurst, p. 317; *Trib.* 7 September 1916.

212 [25 April 1916], OMP/1365.

213 [25 April 1916], CEMP. For the dating of this letter, see note 221 below.

214 For example, C.A., 'Alternative Service', *Ploughshare*, May 1916, reprinted as a leaflet, and abridged in Gilbert, pp. 55–6. See also B.R.'s letter to *Nation*, 15 April 1916, above, p. 52; open letter from the NCF to the Prime Minister, 15 April 1916, copy in BRA; C.A., letter to *Nation*, 10 June 1916.

215 C.A., 'A Personal Word', *Trib.*, 11 May 1916. For editorials in which the emphasis is on the absolutist viewpoint, see *Trib.*, 15 and 22 June 1916.

216 See, for example, a leaflet dated 1 May 1916, copy in BRA.

217 Correspondence on alternative service and related attitudes had been going on in *Friend* sporadically at least since mid-1915. The letters to *LL* are of interest largely because of the socialist viewpoint of most correspondents. For some, their previous advocacy of increased state compulsion was a stumbling-block in their refusal now to obey the state. Letters, especially from H. J. Stenning, 11 and 25 May, refer. *Nation* gave space to a number of highly literate defenders of the COs, but not unnaturally it was rare for this or any other paper of wide circulation to concern itself with the finer points of the alternative service controversy—enough if the more liberal organs countenanced some discussion of the rights and wrongs of conscientious objection or consented to publicise the worst cases of persecution.

218 Cross, p. 145.

219 p/25 April 1916, OMP/1371; *LL*, 27 April 1916. For the importance of Snowden's contribution, see also Kennedy, p. 231. For other disparaging comments on the ILP leaders, especially W. C. Anderson, see B.R. to C.E.M., [11 April 1916], CEMP; [25 April 1916], OMP/1365.

220 B.R. to C.E.M. [25 April 1916] (for dating of this letter see note 221 below); 'Report of Deputation', n.d., CEMP. Other correspondence between C.E.M. and John Dillon, MP (17 and 23 April) also refers, CEMP.

221 C.A. and C.E.M. had originally been invited to lunch with Lloyd George at Walton Heath on 11 April (card dated 10 April, CEMP). B.R.'s note to C.E.M. in which he refers to the visit (clearly as having just taken place) was dated only 'Tues. night' but bears the pencil notation in C.E.M.'s handwriting, 'April 11 1916'. But this must have been added later, when C.E.M. perhaps dated it by reference to the original invitation. 11 April, the day after the end of the National Convention, was also the date of C.A.'s appearance before the London Appeal Tribunal, which can hardly have taken place on the same day. The 25 April date is consistent with an entry in B.R.'s 'Diary' (BRA), and is confirmed by the reference to the deputation, and by the mood of the letter, which is very different from the euphoria which B.R. expressed immediately after the Convention. His letter to O.M., quoted here (OMP/1365, and *Autobiog.*, II, p. 62) is also undated, and while it contains no solid evidence to assist in dating, its whole tone fits

better with the 25 April date, and there is the negative evidence that it
makes no reference to C.A.'s appeal tribunal. The meeting with Lloyd
George has not been described in secondary sources except in a recent
article by Kennedy, where he accepts the earlier date, but with apparent
reservations ('Public Opinion and the Conscientious Objector', p. 115),
and in B.R.'s own autobiography (where he does not assign a date).

222 B.R. to C.E.M., n.d., CEMP. B.R. told C.E.M. that he had written the
incident up in the form of a Sunday School story, but unfortunately this
version has not come to light.

223 24 April 1916, OMP/1371.

224 Ms. in BRA. The title comes from Shakespeare, Sonnet 66.

225 [8 May, 1916], OMP/1374; p/26 May, OMP/1380. References to the
activities described are found chiefly in OMP, with supporting evidence in
B.R.'s 'Diary' and in CEMP. I met Lady Helen Pease, August 1978, and
also consulted material deposited by her in the Imperial War Museum.

226 p/26 May, 1916, OMP/1280; 8 May, OMP/1374. *Proceedings of the Aristotelian Society*, n.s. 16 (1915–16), pp. 301–10.

227 p/30 April, OMP/1373.

228 H. C. Deb., (5), 81(1916), col.45, 21 March 1916.

229 'The "Bodkin" Poster', *Trib.*, 5 October 1916.

230 18 May 1916, OMP/1384.

231 B.R. to C.A., 18 May 1916, AP; original summons to A.F.B. in SCPC/
AFB; extensive material in CEMP. Other accounts can be found in *Trib.*,
18 May; ts. report from London News Agency, CEMP; E. Grubb in *We
Did Not Fight*, p. 148–9; Boulton, p. 181; Hayes, p. 256; Graham, p. 191;
W. J. Chamberlain, *Fighting for Peace* (No More War Movement, London
[1929]), pp. 58–61; Kennedy, p. 222. References to the appeal appear in
Trib., 6 July, 20 July; *LL*, 20 July.

232 18 May 1916, OMP/1384. Frank Russell had been jailed for bigamy in
1901.

233 [14 April 1916], OMP/1367.

234 Some problems later developed within the Non-Combatant Corps over
such matters as the handling of munitions.

235 'Conscientious Objectors and Military Service', drawn up by C. F. N.
Macready, Adjutant-General, and circulated to the Cabinet by Kitchener,
16 May 1916, PRO, WO 32/5491. The passage quoted is an excellent
description of the situation as it first appeared to the Army—in mid-April
—but Macready should have realised by the date of writing that it would
not work.

236 *LL*, 20 April 1916. The NCF's initial reaction to the treatment of Everett
was perhaps unjust. *Trib.* also mocked what was to become the standard
and least persecutory way of dealing with COs, by which an officer gave a
formal order in front of a witness, knowing that it would be disobeyed:
this led directly to a court martial. 'How it is done', *Trib.*, 25 May 1916.
But as late as the end of May one NCF member reported that he had been
told that there would be no more court-martial cases: 'We are going to
make you soldiers, not prisoners, my lad.' *Trib.*, 1 June 1916.

237 n.d., OMP/1123.

238 A number of notes and memos in CEMP relate, especially 'Report from
Mr Philip Snowden (per Mrs Snowden, per telephone, June 20th)';
C.E.M. to Asquith, 19 June; copy of letter from Childs to Commandant
Detention Barracks, July 1916. See also Snowden, *Autobiography*, I, pp.
411–12; *LL*, 22 June, 1916; *Trib.*, 6 July 1916; Kennedy, pp. 241–3;

Graham, pp. 144–6; Boulton, pp. 153–4. Another example of Brooke's inhumanity is given in *Trib.*, 1 June 1916.

239 'Conscientious Objectors', undated and unsigned memorandum, PRO, WO 32/5491, which can confidently be assigned to General Childs, as it refers to the setting up of a special department in the author's directorate. It cannot be dated exactly, but was certainly written during the first few weeks of the operation of conscription.

240 *Trib.*, 1 June 1916.

241 For the circumstances of the introduction of this Bill, see *inter alia* Roy Jenkins, *Asquith* (Collins, London 1967), pp. 439–43; David Lloyd George, *War Memoirs* (Odhams, London [1938]), I, pp. 438–43; Earl of Oxford and Asquith, *Memories and Reflections, 1852–1927* (Little, Brown, Boston 1928), II, pp. 148–51; Kennedy, p. 145.

242 'Conscientious Objectors: 1 June 1916', Kitchener Papers, PRO 30/57/74; 'Conscientious Objectors and Military Service', 16 May 1916, and 'Conscientious Objectors', n.d., PRO, WO 32/5491.

243 p/25 April 1916, OMP/1371.

244 Notes headed 'France', 'For J.A.C. etc.', in C.A.'s hand, n.d., CEMP. See also copies of extracts from letters from men in the NCC at Felixstowe and Shoreham, May 1916, BRA, CEMP; 'Are Men to be Shot for Conscience?', draft pamphlet, several versions, CEMP; *Trib.*, 18 and 25 May 1916.

245 *H. C. Deb.*, (5), 82(1916), col.440, 9 May 1916.

246 'Memorandum for Private Deputation to the Prime Minister', 11 May 1916, CEMP. Philip Morrell and Marshall, who had arranged the deputation, had originally hoped for an interdenominational representation, 'a papist, a non-con[formist] and an Anglican bishop uniting to support conscience'. (The papist was to be John Dillon, the Irish MP, the 'non-com.' John Clifford, and the Anglican the Bishop of Oxford. Only the last materialised.) P. Morrell to B.R., n.d., BRA; Bishop of Oxford to the Prime Minister, 11 May 1916, copy in CEMP. See also C.E.M. to Mennell, 8 May 1916; Mennell to C.E.M., 9 May 1916, both in FH.

247 [12 May 1916], OMP/1383. In *Autobiog.*, II, p. 24, B.R. refers to this occasion and to another when he met Asquith at Garsington just as he (Russell) emerged naked from a pond.

248 Exchange of letters between C.E.M., Asquith, and David Davies, 11–17 May 1916, copies and originals in CEMP, and copies typed on one sheet in CEMP, BRA; Rae, pp. 152–9; Graham, p. 112.

249 H. Peet, 'The Men Sentenced to Death', *Souvenir*, pp. 45–6; *Trib.*, 15 June, 29 June 1916; Boulton, pp. 172–3; Kennedy, p. 252; Rae, p. 155.

250 A party of journalists had been encouraged by the military authorities to visit a non-combatant battalion in France, where they saw and reported on 'a contented force doing useful work' but, of course, learnt nothing relevant to those objectors who could not accept non-combatant service. *Times*, 20 May 1916; *Trib.*, 23 May.

251 *Trib.*, 8 June 1916; *H. C. Deb.*, (5), 82(1916), cols.2891–2, 1 June 1916.

252 *Trib.*, 29 June 1916; *H. C. Deb.*, (5), 82(1916), cols.490–2, 22 June 1916. *H. C. Deb.*, (5), 82(1916), col.523, 26 June 1916.

253 [24 June 1916], OMP/1387.

254 B.R., 'Mr Tennant on the Conscientious Objectors', original, n.d. in CEMP (copy BRA). Probably intended for use in *Trib.*, but does not appear to have been published anywhere.

255 Kennedy, p. 256.

256 For material bearing on this possibility, see Graham, pp. 111–16; Kennedy,

pp. 249–57; Rae, pp. 154–6; Boulton, pp. 164–75. A careful examination of the evidence, including some not previously used, has led the writer to conclude that there was a plot at some level, although it is still difficult to name names with certainty. It is hoped to publish a full discussion of this elsewhere.

257 E. Whitehead to B.R., 23 June 1916, BRA.

258 OMP/1383. An undated memo to C.E.M. in the same vein must also belong to this period, though it is assigned by Keith Robbins, *The Abolition of War*, (University of Wales Press, Cardiff 1976), p. 145, to late 1917).

259 The NCF was also now affiliated to the Peace Negotiations Committee chaired by the Rev. Herbert Dunnico, which had held its inaugural meeting on 28 April 1916, and was committed to co-ordinating a campaign to urge the opening of negotiations.

260 *Trib.*, 11 and 18 May, mimeograph, 'Prosecutions under the D.O.R.A. for distributing leaflets published by the No-Conscription Fellowship', BRA; numerous letters and telegrams in CEMP; draft of private memorandum for MPs, n.d., CEMP; Morgan Jones to B.R., 22 May 1916; Dorothy Waid to B.R., 24 May 1916, BRA; PRO, HO 45/11012/312286.

261 Reprinted in *Autobiog.*, II, pp. 64–5.

262 His 1915 *Atlantic* articles had been followed by the publication as articles of several of his lectures on the *Principles of Social Reconstruction*. 'Religion and the Churches', *Unpopular Review*, April 1916; 'War as an Institution', *Atlantic Monthly*, May 1916; 'Education as a Political Institution', *ibid.* June 1916; 'Marriage and the Population Question', *International Journal of Ethics*, July 1916. Others in the series were offered to *Open Court* (Chicago), but were not accepted, apparently because points of detail seemed incorrect to the editor. Abstract by E. R. Eames of correspondence between P.E.B. Jourdain and Paul Carus, editor of *Open Court*, BRA.

263 Woods to B.R., 23 June 1916, BRA.

264 'The Foreign Office on Bertrand Russell: from The Public Record Office London', ts. compiled by K. Blackwell, August 1967, BRA. In 1967 B.R. was shown the material for the first time and told Blackwell that he had enjoyed reading it. Personal communication.

265 Thursday 1 June 1916, OMP/1402.

266 Addendum by Blackwell, derived from material which follows, but is separate from the Foreign Office minutes relating to the question of Russell's passport. Blackwell writes: 'It was decided to circulate the "short Catholic article" widely and to allow a limited circulation to the second, called "Mugwumpery as Cover", by an army officer who supposedly knew B.R.' But see Clark, p. 296. I am indebted to Conrad Russell for pointing out that the date of Newton's letter does not preclude a prior hint by word of mouth.

267 n.d., OMP/1401; in *Autobiog.*, II, pp. 66–7.

268 1 June 1916, OMP/1402; p/3 June, OMP/1385.

269 Mimeographed letter, dated 1 June 1916, copy in CEMP.

270 E. Whitehead to B.R., 2 and 5 June 1916, BRA; A. N. Whitehead to B.R., 4, 5 and 7 June, BRA; Moya Llewelyn Davies to B.R., 5 June 1916, BRA; *The Journals of Thomas James Cobden-Sanderson* (Doves Press, London 1926; reprinted Franklin, New York 1969), II, pp. 292–3; Holroyd, II, pp. 173–4; S. Pankhurst, p. 368.

271 Notes from C.E.M. to B.R., 5 June 1916; B.R. to C.A., 6 June 1916, BRA. There are several references around this time which suggest that Russell sometimes expected more organisational efficiency than Allen had time or inclination for. See, for example, C.A. to B.R., 27 June 1916, BRA.

272 For a discussion of the different versions, see a note by Blackwell in *Russell*, no.

1 (spring 1971), pp. 7–8. See also C.E.M., 'Russell Case, 5th June 1916' (rough ms. notes), CEMP. *Rex v. Bertrand Russell* was advertised in *Trib.*, only two weeks (6 and 13 July) before it was seized. See also *Trib.*, 17 August 1916, and B.R., letter to *MG*, 14 August 1916.

273 Holroyd, II, p. 174.

274 Leaflet in BRA; reprinted in B.R., 'For Conscience Sake', *Independent Review*, 15 January 1917; in *Autobiog.*, II, p. 164. All that is known of the last paragraph is that it was added by someone in the NCF office.

275 *Rex v. Bertrand Russell* (No-Conscription Fellowship, London 1916), p. 23.

276 *Trib.*, 6 July 1916. B.R. enclosed the ms. of this passage in a letter to C.E.M., n.d., CEMP.

277 E. Whitehead to B.R., 8 June [misdated 8 May] 1916; Holroyd, II, p. 174; Hardy, pp. 34–5.

278 C.E.M. to B.R., 5 June 1916, BRA.

279 [8 June 1916], OMP/1400.

280 Letters in CEMP and BRA; see also *Trib.*, 29 June 1916, where Russell expressed his thanks for the letters he had received; a brief account of the case had appeared in *Trib.*, 8 June 1916.

281 [17 July 1916], OMP/1391; p/22 July 1916, OMP/1403; Hardy, p. 40; *Autobiog.*, II, pp. 32–3. A list of the distrained property is in BRA.

282 Blackwell, 'The Foreign Office on Bertrand Russell'.

283 B.R. to C.E.M., [c. 12 June 1916], CEMP; unpublished ms., 'Principles of Social Reconstruction and Notes for Harvard Lectures', BRA.

284 [7 July 1916], OMP/1395.

285 PRO, HO 45/11012/314670.

286 C.E.M. to B.R., 12 July 1916, BRA.

287 Charles Trevelyan, *H. C. Deb.*, (5), 88(1916), cols.288–9, 28 November 1916. See also *H. C. Deb.*, (5), 85(1916), col.1204, 10 August 1916, where Ponsonby refers to the Harvard appointment accurately, but perhaps misleadingly, as 'purely academic'.

288 [9 July 1916], OMP/1394. For a full discussion of Russell's relationships at Trinity, see Hardy. Two points, sometimes misrepresented, are worth clarifying: (1) Russell was not at this time a Fellow of Trinity College, and therefore lacked tenure; it will be remembered he had rejected a fellowship when the Council wished to attach conditions to his leave of absence; (2) the decision-making body in this issue was the Council, made up of senior fellows holding their positions under certain kinds of title, not elected and not necessarily representative. See also BRA/Trinity College.

289 OMP/1389; 'Tuesday' [probably 8 August 1916], OMP/1193; Hardy, p. 41.

290 [17 July 1916], OMP/1391.

291 Hardy, p. 42; Whitehead to B.R., 14 September 1916, BRA. No copy of the pamphlet is known to have survived.

292 'Tuesday' probably 8 August 1916, OMP/1193; Ward to C.E.M., 11 August 1916. It is not known whether anything came of this project. Some of the information he requested was almost certainly confidential.

293 n.d., BRA.

294 Professor F. Alexander to B.R. 16 July 1916, BRA; in *Autobiog.*, II, p. 68; Cornford to B.R., 23 July 1916, BRA; in *Autobiog.*, II, pp. 69–70. See also *inter alia* M. Llewelyn Davies to B.R., 22 July 1916; E. W. Barnes to B.R., 27 July 1916, BRA.

295 15 July 1916.

296 Leader, *Nation*, 22 July 1916. For other accounts see *Friend*, 21 July 1916;

Trib., 29 July and 17 August; Feinberg and Kasrils, I, pp. 62–3; Clark, pp. 290–2.

297 p/29 May 1916, OMP/1381.

298 See, for example, *MG*, 3 August 1914.

299 'Agenda', National Convention, 8 and 9 April 1916, BRA.

300 [2 July 1916], OMP/1406.

301 [4 July 1916], OMP/1392.

302 [17 July 1916], OMP/1391.

303 [4 July 1916], OMP/1392. It may have been at this point that B.R. wrote the leaflet *Why Not Peace Negotiations?* [July 1916], BRA.

304 [9 July 1916], OMP/1394.

305 Merthyr *Pioneer*, 15 July 1916.

306 [7 July 1916], OMP/1395; [9 July 1916], OMP/1394.

307 W. H. Harries, Chief Inspector, Cardiff City Police to the Head Constable, 6 July 1916; Williams, Head Constable, Cardiff to Home Office (Herbert Samuel), 15 August 1916, PRO, HO 45/11012/314670.

308 *H. C. Deb.*, (5), 88(1916), cols.288–95, 28 November 1916. Samuel's speech on the same occasion departed further from the truth. See Clark, p. 304.

309 Mathews to Sir Ernley Blackwell, 28 August 1916, PRO, HO 45/11012/ 314670.

310 11 August 1916.

311 Copy of Samuel's letter, 14 August 1916, and of the transcribed speech in PRO, HO 45/11012/314670.

312 *H. C. Deb.*, (5), 86(1916), col.880, 19 October 1916.

313 Troup to Mathews, 25 August 1916, PRO, HO 45/11012/314670.

314 Mathews to Blackwell, 28 August 1916; Blackwell to Mathews 31 August 1916. PRO, HO 45/11012/314670.

315 *H. C. Deb.*, (5), 86(1916), col.1127, 25 October 1916; *ibid.* cols.1578–9, 31 October 1916; B.R. to Charles Trevelyan, 22 October 1916, Trevelyan papers, University of Newcastle-upon-Tyne, copy in BRA.

316 15 July 1916.

317 [9 July 1916], OMP/1394.

318 p/29 May 1916, OMP/1381; [19 July 1916], OMP/1390; [15 July, 1916] OMP/1389. There are some unexplained features here that will bear further examination: what has previously been written of wartime Wales would lead one to expect that Russell would have been heckled severely rather than welcomed. See especially Kenneth O. Morgan, *Wales in British Politics 1868–1922* (University of Wales Press, Cardiff 1963) pp. 275–87. Possibly he arrived just at the watershed in Welsh opinion when war-weariness was taking the place of enthusiasm.

319 C.A. used up what little money he had and entered (and emerged from) jail penniless. C.E.M. was supported by her father. Extensive documentation on CEMP refers. There was a distinction of status within the organisation between those who were paid and those who donated their time. Initially, the same situation had prevailed in the UDC, but E. D. Morel, who could not afford to work without a salary—a special handicap which he felt keenly—insisted from the start upon the right to influence policy and rapidly worked himself by his dedication into a position of great power. He was assisted in this by the fact that the other UDC leaders were politicians and dilettantes and did not devote their whole time to the work of the Union.

320 OMP/1389.

321 [17 July 1916], OMP/1391.

322 28 July 1916, OMP/1404; p/29 July OMP/1405; p/30 July, OMP/1407; p/20 August, OMP/1413.
323 Correspondence in PRO, HO 45/11012/314670. My interpretation of the roles of the Home and War Offices differs from that of Clark, pp. 298–300.
324 1 September 1916, OMP/1418.
325 'Sunday night' and 'Monday mg.' [3 and 4 September 1916], OMP/1419.
326 'Mon. night' and 'Tues. mg.' [4 and 5 September 1916], OMP/1423; *Autobiog.*, II, p. 74.
327 'A Sense of Humour' in Harry Ruja (ed.), *Mortals and Others: Bertrand Russell's American Essays, 1931–1935* (Allen & Unwin, London 1975), I, pp. 142–3. Conrad Russell to J. Vellacott, June 1975, also refers.
328 The source for the account of this interview is a report drawn up by Russell immediately after the interview—he enclosed a copy of it in a letter to Ottoline Morrell dated 7 September 1916—but it still of course gives only his recollection of the event.
329 H. C. Deb., (5), 86(1916), cols.880–1, 19 October 1916.
330 5 September 1916, OMP/1420.
331 7 September 1916, OMP/1421.
332 [6 July 1916], OMP/1395; p/7 September 1916, OMP/1421; *Autobiog.*, II, p. 33.
333 [17 September 1916], OMP/1424.
334 The fullest source for the whole of this exchange between Russell and the War Office is their original correspondence in BRA; also a mimeographed collection, 'Mr Russell and the War Office', copies in BRA and CEMP. B.R.'s statement concerning his 5 September meeting with General Cockerill is also reproduced in *Autobiog.*, II, pp. 72–3. The most widely circulated summary of the events is in a leaflet, *Bertrand Russell and the War Office: A Personal Statement*, reprinted as the 'Publisher's Preface' to *Justice in War-Time*, 2nd edition.
335 Carbon copy of a War Office memo (damaged), in PRO, HO 45/11012/314670.
336 n.d., OMP/1430.
337 The NCAC had been raided on 6 June; the NCF had been raided on 5 June, the date of Russell's trial, and was raided again on 4 August; a raid was even made on the private residence of Gladys Rinder, who worked as a secretary for the NCF. There are references to these and innumerable other raids in correspondence and other documents in CEMP. See, in particular, C.E.M. to Snowden, 18 June and 8 August 1916; 'Notice', 4 August 1916; Snowden to C.E.M., 12 June; Henry Davies to C.A., 19 June; all in CEMP. See also mimeographed letter from Adrian Stephen appealing for funds to replenish stationery stocks removed in a raid, in NCAC/SCPC.
338 C.E.M. to B. N. Langdon Davies, 24 October 1916, copy in CEMP; 'Report of Proceedings' NCCL Annual Meeting, 19 January 1917, copy in CEMP.
339 5 September 1916.
340 Correspondence in PRO, HO/45/11012/314670.
341 [17 September 1916], OMP/1424; B.R. to General Cockerill, 12 September, reprinted in 'Mr Russell and the War Office', mimeo, BRA.
342 *Herald*, 18 October 1916. Another (later) account is in Smillie, 'How I Lectured for Bertrand Russell', *Spokesman*, no. 3 (May 1970), pp. 20–1, reprinted from Smillie's *My Life for Labour* (Mills and Boon, London 1924).
343 MG, 16 October 1916; Trib., 26 October 1916.

344 First as magazine articles, then as a book (Century, New York 1917). It was not until 1963 that Allen & Unwin published *Political Ideals* in Britain.

345 *H. C. Deb.*, (5), 85(1916), cols.1204–5, 10 August 1916; *Trib.*, 17 August 1916; n.d., OMP/1437.

346 Ts. document in CEMP, n.d., n.s., filed at 1 June 1916, refers. The approach and the style suggest C.E.M.'s authorship, and the document clearly antedates the Home Office scheme.

347 'Meyer's Scheme', ts., n.d., filed June 1916, CEMP, but probably dates from early July, as it makes a comparison between this and the Home Office scheme. Meyer was not a member of the NCF but must have asked for consideration of his plan. See also 'General Policy', ms. draft in B.R.'s handwriting of a letter to the branches; n.d. but written shortly after B.R. became chairman in January 1917. Letters in FH/FSC also refer.

C.E.M. also drafted a letter covering the same topics, and in this part the printed version finally issued is closer to her version than to B.R.'s, but they are very close in sense. All mss, and copy of letter 'To Divisional and Branch Secretaries', 3 February 1917, CEMP.

348 Ms. draft, 'General Policy', [Jan. 1917] (see note 347 above).

349 [15 July 1916], OMP/1389.

350 Introduction to *On Active Service*, AP. For an excellent account of relations, good and bad, between the FSC and the NCF, see Kennedy, 'Fighting about Peace', forthcoming in *Quaker History*. Kennedy makes use of much new material which has recently come to light at FH; I am grateful to him for drawing it to my attention.

351 *Trib.*, 6 July 1916.

352 Various ms. notes in C.E.M.'s handwriting relating to the meetings of the National Committee on 25 June and 1 July 1916, CEMP.

353 For example, 'COs reported being sent to France weekend 24–26 June', a report sent to Davies on 24 June with a covering letter, and both forwarded to the War Office by Davies, copies in CEMP.

354 Childs to C.E.M., 3 September 1916, CEMP. Childs' office was bombarded with letters asking the result of prisoners' appearances before the Central Tribunal. He agreed to allow all who were returned to prison the privilege of writing a special letter to tell their families the decision.

355 Childs, p. 149; C.A., 'A Word to General Child', *Trib.*, 29 June 1916; Kennedy, pp. 246–7; Graham, pp. 190–1; Rae, pp. 29–30, 116; B.R. to C.E.M., 3 May 1917, not sent, BRA; Grubb, in *We Did Not Fight*, p. 150.

356 Ms. notes on National Committee meeting, 1 July 1916, CEMP; C.E.M. to B.R., 7 July 1916, BRA.

357 B.R.'s letter is not extant, but her reply indicates much of its content. C.E.M. to B.R., 15 July [probably 16 July 1916], BRA.

358 [2 July 1916], OMP/1406; [4 July 1916], OMP/1392; 15 July 1916, OMP/1389.

359 [4 July 1916], OMP/1392; C.E.M. to B.R., 12 July, BRA; [15 July 1916], OMP/1389; B.R., 'General Policy', MS in CEMP; correspondence in FH also refers.

360 See also *Friend*, Supp., 11 August 1916.

361 [15 July 1916], OMP/1389.

362 Wood, p. 96.

363 C.E.M. to B.R., 15 July [probably 15 July 1916], BRA.

364 At one time Hudson had been expected to take the position.

365 p/30 July 1916, OMP/1407. Among other matters, A.F.B. had described what he had seen in prison of Casement, who was in Pentonville awaiting

execution for his part in the Irish Easter Rising. A.F.B. had had no chance to speak to Casement, but saw him brought out for exercise, and saw also the preparations for the execution. See also *Trib.*, 3 August 1916; A.F.B., *Inside the Left*, p. 73–5.

366 B.R., 'General Policy'.

367 Catchpool to C.A., 24 July 1916, AP; C.E.M. to Bryce Leicester, n.d., CEMP; Political Committee circular, 29 July 1916, BRA; Minutes of Staff Meeting, 26 September 1916, CEMP. After resigning from the Friends' Ambulance Unit Catchpool had been refused absolute exemption and was awaiting his arrest, which did not occur until January 1917. The association with the NCF is not mentioned by either of his biographers, both of whom say he spent the time at Woodbrooke, the Quaker Study Centre in Birmingham. Hughes, pp. 34–7; Jean C. Greaves, *Corder Catchpool* (Friends' Home Service Committee, London, 1953), p. 12. Catchpool's letter to C.A. suggests that he did not think the Fellowship was single-minded enough about the peace campaign.

368 *Autobiog.*, II, p. 25; C. Malleson, 'Fifty Years: 1916–1966', in R. Schoenman (ed.), *Bertrand Russell, Philosopher of the Century* (Allen & Unwin, London 1967), p. 17; Malleson, *After Ten Years* (Cape, London 1931), pp. 104–9.

369 Mimeo reports of the hearings of 2 and 11 August 1916, CEMP, AP, BRA; *Trib.*, 10 and 17 August 1916; Kennedy, p. 273; Gilbert, pp. 5, 61; Marwick, *Open Conspirator*, pp. 33, 35.

370 p/20 August 1916, OMP/1413; [24 August 1916], OMP/1414. Allen's brother also visited, and there may have been others.

371 This refers to the preliminary hearing held in private in front of the Commanding Officer. C.E.M. added a note to this effect to Russell's report, in CEMP.

372 CEMP.

373 Letters and notes from Ringer-Hewitt and another sergeant, named Bloomfield to C.E.M., and copies of letters to Ringer-Hewitt, Bloomfield and Mrs Bloomfield from C.E.M., 14 August to 14 December 1916, CEMP. The two sergeants and Mrs Bloomfield continued to write to C.E.M. for some months, expressing warm sympathy with Allen, concern for his health, and admiration for the stand of the COs. They helped her as far as they could with information as to Allen's whereabouts, the time and place of release at the end of his sentence and the destination to which he would be escorted.

374 1 September, 1916, OMP/1417.

375 Ts., 'Chairman's Arrest', n.d., CEMP; extensive material in CEMP, including drafts of letters to MPs and to sympathisers informing them of the date of C.A.'s coming trial, with salient points about his case, some responses to these letters, and 'C.A.'s last Suggestions', ms. in C.A.'s handwriting, in which he says 'use my case widely and often'.

376 C.E.M. drew up a list of the officers, divisional representatives, and associates, noting against each his liabilities (to arrest under the Defence of the Realm Act or the Military Service Act) and where possible the name of a substitute who might take over; in most cases the substitute was also liable to arrest. 'Reconstruction of National Committee', ms. draft in C.E.M.'s handwriting, and ts., n.d., CEMP.

377 p/30 July 1916, OMP/1407. For Lloyd George's statement see *H. C. Deb.*, (5), 84(1916), col.1759, 26 July 1916; *Trib.*, 17 August 1916.

378 *H. C. Deb.*, (5), 85(1916), cols.1837–8, 16 August 1916; *Trib.*, 24 and 31 August 1916. Forster apparently told Meyer on 29 August that he had actually said 'I suppose not' rather than 'I suppose so' in reply to the question

as to whether the men would be sent to France. Ts., n.d. [August 1916], CEMP; A.F.B., 'Stand Firm', *Trib.*, 31 August 1916.

379 p/19 August 1916, OMP/1410.

380 OMP/1417. See also C.E.M. to C.A., 7 November 1916, CEMP.

381 p/28 July 1916, OMP/1404; and see Russell's account of the Committee meeting of 29 July in p/30 July 1916; OMP/1407.

382 The Joint Advisory Committee consisted of representatives of the NCF, the FSC, and the Fellowship of Reconciliation, and met to discuss common problems of policy. It was sometimes called a 'Council' and sometimes a 'Committee'.

383 *H. C. Deb.*, (5), 83(1916), col.1014; *Trib.*, 6 July 1916; 'Prime Minister's statement on the Government's new scheme', ts., CEMP; 'The Prime Minister and the Conscientious Objectors', printed letter issued by the Joint Advisory Council, BRA; *LL*, 6 July; 'Application on Grounds of Conscientious Objection', being a copy of the questions issued by the Central Tribunal, together with a ts. draft of answers, n.s., SCPC/NCF; Kennedy, p. 332. When he introduced the scheme in the House of Commons, Asquith had indicated that those not accepted would be sent to military detention, not back to civil prison. It is possible that the representations of the COs' organisations helped to get this changed, but Rae points out that the Army was now most anxious to have no further dealings with the troublesome objectors, and Childs seems to have been willing to forego his original hope that the 'ungenuine' would be "broken to discipline under the military machine'. Rae, pp. 162–4.

384 [4 July 1916], OMP/1392.

385 'The Present Position; an N.C.F. Letter to the Premier', *Trib.*, 10 August 1916; also issued as a leaflet, *C.O.s and "Alternative Service"*, BRA, CEMP.

386 War Office Orders 23/2695 and 2696 (A.G. 3) refer, copies in CEMP. See also *Trib.*, 3 and 10 August 1916; letters from E. V. Brierley, Brig. Gen., 29 July and B. E. W. Childs, Brig. Gen., July 1916, to commandants of detention barracks, copies in CEMP. Because the Home Office centres were inadequate to handle sufficient men, a few of those released remained on furlough for a considerable time, a situation which filled the War Office with alarm and disgust. Secretary of State to Home Secretary, 10 February 1917, PRO, WO 32/5491.

387 [4 September 1916], OMP/1423.

388 'A Message from Clifford Allen', *Trib.*, 3 August 1916.

389 Mimeos of letter and of additional note, CEMP.

390 Kennedy, pp. 341–2; A.F.B in *Trib.*, 17, 24 and 31 August 1916.

391 CEMP.

392 By mid-October 1000 were occupied under the scheme. The peak employed at any one time was 3000, in December 1917. Rae, p. 173.

393 No full history of the scheme has yet been written. For the best account from the objectors' point of view, see Kennedy, pp. 347–58. Rae's ch. 8 is the best account from the Government side.

394 Rae, pp. 163–6; correspondence in CEMP.

395 For example, in a letter to B.R. dated 26 July, Theodore Neild, formerly a manual training instructor at Sibthorp (a Quaker school), and now released from jail on furlough, admitted that he had filled in the form because he would be willing to go back to that job. But he resented the fact that the idea was being spread abroad that they had had enough of prison and expressed his determination to go back if necessary. CEMP.

396 Brockway recognised the position of this group of men without reservation even in his first leader on the scheme. *Trib.* 24 August 1916.

397 Kennedy, pp. 339–41.

398 28 August 1916, OMP/1416.

399 For an account of Norman's arguments, and A.F.B.'s editorial, see *Trib.*, 7 September 1916. See also Norman, 'Concerning the Scheme', *Trib.*, 28 September 1916.

400 Ts., 'Points of Importance', 15 September 1916, report from Hughes of Dyce; report of a meeting at Dyce, 29 August, CEMP. B.R. later told Trevelyan that he had wanted to go to Haverhill 'where my friend C. H. Norman was, for a purely private and domestic purpose, to try to adjust a personal misunderstanding which had arisen,' a statement which in part prevaricates and in part reflects B.R.'s feeling about the conflict with Norman. B.R. to Charles Trevelyan, 22 October 1916, copy in BRA.

401 PRO, HO 45/11012/314670.

402 28 August 1916, OMP/1417, encl. 1.

403 *Ibid.* encl. 3.

404 'Points of Importance', 15 September, 1916, CEMP.

405 Rae (pp. 172–6) gives the impression that the men suffered from too much freedom to run their own affairs, but this does not stand up in the light of more detail about what went on if it is remembered that the men were supposed to be civilians and neither soldiers nor the schoolboys to whom Rae implicitly compares them.

406 *Trib.*, 7 and 14 September 1916; very extensive material in CEMP, especially CEMP/Dyce Quarry Camp; Rae, p. 177–80; Kennedy, p. 349; Graham, pp. 232–3; Boulton, pp. 211–12.

407 See, for example, 'Concerning the Scheme: C. H. Norman's Opinion', *Trib.*, 28 September 1916; 'The National Committee and Alternativists', *Trib.*, 5 October 1916. See also 'Alternative Service, Oct. 4-', rough notes in C.E.M.'s hand re complaints from Hackney; F. C. Brown to C.E.M., 13 October 1916, describes a meeting of the Hackney branch where only the support of the absolutists present had prevented the resignation of the alternativist members. CEMP.

408 Mimeo, 'Letter from C. A. in Wormwood Scrubs October 21st 1916'. Copy in CEMP.

409 *Ibid.*

410 Rae, p. 167.

411 Rae sets the number of the absolutists in prison at 985 and of the 'ungenuines' at 313. He uncritically accepts the judgment of the Central Tribunal on the invalidity of the objections of the latter, on the ground that the Army Council was putting pressure on the Tribunal to be lenient in its assessments. There must indeed have been some shirkers amongst them, but the belief persisted that a conviction could not be genuine unless it was religiously based and extended to the use of armed force in any situation. While it may be possible to make a case for not extending exemption to such 'political' objectors, it is a different matter to refuse to recognise that their convictions may be real. By this criterion, Russell (for example) would never have qualified to hold conscientious objections. It is also of interest that Rae subscribes to the view that those of the men who made trouble in prison or camp (when some of them were reclassified) could not be genuine objectors. Although they also met with little sympathy from Russell, the logical conclusion of this line of argument is that there has never been a sincere revolutionary. In addition, undoubtedly some of the more inarticu-

late or simple-minded men were unable to satisfy even the supposedly lenient Central Tribunal. Rae, pp. 163–6.

412 For example, on the weekend of 26–7 August the National Committee met on Saturday from 10.30 a.m. to 10.30 p.m., after which a sub-committee went on working until 2.30 a.m., and the whole Committee met again the next day—Sunday—from 9.30 a.m. to 5.00 p.m. p/28 August 1916, OMP/1416.

413 For example, C.E.M. to Rev. Richard Roberts, 1 September 1916, in which she wrote that she had only been to bed for three hours and 'can hardly cope with the mass of urgent work that comes in hour by hour'. Copy in CEMP.

414 A.F.B. to C.E.M., n.d., CEMP; A.F.B. to E. Ellis, 16 November 1916, FH; A.F.B., *Socialism and Pacifists*, (National Labour Press, Manchester 1916).

415 4 September 1916, OMP/1423.

416 p/4 August 1916, OMP/1408; p/28 August 1916, OMP/1416; [3 September 1916], OMP/1419; B.R. to L. Donnelly, 2 November 1916, BRA.

417 This general picture emerges from B.R.'s letters to O.M. over the whole period. *Autobiog.*, II, also refers. See also B.R.'s letters to Lady Constance Malleson, BRA.

418 Letter to branch secretaries, 21 September 1916; C.E.M. to C.A., 7 November, CEMP.

419 [19 September 1916], OMP/1422.

420 *Trib.*, 21 September, 5 October 1916.

421 B.R., 'General Policy'.

422 C.E.M. to C.A., 7 November 1916, CEMP. This letter has an uncertain history. C.A. in jail, like others serving a term at hard labour, was allowed only one letter a month, after the initial period of two months during which no correspondence was permitted. One of his scheduled letters had had to be foregone in lieu of an extra visit on 22 September, which had been claimed on the pretext of business relating to the letting of his flat. C.E.M. was determined to make the most of the precious opportunity to write and had already had one letter returned because of its excessive length. The one cited here is confined to two sides of paper but on these she crowded about 2500 words. Since it was found among C.E.M.'s papers, it is possible that it too was refused delivery, but it is as likely that Allen returned it to her for safe keeping when she saw him at Newhaven in late November.

423 C.E.M., ms. notes on National Committee meeting of 10–11 November 1916. Kennedy, 'Fighting about Peace', *passim*, Tucker, pp. 199–201. It is disappointing that Tucker does not deal more fully with the Quakers' position within the NCF. Although this can be partly excused by a lack of published material, more is available than Tucker has used.

424 Extensive material in CEMP, especially special file 10, 'Birkenhead Cases', filed between August/September 1916; C.E.M. to C.A., 7 November 1916; Conscientious Objectors Information Bureau Report XXXIX, 29 August; *Trib.*, 14 and 28 September 1916; G. L. Dickinson to *Nation*, 9 September 1916; Kennedy, p. 257.

425 Duke and Beardsworth, the two subjects of the enquiry, refused to testify. The finding was that force had been used but all were acquitted and Duke and Beardsworth, charged with refusing to testify, were also acquitted. *Herald*, 20 January 1917; *Trib.*, 18 January 1917. The officer concerned had already been removed by this time and the charges laid were against non-commissioned officers.

426 Ms. notes in C.E.M.'s hand, 'Birkenhead Cases', erroneously filed at 11 August 1916, but should be in special file 10, CEMP.

427 C.E.M. to C.A., 7 November 1916. The article was probably 'The Present

Position of the "C.O."'', which appeared as a leader over A.F.B.'s signature in *Trib.* 5 October 1916. Marshall told Allen that Childs had also been in communication with the Rev. Meyer on the subject.

428 *Ibid.*

429 *Trib*, 12 October 1916.

430 Ms. notes in C.E.M.'s handwriting, dated 14 October, and some by B.R. on the back of his copy of the 'Agenda for Meeting of the National Committee of the N.C.F.', both in CEMP.

431 *Trib.*, 28 September to 9 November 1916; A.F.B., 'The Policy of the N.C.F.', *Trib.*, 16 November 1916.

432 Mrs Wray to C.E.M., 26 October 1916; C.E.M. to Mrs Wray, 23 October 1916, CEMP.

433 B.R., 'General Policy', CEMP; A.F.B., 'The Policy of the N.C.F.', *Trib.*, 16 November 1916. Unfortunately the addresses do not seem to have survived, although other references indicate that they were prepared. See also ms. 'Notes on Proposed Change of N.C.F. Policy', 9 November, apparently by C.E.M., AP; 'C.A.'s Notes on B.B.'s policy', 16 December, AP. Gilbert, p. 65, selects misleadingly and confuses the real import of these notes in describing them as 'smuggled out to Barratt Brown'. They were probably handed quite legitimately to C.E.M. at Newhaven. Gilbert has other such editorial errors. See also, badly damaged, the master copy on which C.E.M. recorded answers to the questionnaire, CEMP.

434 C.A. to C.E.M., 28 November 1916, AP.

435 Childs to T. E. Harvey, 20 October 1916, copy in CEMP.

436 Numerous letters from C.E.M. at this time refer , especially to H. G. Chancellor, MP, 9 February 1917; to Massingham, 4 December 1916, copies in CEMP; C.A. to C.E.M., 28 November 1916, AP; [13 December 1916], OMP/1438. There was one important material aspect in which the guard-room was an improvement on civil prison—that was in the matter of diet.

437 C.E.M.'s pass in CEMP; B.R.'s pass and correspondence with the Competent Military Authority in BRA; p/3 December 1916, OMP/1436; C.E.M. to 'Dear Comrade', 29 November 1916, FH.

438 [13 December 1916], OMP/1438.

439 [29 November 1916], OMP/1437; 7 December, OMP/1439; C.E.M. to C.A., [9 December], copy in CEMP. Victor F. Lenzen, later Professor Emeritus of Physics at Berkeley, who was present at the weekend, describes it in his 'Bertrand Russell at Harvard, 1914', *Russell*, no. 3 (autumn 1971), p. 6.

440 In addition to references given above, there is extensive material in AP and CEMP relating to C.A.'s time at Newhaven, and in CEMP relating to the Non-Combatant Corps disturbances. Special file CEMP/Newhaven contains much but not all of this material. The present writer hopes to give a full account of this little-publicised episode elsewhere. See also C.E.M., 'Events in Newhaven', *Trib.*, 7 December 1916; C.A., 'Weakness and Strength', *Trib.*, 14 December; 'N.C.C. Situation', *Trib.*, 21 December; 'The N.C.C.', *Trib.*, 11 January 1917.

441 Ballott papers and covering letter, 20 December 1916, in 'Scrapbook', BRA. The 'Scrapbook', compiled by an unknown hand, is a recent acquisition by purchase in BRA. It is a large and untidy collection of clippings and documents pasted in a book. The compiler had a close personal interest in both drama and conscientious objection, and some connection with the NCF. The ballot paper—no other copy of which is known to be extant—is marked in Russell's favour.

442 *Justice in War-time*, p. 27.

443 *Political Ideals* (1963), pp. 82–3.

444 B.R. to C.E.M., 25 October 1916; C.E.M. to G. L. Dickinson, 23 October (copy); Dickinson to C.E.M., 24 October; C.E.M. to B.R., 26 October; ts. copy of resolution passed at Women's International League Conference, 26 October; programme of Conference on International Sanctions, Devonshire House, 11 and 12 October 1916, CEMP. Robbins, pp. 107–8, erroneously refers to the latter conference as a 'Quaker Conference' (whereas it was a forum for a variety of views), and describes as 'a statement issued at its conclusion' a passage taken (by him, as his reference shows) from the unpublished ms. Minutes of the Friends' Peace Committee meeting privately in regular session almost two weeks later. Minutes in FH.

445 E. J. Ford to B.R., BRA.

446 *Trib.*, 18 January 1917; *War and Peace*, January 1917, pp. 58–60.

447 B.R. to C.E.M., 3 January 1917, CEMP; see also B.R. to C.E.M., 1 January 1917.

448 She sent this message on a postcard, not extant, but copied the message on to the bottom of B.R.'s letter to her.

449 'On History', published in the *Independent Review*, July 1904, reprinted in *Basic Writings*, p. 527.

450 *The Practice and Theory of Bolshevism* (Allen & Unwin, London 1920), p. 127.

451 'History as an Art', in *Portraits from Memory*, p. 198.

452 *Proceedings of the Aristotelian Society*, 17 (1916–17), p. 482. The contribution, which was on Hume's view of miracles, is not extant.

453 A. N. Whitehead to B.R., 8 January 1917 (2 letters); E. Whitehead to B.R., 10 January 1917, BRA. A. N. Whitehead's first letter is in *Autobiog.*, II, p. 78.

454 17 January 1917, BRA.

455 Letter to divisional and branch secretaries, 3 February 1917. Ts. and ms. drafts in CEMP. This section was drawn up by B.R. and amended by C.E.M. From the ms. we learn that the first of these resolutions was moved by Barratt Brown.

456 [7 December 1916], OMP/1439.

457 B.R., 'The N.C.F. and the Political Outlook', editorial, *Trib.*, 7 December 1916. FSC minutes and correspondence in FH also refer. Such compulsory direction of labour was carried out from the outset of the Second World War with generally good effect on efficiency.

458 Lloyd George, *War Memoirs*, I, ch. 45, pp. 801–16.

459 A. Rose, 'Widen Our Basis', *Trib.*, 21 December 1916; C.E.M., 'The New Issue', editorial, *Trib.*, 4 January 1917; Brown, 'Alter Our Basis', *Trib.*, 4 January 1917; Brown, 'A Correction', *Trib.*, 18 January 1917; Rose to C.E.M., 12 December 1916, with draft of 'Suggested New Basis'; C.E.M. to Brown, 13 December 1916, CEMP; correspondence in FH also refers.

460 Letter to divisional and branch secretaries, 3 February 1917, draft and ts. in CEMP; 'National Committee Meeting', *Trib.*, 22 March 1917.

461 B.R., 'National Service', *Trib.*, 15 February 1917.

462 B.R., 'Liberty and National Service', *Trib.*, 22 February 1917.

463 Grubb may have been another exception, since his position as Treasurer and his service on the National Committee kept him in touch with all sides of the work.

464 She had attended St Leonard's Girls' School, St Andrews, Scotland, an advanced school for its time, her mother was active with her in the suffrage movement and her father was supportive of her work for women and for

peace. Correspondence in CEMP refers. Also private communication from the History Club of St Leonard's School, for which I am indebted to Miss Aylwin Clark.

465 Wood, p. 88, refers to B.R.'s willingness to take on 'humdrum jobs of journalism' on behalf of the COs, but shows no knowledge of the amount of day-to-day work Russell did, or of how much was involved besides writing and speaking.

466 C.E.M. to B.R., 2 October 1916, BRA.

467 C.E.M. to C.A., 7 November 1916, CEMP.

468 There are many references in correspondence, especially Caroline Marshall (C.E.M.'s mother) to C.E.M., 1 November 1916; Frank Marshall to C.E.M., 6 November 1916; C.E.M. to Mr James and to Mr Norrish, 2 December 1916, all in CEMP.

469 For example, in his letter to C.E.M., 3 May 1917, not sent, BRA; to National Committee of NCF, 18 May 1917, not sent, BRA.

470 The Commission and its work are not mentioned in secondary sources because almost all documentation is in CEMP. References occur, *inter alia*, in the following: notes and inter-office memos, especially 20–25 January 1917; E. Frances Lawley to E. Grubb, 5 January [actually 5 February] 1917; E. Grubb to C.E.M., 6 February; B.R. to C.E.M., 6 February; B.R. to C.E.M., n.d. filed early February 1917; ts. 'Work of Headquarters: Memorandum for National Committee, 15 and 16 June 1917'; draft 'Minutes' of National Committee meeting, 16–18 February 1917. All in CEMP.

471 *Autobiog.*, II, p. 33.

472 This description of B.R.'s work for the *Tribunal* is taken from a ts., 'C.E.M.'s Work: Notes for Mr. Hunter, May 1917', CEMP. *Trib.* of 27 September 1917 bears Boothroyd's name, that of 4 October bears Smith's, but other evidence suggests that Smith took over at about mid-summer. The practice of naming the editor was only followed until 18 October. C.E.M.'s 'Memorandum for the National Committee, 15 and 16, June 1917' describes Smith as editor, and gives roughly the same description of Russell's responsibility for the paper.

473 C.E.M. to B.R., 7 March 1917, B.R. to C.E.M., 8 March, both in CEMP.

474 C.E.M. to Ayles, 16 March. Other references occur in C.E.M. to C.P. Trevelyan, 2 March; to Mr Douglas, 16 March; to Ammon, 7 March 1917.

475 OMP/1449. Dated only 'Friday', this letter almost certainly belongs to the first half of March, before the Russian revolution. It also includes a reference to the authorites having refused Russell permission to visit Allen in person, which occurred early in March.

476 A. J. P. Taylor, *First World War* (Penguin, Harmondsworth 1966; first published 1963), pp. 157–8; Lloyd George, *War Memoirs*, I, ch. 31.

477 B.R. to E. Sedgwick, 25 November 1916, copy in BRA; Feinberg and Kasrils, I, p. 65; n.d. OMP/1461 and 1448. Russell, who felt at this time that nothing he could do pleased O.M., hoped that the letter to Wilson might 'help to set me up a little in your eyes'. Probably Katherine Dudley was also the 'young lady who buried . . . in a box of chalk' and brought to the States at this time the ms. of 'For Conscience Sake', an autobiographical article by B.R. on his war-time experiences to date and which appeared (with the above note) in the *Independent*, 15 January 1917. Material in PRO, HO 45/11012/314670 indicates that officials had identified the culprit by 6 February 1917.

478 Feinberg and Kasrils, I, pp. 65–9 and plate 3; Lella Secor Florence, 'The Ford Peace Ship and After' in *We Did Not Fight*, pp. 116–19; *Autobiog.*, II, pp.

27–8, 31. The speaker was William Jennings Bryan, the politician and pacifist.

479 Ms in BRA; reprinted in *Autobiog.*, II, pp. 27–31, and Feinberg and Kasrils, I, pp. 65–8.

480 There were 15 such Notes passed between 12 December 1916 and 16 January 1917. National Peace Council *Circular*, no. 67 (15 January 1917).

481 See especially B.R., 'The Momentum of War', *Trib.*, 14 December 1916.

482 'President Wilson's Statement', *Trib.*, 1 February 1917.

483 'America's Entry into the War', *Trib.*, 19 April 1917. For the reaction of pacifist groups to the issue of a negotiated peace, the Notes exchanged in late 1916 and early 1917, and United States entry into the war, see *inter alia* material in EDMP; Swanwick, pp. 75–88; Feinberg and Kasrils, I, pp. 69–72; Lilian Stevenson, *Towards a Christian International* (International Fellowship of Reconciliation, London 1941), p. 3. For the issues in general, see Taylor, *First World War*, pp. 153–63; Winkler, pp. 139–41; Cooper Willis, pp. 234–41; Armin Rappaport, *The British Press and Wilsonian Neutrality* (Peter Smith, Gloucester, Mass., 1965; 1st edition 1951), *passim*; Fritz Fischer, *Germany's Aims in the First World War* (Chatto & Windus, London 1967; first published in German, 1961), chs. 7–10.

484 'What is Wrong with Western Civilization?', delivered 3 April 1924, ms. in BRA. See also Feinberg and Kasrils, I, pp. 71–2, 94–5.

485 S. R. Graubard, *British Labour and the Russian Revolution* (Harvard University Press, Cambridge, Mass. 1956), pp. 17–18; *H. C. Deb.*, (5), 91(1917), col.2085, 22 March 1917.

486 B.R. to E.D. Morel, 2 July 1917, copy in BRA. The article that suffered the deletion was no doubt 'Why the War Continues', *U.D.C.*, February 1917.

487 BRA. See also B.R., 'Russia Leads the Way', editorial, *Trib.*, 22 March 1917.

488 Milligan, ch. 16. See also Tucker, p. 152.

489 There are a number of items in CEMP bearing the first title, but this writer has found only the second in secondary material.

490 Raymond Postgate, *Life of George Lansbury* (Longmans, Green, London 1951), p. 168.

491 J. A. Leith and C. Dotson (eds.), *Modern Revolutions* (Queen's University, Kingston, Ont. n.d.), pp. 175–6.

492 'Britain's Charter of Freedom', ms. dated (not completely clearly) 17 March 1917. The ms. is in an unidentified handwriting, but bears the annotation in C.E.M.'s handwriting, 'B.R.'s notes for int[erview] with J[ohn] B[urns] etc.'. CEMP..

493 Mimeographed copies of both letters, both dated 21 March 1917, in CEMP.

494 'Sir S. Oliver' was presumably Sir Sydney Olivier, 1859–1943, who was at this time Permanent Secretary at the Board of Agriculture: the notes suggest that he disqualified himself from taking an active part in the campaign because of his appointment. Others approached by C.E.M.—it is not known whether B.R. was with her—included Snowden, whose response was 'very cautious', H. W. Nevinson, John Dillon and H. N. Brailsford, all of whom were described as sympathetic; Holt and Runciman were not favourable.

495 Mss. in C.E.M.'s handwriting, 'Charter Campaign: Suggestions for Organising Committee, Work needed'. This is a list of people to see, annotated with initials of those by whom they will be or have been seen and a short note on the outcome. Also C.E.M. to Brailsford, 20 March 1917; to Meynell, 21 March; to Maude Royden, 21 March; to Lord Farrer, 21 March;

to Ammon, 22 March; 'Notes for Mr Russell', 23 March; 'Points for Mr Russell', 25 March. All in CEMP. *LL* erroneously gave C.E.M. credit for suggesting the Albert Hall, *LL*, 5 April 1917.

496 *Herald*, 7 April 1917; George Lansbury *et al.*, *Russia Free! Ten Speeches delivered at the Royal Albert Hall London on 31 March 1917: Authorized Report* (The Herald Office, London 1917), pp. 20–1; Lady Constance Malleson, personal communication, February 1975; Malleson, *After Ten Years*, p. 112.

497 'Sunday' [1 April 1917], OMP/1459. See also B.R., 'The New Hope', editorial, *Trib.*, 5 April 1917. Russell can hardly have meant the statement about the Russian Jews literally.

498 Ammon to C.E.M., n.d., CEMP. Meynell says that a total of 20,000 tickets were asked for. Francis Meynell, *My Lives* (Bodley Head, London 1971), 104.

499 K. D. Courtney to C.E.M., 6 April 1917, CEMP.

500 *Herald*, 7 April 1917. Not surprisingly, the fullest account was in *Herald*. In addition to sources referred to in previous notes, the following have been used for the activities of the Committee for Anglo-Russian Co-Operation and the organisation of the Albert Hall meeting: 'Programme'; ts. 'Agenda', 20 March; C.E.M. to Pethick-Lawrence, n.d.; proof copy of Smillie's speech; C.E.M. to Lord Weardale, n.d.; all in CEMP. C.E.M. to B.R., [1 April 1917], BRA. Other accounts of the meeting may be found in Postgate, pp. 165–8; Boulton, pp. 232–3; Meynell, *My Lives*, pp. 104–5; Graubard, p. 18. See also B.R., 'The New Hope', *Trib.* 5 April 1917.

501 'Budget from the N.C.F. to delegates', 10 and 21 August 1917, CEMP; C.E.M. attended the 10 August conference and reported on it in 'Summary of News for Prisoners', erroneously dated 1 August 1917, copy in AP. See also E. Hunter's editorial, 'To Stockholm!', *Trib.*, 16 August; B.R.'s front-page article, 'The International Situation', *Trib.*, 23 August; E. Hunter, editorial, 'Long Live the International!' *Trib.*, 23 August 1917.

502 B.R. to C.E.M. 1 June 1917, CEMP.

503 In addition to being Parliamentary Secretary to the NCF, Ammon had heavy commitments with the ILP and was honorary secretary to the trade union section of the NCCL. It is often impossible to be sure which hat he was wearing on any particular occasion.

504 Postgate says that it was in fact the Anglo-Russian Democratic Alliance which organised the Leeds meeting, and this may have been so, but he also states that the Alliance was dissolved, to Lansbury's regret, at that meeting, whereas we know that the conveners were appointed to a Provisional Committee at that time. Postgate, pp. 169–70. The other conveners were H. Alexander, C. Despard, E. C. Fairchild, J. Fineberg, F. W. Jowett, Tom Quelch, P. Snowden and J. R. MacDonald.

505 p/2 April 1917, OMP/1482.

506 For reactions to the Russian revolution, see *inter alia* L. Woolf, *Beginning Again. An Autobiography of the Years 1911–1918* (Hogarth Press, London 1964), p. 209; Cross, pp. 154–7; Swanwick, pp. 85–6; Quentin Bell, *Bloomsbury* (Weidenfeld and Nicolson, London 1968), p. 68; Norman, ch. 7; C. A. Cline, *Recruits to Labour: The British Labour Party, 1914–1931* (Syracuse University Press, Syracuse 1963), p. 17; Malleson, *After Ten Years*, p. 112. One of the responses that proved to be predominantly middle-class and intellectual was the 1917 Club. Bloomsbury was an important element, but it did provide a common social ground for liberals moving left and the ILP. The Snowdens dropped out when the Club applied for a liquor licence. B.R. joined but never seems to have been very active.

507 Letter from B.R. to Herbert Bryan on declining to join the ILP, 6 July 1915, quoted by Swartz, pp. 99–100.

508 Clement J. Bundock, 'Guild Socialism and Education: Interview with Mr Bertrand Russell', *LL*, 22 March 1917. Printed just after the Russian revolution, the lack of any reference in the article to that event makes it safe to assume that the interview took place before the revolution.

509 *Roads to Freedom: Socialism, Anarchism and Syndicalism* (Allen & Unwin, London 1918; in USA as *Proposed Roads to Freedom*, Holt, New York 1919). According to B.R.'s preface, an American publisher invited him to write the book 'before the United States had become a belligerent', so that it must have been in his mind very shortly after the outbreak of the Russian revolution. Preface to 3rd edition (1949), p. 1.

510 *Roads to Freedom*, pp. 124–5. When a new edition was brought out in 1949, Russell stated in the preface that he now felt Anarchism to be less defensible, because of the effects of world scarcity. Guild socialism, however, still seemed to him 'an admirable project', whose advocacy he would like to see revived.

511 'Report', *Trib.*, 24 May 1917. See also 'The Russian Revolution', a single-page ts. marked in B.R.'s handwriting 'Written in the first days of the Russian Revolution'. BRA.

512 B.R., 'Russia and Peace', *Trib.*, 24 May 1917.

513 B.R. estimated the number present at 2500, rather than the 1150 accounted for in this list. 5 June 1917, OMP/1460. This was probably a simple miscalculation, but possibly may reflect the difference between the number of official delegates and the number of attenders. Official figures given in *What Happened at Leeds* (Council of Workers' and Soldiers' Delegates, London 1917; reprinted, with an introduction by Ken Coates, as *British Labour and the Russian Revolution*, Bertrand Russell Peace Foundation, Nottingham [1974]).

514 5 June 1917, OMP/1460.

515 B.R. to C.E.M., 1 June 1917, CEMP.

516 John G. Slater claims that this 'shows how completely the war and its victims had come to dominate his thinking. At best he only alludes to the Russians and their Revolution'. This interpretation does not stand up in the light of the further evidence of Russell's very wide-ranging interest in the Russian revolution which is used here. 'What Happened at Leeds', *Russell*, no. 4 (winter 1971–2), pp. 9–10. The speech is reprinted in full in this short article.

517 *What Happened at Leeds* (1974), pp. 29–30.

518 *Ibid.* p. 32. Williams ended his speech with the words of the *Communist Manifesto*: 'Workers of the world unite! You have nothing to lose but your chains.'

519 The recognition was shared only by the extreme left: or perhaps it was only these who really wanted radical action. Pankhurst wrote a perceptive editorial in *Women's Dreadnought*, 9 June 1917. Walter Kendall, *The Revolutionary Movement in Britain, 1900–21* (Weidenfeld & Nicolson, London 1969), p. 129, gives the impression that the Clydesiders, although they sent delegates, found so 'liberal' a gathering hard to take seriously.

520 Graubard, p. 39.

521 The issues were mainly 'dilution' and exemptions from military service. The Government was sufficiently concerned to set up a commission to investigate industrial unrest. Ken Coates and A. Topham (eds.), *Industrial Democracy in Great Britain: a book of readings and witnesses for workers' control*

(MacGibbon & Kee, London 1968), pp. 95–6; *Trib.*, 23 August 1917; R. K. Middlemas, *The Clydesiders: A Left Wing Struggle for Parliamentary Power* (Hutchinson, London 1965), pp. 75–9. Unrest in the country, and hostility to the Government, were also related to the success of German U-boat warfare and the consequent shortage of food, characterised by the potato queues.

522 B.R. to Bacharach, 7 June 1917, copy in BRA. The principal source of information for the Leeds Conference is *What Happened at Leeds*. The *Herald*, 9 June 1917, also carried a full report, as did *LL*, 9 June, and *Women's Dreadnought*, 9 June. See also 'Leeds and Revolution', n.s., *Trib.*, 7 June. Other first-hand accounts occur in Malleson, *After Ten Years*, pp. 113–14; *Autobiog.*, II, p. 31; Woolf, pp. 210–13; Snowden, *Autobiography*, I, pp. 450–6. In addition to references already noted, see Lansbury, *Miracle of Fleet Street* (Labour Publishing Co., London 1925), pp. 115–16; Boulton, pp. 234–7; Benjamin Sacks, 'The Independent Labour Party During the World War' (PhD dissertation, Stanford University, 1934), pp. 121–3; Cross, pp. 157–8; Ralph Miliband, *Parliamentary Socialism* (Allen & Unwin, London 1961), pp. 54–7; J. J. Macfarlane, *The British Communist Party: Its Origins and Development until 1929* (MacGibbon & Kee, London 1966), p. 21; John McNair, *James Maxton, the Beloved Rebel* (Allen & Unwin, London 1955), p. 76; David Mitchell, *Monstrous Regiment: the story of the women of the first world war* (Macmillan, New York 1965), pp. 308–10; Kendall, p. 129; Postgate, pp. 169–70; Robbins, pp. 120–3.

523 B.R. to H. Wildon Carr, 27 June 1917, copy in BRA; in M. Thompson, 'Some Letters from Bertrand Russell to H. Wildon Carr', *Coranto: Journal of the Friends of the Libraries, University of Southern California*, 10 (1975), pp. 7–19.

524 *Roads to Freedom*, pp. 159–60.

525 Graubard, p. 36.

526 *Autobiography*, I, p. 456.

527 Postgate, pp. 169–70.

528 C.E.M., 'Summary of News for Prisoners', misdated 1 August, actually mid-August, 1917, copy in AP. There is also reference to measures taken by the Army to counter such activity in an NCCL ts., 'Civil Liberties', [January] 1918, copy in CEMP. See also McNair, pp. 76–7; Boulton, pp. 236–7. Boulton's short account is interesting, but as usual lacks documentation. An awareness of the continued life of the movement is found in historians, such as Macfarlane and Kendall, whose subject is politically farther to the left.

529 Mimeographed list of divisional conferences, with NCF circular to branch secretaries, 17 July 1917, copy in BRA; circular headed 'Workers' and Soldiers' Council', 7 July 1917, containing extensive general material together with an agenda for the London District Conference, to be held 28 July. Reference is also made in this to a circular of 15 June. CEMP. It will be noted that the term 'Workmen's' had been re-translated from the Russian into the more appropriately asexual term 'Workers'.

530 B.R. to Carr, 17 June 1917; in Thompson.

531 'Minutes of National Committee', *Trib.*, 21 June 1917. This is the only report known to be extant.

532 Draft letter in BRA.

533 *Trib.*, 5 July 1917. See also S. V. Bracher, letter on 'Non-Resistance and Revolution', *Trib.*, 12 July 1917.

534 Letter to branch secretaries, 19 October 1917, copy in CEMP. That it was thought important, as late as mid-October, to publish the text of the

amendment (which had been omitted from an earlier circular) suggests that the issue was still alive then.

535 Letter to branch secretaries, 17 July 1917, copy in BRA; 'National Committee Meeting', *Trib.*, 19 July 1917.

536 B.R. to C.E.M., 8 August 1917, CEMP. In the same issue of *Trib.*, B.R.'s editorial, 'A Pacifist Revolution?', was on the same theme. Robbins, pp. 123–2, has an interesting discussion of the difficulty of reconciling revolutionary fervour with pacifism.

537 p/13 July 1917, OMP/1463; National Committee minutes, 31 August, 1 September 1917; several drafts of an extremely effusive greeting to the Russians drawn up by C.E.M., CEMP. The actual letter of greeting to all delegates, signed by B.R., C.E.M. and Grubb, is in *Trib.*, 30 August 1917, and is more moderate. See also *Trib.*, 13 September 1917; National Committee minutes, 31 August, 1 September 1917, ts., CEMP.

538 There is room for further research here, in local papers and the records of labour organisations.

539 Macfarlane, p. 21.

540 28 July 1917, OMP/1468; NCCL, 'Civil Liberties', January 1918, ts., CEMP; Malleson, *After Ten Years*, p. 114; Meynell, p. 106; B.R. to C.E.M., n.d., CEMP; B.R., 'Crucify Him! Crucify Him!' *Trib.*, 2 August 1917.

541 2 August 1917, BRA. *Autobiog.*, II, pp. 31–2.

542 Kennedy follows Allen's rather critical view of the NCF executive in its dealings with the Home Office men, which is not justified for the period of B.R.'s chairmanship. Kennedy, pp. 338, 351–2; C.A., 'C.O.'s and Conscription', ch. 3, pp. 13–17, AP.

543 Morgan Jones to C.E.M., 11 March 1917, CEMP. Jones wrote three articles in the Merthyr *Pioneer* on 'Why I accepted Alternative Service'.

544 'Report of interview of Mr Robert Williams with Mr Brace', dated 5 February 1917 (but the interview had taken place in early January), CEMP.

545 Quoted and cited extensively in Rae, ch. 8, *passim*.

546 C.E.M. to C.A., [9 December 1916], CEMP; 'Report on the Relation of the National Committee of the N.C.F. to the Home Office Camps', n.d. [between 18 and 31 May 1917], hereinafter referred to as 'Report on Relation', CEMP. The term 'camp secretaries' means the secretaries of the NCF branches in each of the Home Office camps. There were also elected 'Men's Committees' in each camp, which had the right to make representations on behalf of the men to the Home Office agents, but these included objectors who were not members of the NCF.

547 *Ibid.*; 'Visits of Hunter and Roberts to Llannon and Llanddensant, March 30 and 31 1917', report in BRA; 'National Committee, April 6 and 7', *Trib.*, 3 May.

548 B.R. to camp secretaries, 21 March 1917; see also 'Report on Relation', CEMP.

549 B.R. to camp secretaries, 21 March 1917.

550 'The Position in the Home Office Camps', n.d., for members of the National Committee and camp secretaries, with covering letter from B.R., CEMP.

551 Aylmer Rose to C.E.M., 6 April, 1917, CEMP.

552 *Ibid.*; H. Marten to Ellis, 13 March 1917, copy in CEMP; to Harrop, 18 March, copy in CEMP; to 'Friends', 5 May, BRA. Marten became secretary of the Men's Committee, was one of three appointed to meet with a deputation which came down from the Home Office in April, hoped to see a branch of the Fellowship of Reconciliation formed, was in correspondence

with the FSC and with the NCF, and later became Clerk of the Friends' Meeting which was soon established. 'Home Office Representative at Dartmoor', *News Sheet*, no. 5, copy in CEMP; 'Minute Book: Princetown Allowed Meeting', loaned by courtesy of Plymouth Monthly Meeting; Hughes, pp. 142–3. Marten had earlier been among those sent to France and condemned to death, and also among those who had been released into the Home Office scheme in spite of a refusal to sign the undertaking. Graham, p. 231.

553 Rose to C.E.M., 6 April 1917, CEMP. Rae, pp. 175–6, gives a fair description of the men's attitudes, but in footnote 3, p. 175, makes the curious error of confusing controversy over whether to accept the scheme (canvassed by Harvey and Murray in *Trib.*, 27 July 1916) with 'the arguments for and against cooperation'. A Quaker who arrived a few weeks after the scheme began was told that at the beginning as many as 200–300 had done no work, Keeling to Miss Thomas (FSC) n.d., FH Marten wrote a long analysis of the situation, close in sentiment to Rose's, copy in FH, marked '5. V. 17'.

554 Rose to C.A., 23 February 1919, AP.

555 27 April 1917, copy in CEMP.

556 B.R. to Augustus W. Smith, Men's representative, Princetown, 7 May 1917, copy in CEMP.

557 'News of the Camps', *Trib*, 17 May 1917, reprinted from an article by Lydia Smith in *MG*, 10 May; also quoted in Graham, pp. 235–7, and reprinted as a leaflet by the National Labour Press, copy in SCPC/Wilson. In addition to references already given, the following have been used: A. Rose to C.E.M., 29 April 1917, CEMP; *News Sheet*, nos. 6 and 7, n.d.; Ernest E. Hunter, *The Home Office Compounds*, n.d. [c. June 1917]; 'News from the Camps', *Trib.*, 22 March and 10 May. Also a 'Record Book' which was kept by Sophia Sturge, a well-known Quaker who stayed in Princetown for some time during the early days of the settlement, and ran a hospitality centre for COs and their visiting relatives and friends. In a letter of 1969, when this book changed hands, it is described as 'Papers relating to COs at Princetown collected by Sophia Sturge being a list of autographs, addresses, photos and what is interesting, a list of birds seen March and April 1917'. This, like the Minute Book of the Princetown Friends Allowed Meeting, was loaned to the writer by courtesy of Plymouth Monthly Meeting of the Society of Friends, with whom they are now lodged. Both are of interest in showing the lighter side of life in the Dartmoor settlement, with a Field Club, Saturday afternoon and Sunday outings in fine weather, and occasional opportunities to attend Friends' Monthly Meeting in Plymouth. But the general rather grim picture is confirmed.

558 Marten to Harrop, 18 March 1917; 'News of the Camps', *Trib.*, 26 April 1917.

559 'Press Campaign Against the Home Office Work Settlement at Princetown', 2 May 1917, CEMP. The document gives the exact source of each headline: three were from the *Daily Mail*, others from the *Morning Post, Daily Sketch, Newcastle Daily Journal,* and *Western Morning News*. The *Evening News* was also particularly active in the campaign.

560 C. H. Norman to B. R., 3 May 1917; Graham, p. 238.

561 'News of the Camps', *Trib.*, 26 April 1917.

562 Norman to B. R., 11 July 1917, BRA.

563 'For B.R.', ms. notes, 27 April 1917, CEMP.

564 'Report of Miss Marshall's Interview with General Childs, 26 April 1917',

CEMP. Also 'Notes for C.M.', ms. notes, 26 April, believed to be notes written by C.E.M. to her mother about her ongoing work; 'C.E.M.'s Notes, 26 April 1917', ts.; and C.E.M. to Norman, 9 May 1917, copy, CEMP.

565 C.E.M. to Major Thornton, 27 April 1917, copy in CEMP; 'Report on the Relation'; 'Copy Extract From Letter Sent by Miss Marshall to a Government Official with Whom She Had an Interview Respecting the Reported Reconsideration by the Government of the Whole C.O. Problem', 27 April 1917. Copies in CEMP and BRA. This document and the report on the interview with Gen. Childs was produced in this form after the controversy over the issue developed. Although Thornton is not named here, Marshall's correspondent can be identified from references in other notes and letters. Robbins, p. 126, inaccurately describes the letter as being to 'a Home Office official', and his quotation from it is misleading. C.E.M. had been at pains to make it clear the NCF did not think the Home Office scheme a good one, and had outlined the essential conditions which must be met before a satisfactory scheme might 'evolve from the Dartmoor experiment'. However, even this may have been injudicious.

566 The practice of calling together the London members was followed when there was not time to assemble the full National Committee. Decisions made had to be confirmed by the full Committee as soon as convenient.

567 'Special Meeting of Nat. Com. (London Members) May 1st, 1917', ms. notes in C.E.M.'s handwriting; 'The Attacks on H.O. Camp Men: C.E.M.'s notes for Special Com^{ee} Meeting', CEMP.

568 C.E.M. to B.R., 1 May 1917, BRA.

569 B.R. to C.E.M., 3 May 1917, 'not sent', BRA.

570 See, for example, his analysis in *Authority and the Individual* (Allen & Unwin, London 1949).

571 Eva Kyle refused a job at higher pay and with a more assured future; Hunter expressed pleasure in working with her. Correspondence in CEMP, especially September 1917, refers.

572 BRA.

573 C.A. to B.R., 31 May 1917, BRA.

574 B.R.'s covering letter is addressed, as was the practice, to 'Dear Comrade', but its distribution is clear from the context, and one draft in CEMP bears the annotation 'To Members of Nat. Com^{ee}'; the only known copy of the draft letter itself has no heading or date, but it is marked 'Enclosure E' and can be identified by reference to a budget of material on the issue which was made up later. See 'Report on the Relation', n.d., CEMP. Russell also wrote an editorial for *Trib.*, 3 May 1917, called 'Resistance and Service', in which he made the same points of principle, but couched in more general terms.

575 In CEMP. Unrealistic as this would have been—it would have been rejected out of hand by the War Office, which had no wish to repeat the struggle with the COs—such a wish may have been behind the right-wing press campaign. All sections of the community were feeling the effects of the Government's renewed efforts to squeeze out yet more fighting men.

576 For Norman's claim to be striving to maintain the 'spirit of unity' against the hostility of the head office, see also 'The N.C.F. and the Home Office Men', *News Sheet* no. 7 (n.d.), and Norman to B.R., 3 May 1917, copy in CEMP.

577 'The N.C.F. Executive and the Home Office Men', See also Norman to B.R., 3 May 1917; 'Report on the Relation', CEMP. Norman did not

know that Marshall's interviews with Childs and letter to Thornton had only taken place a week before he wrote, and long after the press attacks began. But he did not wait to find out.

578 'Extract of letter from H. Wood', n.d., copy in CEMP.

579 B.R. to A. W. Smith, 7 May 1917, copy in CEMP.

580 B.R. to C.E.M., 7 May 1917, CEMP.

581 Robbins' account of the events at Dartmoor curiously stops short of the resolution of the conflict, although, like mine, it is based mainly on evidence in CEMP.

582 B.R., 'Report of Visit of Hon. Bertrand Russell to Princetown, May 9' (it is safe to assume that Russell was not responsible for this heading), 11 May 1917, copy in CEMP.

583 Hunter, *The Home Office Compounds*, p. 13; 'Report on the Relation'; Boulton, p. 217. Boulton claims there were nearly 900 men at the meeting, but this seems unlikely (and he does not give his source) as it would represent almost total attendance. There were 856 men at the settlement at the end of April 1917, and 1200 at the peak, in the autumn. Rae, p. 185.

584 'Report on the Relation'. See also H. C. Marten to B.R., 23 May 1917, in which Marten, as secretary of the Men's Committee at Dartmoor, expressed satisfaction at the National Committee resolution, and thanked B.R. for his personal services. BRA.

585 Boulton, p. 217. See also *Trib.*, *passim*, and various material in CEMP.

586 Editorial, 'A Valuable Suggestion by the Bishop of Exeter', *Trib.*, 18 October 1917.

587 Graham, pp. 244–5; Rae, pp. 186–7; Boulton, pp. 216–17; *Trib.*, 19 July 1917.

588 Rae, pp. 188; Graham, pp. 250–1; Kennedy, pp. 355–6.

589 Rae, pp. 188–190.

590 For example, National Committee 'minutes', ms., 13 October 1917, CEMP.

591 *H. C. Deb.*, (5), 86(1916), cols.880–1, 19 October 1916.

592 'To Members of the National Committee', 18 May 1917, ms. In BRA. Some notes in C.E.M.'s hand, 'Notes for C. A. Parkhouse Camp May 1917', although very scrappy also refer to the problems between B.R. and C.E.M. CEMP.

593 Exact figures are elusive, although *Trib.* attempted a weekly estimate. Government sources were also apt to be confused. See especially *Trib.*, 22 February 1917.

594 'The Prospects of the N.-C.F. in the New Year', *Trib.*, 1 February 1917.

595 'Position of the Absolutists', *Trib.*, 1 March 1917; extensive material in CEMP refers.

596 'No. of Court Martial proceedings on Conscientious Objectors up to 30th June, 1917', PRO, WO 32/5491. The number of those rejected rose to just over 300 by 31 March 1918, for which date a similar enumeration exists in the same War Office file. See also Rae, pp. 166–7.

597 'The Government and Absolute Exemption', editorial, *Trib.*, 8 February 1917.

598 There is a full description of conditions in Graham, chs. 8 and 9, borne out by much evidence AP, BRA, and CEMP. See also Boulton, especially ch. 10. The present writer's understanding of the humiliation and sensory deprivation to which the prisoners were subjected was greatly aided by the privilege of studying a series of bleak little watercolour miniatures done in prison by George Gascoigne. The artist served a total of about two and a half

years, at first in Wormwood Scrubs and later in Wandsworth, where he was fortunate to attract the attention of the Roman Catholic chaplain, who employed him on redecorating the chapel. In connection with this work, which occupied almost the whole of his time, he was often locked in, alone, in the chaplain's office, from which he smuggled out tiny quantities of paper and paint to his cell, where he painted these miniatures.

599 Graham, p. 295. Longer sentences were served at penal servitude, where conditions were less repressive.

600 'Extracts from letter from Clifford Allen . . . 12th February 1917', copy in CEMP.

601 The diet of the Home Office men was also cut. Meynell and a friend experimentally went out to dinner at the Ritz, where they found that extra servings of even the scarcest foods were easily obtained. Meynell wrote an article for *Herald* on the experience, which attracted considerable attention. Meynell, *My Lives*, p. 108.

602 Extensive information was collected by the NCF during the summer of 1917. Various reports dated June–August are filed in special file 25, 'Prison Conditions', at July 1917, CEMP. See also C.E.M., 'Insufficiency of Food in Prison', *Trib.*, 6 September 1917. Marwick, *The Deluge*, ch. 6, pp. 203–43 gives a good account of the general effects of shortages from 1917–18.

603 Copies of letters from the men involved are in the Wilson Papers, SCPC. See also 'The Men Sent to France', *Trib.*, 19 July 1917. Other examples of brutality continued to occur from time to time. See *Trib.*, *passim*. It should be noted that 'within the range of shell-fire' does not mean right in the front line. Recent media accounts of COs being forced 'over the top' or tied up in no-man's land between the British and German lines are, to the best of my knowledge, unfounded and seem to be based on a misunderstanding of Field Punishment No. 1.

604 Rae, p. 144.

605 The letter is addressed to 'Sir', and may have been to B.R. as chairman. It appears to date from July 1917, but the evidence is not clear.

606 *Trib.*, 12 July 1917. This issue also contained accounts of the cases of Gray and of Brightmore. The latter suffered at Cleethorpes, which had a bad reputation at the time. The treatment to which he was subjected was bizarre, involving confinement for four days in a deep muddy pit in which he stood on two strips of wood above a foot of water. Other correspondence in CEMP, especially with James Crawshaw, a Yorkshire member of the National Committee who was in touch with both cases, also refers. Questions were asked in the House of Commons. *H. C. Deb.*, (5), 95(1917), cols.403–4, 27 June 1917; 95(1917), cols.1305–6, 5 July 1917; 96(1917), cols.872–5, 23 July 1917.

607 *Herald*, 10 March 1917.

608 Violet Tillard to C.E.M., 11 March 1918, CEMP; *C.O. Clink Chronicle*, n.d., SCPC. Chamberlain had written a cheerful account of jail life after the sentence served by him and other National Committee members in the *Repeal the Act* case. It was serialised in *Trib.* from 1 September to 2 November 1916 as 'Pen Pictures of Prison Life' and reprinted separately as *A C.O. in Prison* (NCF, [London 1916]).

609 Especially 'Letter from Clifford Allen from Maidstone Prison, March 24th., 1917', copies in AP and CEMP. See also Gilbert, pp. 67–9.

610 A.F.B. to C.E.M., March 1917, CEMP; A.F.B. to editor, *Herald*, 31 March. Other correspondence on this topic includes Arthur Gwilliam to B.R., 1 March 1917; B.R. to Gwilliam, 2 March, copy; Ayles to C.E.M.,

28 February; C.E.M. to Ayles, 16 March, copy, CEMP; 'The Wife of a C.O.' to B.R., 4 April, BRA. See also letters in *Trib.*, 15 March 1917, from Ayles and S.V. Bracher; 22 March, from Brown, S. Hobhouse, and 'W.H.F.'; 29 March, from Gwilliam, A.F.B., Mrs S. Cahill and 'Regular Reader'. Letters in FH also refer, especially Wilfrid Hinde to Grubb, 11 March 1917.

611 'The Evils of Persecution', *Trib.*, 29 March 1917.

612 The executive committee of London Yearly Meeting between sessions. Meeting for Sufferings acquired its name and its first function during the imprisonment of many Quakers in the late seventeenth century. Correspondence and minutes in FH refer to the attempts to persuade the Meeting to act on behalf of COs.

613 For the decision of the Meeting for Sufferings, see Tucker, pp. 198–208. The Friends made a full explanation of their stand in *Friend*, 2 November 1917, which Tucker quotes at length. It was reprinted in *Trib.*, 27 December 1917, and somewhat revived the controversy. See Kennedy, p. 372; also Donington, p. 117. I am indebted to Prof. Kennedy for allowing me to read his article 'Fighting about Peace', forthcoming in *Quaker History*, which greatly illuminates the conflict between the FSC and the NCF. Littleboy to Ellis, 27 September 1917, FH.

614 15 May 1917, FH.

615 Brown to B.R., (1) as chairman, (2) personal, 23 May 1917; to B.R., 31 May; to B.R., 12 June, BRA; to C.E.M., 23 May; to 'My dear Rex [C.A.]', 23 May, CEMP. The controversy was labelled as 'Peace or Release', but the present writer has avoided this phrase because of its pejorative overtone. Both factions wanted peace, both wanted release, but Russell and those who thought with him believed the campaign for exemption should continue as part of the peace campaign. Robbins (p. 128) erroneously ascribes Brown's resignation to disagreement over Allen's proposed work-strike.

616 B.R. to Ellis, 11 September 1917, FH; Ellis to Hodgkin, 14 September, FH; Brown to Ellis, 20 September, FH; Ellis to B.R., 22 September, FH (cited by Kennedy, 'Fighting about Peace').

617 'The Position of the Absolutists', editorial, *Trib.*, 1 March 1917; 'The Evils of Persecution', editorial, *Trib.*, 29 March.

618 In his letter of 24 March 1917, he showed an acute awareness of this.

619 'Letter from Clifford Allen' [to C.E.M.], 21 April 1917, with footnote added by C.E.M. Mimeographed copies in AP, CEMP, reprinted in Gilbert, pp. 70–3.

620 C.E.M. to Childs, 4 May 1917, rough draft, CEMP; C.E.M. to E. Ellis (FSC), 30 April 1917, FH.

621 'Open Letter to Lloyd George', dated 31 May, *Trib.*, 14 June 1917; Kennedy, pp. 379–80.

622 Letter from C.A. to B.R. as chairman, 17 May 1917. All the stages of Allen's reasoning are clear from this letter, when it is read with the careful marginal notes made by C.E.M. for presentation to the National Committee on 15 June. Annotated copy in AP. See also C.E.M. to members of the National Committee, carbon copy of ms. draft, 6 June 1917, CEMP.

623 Kennedy, p. 377; Robbins, p. 127.

624 *Trib.*, 28 September 1916; Kennedy, p. 375.

625 C.A., 'C.O.s and Conscription', ch. 3, pp. 19–23; Kennedy, p. 379.

626 See C.E.M.'s letter *Trib.*, 2 August 1917; and her ms. footnote to a letter to Bram Longstaffe, 24 August 1917, CEMP.

627 'The Value of Endurance', *Trib.*, 17 May 1917.

628 B.R. to C.E.M., 6 June 1917, CEMP.

629 C.E.M. to B.R., 7 June 1917, ms. copy in CEMP.

630 Letter in SCPC/Wilson. See also 'Nat. Com. Mtg.', 9 November 1917, rough ms. notes, CEMP. Much later, Hudson endorsed work-striking.

631 'C.E.M.'s notes on Work Strike and Hunger Strike for A.F.B.', 7 September; another document of the same title, but different text, with comments in A.F.B.'s handwriting, CEMP; A.F.B. to B.R., 7 September 1917, BRA.

632 'Refusal to work in prison', *Trib.*, 9 August 1917; 'C.A. on Prison Policy, with comments by W.J.C. and A.F.B.', ts., AP; 'Work Strike and Hunger Strike: Prisoner's Opinions', n.d., CEMP; H. Inman to C.E.M., 9 July; J. D. Davis to 'Dear Comrade', n.d., CEMP; Joseph Dalby to Mr [Alexander] Wilson, dated 5 June [apparently in error for 5 July], SCPC/Wilson. Nearly all of the few who supported the principle of the work strike held that to be valid and effective it must be nationally organised, and admitted that there was not yet sufficient support for it.

633 Bram Longstaffe to C.E.M., marked 'Rec'd. August 30', CEMP.

634 'Opinion of B.R. and C.E.M. on Proposal Received from Comrades in W. S. August 23rd. 1917', ts.; C.E.M. to Bram Longstaffe, the Settlement, Princetown, 24 August 1917, CEMP. In a footnote to this letter, C.E.M. declared that she herself would feel morally obliged to refuse work in prison, but not as an expedient to gain amelioration of conditions. See also Graham, pp., 198–9, also quoted by Boulton, pp. 251–2. This account describes the kite incident, but does not name the jail or give any details of the protest. (The solecism noted, together with two others in parts of the letter not quoted, must be blamed on the typist. Marshall did not commit such errors, nor—it goes without saying—did Russell.)

635 B.R.'s opinion is found in ms. notes made by C.E.M., headed 'Nat Comm^{ee}., 9, 10 November 1917', CEMP. For the resolution, see 'Minutes of National Committee Meeting', [misdated 'Friday, November 11th. 1917' and 'Saturday . . . (November 12th 1917)'], ts. signed by B.R., CEMP; 'Notes from N.-C.F. Headquarters', *Trib.*, 22 November 1917; Kennedy, p. 382.

636 Meynell, one of those who abstained from the vote on 10 November, owed his liberty to a hunger and thirst strike of eleven days. Meynell, *My Lives*, pp. 99–103; *Trib.*, 1 February, 8 March 1917; Meynell to C.A., n.d. January 1918, and 31 January 1918, AP. Other hunger-strikers were force-fed. For the notorious case of Emanuel Ribeiro, see *Trib.*, 21 February, 20 June 1918. In CEMP there is a copy of an appeal to the Prime Minister on Ribeiro's behalf, with a covering letter from Emily Lutyens to Mrs Despard dated 20 July 1917. It bears the autographs of a number of people, of whom the last are C.E.M. and B.R., and should clearly have been returned. See also Kennedy, pp. 388–9. For other cases of hunger and work strikes, see *Trib.*, *passim*, and miscellaneous material in CEMP.

637 See *inter alia* 'Extracts from a Letter by A. Fenner Brockway to His Wife, Dated May 12th.', mimeographed copies in AP and SCPC/Brockway; A.F.B. to Sir George Cave, 13 May 1918, AP, reprinted in *Trib.*, 23 May 1918; Kennedy, pp. 385–7, 394–5; A.F.B., *Inside the Left*, pp. 103–15; 'Programme' of (an illicit Christmas concert), SCPC; Graham, pp. 304–9; *Trib.*, 23 January 1919.

638 'Conscientious Objectors', PRO, W.O./G.T. 677. My account of Russell's part in these transactions appeared in *Russell*, no. 15 (autumn 1974).

639 pp. 207–25.

640 S. Hobhouse, *Forty Years and an Epilogue: An Autobiography, 1881–1951*

(James Clarke, London 1951), p. 171; W. David Wills, *Stephen Hobhouse: a Twentieth-Century Quaker Saint* (Friends' Home Service Committee, London 1972), pp. 52–3. See also S. Hobhouse, 'Fourteen Months' Service with the Colours', in *We Did Not Fight*, pp. 157–75; Graham, p. 94.

641 'Notes for C.M.', in C.E.M.'s handwriting, 26 April 1917, CEMP; C.E.M. to Major Thornton, 2 May 1917, copy, BRA. It is of interest that the many Government documents and papers of officials consulted by Rae revealed nothing of the extent to which, again and again, members of the Administration and the public service turned to the NCF for information.

642 'Conscientious Objectors', 16 June 1917, W.O. 32/5472. See also Rae, pp. 213–14.

643 Ms. notes headed 2 May, believed to be notes made by C.E.M. for her mother, Caroline Marshall, CEMP. Also C.E.M. to Childs, rough draft, 4 May 1917, CEMP.

644 n.d., marked in pencil 'June? 1917', OMP/1455.

645 Rae, pp. 213–14.

646 'Minute', 13 June 1917, W.O. 32/5472. See also [Childs] to Kerr, 18 June 1917, n.s., copy, W.O. 32/5472; Derby to Emmett, 22 June 1917, copy; Emmett to Derby, 29 June, both in W.O. 32/5473; Rae, p. 214.

647 All three documents are in W.O. 32/5472. General Macready is the other person who might have wielded the green pencil.

648 Other possibilities exist, but without supportive evidence. There is no copy among surviving War Office documents of any letter that is recognisably the one that Childs is purported to have read to C.E.M. It may have been that Derby or Macready, both Childs' superiors and unalterably opposed to the release of COs, did not allow it to go forward, and pulled Childs back into line. It is tempting to think that while Marshall was having her knuckles rapped by the NCF for her connection with Childs, he was having his rapped by the War Office for the same association.

649 p/13 July 1917, OMP/1463. See also C.E.M. to B.R., 11 July, draft in CEMP, ts. 'Matters upon which the line to be taken needs to be much more clearly defined', n.d., FH.

650 p/7 July 1917, OMP/1462; Sassoon to O.M., 8 July [1917], OMP.

651 Draft of statement by Sassoon (revised in B.R.'s hand), BRA; copy of statement in OMP; *H. C. Deb.*, (5), 96(1917), cols.1797–9, 30 July 1917; *Times*, 31 July; *Trib.*, 16 August; reprinted from *Bradford Pioneer*, 27 July, in Robert Graves, *Goodbye to All That* (Cape, London 1929), ch. 24; *Trib.*, 16 August 1917.

652 Letters from Sassoon to O.M., OMP, *passim*; p/25 April 1917, OMP/1483; 21 July, OMP/1464; p/23 July, OMP/1491; n.d., OMP/1472. See also Sassoon, *Collected Poems* (Faber & Faber, London 1947), especially 'Banishment', p. 86; Sassoon, *Memoirs of an Infantry Officer* (Faber & Faber, London 1936), pp. 13–89. Sassoon wrote his autobiography first in a fictionalised form, but very close to actual events. Russell appears as 'Thornton Tyrrell' and is described on p. 283 of *Memoirs of an Infantry Officer*. For Sassoon's non-fictional memoirs, see *Siegfried's Journey: 1916–1920* (Faber & Faber, London 1945), pp. 50–7. See also Graves, ch. 24; Meynell, *My Lives*, p. 103. See also Sassoon correspondence in Imperial War Museum.

653 B.R., ms. note with Hobhouse correspondence, BRA.

654 Stephen Hobhouse writes briefly of his struggle to prevent his family from keeping him out of jail altogether by the use of their influence. *Forty Years*, p. 155; *We Did Not Fight*, p. 165; Wills, p. 43.

655 B.R. to C.E.M., 6 June 1917; C.E.M. to B.R., n.d., copy, CEMP.

656 (Allen & Unwin, London 1917), 86 pages. '*I Appeal Unto Caesar*' was first advertised in *Trib.* 30 August 1917.

657 M. Hobhouse to B.R., n.d., BRA. Constance Malleson, in a letter to the Russell Archives of 19 August 1974, reports that she was told nothing of B.R.'s authorship, though she (faintly) recalled the book.

658 B.R. to M. Hobhouse, 6 June 1917, copy in BRA. Russell also said in this letter that he had the pamphlet well in hand, and that he thought that he quite understood the sort of thing she wished it to be. In letters to him, she mentioned receiving his manuscript, referred to the supporting letters she was soliciting (Smuts and McKenna were approached unsuccessfully, although the former gave support in other ways), and discussed the foreword she was to write. She had some slight accident at about this time, which may have increased her dependence on Russell's help. A few of the letters bear dates in early June 1917, others are undated. All are in BRA. An effort, so far unsuccessful, has recently been made to locate the other side of the exchange (a copy of only one of B.R.'s letters to Mrs Hobhouse is present), but she probably obeyed her own advice and destroyed the evidence.

659 Lilla Brockway to C.E.M., n.d., CEMP.

660 '*I Appeal Unto Caesar*', pp. 7, 6. The nature of the reference to Spinoza also strongly indicates Russell's authorship. He constantly returned to the thought contained in Prop. XLIII of Part III of the *Ethic* (Oxford, London 1910), 'Hatred is increased through return of hatred, but may be destroyed by love.' (See p. 41 above and Russell's discussion in *History of Western Philosophy*). An account of the importance to Russell's thought will be developed in K. Blackwell's doctoral thesis, forthcoming, University of Guelph, Ontario.

661 *Spectator*, 15 September 1917. See also 'A Notable Book and Some Opinions Concerning It', n.s., *Trib.*, 23 August 1917; Kennedy, p. 390; Wills, p. 53; Rae, p. 215.

662 Receipt and covering letter from C.E.M., date illegible, not sent, CEMP; 'Propaganda Report: July and August 1917'; 'Propaganda Report', 9, 10 November, CEMP.

663 'A New Tribunal for Gaol Delivery', *Trib.*, 15 November 1917.

664 Quoted in Tucker, p. 206.

665 Wilfred Littleboy to Ellis, 27 September 1917, FH.

666 (C. W. Daniel, London [1917]).

667 [19 September 1916], OMP/1422.

668 Hunter to C.E.M., 11 September 1917, CEMP.

669 Articles and supporting evidence researched by K. Blackwell. 'The Fall of Bethmann-Hollweg, *Herald*, 21 July 1917; 'Chancellor and Premier', *Herald*, 28 July 1917; letters which refer include B.R. to C. Malleson, p/5 July and p/10 July, B.R. to O.M. [12 July], OMP/1523.

670 C.E.M. to B.R., 17 August 1917, copy in CEMP.

671 Extensive material in CEMP refers.

672 National Committee minutes, 9, 10 November 1917, CEMP.

673 Hunter to C.E.M., 11 September 1917, CEMP.

674 Childs to Wigram, 17 September 1917, quoted by Rae, p. 215. For a fuller discussion of the political and administrative aspects of the issue, see Rae, pp. 215–18.

675 See also C.E.M., 'Newsletter for Prisoners', August 1917; W.O. 32/5474 contains the documents relating to these negotiations.

676 In September 1918 the Home Office made an attempt to relieve the absolutists who had served more than two years by placing them together in Wakefield prison under greatly relaxed discipline. After about two weeks of

enjoyable confusion the men were told the conditions of continuing their stay there: they rejected them and were returned to hard labour. Extensive material in AP, CEMP and SCPC; also Kennedy, pp. 391–3.

677 The concessions were announced by Lord Curzon, the Coalition Government's leader in the House of Lords. *H. L. Deb.*, (5), 27(1917–18), cols. 53–6, 4 December 1917; 'Conscientious Objectors suffering ill-health in Prison', 15 December 1917, CEMP; B.R., 'The Government's "Concessions"', *Trib.*, 13 December 1917; C.E.M., 'Adding Insult to Injury', letter to editor, *Trib.*, 3 January 1918; 'Statement issued by the Parliamentary Department', n.d., signed by Charles Ammon, CEMP. See also Scott Duckers to C.E.M., 1 December 1917; A.F.B. in the *Walton Leader* (one of several prison papers edited by A.F.B. during his imprisonment). This issue was smuggled out and mimeographed. Copy in SCPC.

678 Copy of letter, which is dated 29 November, in W.O. 32/5474. The copy has been marked with the same expressive green pencil as we have noted before. In justice to Mrs Hobhouse, it should be noted that the COs' friends recognised that the release of any absolutist would make it difficult for the Government to justify keeping other sick men in jail, and that release of those identified as 'religious' would provide an argument for release of the rest. Hunter to C.E.M. 11 September 1917, CEMP..

679 Rae, pp. 220–3.

680 Untitled report of meeting between Curzon, Cave and Childs on 19 November 1917, W.O. 32/5474, at which it was stated 'of course, at the present moment Stephen Hobhouse's health has never been such as to warrant his discharge from prison on medical grounds'; *Trib.*, 20 December 1917, and material in CEMP. For Stephen's own view of his release, see brief accounts in *We Did Not Fight*, p. 174; *Forty Years*, p. 171.

681 *Trib.*, 13 December 1917 announced that Hobhouse had been released 'in the same manner' as C.A., an error which C.A. was quick to correct. C.A. to B.R., 17 December 1917; B.R. to C.A., 18 December, BRA; *Trib.*, 10, 31 January 1918; Graham, p. 309. Mental cases were usually given a complete discharge, as had been done for a few even before this time, in accordance with a regular Army procedure.

682 Governor of Winchester prison to C.E.M., 1 July 1917; C.E.M. to Lord Lytton, 27 November, copy; Frank Marshall to C.E.M., 29 November, all in CEMP. A fellow-prisoner and patient later bore witness to the humanising effect of Allen's personality even within the notoriously harsh and unfeeling atmosphere of Winchester jail. John Mitchell, ts. in AP; Kennedy, p. 383. Harold Bing, who thought C.A. 'one of the gentlest, most lovable, most loving people I've ever known', was able, as a fellow-prisoner, to smuggle Horlicks tablets to him with the connivance of a warder. Taped interview, Imperial War Museum.

683 18 December 1917, OMP/1478. See also B.R. to C.A., December 1917, BRA; Wood, p. 95.

684 E. Bolton to C.E.M., 1 December 1917, CEMP.

685 Swanwick to B.R., 4 December 1917, BRA; to C.E.M., 27, 29 November 1917, CEMP.

686 18 December 1917, OMP/1478.

687 B.R. to C.E.M., [29 November 1917], CEMP. B.R., 'Lord Lansdowne's Letter', editorial, *Trib*, 6 December 1917.

688 B.R.'s 1917 letters to O.M. reflect the struggle; O.M.'s bitterness can be seen in comments she pencilled on the envelopes of some. B.R.'s letters to Colette, now in BRA, reveal more of the tangled web.

689 Dated '1917' but with pencil date '1918?' added, and clearly belongs to the latter year. OMP/1479.

690 [4 August 1917], OMP/1458; n.d., OMP/1466; n.d. [probably 21 August], OMP/1492.

691 p/26 November 1917, OMP/1476.

692 The help and support he had offered to Mrs Hobhouse and Siegfried Sassoon take extra significance from this comment.

693 B.R. to L. Woolf, 6 September 1917, BRA; also Clark, p. 333.

694 n.d., OMP/1472.

695 For example, Wrinch continued to work under him. Lenzen has already been noted. Raphael Demos, later Professor of Philosophy at Harvard, showed up in 1917 and spent much time with B.R.

696 23 December 1917, OMP/1477.

697 Carr to B.R., 21 November 1917, BRA (in Thompson); 20 September 1917, OMP/1743; Wrinch to B.R., 10 September 1917, BRA. The idea of freelance lecturing in philosophy had occurred to B.R. as he awaited news of his dismissal from Trinity. n.d. [probably 10 July 1916], OMP/1388.

698 *The Monist*, 1918–19; B.R., *Logic and Knowledge*, ed. R. C. Marsh (Allen & Unwin, London 1956).

699 Reviews of May Sinclair, *A Defense of Idealism* appeared in *Nation*, 8 September 1917, and *English Review*, October 1917, under the titles, respectively, of 'Idealism on the Defensive' and 'Metaphysics'. *Nation*, 10 November 1917, contained a review of John Laird's *Problems of the Self*.

700 n.d. [early 1916], OMP/1123, reprinted in *Autobiog.*, II, pp. 56–7; 27 July 1917, OMP/1467. B.R.'s philosophical development is outside the scope of this work. The writer's attention was drawn to the importance of B.R.'s renewed philosophical vitality at this period by K. Blackwell (personal communication). For our purpose, it is particularly significant in correcting a possible impression that the return to philosophy was no more than escapism for B.R.

701 See Wittgenstein to Russell, [June 1913] and 27 July 1913, in L. Wittgenstein, *Letters to Russell, Keynes and Moore*, ed. G. H. von Wright (Blackwell, Oxford 1974), pp. 23–4, 59–66.

702 The exact date is not clear. Salter occasionally signed as 'Interim Chairman' as early as 17 December 1917 (material in CEMP).

703 *Trib.*, 14 November, 6 December 1917.

704 The ballot paper for this election was much simpler than the ballot paper used the previous time. Copy in CEMP. As usual, officers in prison were declared elected. Allen remained chairman, Brockway honorary secretary, Grubb honorary treasurer. See 'National Committee News', *Trib.*, 17 January 1918; National Committee notes, 11 January, CEMP.

705 Extensive material in CEMP refers.

706 OMP/1477.

707 The discussion began on Saturday morning, and Salter asked time to consider until the afternoon session, when he agreed to accept, but only for a period of three months. In fact he remained Acting Chairman until after the end of the war.

708 *Autobiog.*, II, p. 33.

709 Reprinted in *Autobiog.*, II, pp. 79–81.

710 Childs regularly received copies of *Trib.*, *LL* and *Herald*. 'Our Prosecution', n.s., *Trib.*, 9 May 1918.

711 Wood, p. 97.

712 B.R. to C.A., 2 February 1918, BRA.

713 Hunter to C.E.M., 4, 7 February 1918, CEMP.

714 B.R. had written remarks just as insulting to the American Army on a previous occasion. See 'Imperialist Anxieties', editorial, *Trib.*, 30 August 1917, to which attention is drawn by John G. Slater in his Introduction to the Kraus reprint of *Trib.*

715 [4 February 1918], OMP/1488.

716 'Our Prosecution', *Trib.*, 14 February 1918.

717 Wood, p. 97.

718 Quoted by Wood, p. 97.

719 9 February 1918, OMP/1480. Wood, p. 97, quotes from another of B.R.'s letters on the event.

720 Ammon to C.E.M., 18 February 1918, CEMP; Holroyd, p. 253. Almost all accounts comment in the same vein.

721 Graham, pp. 199–200.

722 Frank Russell and Cobden-Sanderson were the sureties.

723 Ammon to C.E.M., 18 February 1918, badly damaged ms. letter, CEMP.

724 Correspondence in AP. I am indebted to Conrad Russell for enlarging my understanding of General Childs and for drawing my attention to the significance of 'the breakdown of the Marshall-Childs exchanges as . . . an important part of the strange death of Liberal England'.

725 *Trib.*, 14 February 1918. See also C.A. to B.R., 11 February 1918; 'Extracts from C.A.'s Diary', 9, 11 February 1918, AP; Rinder to C.E.M., n.d., 'rec'd Feb. 21', CEMP; Wood pp. 96–8; Holroyd, II, pp. 252–3; Graham, p. 199.

726 9 February 1918, OMP/1480.

727 'Monday' [probably 11 February 1918], OMP/1446.

728 F. M. Cornford to B.R., 13 February 1918, BRA. See also C.A. to B.R., 6 February, BRA. Anna Barlow felt that the quotation from the article must have been garbled as given in the press. Anna Barlow to B.R., 26 February 1918, BRA.

729 C.A. to B.R., 11 February 1918, BRA.

730 G.M. to B.R., 10 February 1918, copy in BRA.

731 B.R. to G.M., 15 February 1918, copy in BRA; also B.R. to E. S. P. Haynes, 18 February 1918, quoted by Clark, p. 340. Others who wrote in support at this time included Lucy Silcox, E. Whitehead, C. P. Sanger, Grubb, Armstrong, Barratt Brown, Joan Mary Fry and spokesmen for several NCF branches and the Irishwoman's International League. Correspondence in BRA.

732 Kennedy, pp. 312–27. PRO, HO 45/11012/314670. Frank Russell had made representations on B.R.'s behalf in December 1917.

733 Rinder to C.E.M., 'rec'd. 21 February', CEMP. The incident is also referred to in *The Letters of Katherine Mansfield*, ed. J. M. Murry (Knopf, New York 1929), I, p. 120.

734 B.R. to C.A., 9 March 1918, BRA. The 'ode' could possibly be the one quoted at the beginning of Newberry (Vellacott), 'Russell and the Pacifists' in *Russell in Review*, ed. J. E. Thomas and Kenneth Blackwell (Toronto; Hakkert, 1976), p. 33.

735 C.A. to B.R., 11 March 1918, BRA; C.E.M. to B.R., 23 March, BRA.

736 n.d., OMP/1447; Stanley Unwin to B.R., 15 April 1918 BRA.

737 Significantly, the writer has come across no criticism from friend or opponent along these lines.

738 Untitled two-page ts., n.d., n.s., OMP, copy in BRA. Probably drawn up before B.R.'s entry into jail. Although unquestionably of B.R.'s authorship it has some unusual style lapses (there is for instance no identifiable

antecedent for the pronoun 'them' in line 3 of the above quotation), and may be incomplete.

739 9 February 1918, OMP/1480.

740 'Monday' [probably 11 February 1918], OMP/1446.

741 The sentence was a six-month one, with one month's remission for good conduct.

742 B.R. to G.M., 27 March 1918, copy in BRA; in *Autobiog.*, II, p. 82.

743 Swartz, p. 179 and n. 34. Swartz cites convincing evidence that Morel's hair was white before he went to jail.

744 See, for example, *Autobiog.*, II, p. 39; B.R., *Freedom and Organization, 1814–1914* (Allen & Unwin, London 1934), p. 455.

745 For further evidence that Morel was seriously affected by his imprisonment see Murray to B.R. 29 March 1917, copy in BRA; material in EDMP, especially the following: pencil notes in the hand of Mrs Morel on back of book list, c. 15 October 1917; the prison doctor to Mrs Morel, 23 October 1917; Mrs Morel to 'Dear Arthur', 1 February 1918. See also 'Stoning a Prophet', n.s., *Trib.*, 6 September 1917; extensive material on Morel's trial in EDMP.

746 27 March 1918.

747 G.M. to B.R., 6 March 1918, copy in BRA.

748 G.M. to B.R., 20 March 1918, copy in BRA.

749 B.R. to G.M., 27 March 1918, copy in BRA; *Autobiog.*, II, p. 82.

750 This was enacted on 18 April 1918.

751 A Cambridge mathematician who had been exempted in 1916.

752 OMP/1489.

753 According to C.A., the reason why they could not spend it at Frank Russell's house, where B.R. was staying, was because the Earl feared 'the disrepute of pacifist intrigues'. C.A., 'Diary' (extracts), 30 March 1918, AP; reprinted in Gilbert, p. 110. If true, this is rather surprising in view of the amount of sympathy and support given by Frank to B.R. at this time. Certainly B.R. does not seem to have invited C.A. to spend the night at his brother's house, although they had tea there before leaving for Marlow. B.R. to C.A., n.d., BRA.

754 2 April 1918, OMP/1481. See also C.E.M. to B.R., 23 March 1918, BRA.

755 C.A., 'Diary' (extracts), 30, 31 March, 1 April 1918, AP; in Gilbert, pp. 110–11; C.A., 'M.S.A., Prison Treatment', ms. notes, n.d.; B.R. to C.A., n.d., BRA; C.A. to B.R., 10 April 1918, BRA.

756 B.R. to G.M., 30 March 1918; G.M. to B.R., 30 March, copies in BRA.

757 'Statement by B.R.', 30 March 1918, BRA.

758 Copy in BRA.

759 B.R. to G.M., 4 April 1918, copy in BRA.

760 G.M. to B.R., 9 April 1918, copy in BRA.

761 Carr to G.M., 9 April 1918, copy in BRA. See also Carr to B.R., 5 April 1918, in Thompson; G.M. to B.R., 7 April, enclosing copy of petition; B.R. to Carr, 8 April, in Thompson; copies of all in BRA. That B.R may have had some grounds for his fear is borne out by a letter from Bernard Bosanquet to G.M., in which he agreed to sign but said that he understood B.R. had desisted from pacifist propaganda and that he (Bosanquet) could say or do nothing except on that basis. 7 April 1918, BRA/Murray.

762 n.d., OMP/1442; B.R. to C.A., n.d., BRA.

763 G.M. to B.R., 9 April 1918, BRA.

764 Signatories included Bosanquet, Alexander, A.C. Bradley (not the eminent philosopher but his brother, the literary critic). McTaggart declined—unless

health could be made the prime plea—and Sir Oliver Lodge wrote that he felt second division treatment would suffice. Correspondence in BRA/ Murray.

765 B.R. to G.M., 11 April 1918, copy in BRA.

766 B.R. to C.A., n.d., BRA.

767 'Statement by Bertrand Russell', 8 April 1918, copy in BRA. Covering letter to G.M., 11 April, copy in BRA.

768 B.R. to Carr, 17 April 1918, in Thompson.

769 See, for example, B.R. to M. Llewelyn Davies, 15 April 1918; M. Llewelyn Davies to B.R., 16 April, BRA; 16 April, OMP/1484; Cooper Willis to B.R., 18 April, BRA.

770 'Use of United States Military in Industrial Disputes', extracts from the 'Final Report of the Commission on Industrial Relations (1915) appointed by the United States Congress', ts. in BRA, with ms. note by B.R. BRA/Rex v Russell, 1918. See also *Autobiog.*, II, pp. 33–4; and *Roads to Freedom*, pp. 89–90, where B.R. cited the same publication in discussing military strike-breaking. Feinberg and Kasrils, I, pp. 73–4, presumably following the statement in Russell's note, also say that B.R. was not allowed to cite this report, but the account in 'Our Prosecution', n.s., *Trib.*, 9 May 1918, makes it clear that extensive use was made of it in the appeal. B.R. did not conduct his own defence on either occasion.

771 The stickleback is a 'small fish with sharp spines on back' (*Concise O.E.D.*), and aggressive in habit. Joan Beauchamp later referred to B.R. as 'my fellow stickleback'.

772 'Our Prosecution', *Trib.*, 9 May 1918. B.R. later asked if Lawrie's complimentary references had been inspired. B.R. to Frank Russell, 16 May 1918, BRA.

773 II, pp. 33–4.

774 *Bertrand Russell Speaks His Mind* (Barker, London [1960]), p. 121.

775 His principal correspondents were Frank Russell, Ottoline Morrell, Constance Malleson and Gladys Rinder, who passed messages to and from his other friends. The correspondence is in BRA.

776 See, for example, S. Hobhouse and F. Brockway (eds.), *English Prisons Today: Being the Report of the Prison System Enquiry Committee* (Longmans, Green, London 1922), pp. 220–2.

777 B.R. to F. Russell, 6 May 1918; F. Russell to B.R., 7 May, BRA.

778 Wood, p. 100, PRO, HO 45/11012/314670; Clark, p. 345.

779 *Autobiog.*, II, p. 34–5.

780 'Messages from Constance Malleson to Bertrand Russell in Brixton Prison, 1918, inserted in "The Times"', researched by K. Blackwell, BRA. For a full account, see Clark, p. 346.

781 C.E.M. to B.R., 10 April [1918], BRA.

782 *Autobiog.*, II, p. 34.

783 B.R. to Frank Russell, 3 June 1918, BRA; Wood, pp. 98–9.

784 Many of the prison letters refer, especially B.R. to Frank Russell, 15 July 1918, BRA, and a number of Rinder's to B.R., BRA.

785 See, for example, B.R. to Frank Russell, 29 July 1918, BRA, where he complains he has been waiting a month for certain books.

786 Raphael Demos, 'Early Memories of T.S. Eliot', ts., n.d., Harvard University Archives, copy in BRA.

787 B.R. to Frank Russell, 29 July 1918, BRA.

788 *Journal of Philosophy*, 16 (2 January 1919), pp. 5–26.

789 *Nation*, 27 July 1918. B.R.'s letter of 14 July 1918 to O.M. identifies the letter as his, although it bears the pseudonym 'Philalethes'.

790 n.d. [c. August 1917], OMP/1492.

791 'Are Criminals Worse than Other People?', 7 December 1932, in Ruja.

792 B.R. to F. Russell, 12 August 1918; to Rinder, 5 August and 19 August, BRA.

793 Clark, pp. 349–50, gives a full account of this episode.

794 B.R. to F. Russell, 'Message for Lady Ottoline', 3 June 1918, BRA.

795 B.R. to F. Russell, 24 June 1918, BRA.

796 Sassoon to O.M., 27 August 1918, OMP. See also Sassoon to O.M., 'Sunday', 4 September, 25 September, OMP; John Withers to C. Trevelyan, 20 September 1918, copy in BRA; Rinder to B.R., 6 September 1918, and other undated letters from Rinder, BRA.

797 [Probably 23 September 1918], OMP/1493.

798 30 October 1918, OMP/1497. The source and nature of the assurance are not known for certain, but Rinder to B.R., 'Thursday', n.d., suggests that someone (possibly Mrs Hobhouse?) would approach Milner. Clark, p. 353.

799 Rinder to B.R., 14 September 1918, BRA; Clark, p. 353.

800 *Autobiog.*, II, p. 40 (this part was written in 1931—see *ibid*, II, p. 159).

801 A tangible—if small and infinitely bitter—fruit of their struggle was to be the conscience clauses of the 1939 National Service Act, which avoided the administrative tangle and the direct confrontation between objectors and the Army which had resulted from the Military Service Act of the First World War. In the doctoral thesis on which his book *Conscience and Politics* was based, John Rae made a full comparison between the administration of conscription in the two periods. Rae, 'The Development of Official Treatment of Conscientious Objectors to Military Service, 1916–1945' (unpublished PhD dissertation, University of London, 1965).

802 Introduction, *Selected Papers of Bertrand Russell* (Random House, New York 1927), p. xii.

803 C.E.M. to B.R., 8 February 1918, BRA.

804 C.A. to B.R., 10 April 1918, BRA.

805 Fry to B.R., 21 February 1918, BRA.

806 *Autobiog.* II, p. 17.

807 Allen & Unwin, London 1920.

808 Bosanquet to G.M., 7 April 1918, copy in BRA.

809 B.R. to Donnelly, 18 March 1908, BRA.

810 *Principles*, p. 208.

811 Untitled two-page ts., n.d., n.s., OMP, copy in BRA. This appears to be a message sent from prison to C.A., possibly in connection with B.R.'s resignation from the National Committee. Rinder to B.R., n.d., (BRA), comments: 'CA sent me that note and asked me to have part of it copied. You have put into words what many of us have been grasping for. . . . If we are to be of value at all we must be creative, it isn't enough to pull down incessantly. I always felt that yr. influence in the offices was in some sense creative: it brought harmony and good feeling where before and *afterwards* there was friction, and it seems to me that will be a very valuable asset for the afterwar time . . . if we can't manage it on a small scale . . . we shall only fail with bigger things . . . I . . . wish one were sure one was really 'nourishing life in the world' in your sense.'

BIBLIOGRAPHY

This bibliography of source materials and printed matter is confined to what has been cited in the foregoing pages.

Unpublished Sources

Collections

Bertrand Russell Archives. McMaster University, Hamilton, Ontario, Canada.
Catherine E. Marshall papers. Cumbria Record Office, Carlisle, Cumberland, England.
Ottoline Morrell papers. Humanities Research Center, University of Texas, Austin, Texas, USA.
Clifford Allen papers. University of South Carolina, Columbia, South Carolina, USA.
Women's International League for Peace and Freedom, International Section, Archives. University of Colorado Library, Boulder, Colorado.
Swarthmore College Peace Collection (containing numerous sub-collections of British papers). Swarthmore College, Swarthmore, Pennsylvania, USA.
E. D. Morel papers. British Library of Economics and Political Science, University of London, London, England.
War Office papers; Cabinet minutes and papers; Kitchener papers; Home Office papers. Public Record Office, London, England.
Various collections and minute books, Friends' House, Euston Road, London, England.
Collection of tapes and mss. relating to opposition to the First World War. Imperial War Museum, London, England.
Sassoon papers. Imperial War Museum, London, England.
Papers in the possession of Plymouth Monthly Meeting, Society of Friends, Plymouth, England.

Individual writings by Bertrand Russell

Appointments 'Diary'. 1913–14, 1914–15, 1915–16, 1917–18. BRA.
'Folly, Doctor-like, Controlling Skill', [1916]. Ms. in BRA.
'How America Can Help to Bring Peace', July 1915. Ts. and galleys in BRA.
'Introduction' to proposed booklet, On Active Service, by C.A. Ms in AP.
'Journal', November 1902–April 1905. Transcription by Kadriin Timusk in BRA; ms. in OMP.
'Mr Tennant on the Conscientious Objectors', [1916]. Ms. in CEMP (copy in BRA).
'Principles of Social Reconstruction and Notes for Harvard Lectures', [1916]. Ms. in BRA.
'The Russian Revolution', [1917]. Ts. in BRA.
'To the editor of the Nation', 4 August 1914. Ms. in BRA.
'What is Wrong with Western Civilization?', April 1924. Ms. in BRA.

Individual writings by others

Allen, Clifford, 'Conscientious Objectors and Conscription'. Book-length ms. in AP.

Anonymous, 'Application on Grounds of Conscientious Objection', [1916]. A copy of the questions issued by the Central Tribunal with ts. draft of answers. In SCPC/NCF.

'Are Men to be Shot for Conscience?', [1916]. Draft pamphlet in several versions. In CEMP.

'Conscience and Character', 21 June 1916. In CEMP.

'Conscientious Objectors: June 1, 1916'. In Kitchener papers, PRO 30/57/74.

'Memorandum for Private Deputation to the Prime Minister', 11 May 1916. In CEMP.

'Minute Book: Princetown Allowed Meeting'. Plymouth Monthly Meeting, Swarthmore Hall, Plymouth, England.

'Mr Russell and the War Office'. Mimeographed collection of correspondence, 1916. In BRA and CEMP.

Barlow, Anna, 'Extract from the diary of Anna Barlow'. In AP.

Blackwell, K., 'The Foreign Office on Bertrand Russell: from the Public Record Office London', August 1967. Ts. in BRA.

Childs, Wyndham, 'Conscientious Objectors', [1916]. PRO, WO32/5491.

Demos, Raphael, 'Early Memories of T. S. Eliot', n.d. Ts. in Harvard University Archives (copy in BRA).

Macready, C.F.N., 'Conscientious Objectors and Military Service'. 16 May 1916. Circulated to the Cabinet by Kitchener. PRO, WO32/5491.

Milligan, Edward, 'Biography of T. E. Harvey', n.d. Ts. in author's possession.

Sturge, Sophia, 'Record Book: Papers relating to COs at Princetown collected by Sophia Sturge being a list of autographs, addresses, photos, and what is interesting, a list of birds seen March and April 1917'. In possession of Plymouth Monthly Meeting, Swarthmore Hall, Plymouth, England.

Weston-super-Mare Peace Society. 'Minute Book'. In SCPC/Weston-super-Mare.

Published sources

Official publications

Committee on Alleged German Outrages, *Report of the Committee on Alleged German Outrages*. Parl. Pubs., 1914–16. vol. 23, Cd.7894. HMSO, London, 1915.

Correspondence Respecting the European Crisis. Parl. Pubs., 1914. vol. 101 (Misc. no. 6), Cd.7467. HMSO, London, 1914.

House of Commons Debates. Series 5. 1914–17.

House of Lords Debates. Series 5. 1916–17.

Periodicals

Conscientious Objectors' Information Bureau, Weekly Reports

C.O.s' Hansard.

Daily Express.

Friend.

Herald.

Labour Leader.

Manchester Guardian.

Nation.

National Peace Council *Circular.*

News Sheet (published by Dartmoor Home Office settlement)
Suffragette.
The Times.
The Tribunal (available in single-volume reprint, Kraus, New York 1970; intro-
   duction by John G. Slater).

Writings by Bertrand Russell

'*Adsum Qui Feci*', *Times*, 17 May 1916. Reprinted in *Autobiog.*, II, pp. 64–5.
'America's Entry into the War', *Trib.*, 19 April 1917.
'Are Criminals Worse than Other People?', in Harry Ruja (ed.) *Mortals and
   Others,* Allen & Unwin, London, 1975.
'Armaments and National Security', *LL*, 15 October 1914.
Authority and the Individual, Allen & Unwin, London, 1949.
The Autobiography of Bertrand Russell, 1872–1914, I, Allen & Unwin, London,
   1967.
The Autobiography of Bertrand Russell, 1914–1944, II, Allen & Unwin, London,
   1968.
The Basic Writings of Bertrand Russell, ed. Robert E. Egner and Lester E. Denonn,
   Allen & Unwin, London, 1961.
'Belgian Professors in Cambridge', *Cambridge Magazine,* 24 October 1914.
Bertrand Russell and the War Office: A Personal Statement, National Council for
   Civil Liberties, London, 1916. Reprinted as 'Publisher's Preface' to *Justice in
   War-Time,* 2nd edition.
'The Bolsheviks and Mr Lloyd George', *Trib.*, 10 January 1918.
'Can England and Germany be Reconciled after the War?', *Cambridge Review,*
   10 February 1915.
'Chancellor and Premier', *Herald,* 28 July 1917 [attributed].
'Christmas message', *LL*, 24 December 1914.
'A Clash of Consciences', *Nation,* 15 April 1916.
'Clifford Allen and Mr Lloyd George', *Trib.*, 17 August 1916.
A Course of Eight Lectures on Principles of Social Reconstruction, London [1915].
   Syllabus for lecture series.
'"Crucify Him! Crucify Him!"', *Trib.*, 2 August 1917.
'Education as a Political Institution', *Atlantic Monthly,* June 1916. Reprinted in
   Principles of Social Reconstruction.
'The Ethics of War', in *Justice in War-Time.*
'The Evils of Persecution', *Trib.*, 29 March 1917.
'The Fall of Bethmann-Hollweg', *Herald,* 21 July 1917 [attributed].
'A Fifty-Six Year Friendship', in G.M., *An Unfinished Autobiography: with
   Contributions by his Friends.* Allen & Unwin, London, 1960.
'For Conscience Sake', *Independent,* 15 January 1917.
Freedom and Organization, 1814–1914. Allen & Unwin, London, 1934.
'A Free Man's Worship', *Independent Review,* December 1903. Reprinted in *Basic
   Writings.*
'The Future of Anglo-German Rivalry', *Atlantic Monthly,* July 1915. Reprinted in
   Justice in War-Time.
'The German Peace Offer', *Trib.*, 3 January 1918. Reprinted in *Autobiog.*, II,
   pp. 79–81.
German Social Democracy, Longmans, Green, London, 1896.
'The Government and Absolute Exemption', *Trib.*, 8 February 1917.
'The Government's "Concessions"', *Trib.*, 13 December 1917.
'History as an Art', in *Portraits from Memory.*
'Imperialist Anxieties', *Trib.*, 30 August 1917.

'The International Situation', *Trib.*, 23 August 1917.
'Is a Permanent Peace Possible?', *Atlantic Monthly*, March 1915. Reprinted in *Justice in War-Time*.
Justice in War-Time, Open Court, Chicago, 1916. 2nd edition, 1917. Reissued, Allen & Unwin, London, 1924. Reprinted, with additions, as *The Ethics of War*, ed. Charles Chatfield, Garland Library of War and Peace, New York, 1972; also reprinted: Haskell House, New York, 1974.
'Liberty and National Service', *Trib.*, 22 February 1917.
'Lord Lansdowne's Letter', *Trib.*, 6 December 1917.
'Marriage and the Population Question', *International Journal of Ethics*, July 1916. Reprinted in *Principles of Social Reconstruction*.
'The Momentum of War', *Trib.*, 14 December 1916.
Mortals and Others: Bertrand Russell's American Essays, 1931–1935, I, ed. Harry Ruja, Allen & Unwin, London, 1975.
'Mr. Russell's Reply to His Critics', *Cambridge Review*, 24 February 1915.
Mysticism and Logic, Longmans, Green, London, 1918.
'National Service', *Trib.*, 15 February 1917.
'The Nature of the State in View of Its External Relations', *Proceedings of the Aristotelian Society*, n.s. 16 (1915–16), pp. 301–10.
'The NCF and the Political Outlook', *Trib.*, 7 December 1916.
'The New Hope', *Trib.*, 5 April 1917.
'A New Tribunal for Gaol Delivery', *Trib.*, 15 November 1917.
'On History', *Independent Review*, July 1904. Reprinted in *Basic Writings*.
On a review of Siegfried Sassoon's *Counter-Attack*. *Nation*, 27 July 1918. A letter signed 'Philalethes', identified as B.R.'s through his letter of 14 July 1918 to O.M., in OMP.
'Our Foreign Office', *LL*, 8 October 1914.
'Pacifism and Economic Revolution', *Trib.*, 5 July 1917.
'Pacifism and Revolution', *Trib.*, 19 July 1917.
The Philosophy of Pacifism. Peace and Freedom Pamphlets, no. 1. League of Peace and Freedom, London, [1915]. Also in *Towards Ultimate Harmony: Report of Conference on Pacifist Philosophy of Life, Caxton Hall, London, 8 and 9 July 1915*, Headley Bros., for League of Peace and Freedom, London, [1915].
The Policy of the Entente, 1904–14: a Reply to Professor Gilbert Murray. National Labour Press, Manchester and London, [1915]. Reprinted as 'The Entente Policy' in *Justice in War-Time*.
'Political Ideals'', *North American Review*, February 1917. First published as a pamphlet, National Council for Civil Liberties, London, [1916]. Reprinted in *Political Ideals*.
Political Ideals, Century, New York, 1917. In Britain: Allen & Unwin, London, 1963.
Portraits from Memory, Simon and Schuster, New York, 1963 (first published 1956).
'The Position of the Absolutists', *Trib.*, 1 March 1917.
'Practical War Economy', *LL*, 20 April 1916. A letter signed 'F.R.S.', identified as B.R.'s by the style and by A.F.B.
The Practice and Theory of Bolshevism, Allen & Unwin, London, 1920.
'President Wilson's Statement', *Trib.*, 1 February 1917.
Principles of Social Reconstruction, Allen & Unwin, London, 1916. In USA as *Why Men Fight*, Century, New York, 1917. Reprinted, with an Introduction by Jo Newberry, Garland Library of War and Peace, New York, 1971.
'The Prospects of the N.-C.F. in the New Year', *Trib.*, 1 February 1917.
'Religion and the Churches', *Unpopular Review*, April 1916. Reprinted in *Principles of Social Reconstruction*.
'The Renewed Ill-Treatment of 'C.O.'s', *Trib.*, 12 July 1917.

'Reply to Criticisms', in P. A. Schilpp (ed.), *The Philosophy of Bertrand Russell*, Northwestern University, Evanston and Chicago, 1944.

'Resistance and Service', *Trib.*, 3 May 1917.

Review of William James' *Memories and Studies, Cambridge Review*, 16 November 1911.

Rex v. Bertrand Russell, No-Conscription Fellowship, London, 1916. Pamphlet.

'Rex v. Russell', *MG*, 14 August 1916. A letter.

'The Rights of the War', *Nation*, 15 August 1914. A letter.

Roads to Freedom: Socialism, Anarchism and Syndicalism. Allen & Unwin, London, 1918. 3rd edition, 1949. In USA as *Proposed Roads to Freedom*, Henry Holt, New York, 1919.

'Russia and Peace', *Trib.*, 24 May 1917.

'Russia Leads the Way', *Trib.*, 22 March 1917.

'A Sense of Humour' in Harry Ruja (ed.), *Mortals and Others*, Allen & Unwin, London, 1975.

'Some Psychological Difficulties of Pacifism in Wartime', in Julian Bell (ed.), *We Did Not Fight*.

Speech at Leeds Conference. *Herald*, 9 June 1917. Reprinted in *What Happened at Leeds*, (see Coates, *British Labour and the Russian Revolution* below).

'To the President of the United States', in 'Mysterious Girl Brings Russell's Peace Plea Here', *New York Times*, 23 December 1916. Reprinted in *Autobiog.*, II, pp. 28–31; in Feinberg and Kasrils, pp. 65–8.

'A True History of Europe's Last War', *LL*, 11 March 1915.

Two Years' Hard Labour for Not Disobeying the Dictates of Conscience. National Labour Press, London, [1916]. The 'Everett' leaflet, reprinted in *Autobiog.*, II, pp. 63–4.

'A Valuable Suggestion by the Bishop of Exeter', *Trib.*, 18 October 1917.

'The Value of Endurance', *Trib.*, 17 May 1917.

'War and Non-Resistance', *Atlantic Monthly*, August 1915. Reprinted in *Justice in War-Time*.

'War as an Institution', *Atlantic Monthly*, May 1916. Reprinted in *Principles of Social Reconstruction*.

'War: the Cause and the Cure', *LL*, 24 September 1914.

War: the Offspring of Fear, Union of Democratic Control, London [1914]. Pamphlet. Reprinted in P. Stansky (ed.), *The Left and War: The British Labour Party and World War I*, Oxford, New York, 1969.

'What Bertrand Russell Was Not Allowed to Say', *Trib.*, 6 July 1916.

'What We Stand For', *Trib.*, 12 October 1916.

Why Not Peace Negotiations?, National Labour Press, London [1916]. Leaflet.

'Why the War Continues', *U.D.C.*, February 1917.

'Will They Be Shot?', *Herald*, 6 May 1916. A letter.

'Will This War End War?', *LL*, 10 September 1914.

Writings by others

Addams, Jane, *Peace and Bread in Time of War*, King's Crown Press, New York, 1945.

Addams, Jane, E. Balch and A. Hamilton, *Women at The Hague*, Macmillan, New York, 1915.

Allen, Clifford, 'Alternative Service', *Ploughshare*, May 1916.

'The Conscientious Objectors' Struggle', *LL*, 20 July 1916.

'Chairman's Address to N.C.F. Convention, November, 27 1915', in Graham.

'The Faith of the N.C.F.', in *Souvenir*.

'A Message from Clifford Allen', *Trib.*, 3 August 1916.
'No Compromise', *Trib.*, 6 April 1916.
'Open Letter to Lloyd George', *Trib.*, 14 June 1917.
'Pacifism', in Bell, (ed.), *We Did Not Fight.*
'A Personal Word', *Trib.*, 11 May 1916.
'Weakness and Strength', *Trib.*, 14 December 1916.
'A Word to General Childs', *Trib.*, 29 June 1916.
'A Word to the Government', *Trib.*, 23 March 1916.
Angell, Norman, *After All: The Autobiography of Norman Angell*, Hamish Hamilton, London, 1952.
'War and Peace, 1914', in Bell (ed.), *We Did Not Fight.*
Anonymous, 'At Keddington and Dyce', *Trib.*, 7 September 1916.
'The "Bodkin" Poster', *Trib.*, 5 October 1916.
'Concerning the Scheme: C. H. Norman's Opinion', *Trib.*, 28 September 1916.
'Conditions at Dyce', *Trib.*, 14 September 1916.
'Conscientious Objectors: The "Absolutists" and the "Ungenuines"', [1917]. Leaflet.
'Home Office Representative at Dartmoor'. *News Sheet*, no. 5.
'How it is done', *Trib.*, 25 May 1916.
'Leeds and Revolution', *Trib.*, 7 June 1917.
'Men Released After Sentence', *Trib.*, 3 August 1916.
'The Men Sent to France', *Trib.*, 19 July 1917.
'The N.C.C.', *Trib.*, 11 January 1917.
'N.C.C. Situation', *Trib.*, 21 December 1916.
'The N.-C.F. and Political Action', *Trib.*, 3 August 1916.
'The National Committee and Alternativists', *Trib.*, 5 October 1916.
'The New Crime', *Trib.*, 18 January 1917.
'A Notable Book and Some Opinions on It', *Trib.*, 23 August 1917.
'The Present Position': an N.C.F. Letter to the Premier', *Trib.*, 10 August 1916. Reprinted as a leaflet: 'C.O.'s and "Alternative Service"'.
'A Reply to Mr Harvey', *Trib.*, 27 July 1916.
'Statement of Principles'. No-Conscription Fellowship, London, [1916]. Leaflet.
'Stoning a Prophet', *Trib.*, 6 September 1917.
'The Treatment of C.O.'s', *Trib.*, 28 September 1916.
'Treatment of C.O.'s on Expiration of Sentences', *Trib.*, 10 August 1916.
U.D.C. Motives, Object, Policy, UDC, London, n.d. Pamphlet.
'Urgent Call to Members', *Trib.*, 20 July 1916.
'The Working of the Scheme', *Trib.*, 14 September 1916.
Bell, Julian (ed.), *We Did Not Fight: 1914–18 Experiences of War Resisters*, Cobden-Sanderson, London, 1935.
Bell, Quentin, *Bloomsbury*, Weidenfeld and Nicolson, London, 1968.
Blackwell, Kenneth, '[The Text of *Rex v. Bertrand Russell*]', *Russell*, no. 1 (spring 1971), pp. 7–8.
'[Unsigned Russell Material]', *Russell*, no. 2 (summer 1971), pp. 10–11.
Boulton, David, *Objection Overruled*, MacGibbon & Kee, London, 1967.
Bracher, S. V., 'Non-Resistance and Revolution', *Trib.*, 12 July 1917.
Brailsford, H. N., *The War of Steel and Gold*, Bell, London, 1914.
Brink, Andrew, 'Russell to Lady Ottoline Morrell' in *Russell*, no. 21–22 (1976), pp. 3–15.
Brinton, Howard, *Friends for 300 Years*, Pendle Hill Publications, Philadelphia, 1965.

Brittain, Vera, *The Rebel Passion: A Short History of Some Pioneer Peace-Makers*, Allen & Unwin, London, 1964.

Brock, Peter, *Pacifism in the United States from the Colonial Era to the First World War*. Princeton University Press, Princeton, N.J., 1968.

Twentieth-Century Pacifism, Van Nostrand Reinhold, New York, 1970.

Brockway, A. Fenner, Lord, 'The Home Office Scheme', *Trib.*, 7 September 1916.

Inside the Left, Allen & Unwin, London, 1942.

'On Russell's Unpublished [*sic*] Letter', *Russell*, no. 6 (summer 1972), p. 5.

'Pacifism—Conscience on Trial', in Peter Young (ed.), *History of the First World War*, V, no. 15 (1971).

'The Past and the Future', *Trib.*, 17 August 1916.

'The Policy of the N.C.F.', *Trib.*, 16 November, 1916.

'The Present Position of the "C.O."', *Trib.*, 5 October 1916.

'Sentence of Death', *Trib.*, 24 August 1916.

Socialism for Pacifists, National Labour Press, Manchester, 1916.

'Stand Firm', *Trib.*, 31 August 1916.

Brown, A. Barratt, 'Alter Our Basis', *Trib.*, 4 January 1917.

'A Correction', *Trib.*, 18 January 1917.

Bundock, Clement J., 'Guild Socialism and Education: Interview with Mr Bertrand Russell', *LL*, 22 March 1917.

Bussey, Gertrude and Tims, Margaret, *The Women's International League for Peace and Freedom*, Allen & Unwin, London, 1965.

Carnegie Endowment for International Peace. *Report of the International Commission to Inquire into the Causes and Conduct of the Balkan Wars*, The Carnegie Endowment for International Peace, Washington, 1914.

Catchpool, Corder, *On Two Fronts: Letters of a Conscientious Objector*, Headley, London, 1918.

Chamberlain, William J., *Fighting for Peace*, No More War Movement, London, [1929].

'Pen Pictures of Prison Life', *Trib.*, 1 September–2 November 1916. Reprinted as *A C.O. in Prison*, NCF, [London], [1916].

Childs, Wyndham, *Episodes and Reflections*, Cassell, London, 1930.

Clark, Ronald W., *The Life of Bertrand Russell*, Jonathan Cape and Weidenfeld & Nicholson, London, 1975.

Cline, C. A., *Recruits to Labour: The British Labour Party, 1914–1931*. Syracuse University Press, Syracuse, 1963.

Coates, Ken (ed.), *British Labour and the Russian Revolution*, Bertrand Russell Peace Foundation, Nottingham, [1974]. A reprint, with an Introduction by Coates, of *What Happened at Leeds*, Council of Workers' and Soldiers' Delegates, London, 1917.

Coates, Ken and Topham, A. (eds.), *Industrial Democracy in Great Britain: a book of readings and witnesses for workers' control*. MacGibbon & Kee, London, 1968.

Cobden-Sanderson, T. J., *The Journals of Thomas James Cobden-Sanderson*, Doves Press, London, 1926. Reprinted: Franklin, New York, 1969.

Cole, Margaret (ed.), *Beatrice Webb's Diaries: 1912–1924*, Longmans, Green, London, 1952.

Cooper Willis, Irene, *England's Holy War*, Garland Library of War and Peace, New York, 1971 (first published 1928).

Courtney, K., *Extracts from a Diary during the War*. Printed for private circulation, 1927.

Cross, Colin, *Philip Snowden*, Barrie & Rockliff, London, 1966.

Donington, Robert and Barbara, *The Citizen Faces War*, Gollancz, London, 1936.

Ensor, R. C. K., *England: 1870–1914*, Oxford University Press, Oxford, 1936.

Feinberg, Barry and Kasrils, Ronald, *Bertrand Russell's America: His Trans-Atlantic Travels and Writings*, I: 1896–1945, Allen & Unwin, London, 1973.

Florence, Lella Secor, 'The Ford Peace Ship and After' in Bell (ed.), *We Did Not Fight*.

Forster, E. M., *Goldsworthy Lowes Dickinson*, Arnold, London, 1934.

Gilbert, Martin, *Plough My Own Furrow: The Story of Lord Allen of Hurtwood as told through his writings and correspondence*. Longmans, Green, London, 1965.

Graham, John, *Conscription and Conscience*, Allen & Unwin, London, 1922.

Graubard, S. R., *British Labour and the Russian Revolution*, Harvard University Press, Cambridge, Mass., 1956.

Graves, Robert, *Goodbye to All That*, Cape, London, 1929.

Greaves, Jean C., *Corder Catchpool*, Friends' Home Service Committee, London, 1953.

Greenspan, Louis, *The Incompatible Prophecies: Science and Liberty in the Political Writings of Bertrand Russell*, Mosaic Press/Valley Editions, Oakville, Ont., 1978.

Grubb, Edward, 'War Resistance' in Bell (ed.), *We Did Not Fight*.

Halévy, E., *History of the English People*, VI: *The Rule of Democracy (1905–1914)*. Benn, London, 1961.

Hanak, H., 'The Union of Democratic Control during the First World War', *Bulletin of the Institute of Historical Research*, 36 (November 1963), pp. 168–80.

Hardy, G. H., *Bertrand Russell and Trinity*, Cambridge University Press, Cambridge, 1970 (first printed privately in 1942).

Harvey, T. E., 'Alternative Service', *Trib.*, 27 July 1916.

Hayes, Denis, *Conscription Conflict*, Sheppard Press, London, 1949.

Heasman, Kathleen, *Evangelicals in Action*, Geoffrey Bles, London, 1962.

Hirst, M. E., *Quakers in Peace and War*, Swarthmore Press, London, 1923.

Hobhouse, Margaret (Mrs Henry), *'I Appeal Unto Caesar': The Case of the Conscientious Objector*, Allen & Unwin, London, 1917.

Hobhouse, Stephen, *Forty Years and an Epilogue: an Autobiography, 1881–1951*. James Clarke, London, 1951.

'Fourteen Months' Service with the Colours', in Bell (ed.), *We Did Not Fight*.

Hobhouse, S. and Brockway, F. (eds.), *English Prisons Today: Being the Report of the Prison Enquiry Committee*, Longmans, Green, London, 1922.

Holroyd, Michael, *Lytton Strachey, a Critical Biography*, 2 vols., Heinemann, London, 1967–8.

Hughes, William R., *Indomitable Friend: Corder Catchpool, 1883–1952*, Housmans, London, 1964.

Sophia Sturge, Allen & Unwin, London, 1940.

Hunter, Ernest E., *The Home Office Compounds: A Statement as to How Conscientious Objectors are Penalized*, No-Conscription Fellowship, London, 1917.

'Long Live the International!', *Trib.*, 23 August 1917.

'To Stockholm!', *Trib.*, 16 August 1917.

James, Stanley, *The Men Who Dared*, C. W. Daniel, London, [1917].

Jannaway, Frank G., *Without the Camp: Being the Story of Why and How the Christadelphians were Exempted from Military Service,* privately published, London, 1917.

Jenkins, Roy, *Asquith*, Collins, London, 1967.

Johnstone, J. K., *The Bloomsbury Group*, Secker & Warburg, London, 1954.

Jones, Peter d'Arcy, *The Christian Socialist Revival, 1877–1914*, Princeton University Press, Princeton, N. J., 1968.

Jones, Rufus M., *The Later Periods of Quakerism*, Macmillan, London, 1921.

Kendall, Walter, *The Revolutionary Movement in Britain, 1900–1921*, Weidenfeld & Nicolson, London, 1969.

Kennedy, Thomas C., 'Public Opinion and the Conscientious Objector, 1915–1919', *Journal of British Studies*, 12 (May 1973), pp. 105–19.

'The Women's Man for Wimbledon, 1907: Russell as Parliamentary Candidate', *Russell*, no. 14 (summer 1974), pp. 19–26.

Langdon-Davies, B. N., 'Alternative Service', in Bell (ed.), *We Did Not Fight*.

Lansbury, George, *The Miracle of Fleet Street*, Labour Publishing Co., London, 1925.

Leith, J. A. and Dotson, C. (eds.), *Modern Revolutions*, Queen's University, Kingston, Ont., n.d.

Lenzen, Victor F., 'Bertrand Russell at Harvard, 1914', *Russell*, no. 3 (autumn 1971), pp. 4–6.

Lloyd George, David, *War Memoirs*, 2 vols, Odhams, London, [1938].

Macfarlane, J. J., *The British Communist Party: Its Origins and Development until 1929*, MacGibbon & Kee, London, 1966.

Malleson, Constance, *After Ten Years*, Cape, London, 1931.

'Fifty Years: 1916–1966', in Ralph Schoenman (ed.), *Bertrand Russell, Philosopher of the Century*, Allen & Unwin, London, 1967.

Marchant, James, *Dr. John Clifford: Life, Letters and Reminiscences*, Cassell, London, 1924.

Marshall, Catherine E., 'Adding Insult to Injury', *Trib.*, 3 January 1918.

'Events in Newhaven', *Trib.*, 7 December 1916.

'Insufficiency of Food in Prison', *Trib.*, 6 September 1917.

'The New Issue', *Trib.*, 4 January 1917.

'Refusal to Work in Prison', *Trib.*, 9 August 1917.

Marwick, Arthur, *Clifford Allen: The Open Conspirator*, Oliver and Boyd, Edinburgh and London, 1964.

The Deluge: British Society and the First World War, Penguin, Harmondsworth, 1967.

McNair, John, *James Maxton, the Beloved Rebel*, Allen & Unwin, London, 1955.

Meyer, Frederick B., *The Majesty of Conscience*, National Labour Press, Manchester, 1917.

Meynell, Francis, *My Lives*, Bodley Head, London, 1971.

Middlemas, R. K., *The Clydesiders: A Left Wing Struggle for Parliamentary Power*, Hutchinson, London, 1965.

Miliband, Ralph, *Parliamentary Socialism*, Allen & Unwin, London, 1961.

Mitchell, David, *Monstrous Regiment: The Story of the Women of the First World War*, Macmillan, New York, 1965.

Moore, G. E., 'Suggestions for the Council of Trinity College', *Cambridge Magazine*, 27 November 1915.

Moore, Harry T. (ed.), *D. H. Lawrence's Letters to Bertrand Russell*, Gotham Book Mart, New York, 1948.

Morel, E. D., *Morocco in Diplomacy*, Smith, Elder, London, 1912.

Morgan, Kenneth O., *Wales in British Politics, 1868–1922*, University of Wales Press, Cardiff, 1963.

Morrell, Ottoline, *Ottoline: The Early Memoirs of Lady Ottoline Morrell*, ed. Robert Gathorne-Hardy, Faber & Faber, London, 1963.

Murray, Gilbert, *The Foreign Policy of Sir Edward Grey, 1906–15*, Clarendon Press, Oxford, 1915.

Newberry, Jo Vellacott, 'Anti-War Suffragists', *History*, vol. 62, October 1977.

Newberry (Vellacott), Jo, 'Introduction' to I. Cooper Willis, *England's Holy War*, 1971.

'Introduction' to B. R. *Why Men Fight*. Garland Library of War and Peace, New York, 1971.

'Voteless Women of No Degree' in *Lucely Speaking*, March 1977 (privately published house journal of Lucy Cavendish College, Cambridge).

No-Conscription Fellowship, A Souvenir of Its Work during the Years 1914–1919. NCF, London [1920].

Norman, C. H., 'Concerning the Scheme', *Trib.*, 28 September 1916.

'The N.C.F. and the Home Office Men', *News Sheet*, no. 7, n.d.

A Searchlight on the European War, Labour Publishing Co., London, 1924.

Oxford and Asquith, Earl of, *Memories and Reflections, 1852–1927*, 2 vols., Little, Brown, Boston, 1928.

Pankhurst, Christabel, 'Go to Germany', *Suffragette* 14 May 1915.

Pankhurst, Sylvia, *The Home Front*, Hutchinson, London [1932].

Peet, H., 'The Men Sentenced to Death', in *Souvenir.*

Playne, Caroline, *The Pre-War Mind in Britain*, Allen & Unwin, London, 1928.

Postgate, Raymond, *Life of George Lansbury*, Longmans, Green, London, 1951.

Prasad, Devi and Smythe, Tony (eds.), *Conscription: a World Survey: Compulsory Military Service and Resistance to It*, War Resisters International, London, 1968.

Rae, John, *Conscience and Politics*, Oxford University Press, London, 1970.

Randall, Mercedes, *Improper Bostonian: Emily Greene Balch*, Twayne Publishers, New York, 1964.

Rappaport, Armin, *The British Press and Wilsonian Neutrality*, Peter Smith, Gloucester, Mass.; 1965 (first edition 1951).

Rempel, Richard, 'From Imperialism to Free Trade: Couturat, Halévy, and Russell's First Crusade', *Journal of the History of Ideas*, 40 (July 1979), pp. 67–87.

Repeal the Act, No-Conscription Fellowship, London, 1916.

Robbins, Keith, *The Abolition of War*, University of Wales Press, Cardiff, 1976.

Rose, Aylmer, 'Widen Our Basis', *Trib.*, 21 December 1916.

Ruja, Harry, *Mortals and Others: Bertrand Russell's American Essays, 1931–1935*, I, Allen & Unwin, London, 1975.

Russell, John Francis Stanley, 2nd Earl, *My Life and Adventures*. Cassell, London, 1923.

Sassoon, Siegfried, *Collected Poems*, Faber & Faber, London, 1947.

Memoirs of an Infantry Officer, Faber & Faber, London, 1930.

Sherston's Progress, Faber & Faber, London, 1936.

Siegfried's Journey: 1916–1920, Faber & Faber, London, 1945.

Simon, Bennett and Nancy, 'The Pacifist Turn', *Russell*, no. 13 (spring 1974).

Simon, Viscount, *Retrospect*, Hutchinson, London, 1952.

Slater, John G., 'What Happened at Leeds?', *Russell*, no. 4 (winter 1971–2), pp. 9–10.

Smillie, R., 'How I Lectured for Bertrand Russell', *Spokesman*, no. 3 (May 1970), pp. 20–1. Reprinted from Smillie's *My Life for Labour*, Mills & Boon, London, 1924.

Snowden, Philip, *Autobiography*, 2 vols. Nicholson & Watson, London, 1934.

British Prussianism, National Labour Press, London, 1916.

Stapledon, Olaf, 'Experiences in the Friends' Ambulance Unit' in Bell (ed.), *We Did Not Fight.*

Steed, H. Wickham, *Through Thirty Years*, Doubleday, New York, 1925.

Stevenson, Lillian, *Towards a Christian International*, International Fellowship of Reconciliation, London, 1941.

Stromberg, R. N., 'The Intellectuals and the Coming of War', *Journal of European Studies*, 3 (1973), pp. 109–22.

Stansky, Peter (ed.), *The Left and War: The British Labour Party and World War I*, Oxford, New York, 1969.

Swanwick, Helena M., *Builders of Peace*, Swarthmore Press, London, 1924.

Swartz, Marvin, *The Union of Democratic Control in British Politics during the First World War*, Oxford University Press, London, 1971.

Tatham, Meaburn, and Miles, James E., *The Friends' Ambulance Unit, 1914–1919*, Swarthmore Press, London, [1919].

Taylor, A. J. P., *English History: 1914–1945*, Clarendon Press, Oxford, 1965.
First World War, Penguin, Harmondsworth, 1966 (first published in 1963).
The Trouble Makers, Hamish Hamilton, London, 1957.

Thompson, Michael, 'Some Letters from Bertrand Russell to H. Wildon Carr', *Coranto: Journal of the Friends of the Libraries, University of Southern California*, 10 (1975), pp. 7–19.

Tolstoy, Leo, 'Count Tolstoy on the War', *Times*, 27 June, 1904.

Vellacott, Jo. See Newberry.

Webb, Beatrice, *Beatrice Webb's Diaries (1912–1924)*. See Cole.
Our Partnership, Longmans, Green, London, 1948.

West, Arthur Graeme, *The Diary of a Dead Officer*, Allen & Unwin, London, [1919].

Willis, W. David, *Stephen Hobhouse: A Twentieth-Century Quaker Saint*. Friends' Home Service Committee, London, 1972.

Winkler, Henry R., *The League of Nations Movement in Great Britain: 1914–1919*, Scarecrow Reprint Corp., Metuchen, N.J., 1967 (first published in 1952).

Wittgenstein, Ludwig, *Letters to Russell, Keynes and Moore*, ed. G. H. von Wright, Blackwell, Oxford, 1974.

Woolf, Leonard, *Beginning Again. An Autobiography of the Years 1911–1918*. Hogarth Press, London, 1964.
Sowing: An Autobiography of the Years 1880–1904, Hogarth Press, London, 1961.

Wood, Alan, *Bertrand Russell, The Passionate Sceptic*, Allen & Unwin, London, 1963 (first published in 1957).

Dissertations

Berkman, Joyce Avrech, 'Pacifism in England: 1914–1939', Ph.D dissertation, Yale University, 1967.

Blackwell, Kenneth, 'Wittgenstein's Impact on Russell's Theory of Belief', MA thesis, McMaster University, 1974.

Kennedy, Thomas C., 'The Hound of Conscience: A History of the No-Conscription Fellowship, 1914–1919', PhD dissertation, University of South Carolina, 1967. Revised and forthcoming, Kentucky University Press, 1980.

Lindsay, J. E., 'The Failure of Liberal Opposition to British Entry into World War I', PhD dissertation, Columbia University, 1969.

Pollock, Marvin Ronald, 'British Pacifism during the First World War: The Cambridge-Bloomsbury Contribution', PhD dissertation, Columbia University, 1971.

Rae, John Malcolm, 'The Development of Official Treatment of Conscientious Objection to Military Service, 1916–1945', PhD dissertation, University of London, 1965.

Sacks, Benjamin, 'The Independent Labour Party during the World War', PhD dissertation, Stanford University, 1934.

Tucker, Leigh R., 'The English Quakers and World War I, 1914–1920', PhD dissertation, University of North Carolina, 1972.

INDEX

Russell, Bertrand, (*contd.*)
  *Introduction to Mathematical
    Philosophy*, 238
  Justice in War-Time, 134, n66
  Logic and Knowledge (*The
    Philosophy of Logical Atomism*),
    221
  Mysticism and Logic, n52
  *Our Knowledge of the External
    World*, 14
  *The Policy of the Entente: A Reply
    to Professor Gilbert Murray*, 16,
    n12
  Political Ideals, 99, 169, n344, n433
  Portraits from Memory, 29 (n125)
  *The Practice and Theory of
    Bolshevism*, 249, n450
  Principles of Social Reconstruction
    (*Why Men Fight*), 11, 24, 26, 27,
    28, 33, 64–5, 100, 123, 159, 169,
    208, 220, 248, 249, n262
  Problems of Philosophy, 92
  Roads to Freedom, 160, 163–5, 171,
    220, 222, 229, n509, n510, n770
Lectures, Articles, Editorials, etc.:
  'Adsum Qui Feci', letter to editor,
    78
  'Are Criminals Worse than Other
    People?', article, 238–9 (n791)
  'Can England and Germany be
    Reconciled After the War?',
    article, 19
  'The Causes of the War', lecture,
    18
  'A Clash of Consciences', letter to
    editor, 52, n214
  'Clifford Allen and Mr. Lloyd
    George', *Trib.* article, 112
  'Education as a Political
    Institution', article, n262
  'The Ethics of War', article, 134
  'The Evils of Persecution', *Trib.*
    editorial, 196, 197 (n611, n617)
  'F.R.S.', letter to editor, 58
  'A Fifty-Six Year Friendship',
    essay, 16 (n63)
  'Folly, Doctor-like, Controlling
    Skill', article, 66
  'For Conscience' Sake', article,
    n274, n477
  'A Free Man's Worship', essay, 3
  'The Future of Anglo-German
    Rivalry', article, 17

'The German Peace Offer', *Trib.*
  article, 223–8
'The Government and Absolute
  Exemption', *Trib.* editorial, 191
  (n597)
'History as an Art', essay, n451
'How America Can Help to Bring
  Peace', article, 17
'Idealism on the Defensive',
  review, 221 (n699)
'Imperialist Anxieties', *Trib.*
  editorial, n714
'Is a Permanent Peace Possible?',
  article, 16
'Liberty and National Service',
  Trib. editorial, 141 (n462)
'Marriage and the Population
  Question', article, n262
'Metaphysics', review, 221 (n699)
'Mr. Tennant on the
  Conscientious Objectors',
  article, 65 (n254)
'Nationality', lecture, 18
'National Dependence and
  Internationalism', lecture,
  134–5
'National Service', *Trib.* editorial,
  140 (n461)
'The Nature of the State in View
  of Its External Relations',
  speech, 66
'A New Tribunal for Gaol
  Delivery', *Trib.* article, 212
  (n633)
'The N.C.F. and the Political
  Outlook', *Trib.* editorial, n457
'N.C.F. Ideals', lecture, 110
'On History', essay, 136–7
'Pacifism and Economic
  Revolution', *Trib.* editorial, 167
'A Pacifist Revolution?', *Trib.*
  editorial, n536
'The Philosophy of Pacifism',
  lecture, 23 (n100)
'The Position of the Absolutists',
  Trib. editorial, 197 (n617)
'The Principles of Peace', lecture,
  18
'The Prospects of the N.C.F. in
  the New Year', *Trib.* editorial,
  190 (n594)
'Religion and the Churches',
  article, n262